STUDENT SOLUTIONS MANUAL

COST ACCOUNTING

A Managerial Emphasis

STUDENT SOLUTIONS MANUAL

Charles T. Horngren *Stanford University*   Srikant M. Datar *Harvard University*

George Foster *California State University*   M. Zafar Iqbal *San Luis Obispo*

COST ACCOUNTING

A Managerial Emphasis

Eleventh Edition

HORNGREN   DATAR   FOSTER

Upper Saddle River, New Jersey 07458

Acquisitions editor: Thomas Sigel
Assistant editor: Sam Goffinet
Production editor: Wanda Rockwell
Manufacturer: Victor Graphics

ISBN 0-13-065006-4

10 9 8 7 6 5 4 3 2

CONTENTS

This Student Solutions Manual by Charles T. Horngren, Srikant M. Datar, George Foster, and M. Zafar Iqbal, assists with even-numbered end-of-chapter problems.

CHAPTER 1
THE ACCOUNTANT'S ROLE IN THE ORGANIZATION

1-2 *Management accounting* measures and reports financial and nonfinancial information that helps managers make decisions to fulfill the goals of an organization. It focuses on internal reporting.

Financial accounting focuses on reporting to external parties. It measures and records business transactions and provides financial statements that are based on generally accepted accounting principles (GAAP).

Other differences include: (1) management accounting emphasizes the future, (2) management accounting influences the behavior of managers and employees (3) management accounting is not restricted by Generally Accepted Accounting Principles and (4) management accounting covers more topics.

1-4 The three roles are:
1. Problem solving—comparative analysis for decision making.
2. Scorekeeping—accumulating data and reporting results to all levels of management describing how the organization is doing.
3. Attention directing—helping managers to focus on opportunities and problems.

1-6 The business functions in the value chain are:
- **Research and development**—generating and experimenting with ideas related to new products, services, or processes.
- **Design of products, services, and processes**—the detailed planning and engineering of products, services, or processes.
- **Production**—acquiring, coordinating, and assembling resources to produce a product or deliver a service.
- **Marketing**—promoting and selling products or services to customers or prospective customers.
- **Distribution**—delivering products or services to customers.
- **Customer service**—providing after-sales support to customers.

1-8 The four themes are:
1. Customer focus.
2. Value-chain and supply-chain analysis.
3. Key success factors (such as cost and efficiency, quality, time, and innovation).
4. Continuous improvement and benchmarking.

1-10 The three guidelines for management accountants are:
1. Employ a cost-benefit approach.
2. Recognize behavioral and technical considerations.
3. Adopt the "different costs for different purposes" notion.

1-12 The new controller could reply in one or more of the following ways:

1-12   The new controller could reply in one or more of the following ways:

(a)   Demonstrate to the plant manager how he or she could make better decisions if the plant controller was viewed as a resource rather than a deadweight. In a related way, the plant controller could show how the plant manager's time and resources could be saved by viewing the new plant controller as a team member.

(b)   Demonstrate to the plant manager a good knowledge of the technical aspects of the plant. This approach may involve doing background reading. It certainly will involve spending much time on the plant floor speaking to plant personnel.

(c)   Show the plant manager examples of the new plant controller's past successes in working with line managers in other plants. Examples could include:
   • assistance in preparing the budget,
   • assistance in analyzing problem situations and evaluating financial and nonfinancial aspects of different alternatives, and
   • assistance in submitting capital budget requests.

(d)   Seek assistance from the corporate controller to highlight to the plant manager the importance of many tasks undertaken by the new plant controller. This approach is a last resort but may be necessary in some cases.

1-14   The Institute of Management Accountants (IMA) sets standards of ethical conduct for management accountants in the following areas:
• Competence
• Confidentiality
• Integrity
• Objectivity

1-16   (15 min.)   **Planning and control decisions.**

1.   (a) Planning—decision by Barnes & Noble (B&N) about cash needs for the future.
     (b) Control—performance evaluation of B&N for the year.
2.   (a) Planning—decision to increase or decrease local marketing support.
     (b) Control—decision on whether recent sales promotion led to an increase in revenues.
3.   (a) Planning—decision about whether or not to expand B&N's Internet lines of business.
     (b) Control—evaluation by VP of New Business Development of the performance of managers of individual lines of business.
4.   (a) Planning—decision on which books to advertise more or which books to include in a special chat-room site.
     (b) Control—decision by publisher to pay additional bonuses to authors due to their book being on a bestseller list.
5.   (a) Planning—decision by B&N on the amount and type of insurance to purchase next year.
     (b) Control—follow up by B&N with the insurance company regarding a cash payment to B&N.

1-18 (15 min.) **Problem solving, scorekeeping, and attention directing.**

The accountant's duties are often not sharply defined, so some of these answers might be challenged:

1. Attention directing
2. Problem solving
3. Scorekeeping
4. Scorekeeping
5. Scorekeeping
6. Attention directing
7. Problem solving
8. Scorekeeping
9. Problem solving
10. Attention directing

1-20 (15 min.) **Value chain and classification of costs, pharmaceutical company.**

Cost Item	Value Chain Business Function
a.	Design
b.	Marketing
c.	Customer Service
d.	Research and Development
e.	Marketing
f.	Production
g.	Marketing
h.	Distribution

1-22 (15 min.) **Management themes and changes in management accounting.**

Change in Management Accounting	Key Theme
a.	Value-chain and supply-chain analysis
b.	Key success factors (quality)
c.	Key success factors (cost) and continuous improvement and benchmarking.
d.	Continuous improvement and benchmarking and key success factor (cost).
e.	Customer focus

1-24 (15 min.) **Management accounting guidelines.**

1. Cost-benefit approach

2. Behavioral and technical considerations

3. Different costs for different purposes

4. Cost-benefit approach

5. Behavioral and technical considerations

6. Cost-benefit approach

7. Behavioral and technical considerations

8. Different costs for different purposes

9. Behavioral and technical considerations

1-26 (30 min.) **Problem solving, scorekeeping, attention directing, and feedback, Internet company (continuation of 1-25).**

1.   *Problem solving* – comparative analysis for decision making.
Scorekeeping – accumulating data and reporting results to all levels of management describing how the organization is doing.
Attention directing – helping managers focus on opportunities and problems.

2.   (a) and (e) Decisions to change subscription fee.
Problem solving – report outlining expected revenues from subscribers and advertising with different monthly fee amounts.
Scorekeeping – report with monthly subscribers and their revenues in prior months.
Attention directing – report showing the change in the number of subscribers of Internet companies at the time they change their monthly fees.

(b) Decision to inform existing subscribers of $24.95 fee from July onwards.
Problem solving – report analyzing different ways (e-mail, regular mail) of informing subscribers.
Scorekeeping – report indicating how many subscribers have been contacted.
Attention directing – report showing how many subscribers have cancelled their subscriptions following notification of the increase in fees.

(c) Decision to upgrade content of online services and to offer better Internet mail services.
Problem solving – report outlining expected revenues from subscribers and advertisers as a result of upgrading service.
Scorekeeping – report with monthly subscribers and revenues before and after upgrading service.
Attention directing – report showing the change in the number of subscribers of Internet companies after they upgraded service.

1-26 (Cont'd.)

(d) Decision to demote vice president of marketing.

Problem solving and *attention directing* – report analyzing growth in subscribers at competing Internet companies.

3. As a result of the feedback, WebNews.com made the following decisions:

a. Decision to change subscription fee from $24.95 per month in September 2003 to $21.95 in October 2003.

b. Demotion of Vice President of Marketing after significant slowing of subscriber growth in accounts and revenues.

4. WebNews.com overestimated the number of subscribers for the July to September 2003 period. It might examine the methodology it uses to estimate the sensitivity of subscriptions to price changes and upgrade of its services.

1-28   (30 min.)   Software procurement decisions, ethics.

1.   Michael faces an ethical problem. The trip appears to be a gift which could influence his purchase decision. The ethical standard of integrity requires Michaels to refuse the gift. Companies with "codes of conduct" frequently have a "supplier clause" that prohibits their employees from accepting "material" (in some cases, any) gifts from suppliers. The motivations include:

(a)   Integrity/conflict of interest. Suppose Michaels recommends that a Horizon 1-2-3 product subsequently be purchased by Fiesta. This recommendation could be because he felt obligated to them as his trip to the Cancun conference was fully paid by Horizon.

(b)   The appearance of a conflict of interest. Even if the Horizon 1-2-3 product is the superior one at that time, other suppliers likely will have a different opinion. They may believe that the way to sell products to Fiesta is via "fully-paid junkets to resorts." Those not wanting to do business this way may downplay future business activities with Fiesta even though Fiesta could gain much from such activities.

Some executives view the meeting as "suspect" from the start given the Caribbean location and its "rest and recreation" tone.

2.   I do not think Fiesta should allow executives to attend user meetings while negotiating with other vendors about a purchase decision. The payment of expenses for the trip constitutes a gift that could appear to influence their purchase decision.

Pros of attending user meeting

(a)   Opportunity to learn more about Horizon's software products.

(b)   Opportunity to interact with other possible purchasers and get their opinions.

(c)   Opportunity to influence the future product development plans of Horizon in a way that will benefit Fiesta. An example is Horizon subsequently developing software modules tailored to food product companies.

(d)   Saves Fiesta money. Visiting suppliers and their customers typically cost money, whereas Horizon is paying for the Cancún conference.

Cons of Attending
(a) The ethical issues raised in requirement 1.
(b) Negative morale effects on other Fiesta employees who do not get to attend the Cancún conference. These employees may reduce their trust and respect for Michaels's judgment, arguing he has been on a "supplier-paid vacation."

Conditions on Attending that Fiesta Might Impose
(a) Sizable part of that time in Cancun has to be devoted to business rather than recreation.
(b) Decision on which Fiesta executive attends is <u>not</u> made by the person who attends (this reduces the appearance of a conflict of interest).
(c) Person attending (Michaels) does not have final say on purchase decision (this reduces the appearance of a conflict of interest).
(d) Fiesta executives go only when a new major purchase is being contemplated (to avoid the conference becoming a regular "vacation").

A Conference Board publication on *Corporate Ethics* asked executives about a comparable situation:
• 76% said Fiesta and Michaels face an ethical consideration in deciding whether to attend.
• 71% said Michaels should not attend, as the payment of expenses is a "gift" within the meaning of a credible corporate ethics policy.

1. I think the company does not need its own code of ethics. They can use the code of ethics developed by the IMA.

Pros of having a written code
The Conference Board outlines the following reasons why companies adopt codes of ethics:
(a) Signals commitment of senior management to ethics.
(b) Promotes public trust in the credibility of the company and its employees.
(c) Signals the managerial professionalism of its employees.
(d) Provides guidance to employees as to how difficult problems are to be handled. If adhered to, employees will avoid many actions that are unethical or appear to be unethical.
(e) Drafting of the policy (and its redrafting in the light of ambiguities) can assist management in anticipating and preparing for ethical issues not yet encountered.

Cons of having a written code
(a) Can give appearance that all issues have been covered. Issues not covered may appear to be "acceptable" even when they are not.
(b) Can constrain the entrepreneurial activities of employees. Forces people to always "behave by the book."
(c) Cost of developing code can be "high" if it consumes a lot of employee time.

1-30 (40 min.) **Global company, ethical challenges with bribery.**

1.   It is clear that bribes are illegal according to U.S. laws. It is not clear from the case whether bribes are illegal in Safistan. However, knowledgeable people in global business would attest to the fact that it is virtually impossible to find any country in the world which specifically sanctions bribery. The major point, however, that deserves discussion is: Should Norris engage in any unethical activities even if they are not illegal?

It is difficult to make a generalization about all shareholders of the company. It is, however, safe to assume that not all shareholders would want to keep their investment in a company that is engaged in unethical and/or illegal activities. There is historical evidence to substantiate this point: When apartheid laws were in effect in South Africa, many investors divested shares of companies doing business in South Africa.

Apart from the ethical issues, it should also be noted that bribery can be very costly in some parts of the world. Bribes may not generate revenues sufficient enough to offset their cost.

2.   Apparently Short thinks that local culture and common practice are one and the same. This, in fact, is not the case. There are many common practices in developing countries, which are against the native culture.

Specifically, bribery often leads to decisions that are not made on the basis of the merits of the alternative selected. This results in misallocation of meager resources of the developing country. Misallocation of resources has adverse effects on the economy of a country and the living standard of its population. The negative impact is intensified in developing countries because they can least afford the misallocation of resources.

3.   Norris might have an articulated corporate policy against such payments to get the message across that regardless of laws, the top management would not tolerate any bribery payments made by its employees. A strong and consistent message from the top often has a noticeable effect on the corporate culture and employee behavior.

U.S. laws specifically prohibit bribery payments. Such payments can result in heavy penalties to the corporation making the payments.

CHAPTER 2
AN INTRODUCTION TO COST TERMS AND PURPOSES

2-2   Cost assignment is a general term that encompasses the assignment of both direct costs and indirect costs to a cost object. Direct costs are *traced* to a cost object while indirect costs are *allocated* to a cost object.

- Direct costs of a cost object are related to the particular cost object and can be traced to that cost object in an economically feasible (cost-effective) way.
- Indirect costs of a cost object are related to the particular cost object but cannot be traced to that cost object in an economically feasible (cost-effective) way.

2-4   Factors affecting the classification of a cost as direct or indirect include:
- the materiality of the cost in question,
- available information-gathering technology,
- design of operations, and
- contractual arrangements.

2-6   A *cost driver* is a variable, such as the level of activity or volume, that causally affects costs over a given time span. A change in the cost driver results in a change in the level of total costs. For example, number of vehicles assembled is a driver of the costs of steering wheels on a motor-vehicle assembly line.

2-8   The *relevant range* is the band of normal activity level or volume in which there is a specific relationship between the level of activity or volume and the cost in question. Costs are described as variable or fixed with respect to a particular relevant range.

2-10   Manufacturing companies typically have one or more of the following three types of inventory.
1. *Direct materials inventory.* Direct materials in stock and awaiting use in the manufacturing process.
2. *Work-in-process inventory.* Goods partially worked on but not yet fully completed. Also called *work in progress*.
3. *Finished goods inventory.* Goods fully completed but not yet sold.

2-12   No. Service sector companies have no inventories and, hence, no inventoriable costs.

2-14   *Overtime premium* is the wage rate paid to workers (for both direct labor and indirect labor) in excess of their straight-time wage rates.

   Idle time is a subclassification of indirect labor that typically represents wages paid for unproductive time caused by lack of orders, machine breakdowns, material shortages, poor scheduling, and the like.

2-16 (15 min.) **Computing and interpreting manufacturing unit costs.**

1.

	(in Millions)		
	Supreme	**Deluxe**	**Regular**
Direct materials costs	$ 84.00	$ 54.00	$62.00
Direct manuf. labor costs	14.00	28.00	8.00
Indirect manuf. costs	42.00	84.00	24.00
Total manuf. costs	$140.00	$166.00	$94.00
Units produced (millions)	80	120	100
Cost per unit (Total manuf. costs ÷ units produced)	$1.7500	$1.3833	$0.9400

2.   The unit costs in requirement 1 includes $20 million of indirect manufacturing costs that are fixed irrespective of changes in the volume of output per month, while the remaining variable indirect manufacturing costs change with the production volume. Given the unit volume changes for August 2004, the use of unit costs from the past month at a different unit volume level (both in aggregate and at the individual product level) will yield incorrect estimates of total costs in August 2004.

2-18   (15-20 min.) **Classification of costs, service sector.**

Cost object: Each individual focus group
Cost variability: With respect to changes in the number of focus groups
        There may be some debate over classifications of individual items. Debate is more likely as regards cost variability.

Cost Item	D or I	V or F
A	D	V
B	I	F
C	I	V[a]
D	I	F
E	D	V
F	I	F
G	D	V
H	I	V[b]

[a] Some students will note that phone call costs are variable when each call has a separate charge. It may be a fixed cost if Consumer Focus has a flat monthly charge for a line, irrespective of the amount of usage.

[b] Gasoline costs are likely to vary with the number of focus groups. However, vehicles likely serve multiple purposes, and detailed records may be required to examine how costs vary with changes in one of the many purposes served.

2-20   (15-20 min.) **Classification of costs, manufacturing sector.**

Cost object: Type of car assembled (Corolla or Geo Prism)
Cost variability: With respect to changes in the number of cars assembled
     There may be some debate over classifications of individual items. Debate is more likely as regards cost variability.

Cost Item	D or I	V or F
A	D	V
B	I	F
C	D	F
D	D	F
E	D	V
F	I	V
G	D	V
H	I	F

2-22   (15 min)   **Cost drivers and the value chain.**

1.

Business Function	Representative Cost Driver
Production	• Hours the Tylenol packaging line is in operation
Research and development	• Number of patents filed with U.S. Patent office
Marketing	• Minutes of TV advertising time on "60 Minutes"
Distribution	• Number of packages shipped
Design of products/processes	• Hours spent designing tamper-proof bottles
Customer service	• Number of calls to toll-free customer phone line

2-22 (Cont'd.)

2.

Business Function	Representative Cost Driver
Research and development	• Hours of laboratory work • Number of new drugs in development
Design of products/processes	• Number of focus groups on alternative package designs • Hours of process engineering work
Production	• Number of units packaged • Number of tablets manufactured
Marketing	• Number of promotion packages mailed • Number of sales personnel
Distribution	• Weight of packages shipped • Number of supermarkets on delivery route
Customer service	• Number of units of a product recalled • Number of personnel on toll-free customer phone lines

2-24 (10 min.) Total costs and unit costs.

1. Total cost, $4,000. Unit cost per person, $4,000 ÷ 500 = $8.00

2. Total cost, $4,000. Unit cost per person, $4,000 ÷ 2,000 = $2.00

3. The main lesson of this exercise is to alert the student early in the course to the desirability of thinking in terms of total costs rather than unit costs wherever feasible. Changes in the denominator (the level of total activity or volume in this case attendance) will affect *total variable costs* but not *total fixed costs*. In our example, it would be perilous to use either the $8.00 or the $2.00 unit cost to predict the total cost because the total costs are not affected by the attendance. Instead, the student association should use the $4,000 total cost. Obviously, if the musical group agreed to work for, say, $4.00 per person, such a unit variable cost could be used to predict the total cost.

2-26 (20-30 min.)**Inventoriable costs versus period costs.**

1. *Manufacturing-sector companies* purchase materials and components and convert them into different finished goods.

    Merchandising-sector companies purchase and then sell tangible products without changing their basic form.

    Service-sector companies provide services or intangible products to their customers—for example, legal advice or audits.

    Only manufacturing and merchandising companies have inventories of goods for sale.

2. *Inventoriable costs* are all costs of a product that are regarded as an asset when they are incurred and then become cost of goods sold when the product is sold. These costs for a manufacturing company are included in work-in-process and finished goods inventory (they are "inventoried") to build up the costs of creating these assets.

    Period costs are all costs in the income statement other than cost of goods sold. These costs are treated as expenses of the period in which they are incurred because they are presumed not to benefit future periods (or because there is not sufficient evidence to conclude that such benefit exists). Expensing these costs immediately best matches expenses to revenues.

1.   (a) Mineral water purchased for resale by Safeway—inventoriable cost of a merchandising company. It becomes part of cost of goods sold when the mineral water is sold.

    (b) Electricity used at GE assembly plant—inventoriable cost of a manufacturing company. It is part of the manufacturing overhead that is included in the manufacturing cost of a refrigerator finished good.

    (c) Depreciation on AOL's computer equipment—period cost of a service company. AOL has no inventory of goods for sale and, hence, no inventoriable cost.

    (d) Electricity for Safeway's store aisles—period cost of a merchandising company. It is a cost that benefits the current period and is not traceable to goods purchased for resale.

    (e) Depreciation on GE's assembly testing equipment—inventoriable cost of a manufacturing company. It is part of the manufacturing overhead that is included in the manufacturing cost of a refrigerator finished good.

    (f) Salaries of Safeway's marketing personnel—period cost of a merchandising company. It is a cost that is not traceable to goods purchased for resale. It is presumed not to benefit future periods (or at least not to have sufficiently reliable evidence to estimate such future benefits).

    (g) Water consumed by AOL's engineers—period cost of a service company. AOL has no inventory of goods for sale and, hence, no inventoriable cost.

    (h) Salaries of AOL's marketing personnel—period cost of a service company. AOL has no inventory of goods for sale and, hence, no inventoriable cost.

2-28 (30-40 min.) **Cost of goods manufactured.**

1.

Canseco Company
Schedule of Cost of Goods Manufactured for the Year Ended December 31, 2004
(in thousands)

Direct materials costs:		
Beginning inventory, Jan. 1, 2004	$22,000	
Purchases of direct materials	75,000	
Cost of direct materials available for use	97,000	
Ending inventory, Dec. 31, 2004	26,000	
Direct materials used		$ 71,000
Direct manufacturing labor costs		25,000
Indirect manufacturing costs:		
Indirect manufacturing labor costs	15,000	
Plant insurance	9,000	
Depreciation—plant building and equipment	11,000	
Repairs and maintenance—plant	4,000	39,000
Manufacturing costs incurred during 2004		135,000
Add beginning work-in-process inventory, Jan. 1, 2004		21,000
Total manufacturing costs to account for		156,000
Deduct ending work-in-process inventory, Dec. 31, 2004		20,000
Cost of goods manufactured		$136,000

2.

Canseco Company
Income Statement for the Year Ended December 31, 2004
(in thousands)

Revenues		$300,000
Cost of goods sold:		
Beginning finished goods, Jan. 1, 2004	$ 18,000	
Cost of goods manufactured (requirement 1)	136,000	
Cost of goods available for sale	154,000	
Ending finished goods, Dec. 31, 2004	23,000	131,000
Gross margin		169,000
Operating costs:		
Marketing, distribution, and customer service	93,000	
General and administrative	29,000	122,000
Operating income		$ 47,000

2-28 Excel Application

Canseco Company
Income Statement For the Year Ended December 31, 2004

Revenues		$300,000
Cost of goods sold:		
Beginning finished goods	$18,000	
Cost of goods manufactured	136,000	
Cost of goods available for sale	154,000	
Ending finished goods	23,000	131,000
Gross margin		169,000
Operating costs:		
Marketing, distribution, and customer service costs	93,000	
General and administrative costs	29,000	122,000
Operating Income		$47,000

Canseco Company
Schedule of Cost of Goods Manufactured For the Year Ended 2004

Direct Materials:		
Beginning direct materials inventory		$ 22,000
Purchases of direct materials		75,000
Cost of direct materials available for use		97,000
Ending direct materials inventory		26,000
Direct materials used		71,000
Direct manufacturing labor		25,000
Indirect manufacturing costs:		
Indirect manufacturing labor	$15,000	
Plant insurance	9,000	
Depreciation	11,000	
Repairs and Maintenance	4,000	39,000
Manufacturing costs incurred during 2004		135,000
Add beginning work in process		21,000
Total manufacturing costs to account for		156,000
Deduct ending work in process		20,000
Cost of goods manufactured		$136,000

2-30 (15-20 min.) **Interpretation of statements** (continuation of 2-29).

1.   The schedule in 2-29 can become a Schedule of Cost of Goods Manufactured and Sold simply by including the beginning and ending finished goods inventory figures in the supporting schedule, rather than directly in the body of the income statement. Note that the term *cost of goods manufactured* refers to the cost of goods brought to completion (finished) during the accounting period, whether they were started before or during the current accounting period. Some of the manufacturing costs incurred are held back as costs of the ending work in process; similarly, the costs of the beginning work in process inventory become a part of the cost of goods manufactured for 2004.

2.   The sales manager's salary would be charged as a marketing cost as incurred by both manufacturing and merchandising companies. It is basically an operating cost that appears below the gross margin line on an income statement. In contrast, an assembler's wages would be assigned to the products worked on. Thus, the wages cost would be charged to Work in process and would not be expensed until the product is transferred through Finished Goods Inventory to Cost of Goods Sold as the product is sold.

3.   The direct-indirect distinction can be resolved only with respect to a particular cost object. For example, in defense contracting, the cost object may be defined as a contract. Then, a plant supervisor working only on that contract will have his or her salary charged directly and wholly to that single contract.

4.   Direct materials used   = \$320,000,000 ÷ 1,000,000 units = \$320 per unit
      Depreciation   = \$ 80,000,000 ÷ 1,000,000 units = \$ 80 per unit

5.   Direct materials unit cost would be unchanged at \$320. Depreciation cost per unit would be \$80,000,000 ÷ 1,200,000 = \$66.67 per unit. Total direct materials costs would rise by 20% to \$384,000,000 (\$320 per unit × 1,200,000 units), whereas total depreciation would be unaffected at \$80,000,000.

6.   Unit costs are averages, and they must be interpreted with caution. The \$320 direct materials unit cost is valid for predicting total costs because direct materials is a variable cost; total direct materials costs indeed change as output levels change. However, fixed costs like depreciation must be interpreted quite differently from variable costs. A common error in cost analysis is to regard all unit costs as one—as if all the total costs to which they are related are variable costs. Changes in output levels (the denominator) will affect *total variable costs*, but not *total fixed costs*. Graphs of the two costs may clarify this point; it is safer to think in terms of total costs rather than in terms of unit costs.

2-32 (15-20 min.) **Terminology, interpretation of statements**
(continuation of 2-31).

1.

Direct materials used	$105 million
Direct manufacturing labor costs	40 million
Prime costs	$145 million

Direct manufacturing labor costs	$ 40 million
Indirect manufacturing costs	51 million
Conversion costs	$ 91 million

2. Inventoriable costs (in millions) for Year 2004

Plant utilities	$ 5
Indirect manufacturing labor	20
Depreciation—plant, building, and equipment	9
Miscellaneous manufacturing overhead	10
Direct materials used	105
Direct manufacturing labor	40
Plant supplies used	6
Property tax on plant	1
Total inventoriable costs	$196

Period costs (in millions) for Year 2004

Marketing, distribution, and customer-service costs	$ 90

3. Design costs and R&D costs may be regarded as product costs in case of contracting with a governmental agency. For example, if the Air Force negotiated to contract with Lockheed to build a new type of supersonic fighter plane, design costs and R&D costs may be included in the contract as product costs.

4. Direct materials used $\quad = \quad \$105,000,000 \div 1,000,000$ units $= \$105$ per unit
Depreciation $\qquad\qquad = \quad \$\ \ 9,000,000 \div 1,000,000$ units $= \$\ \ 9$ per unit

5. Direct materials unit cost would be unchanged at $105. Depreciation unit cost would be $9,000,000 \div 1,500,000 = \$6$ per unit. Total direct materials costs would rise by 50% to $157,500,000 ($105 per unit $\times$ 1,500,000 units). Total depreciation cost of $9,000,000 would remain unchanged.

6. In this case, equipment depreciation is a variable cost in relation to the unit output. The amount of equipment depreciation will change in direct proportion to the number of units produced.

(a) Depreciation will be $4 million (1 million $\times$ $4) when 1 million units are produced.
(b) Depreciation will be $6 million (1.5 million $\times$ $4) when 1.5 million units are produced.

2-34 (20-25 min.) **Finding unknown amounts.**

Let G = given, I = inferred

	Case 1	Case 2
Step 1: Use gross margin formula		
Revenues	$ 32,000 G	$31,800 G
Cost of goods sold	**A** 20,700 I	20,000 G
Gross margin	$ 11,300 G	**C** $11,800 I
Step 2: Use schedule of cost of goods manufactured formula		
Direct materials used	$ 8,000 G	$ 12,000 G
Direct manufacturing labor costs	3,000 G	5,000 G
Indirect manufacturing costs	7,000 G	**D** 6,500 I
Manufacturing costs incurred	18,000 I	23,500 I
Add beginning work in process, 1/1	0 G	800 G
Total manufacturing costs to account for	18,000 I	24,300 I
Deduct ending work in process, 12/31	0 G	3,000 G
Cost of goods manufactured	$ 18,000 I	$ 21,300 I
Step 3: Use cost of goods sold formula		
Beginning finished goods inventory, 1/1	$ 4,000 G	4,000 G
Cost of goods manufactured	18,000 I	21,300 I
Cost of goods available for sale	22,000 I	25,300 I
Ending finished goods inventory, 12/31	**B** 1,300 I	5,300 G
Cost of goods sold	$ 20,700 I	$ 20,000 G

For case 1, do steps 1, 2, and 3 in order.
For case 2, do steps 1, 3, and then 2.

2-36 (30 min.)   **Comprehensive problem on unit costs, product costs.**

1.   If 2 pounds of direct materials are used to make each unit of finished product, 100,000 units × 2 lbs., or 200,000 lbs. were used at $0.70 per pound of direct materials ($140,000 ÷ 200,000 lbs.). (The direct material costs of $140,000 are direct materials used, not purchased.) Therefore, the ending inventory of direct materials is 2,000 lbs. × $0.70 = $1,400.

2.

	Manufacturing Costs for 100,000 units		
	Variable	**Fixed**	**Total**
Direct materials costs	$140,000	$ –	$140,000
Direct manufacturing labor costs	30,000	–	30,000
Plant energy costs	5,000	–	5,000
Indirect manufacturing labor costs	10,000	16,000	26,000
Other indirect manufacturing costs	8,000	24,000	32,000
Cost of goods manufactured	$193,000	$40,000	$233,000

Average unit manufacturing cost: $233,000 ÷ 100,000 units
= $2.33 per unit

$$\text{Finished goods inventory in units:} = \frac{\$20,970\ (\text{given})}{\$2.33\ \text{per unit}}$$
= 9,000 units

3.   Units sold in 2004 = Beginning inventory + Production – Ending inventory
= 0 + 100,000 – 9,000 = 91,000 units
Selling price per unit in 2004 = $436,800 ÷ 91,000
= $4.80 per unit

4.
Revenues (91,000 units sold × $4.80)		$436,800
Cost of units sold:		
Beginning finished goods, Jan. 1, 2004	$ 0	
Cost of goods manufactured	233,000	
Cost of goods available for sale	233,000	
Ending finished goods, Dec. 31, 2004	20,970	212,030
Gross margin		224,770
Operating costs:		
Marketing, distribution, and customer-service costs	162,850	
Administrative costs	50,000	212,850
Operating income		$ 11,920

Note: Although not required, the full set of unit variable costs is:

Direct materials costs	$1.40	
Direct manufacturing labor costs	0.30	
Plant energy costs	0.05	Per unit manufactured
Indirect manufacturing labor costs	0.10	
Other indirect manufacturing costs	0.08	
Marketing, distribution, and customer-service costs	$1.35	Per unit sold

2-38 (30 min.)   **Cost analysis, litigation risk, ethics.**

1.   Reasons for Savage not wanting Nash to include the potential litigation costs include:
   (a)   Genuine belief that the product has no risk of future litigation. Note that she asserts "she has total confidence in her medical research team."
   (b)   Concern that the uncertainties about litigation are sufficiently high to make any numerical estimate "meaningless."
   (c)   Concern that inclusion of future litigation costs would cause the board of directors to vote against the project. Savage may be "overly committed" to the project and wants to avoid showing information that prompts questions she prefers not to be raised.
   (d)   Avoid "smoking gun" memos being included in the project evaluation file. Savage may believe that if subsequent litigation occurs, the plaintiffs will "inappropriately" use a litigation cost line item as "proof" FY "knew the product had health problems" that were known to management at the outset.

2.
Unit costs excluding litigation costs	$100
Add unit litigation costs	110
Total unit costs	210
Add 20% markup	42
Selling price per unit	$252

Since each treatment is planned to cost patients $300, the new selling price of $252 will drop the doctors' margin to only $48 from the planned margin of $180 based on the planned selling price of $120. This would probably result in the doctors not having much incentive to promote the product. In fact, it may be quite possible that the doctors may not attempt to prescribe the treatment at such low margin because of their own exposure to liability.

3.   Nash has already registered his concern to Savage. The difficulty is that Savage asked Nash to not include the possible litigation in his presentation. If there is no record of this presentation, then Nash may have several concerns.
   (a)   He may be accused at a later stage of not anticipating the costs of litigation. If litigation does occur, some people will try to distance themselves from the problems. It may be to Nash's advantage to have a record of his early concerns. (Although plaintiffs may make Nash's life very difficult if they get access to Nash's files.) Nash may want to keep some record of his presentation to Savage.
   (b)   He may be portrayed as not being a "team player" if he continues his objections. Savage may have to silence his concerns if he decides to stay at FY.
   (c)   He may have difficult ethical objections with Savage's behavior. If he thinks she is acting unethically, his main options are to speak to her first (at least one time), speak to her supervisor (probably chairman of the company), or, as a final resort, resign.

CHAPTER 3
COST-VOLUME-PROFIT ANALYSIS

3-2   The assumptions underlying the CVP analysis outlined in Chapter 3 are:

1.   Changes in the level of revenues and costs arise only because of changes in the number of product (or service) units produced and sold.
2.   Total costs can be separated into a fixed component that does not vary with the output level and a component that is variable with respect to the output level.
3.   When represented graphically, the behavior of total revenues and total costs are linear (represented as a straight line) in relation to output units within a per unit relevant range and time period.
4.   The selling price, variable cost per unit, and fixed costs are known and constant.
5.   The analysis either covers a single product or assumes that the sales mix, when multiple products are sold, will remain constant as the level of total units sold changes.
6.   All revenues and costs can be added and compared without taking into account the time value of money.

3-4   Contribution margin is the difference between total revenues and total variable costs. Contribution margin per unit is the difference between selling price and variable cost per unit. Contribution-margin percentage is the contribution margin per unit divided by selling price.

3-6   Breakeven analysis denotes the study of the breakeven point, which is often only an incidental part of the relationship between cost, volume, and profit. Cost-volume-profit relationship is a more comprehensive term than breakeven analysis.

3-8   An increase in the income tax rate does not affect the breakeven point. Operating income at the breakeven point is zero, and no income taxes are paid at this point.

3-10   Examples include:
Manufacturing—substituting a robotic machine for hourly wage workers.
Marketing—changing a sales force compensation plan from a percent of sales dollars to a fixed salary.
Customer service—hiring a subcontractor to do customer repair visits on an annual retainer basis rather than a per-visit basis.

3-12   Operating leverage describes the effects that fixed costs have on changes in operating income as changes occur in units sold, and hence, in contribution margin. Knowing the degree of operating leverage at a given level of sales helps managers calculate the effect of fluctuations in sales on operating incomes.

3-14   A company with multiple products can compute a breakeven point by assuming there is a constant mix of products at different levels of total revenue.

3-16 (10 min.) CVP computations.

	Revenues	Variable Costs	Fixed Costs	Total Costs	Operating Income	Contribution Margin	Contribution Margin %
a.	**$2,000**	$ 500	**$300**	$ 800	$1,200	$1,500	**75.0%**
b.	2,000	**1,500**	300	**1,800**	200	500	**25.0%**
c.	1,000	700	**300**	1,000	**0**	300	**30.0%**
d.	1,500	**900**	300	**1,200**	300	600	40.0%

3-18 (35-40 min.) CVP analysis, changing revenues and costs.

1a.
$$SP = 8\% \times \$1,000 = \$80 \text{ per ticket}$$
$$VCU = \$35 \text{ per ticket}$$
$$CMU = \$80 - \$35 = \$45 \text{ per ticket per ticket}$$
$$FC = \$22,000 \text{ a month}$$

$$Q = \frac{FC}{CMU} = \frac{\$22,000}{\$45 \text{ per ticket}}$$

$$= 489 \text{ tickets (rounded up)}$$

1b.
$$Q = \frac{FC + TOI}{CMU} = \frac{\$22,000 + \$10,000}{\$45 \text{ per ticket}}$$

$$= \frac{\$32,000}{\$45 \text{ per ticket}}$$

$$= 712 \text{ tickets (rounded up)}$$

2a.
$$SP = \$80 \text{ per ticket}$$
$$VCU = \$29 \text{ per ticket}$$
$$CMU = \$80 - \$29 = \$51 \text{ per ticket}$$
$$FC = \$22,000 \text{ a month}$$

$$Q = \frac{FC}{CMU} = \frac{\$22,000}{\$51 \text{ per ticket}}$$

$$= 432 \text{ tickets (rounded up)}$$

2b.
$$Q = \frac{FC + TOI}{CMU} = \frac{\$22,000 + \$10,000}{\$51 \text{ per ticket}}$$

3-18 (Cont'd.)

$$= \frac{\$32,000}{\$51 \text{ per ticket}}$$

$$= 628 \text{ tickets (rounded up)}$$

3a. SP   = \$48 per ticket
VCU   = \$29 per ticket
CMU   = \$48 − \$29 = \$19 per ticket
FC   = \$22,000 a month

$$Q = \frac{FC}{CMU} = \frac{\$22,000}{\$19 \text{ per ticket}}$$

$$= 1,158 \text{ tickets (rounded up)}$$

3b. $$Q = \frac{FC + TOI}{CMU} = \frac{\$22,000 + \$10,000}{\$19 \text{ per ticket}}$$

$$= \frac{\$32,000}{\$19 \text{ per ticket}}$$

$$= 1,685 \text{ tickets (rounded up)}$$

The reduced commission sizably increases the breakeven point and the number of tickets required to yield a target operating income of \$10,000:

	8% Commission (Requirement 2)	Fixed Commission of \$48
Breakeven point	432	1,158
Attain OI of \$10,000	628	1,685

4a.   The \$5 delivery fee can be treated as either an extra source of revenue (as done below) or as a cost offset. Either approach increases UCM by \$5:

SP   = \$53 (\$48 + \$5) per ticket
VCU = \$29 per ticket
CMU = \$53 − \$29 = \$24 per ticket
FC   = \$22,000 a month

$$Q = \frac{FC}{CMU} = \frac{\$22,000}{\$24 \text{ per ticket}}$$

$$= 917 \text{ tickets (rounded up)}$$

3-18 (Cont'd.)

4b. $\quad Q = \dfrac{FC + TOI}{CMU} = \dfrac{\$22,000 + \$10,000}{\$24 \text{ per ticket}}$

$\qquad\qquad = \dfrac{\$32,000}{\$24 \text{ per ticket}}$

$\qquad\qquad = 1,334 \text{ tickets (rounded up)}$

The $5 delivery fee results in a higher contribution margin which reduces both the breakeven point and the tickets sold to attain operating income of $10,000.

3-20 (20 min.) CVP exercises.

	Revenues	Variable Costs	Contribution Margin	Fixed Costs	Budgeted Operating Income
Orig.	$10,000,000[G]	$8,200,000[G]	$1,800,000	$1,700,000[G]	$100,000
1.	10,000,000	8,020,000	1,980,000[a]	1,700,000	280,000
2.	10,000,000	8,380,000	1,620,000[b]	1,700,000	(80,000)
3.	10,000,000	8,200,000	1,800,000	1,785,000[c]	15,000
4.	10,000,000	8,200,000	1,800,000	1,615,000[d]	185,000
5.	10,800,000[e]	8,856,000[f]	1,944,000	1,700,000	244,000
6.	9,200,000[g]	7,544,000[h]	1,656,000	1,700,000	(44,000)
7.	11,000,000[i]	9,020,000[j]	1,980,000	1,870,000[k]	110,000
8.	10,000,000	7,790,000[l]	2,210,000	1,785,000[m]	425,000

[G]stands for given.

[a]$1,800,000 × 1.10; [b]$1,800,000 × 0.90; [c]$1,700,000 × 1.05; [d]$1,700,000 × 0.95; [e]$10,000,000 × 1.08; [f]$8,200,000 × 1.08; [g]$10,000,000 × 0.92; [h]$8,200,000 × 0.92; [i]$10,000,000 × 0.10; [j]$8,200,000 × 1.10; [k]$1,700,000 × 1.10; [l]$8,200,000 × 0.95; [m]$1,700,000 × 1.05

3-22 (10–15 min.) CVP analysis, income taxes.

1. Operating income $= \text{Net income} \div (1 - \text{tax rate})$
   $\qquad\qquad\qquad\quad = \$84,000 \div (1 - 0.40) \quad = \$140,000$

2. Contribution margin – Fixed costs = Operating income
   Contribution margin – $300,000 = $140,000
   $\qquad\qquad$ Contribution margin = $440,000

3. Revenues – Variable costs = Contribution margin
   Revenues – 0.80 Revenues = Contribution margin
   $\qquad$ 0.20 Revenues = $440,000
   $\qquad\qquad$ Revenues = $2,200,000

4. Breakeven revenues = Fixed costs ÷ Contribution margin percentage
   Breakeven revenues = $300,000 ÷ 0.20 = $1,500,000

3-24 (30 min.) **CVP analysis, sensitivity analysis.**

1.   SP = $30.00 × (1 – 0.30 margin to bookstore)
           = $30.00 × 0.70 = $21.00

   VCU = $ 4.00 variable production and marketing cost
              <u>3.15</u> variable author royalty cost (0.15 × $30.00 × 0.70)
           <u>$ 7.15</u>

   CMU = $21.00 – $7.15 = $13.85 per copy

   FC   = $ 500,000 fixed production and marketing cost
           <u>3,000,000</u> up-front payment to Washington
           <u>$3,500,000</u>

Exhibit 3-24A shows the PV graph.

EXHIBIT 3-24A
PV Graph for Media Publishers

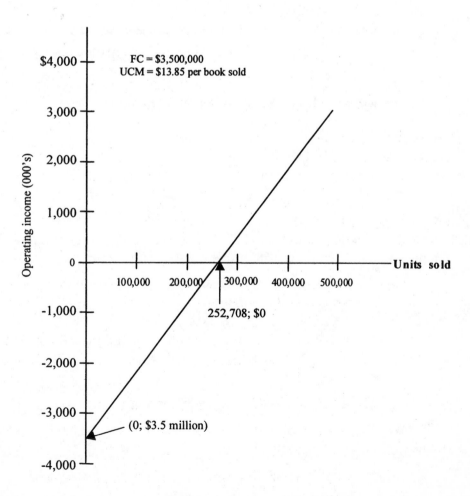

3-24 (Cont'd.)

2a.

$$\text{Breakeven number of units} = \frac{FC}{CMU}$$

$$= \frac{\$3,500,000}{\$13.85}$$

$$= 252,708 \text{ copies sold (rounded up)}$$

2b.

$$\text{Target OI} = \frac{FC + OI}{CMU}$$

$$= \frac{\$3,500,000 + \$2,000,000}{\$13.85}$$

$$= \frac{\$5,500,000}{\$13.85}$$

$$= 397,112 \text{ copies sold (rounded up)}$$

3a. Decreasing the normal bookstore margin to 20% of the listed bookstore price of $30 has the following effects:

SP $= \$30.00 \times (1 - 0.20)$
     $= \$30.00 \times 0.80 = \$24.00$

VCU $= \$\ 4.00$ variable production and marketing cost
     $\underline{+\ \ 3.60}$ variable author royalty cost $(0.15 \times \$30.00 \times 0.80)$
     $\underline{\$\ 7.60}$

CMU $= \$24.00 - \$7.60 = \$16.40$ per copy

$$\text{Breakeven number of units} = \frac{FC}{CMU}$$

$$= \frac{\$3,500,000}{\$16.40}$$

$$= 213,415 \text{ copies sold (rounded)}$$

The breakeven point decreases from 252,708 copies in requirement 2 to 213,415 copies.

3b. Increasing the listed bookstore price to $40 while keeping the bookstore margin at 30% has the following effects:

SP $= \$40.00 \times (1 - 0.30)$
     $= \$40.00 \times 0.70 = \$28.00$

VCU $= \$\ 4.00$ variable production and marketing cost
     $\underline{+\ \ 4.20}$ variable author royalty cost $(0.15 \times \$40.00 \times 0.70)$
     $\underline{\$\ 8.20}$

CMU $= \$28.00 - \$8.20 = \$19.80$ per copy

$$\text{Breakeven number of units} = \frac{\$3,500,000}{\$19.80}$$

3-24 (Cont'd.)

$$= 176{,}768 \text{ copies sold (rounded)}$$

The breakeven point decreases from 252,708 copies in requirement 2 to 176,768 copies.

3c.   The answer to requirements 3a and 3b decreases the breakeven point relative to requirement 2 because in each case fixed costs remain the same at $3,500,000 while contribution margin per unit increases.

3-26   (25 min.)   Operating leverage.

1a.   Let Q denote the quantity of carpets sold

Breakeven point under Option 1
$$\$500Q - \$350Q = \$5{,}000$$
$$\$150Q = \$5{,}000$$
$$Q = \$5{,}000 \div \$150 = 34 \text{ carpets (rounded)}$$

1b.   Breakeven point under Option 2
$$\$500Q - \$350Q - (0.10 \times \$500Q) = 0$$
$$100Q = 0$$
$$Q = 0$$

2.   Operating income under Option 1 = $150Q – $5,000
Operating income under Option 2 = $100Q

Find Q such that $150Q – $5,000 = $100Q
$$\$50Q = \$5{,}000$$
$$Q = \$5{,}000 \div \$50 = 100 \text{ carpets}$$

For Q = 100 carpets, operating income under both Option 1 and Option 2 = $10,000

3a.   For Q > 100, say, 101 carpets,
Option 1 gives operating income   = $150 × 101 – $5,000 = $10,150
Option 2 gives operating income   = $100 × 101   = $10,100
So Color Rugs will prefer Option 1.

3b.   For Q < 100, say, 99 carpets,
Option 1 gives operating income   = $150 × 99 – $5,000 = $9,850
Option 2 gives operating income   = $100 × 99   = $9,900
So Color Rugs will prefer Option 2.

3-26 (Cont'd.)

4. Degree of operating leverage $= \dfrac{\text{Contribution margin}}{\text{Operating income}}$

Under Option 1, degree of operating leverage $= \dfrac{\$150 \times 100}{\$10,000} = 1.5$

Under Option 2, degree of operating leverage $= \dfrac{\$100 \times 100}{\$10,000} = 1.0$

5. The calculations in requirement 4 indicate that when sales are 100 units, a percentage change in sales and contribution margin will result in 1.5 times that percentage change in operating income for Option 1, but the same percentage change in operating income for Option 2. The degree of operating leverage at a given level of sales helps managers calculate the effect of fluctuations in sales on operating incomes.

3-28 (30 min.) Sales mix, new and upgrade customers.

1.

	New Customers	Upgrade Customers
SP	$210	$120
VCU	90	40
CMU	120	80

Let S = Number of units sold to upgrade customers
$1.5S$ = Number of units sold to new customers
Revenues – Variable costs – Fixed costs = Operating income
$[\$210\,(1.5S) + \$120S] - [\$90\,(1.5S) + \$40S] - \$14,000,000 = \text{OI}$
$\$435S - \$175S - \$14,000,000 = \text{OI}$
Breakeven point is 134,616 units when OI = 0
$\$260S$ = $\$14,000,000$
 S = 53,846 units sold to upgrade customers
 $1.5S$ = 80,770 units sold to new customers
 134,616 units

Check

Revenues ($210 × 80,770; $120 × 53,846)	$23,423,220
Variable costs ($90 × 80,770; $40 × 53,846)	9,423,140
Contribution margin	14,000,080
Fixed costs	14,000,000
Operating income (subject to rounding)	$ 0

3-28 (Cont'd.)

2.   When 200,000 units are sold, mix is:

Units sold to new customers (60% × 200,000)	120,000
Units sold to upgrade customers (40% × 200,000)	80,000

Revenues ($210 × 120,000; $120 × 80,000)	$34,800,000
Variable costs ($90 × 120,000; $40 × 80,000)	14,000,000
Contribution margin	20,800,000
Fixed costs	14,000,000
Operating income	$ 6,800,000

3a.   Let S = Number of units sold to upgrade customers
      then S = Number of units sold to new customers

$$[\$210S + \$120S] - [\$90S + \$40S] - \$14,000,000 = OI$$

$330S - 130S$	=	$14,000,000
$200S$	=	$14,000,000
S	=	70,000 units sold to upgrade customers
S	=	70,000 units sold to new customers
		140,000 units

Check

Revenues ($210 × 70,000; $120 × 70,000)	$23,100,000
Variable costs ($90 × 70,000; $40 × 70,000)	9,100,000
Contribution margin	14,000,000
Fixed costs	14,000,000
Operating income	$ 0

3b.   Let S = Number of units sold to upgrade customers
      then $9S$ = Number of units sold to new customers

$$[\$210\,(9S) + \$120S] - [\$90\,(9S) + \$40S] - \$14,000,000 = OI$$

$2,010S - 850S$	=	$14,000,000
$1,160S$	=	$14,000,000
S	=	12,069 units sold to upgrade customers
$9S$	=	108,621 units sold to new customers
		120,690 units

Check

Revenues ($210 × 108,621; $120 × 12,069)	$24,258,690
Variable costs ($90 × 108,621; $40 × 12,069)	10,258,650
Contribution margin	14,000,040
Fixed costs	4,000,000
Operating income (subject to rounding)	$ 0

3-28 (Cont'd.)

3c. As Zapo increases its percentage of new customers, which have a higher contribution margin per unit than upgrade customers, the number of units required to break even decreases:

	New Customers	Upgrade Customers	Breakeven Point
Requirement 3(a)	50%	50%	140,000
Requirement 1	60	40	134,616
Requirement 3(b)	90	10	120,690

3-30   (20 min.)   CVP analysis, multiple cost drivers.

1a.
$$\text{Operating income} = \text{Revenues} - \left(\begin{array}{c}\text{Cost of picture}\\\text{frames}\end{array} \times \begin{array}{c}\text{Quantity of}\\\text{picture frames}\end{array}\right) - \left(\begin{array}{c}\text{Cost of}\\\text{shipment}\end{array} \times \begin{array}{c}\text{Number of}\\\text{shipments}\end{array}\right) - \begin{array}{c}\text{Fixed}\\\text{costs}\end{array}$$

$$= (\$45 \times 40{,}000) - (\$30 \times 40{,}000) - (\$60 \times 1{,}000) - \$240{,}000$$
$$= \$1{,}800{,}000 - \$1{,}200{,}000 - \$60{,}000 - \$240{,}000 = \$300{,}000$$

1b. Operating income $= (\$45 \times 40{,}000) - (\$30 \times 40{,}000) - (\$60 \times 800) - \$240{,}000 = \$312{,}000$

2. Denote the number of picture frames sold by Q, then

$$\$45Q - \$30Q - 500 \times \$60 - \$240{,}000 = 0$$
$$\$15Q = \$30{,}000 + \$240{,}000 = \$270{,}000$$
$$Q = \$270{,}000 \div \$15 = 18{,}000 \text{ picture frames}$$

3. Suppose Susan had 1,000 shipments.

$$\$45Q - \$30Q - (1000 \times \$60) - \$240{,}000 = 0$$
$$15Q = \$300{,}000$$
$$Q = 20{,}000 \text{ picture frames}$$

The breakeven point is not unique because there are two cost drivers—quantity of picture frames and number of shipments. Various combinations of the two cost drivers can yield zero operating income.

3-32 (15–20 min.) **Uncertainty, CVP analysis.**

1. King pays Foreman $2 million plus $4 (25% of $16) for every home purchasing the pay-per-view. The expected value of the variable component is:

Demand (1)	Payment (2) = (1) × $4	Probability (3)	Expected Payment (4)
100,000	$ 400,000	0.05	$ 20,000
200,000	800,000	0.10	80,000
300,000	1,200,000	0.30	360,000
400,000	1,600,000	0.35	560,000
500,000	2,000,000	0.15	300,000
1,000,000	4,000,000	0.05	200,000
			$1,520,000

The expected value of King's payment is $3,520,000 ($2,000,000 fixed fee + $1,520,000).

2.
$$SP = \$16$$
$$VCU = \$\ 6\ (\$4\text{ payment to Foreman} + \$2\text{ variable cost})$$
$$CMU = \$10$$
$$FC = \$2,000,000 + \$1,000,000 = \$3,000,000$$
$$Q = \frac{FC}{UCM}$$
$$= \frac{\$3,000,000}{\$10}$$
$$= 300,000 \text{ homes}$$

If 300,000 homes purchase the pay-per-view, King will break even.

3-34 (30 min.) **CVP, target income, service firm.**

1.
Revenue per child	$600
Variable costs per child	200
Contribution margin per child	$400

$$\text{Breakeven quantity} = \frac{\text{Fixed costs}}{\text{Contribution margin per child}}$$

$$= \frac{\$5,600}{\$400} = 14 \text{ children}$$

2.
$$\text{Target quantity} = \frac{\text{Fixed costs} + \text{Target operating income}}{\text{Contribution margin per child}}$$

$$= \frac{\$5,600 + \$10,400}{\$400} = 40 \text{ children}$$

3-34 (Cont'd.)

3.
Increase in rent ($3,000 – $2,000)	$1,000
Field trips	1,000
Total increase in fixed costs	$2,000
Divide by the number of children enrolled	÷ 40
Increase in fee per child	$ 50

Therefore the fee per child will increase from $600 to $650.
Alternatively,

$$\text{New contribution margin per child} = \frac{\$5,600 + \$2,000 + \$10,400}{40} = \$450$$

New fee per child = Variable costs per child + New contribution margin per child
$$= \$200 + \$450 = \$650$$

3-36 (30-40 min.) CVP analysis, income taxes.

1. Revenues – Variable costs – Fixed costs $= \dfrac{\text{Target net income}}{1 - \text{Tax rate}}$

Let X = Net income for 2003

$$20,000(\$25.00) - 20,000(\$13.75) - \$135,000 = \frac{X}{1 - 0.40}$$

$$\$500,000 - \$275,000 - \$135,000 = \frac{X}{0.60}$$

$$\$300,000 - \$165,000 - \$81,000 = X$$

$$X = \$54,000$$

Alternatively,
Operating income = Revenues – Variable costs – Fixed costs
$$= \$500,000 - \$275,000 - \$135,000 = \$90,000$$
Income taxes = $0.40 \times \$90,000 = \$36,000$
Net income = Operating income – Income taxes
$$= \$90,000 - \$36,000 = \$54,000$$

2. Let Q = Number of units to break even

$\$25.00Q - \$13.75Q - \$135,000 = 0$
$Q = \$135,000 \div \$11.25 = 12,000$ units

3-36 (Cont'd.)

3. Let X = Net income for 2004

$$22{,}000(\$25.00) - 22{,}000(\$13.75) - (\$135{,}000 + \$11{,}250) = \frac{X}{1-0.40}$$

$$\$550{,}000 - \$302{,}500 - \$146{,}250 = \frac{X}{0.60}$$

$$\$101{,}250 = \frac{X}{0.60}$$

$$X = \$60{,}750$$

4. Let Q = Number of units to break even with new fixed costs of $146,250

$$\$25.00Q - \$13.75Q - \$146{,}250 = 0$$
$$Q = \$146{,}250 \div \$11.25 = 13{,}000 \text{ units}$$
$$\text{Breakeven revenues} = 13{,}000 \times \$25.00 = \$325{,}000$$

5. Let S = Required sales units to equal 2003 net income

$$\$25.00S - \$13.75S - \$146{,}250 = \frac{\$54{,}000}{0.60}$$

$$\$11.25S = \$236{,}250$$
$$S = 21{,}000 \text{ units}$$
$$\text{Revenues} = 21{,}000 \text{ units} \times \$25.00 = \$525{,}000$$

6. Let A = Amount spent for advertising in 2004

$$\$550{,}000 - \$302{,}500 - (\$135{,}000 + A) = \frac{\$60{,}000}{0.60}$$

$$\$550{,}000 - \$302{,}500 - \$135{,}000 - A = \$100{,}000$$
$$\$550{,}000 - \$537{,}500 = A$$
$$A = \$12{,}500$$

3-38 (10-15 min.) **Margin of safety.**

1.

Selling price ($1,000,000 ÷ $10,000)	$100
Variable cost per unit ($600,000 ÷ $10,000)	60
Contribution margin	$ 40

$$\text{Breakeven point in units} = \frac{\text{Fixed costs}}{\text{Contribution margin per unit}}$$

$$= \frac{\$250{,}000}{\$40 \text{ per unit}} = 6{,}250 \text{ footballs}$$

3-38 (Cont'd.)

Breakeven point in dollars = 6,250 × $100 = $625,000

2. Margin of safety in units = 10,000 − 6,250 = 3,750 footballs

Margin of safety in dollars = $100 × 3,750 = $375,000

3. Contribution margin ratio = $\dfrac{\text{Contribution margin per unit}}{\text{Selling price}} = \dfrac{\$40}{\$100} = 40\%$

Incremental operating income = 40% × $200,000 = $80,000

3-40 (20–25 min.) **CVP analysis, shoe stores (continuation of 3-39).**

1. Because the unit sales level at the point of indifference would be the same for each plan, the revenue would be equal. Therefore, the unit sales level sought would be that which produces the same total costs for each plan.

$$
\begin{aligned}
\text{Let } Q &= \text{unit sales level} \\
\$19.50Q + \$360,000 + \$81,000 &= \$21.00Q + \$360,000 \\
\$81,000 &= \$1.50Q \\
Q &= 54,000 \text{ pairs}
\end{aligned}
$$

2.

	Commission Plan		Salary Plan	
Sales in units	50,000	60,000	50,000	60,000
Revenues at $30.00	$1,500,000	$1,800,000	$1,500,000	$1,800,000
Variable costs at $21.00 and at $19.50	1,050,000	1,260,000	975,000	1,170,000
Contribution margin	450,000	540,000	525,000	630,000
Fixed costs	360,000	360,000	441,000	441,000
Operating income	$ 90,000	$ 180,000	$ 84,000	$ 189,000

The decision regarding the plans will depend heavily on the unit sales level that is generated by the fixed salary plan. For example, as part (1) shows, at identical unit sales levels in excess of 54,000 units, the fixed salary plan will always provide a more profitable final result than the commission plan.

3. Let TQ = Target number of units

$$
\begin{aligned}
\$30.00TQ - \$19.50TQ - \$441,000 &= \$168,000 \\
\$10.50TQ &= \$609,000 \\
TQ &= \$609,000 \div \$10.50 \\
TQ &= 58,000 \text{ units}
\end{aligned}
$$

3-40 (Cont'd.)

$$\$30.00TQ - \$21.00TQ - \$360,000 \quad = \$168,000$$
$$\$9.00TQ \quad = \$528,000$$
$$TQ \quad = \$528,000 \div \$9.00$$
$$TQ \quad = 58,667 \text{ units (rounded)}$$

The decision regarding the salary plan depends heavily on predictions of demand. For instance, the salary plan offers the same operating income at 58,000 units as the commission plan offers at 58,667 units.

3-42   (30 min.)   CVP analysis, income taxes, sensitivity.

1a.   In order to break even, Almo Company must sell 500 units. This amount represents the point where revenues equal total costs.

Let Q denote the quantity of canopies sold.

$$\begin{aligned}
\text{Revenue} &= \text{Variable costs} + \text{Fixed costs} \\
\$400Q &= \$200Q + \$100,000 \\
\$200Q &= \$100,000 \\
Q &= 500 \text{ units}
\end{aligned}$$

Breakeven can also be calculated using contribution margin per unit.

Contribution margin per unit = Selling price – Variable cost per unit = $400 – $200 = $200

$$\begin{aligned}
\text{Breakeven} &= \text{Fixed Costs} \div \text{Contribution margin per unit} \\
&= \$100,000 \div \$200 \\
&= 500 \text{ units}
\end{aligned}$$

1b.   In order to achieve its net income objective, Almo Company must sell 2,500 units. This amount represents the point where revenues equal total costs plus the corresponding operating income objective to achieve net income of $240,000.

$$\begin{aligned}
\text{Revenue} &= \text{Variable costs} + \text{Fixed costs} + [\text{Net income} \div (1 - \text{Tax rate})] \\
\$400Q &= \$200Q + \$100,000 + [\$240,000 \div (1 - 0.4)] \\
\$400\ Q &= \$200Q + \$100,000 + \$400,000 \\
Q &= 2,500 \text{ units}
\end{aligned}$$

2.   To achieve its net income objective, Almo Company should select the first alternative where the sales price is reduced by $40, and 2,700 units are sold during the remainder of the year. This alternative results in the highest net income and is the only alternative that equals or exceeds the company's net income objective. Calculations for the three alternatives are shown below.

3-42 (Cont'd.)

Alternative 1

$$
\begin{aligned}
\text{Revenues} &= (\$400 \times 350) + (\$360^a \times 2,700) = \$1,112,000 \\
\text{Variable costs} &= \$200 \times 3,050^b = \$610,000 \\
\text{Operating income} &= \$1,112,000 - \$610,000 - \$100,000 = \$402,000 \\
\text{Net income} &= \$402,000 \times (1 - 0.4) = \$241,200
\end{aligned}
$$

$^a\$400 - \$40;\ ^b350$ units $+ 2,700$ units.

Alternative 2

$$
\begin{aligned}
\text{Revenues} &= (\$400 \times 350) + (\$370^c \times 2,200) = \$954,000 \\
\text{Variable costs} &= (\$200 \times 350) + (\$190^d \times 2,200) = \$488,000 \\
\text{Operating income} &= \$954,000 - \$488,000 - \$100,000 = \$366,000 \\
\text{Net income} &= \$366,000 \times (1 - 0.4) = \$219,600
\end{aligned}
$$

$^c\$400 - \$30;\ ^d\$200 - \$10.$

Alternative 3

$$
\begin{aligned}
\text{Revenues} &= (\$400 \times 350) + (\$380^e \times 2,000) = \$900,000 \\
\text{Variable costs} &= \$200 \times 2,350^f = \$470,000 \\
\text{Operating income} &= \$900,000 - \$470,000 - \$90,000^g = \$340,000 \\
\text{Net income} &= \$340,000 \times (1 - 0.4) = \$204,000
\end{aligned}
$$

$^e\$400 - 0.05 \times \$400 = 400 - \$20;\ ^f350$ units $+ 2,000$ units; $^g\$100,000 - \$10,000$

3-44 (15–25 min.) Sales mix, three products.

1. Sales of A, B, and C are in ratio 20,000 : 100,000 : 80,000. So for every 1 unit of A, 5 (100,000 ÷ 20,000) units of B are sold, and 4 (80,000 ÷ 20,000) units of C are sold.

Let Q = Number of units of A to break even
5Q = Number of units of B to break even
4Q = Number of units of C to break even

Contribution margin – Fixed costs = Zero operating income

$$
\begin{aligned}
\$3Q + \$2(5Q) + \$1(4Q) - \$255,000 &= 0 \\
\$17Q &= \$255,000 \\
Q &= 15,000\ (\$255,000 \div \$17)\ \text{units of A} \\
5Q &= 75,000\ \text{units of B} \\
4Q &= \underline{60,000}\ \text{units of C} \\
\text{Total} &= \underline{150,000}\ \text{units}
\end{aligned}
$$

2. Contribution margin:

A: 20,000 × $3	$ 60,000	
B: 100,000 × $2	200,000	
C: 80,000 × $1	80,000	
Contribution margin		$340,000
Fixed costs		255,000
Operating income		$ 85,000

3-44 (Cont'd.)

3.   Contribution margin

A:	20,000 × $3	$ 60,000
B:	80,000 × $2	160,000
C:	100,000 × $1	100,000
	Contribution margin	$320,000
Fixed costs		255,000
Operating income		$ 65,000

Let Q   =   Number of units of A to break even
4Q   =   Number of units of B to break even
5Q   =   Number of units of C to break even

Contribution margin – Fixed costs = Breakeven point

$$\$3Q + \$2(4Q) + \$1(5Q) - \$255,000 = 0$$
$$\$16Q = \$255,000$$
$$Q = 15,938 \ (\$255,000 \div \$16) \text{ units of A (rounded)}$$
$$4Q = 63,752 \text{ units of B}$$
$$5Q = 79,690 \text{ units of C}$$
$$\text{Total} = 159,380 \text{ units}$$

Breakeven point increases because the new mix contains less of the higher contribution margin per unit, product B, and more of the lower contribution margin per unit, product C.

3-46   (20–25 min.)Sales mix, two products.

1.   Let Q   = Number of units of Deluxe carrier to break even
      3Q   = Number of units of Standard carrier to break even

Revenues – Variable costs – Fixed costs = Zero operating income

$$\$20(3Q) + \$30Q - \$14(3Q) - \$18Q - \$1,200,000 = 0$$
$$\$60Q + \$30Q - \$42Q - \$18Q = \$1,200,000$$
$$\$30Q = \$1,200,000$$
$$Q = 40,000 \text{ units of Deluxe}$$
$$3Q = 120,000 \text{ units of Standard}$$

The breakeven point is 120,000 Standard units plus 40,000 Deluxe units, a total of 160,000 units.

2a.   Unit contribution margins are: Standard: $20 – $14 = $6; Deluxe: $30 – $18 = $12
        If only Standard carriers were sold, the breakeven point would be:
        $1,200,000 ÷ $6 = 200,000 units.
2b.   If only Deluxe carriers were sold, the breakeven point would be:
        $1,200,000 ÷ $12 = 100,000 units

3-46 (Cont'd.)

3.
$$\begin{aligned}
\text{Operating income} &= \text{Contribution margin of Standard} + \text{Contribution margin of Deluxe} - \text{Fixed costs} \\
&= 180,000(\$6) + 20,000(\$12) - \$1,200,000 \\
&= \$1,080,000 + \$240,000 - \$1,200,000 \\
&= \$120,000
\end{aligned}$$

Let Q = Number of units of Deluxe product to break even
$9Q$ = Number of units of Standard product to break even

$$\begin{aligned}
\$20(9Q) + \$30Q - \$14(9Q) - \$18Q - \$1,200,000 &= 0 \\
\$180Q + \$30Q - \$126Q - \$18Q &= \$1,200,000 \\
\$66Q &= \$1,200,000 \\
Q &= 18,182 \text{ units of Deluxe (rounded)} \\
9Q &= 163,638 \text{ units of Standard}
\end{aligned}$$

The breakeven point is 163,638 Standard + 18,182 Deluxe, a total of 181,820 units.

The major lesson of this problem is that changes in the sales mix change breakeven points and operating incomes. In this example, the budgeted and actual total sales in number of units were identical, but the proportion of the product having the higher contribution margin declined. Operating income suffered, falling from $300,000 to $120,000. Moreover, the breakeven point rose from 160,000 to 181,820 units.

3-48 (30 min.) Ethics, CVP analysis.

1.
$$\begin{aligned}
\text{Contribution margin percentage} &= \frac{\text{Revenues} - \text{Variable costs}}{\text{Revenues}} \\
&= \frac{\$5,000,000 - \$3,000,000}{\$5,000,000} \\
&= \frac{\$2,000,000}{\$5,000,000} = 40\%
\end{aligned}$$

$$\begin{aligned}
\text{Breakeven revenues} &= \frac{\text{Fixed costs}}{\text{Contribution margin percentage}} \\
&= \frac{\$2,160,000}{0.40} = \$5,400,000
\end{aligned}$$

2. If variable costs are 52% of revenues, contribution margin percentage equals 48% (100% − 52%)

$$\begin{aligned}
\text{Breakeven revenues} &= \frac{\text{Fixed costs}}{\text{Contribution margin percentage}} \\
&= \frac{\$2,160,000}{0.48} = \$4,500,000
\end{aligned}$$

3-48 (Cont'd.)

3.	Revenues	$5,000,000
	Variable costs (0.52 × $5,000,000)	2,600,000
	Fixed costs	2,160,000
	Operating income	$ 240,000

4.   Incorrect reporting of environmental costs with the goal of continuing operations is unethical. In assessing the situation, the specific "Standards of Ethical Conduct for Management Accountants" (described in Exhibit 1-7) that the management accountant should consider are listed below.

Competence
Clear reports using relevant and reliable information should be prepared. Preparing reports on the basis of incorrect environmental costs in order to make the company's performance look better than it is violates competence standards.   It is unethical for Bush to not report environmental costs in order to make the plant's performance look good.

Integrity
The management accountant has a responsibility to avoid actual or apparent conflicts of interest and advise all appropriate parties of any potential conflict. Bush may be tempted to report lower environmental costs to please Lemond and Woodall and save the jobs of his colleagues. This action, however, violates the responsibility for integrity.   The Standards of Ethical Conduct require the management accountant to communicate favorable as well as unfavorable information.

Objectivity
The management accountant's Standards of Ethical Conduct require that information should be fairly and objectively communicated and that all relevant information should be disclosed. From a management accountant's standpoint, underreporting environmental costs to make performance look good would violate the standard of objectivity.

Bush should indicate to Lemond that estimates of environmental costs and liabilities should be included in the analysis. If Lemond still insists on modifying the numbers and reporting lower environmental costs, Bush should raise the matter with one of Lemond's superiors. If after taking all these steps, there is continued pressure to understate environmental costs, Bush should consider resigning from the company and not engage in unethical behavior.

CHAPTER 4
JOB COSTING

4-2   In a *job-costing system,* costs are assigned to a distinct unit, batch, or lot of a product or service. In a *process-costing system,* the cost of a product or service is obtained by using broad averages to assign costs to masses of identical or similar units.

4-4   The seven steps in job costing are: (1) identify the job that is the chosen cost object, (2) identify the direct costs of the job, (3) select the cost-allocation bases to use for allocating indirect costs to the job, (4) identify the indirect costs associated with each cost-allocation base, (5) compute the rate per unit of each cost-allocation base used to allocate indirect costs to the job, (6) compute the indirect costs allocated to the job, and (7) compute the total cost of the job by adding all direct and indirect costs assigned to the job.

4-6   Three major source documents used in job-costing systems are: (1) job cost record or job cost sheet, a document that records and accumulates all costs assigned to a specific job, starting when work begins (2) materials requisition record, a document that contains information about the cost of direct materials used on a specific job and in a specific department; and (3) labor-time record, a document that contains information about the labor time used on a specific job and in a specific department.

4-8   Two reasons for using an annual budget period are:
a.   The numerator reason—the longer the time period, the less the influence of seasonal patterns, and
b.   The denominator reason—the longer the time period, the less the effect of variations in output levels on the allocation of fixed costs.

4-10   A house construction firm can use job cost information (a) to determine the profitability of individual jobs, (b) to assist in bidding on future jobs, and (c) to evaluate professionals who are in charge of managing individual jobs.

4-12   Debit entries to Work-in-Process Control represent increases in work in process. Examples of debit entries under normal costing are: (a) direct materials used (credit to Materials Control), (b) direct manufacturing labor billed to job (credit to Wages Payable Control), and (c) manufacturing overhead allocated to job (credit to Manufacturing Overhead Allocated).

4-14   A company might use budgeted costs rather than actual costs to compute direct labor rates because it may be difficult to trace direct labor costs to jobs as they are completed (for example, because bonuses are only known at the end of the year).

4-16 (10 min) **Job order costing, process costing.**

a.	Job costing		l.	Job costing
b.	Process costing		m.	Process costing
c.	Job costing		n.	Job costing
d.	Process costing		o.	Job costing
e.	Job costing		p.	Job costing
f.	Process costing		q.	Job costing
g.	Job costing		r.	Process costing
h.	Job costing (but some process costing)		s.	Job costing
i.	Process costing		t.	Process costing
j.	Process costing		u.	Job costing
k.	Job costing			

4-18 (20 -30 min.) **Job costing, normal and actual costing.**

1.
$$\text{Budgeted indirect - cost rate} = \frac{\text{Budgeted indirect costs}}{\text{Budgeted direct labor - hours}} = \frac{\$8,000,000}{160,000 \text{ hours}}$$

$$= \$50 \text{ per direct labor-hour}$$

$$\text{Actual indirect - cost rate} = \frac{\text{Actual indirect costs}}{\text{Actual direct labor - hour}} = \frac{\$6,888,000}{164,000 \text{ hours}}$$

$$= \$42 \text{ per direct labor-hour}$$

These rates differ because both the numerator and the denominator in the two calculations are different—one based on budgeted numbers and the other based on actual numbers.

2a.		**Laguna Model**	**Mission Model**
	Normal costing		
	Direct costs		
	Direct materials	$106,450	$127,604
	Direct labor	36,276	41,410
		142,726	169,014
	Indirect costs		
	Assembly support ($50 × 900; $50 × 1,010)	45,000	50,500
		45,000	50,500
	Total costs	$187,726	$219,514
2b.	Actual costing		
	Direct costs		
	Direct materials	$106,450	$127,604
	Direct labor	36,276	41,410
		142,726	169,014
	Indirect costs		
	Assembly support ($42 × 900; $42 × 1,010)	37,800	42,420
		37,800	42,420
	Total costs	$180,526	$211,434

3.   Normal costing enables Anderson to report a job cost as soon as the job is completed, assuming that both the direct materials and direct labor costs are known at the time of use/work. Once the 900 direct labor-hours are known for the Laguna Model (June 2004), Anderson can compute the $187,726 cost figure using normal costing. Anderson can use this information to manage the costs of the Laguna Model job as well as to bid on similar jobs later in the year. In contrast, Anderson has to wait until the December 2004 year-end to compute the $180,526 cost of the Laguna Model using actual costing.

    Although not required, the following overview diagram summarizes Anderson Construction's job-costing system.

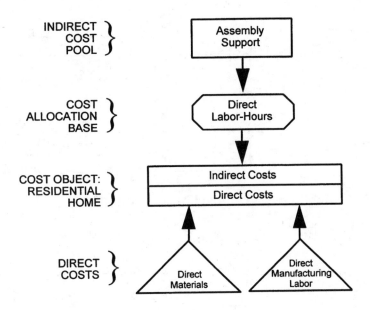

4-20 (20-30 min.) **Job costing, accounting for manufacturing overhead, budgeted rates.**

1. An overview of the product costing system is:

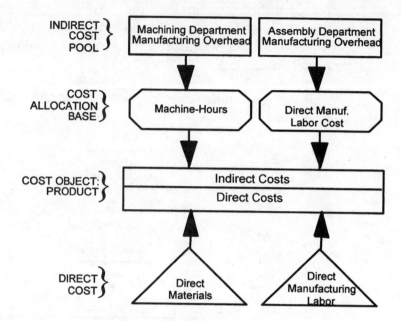

Budgeted manufacturing overhead divided by allocation base:

Machining overhead $\dfrac{\$1,800,000}{50,000} = \$36$ per machine-hour

Assembly overhead: $\dfrac{\$3,600,000}{\$2,000,000} = 180\%$ of direct manuf. labor costs

2.

Machining department, 2,000 hours × $36	$72,000
Assembly department, 180% × $15,000	27,000
Total manufacturing overhead allocated to Job 494	$99,000

3.

	Machining	Assembly
Actual manufacturing overhead	$2,100,000	$ 3,700,000
Manufacturing overhead allocated,		
55,000 × $36	1,980,000	
180% × $2,200,000		3,960,000
Underallocated (Overallocated)	$ 120,000	$ (260,000)

4-22   (20–30 min.) **Computing indirect-cost rates, job costing.**

1a.

	Budgeted Fixed Indirect Costs	Budgeted Hours	Budgeted Fixed Indirect Cost Rate per Hour	Budgeted Variable Indirect Cost Rate per Hour	Budgeted Total Indirect Cost Rate per Hour
Jan.–March	$ 50,000	20,000	$ 2.50	$10	$12.50
April–June	50,000	10,000	5.00	10	15.00
July–Sept.	50,000	4,000	12.50	10	22.50
Oct.–Dec.	50,000	6,000	8.33	10	18.33
b.	$200,000	40,000	$ 5.00	$10	$15.00

2a.   All four jobs use 10 hours of professional labor time. The only difference in job costing is the indirect cost rate. The quarterly-based indirect job costs are:

Hansen:	$(10 \times \$12.50)$	= $125.00
Kai:	$(6 \times \$12.50) + (4 \times \$15.00)$	= $135.00
Patera:	$(4 \times \$15.00) + (6 \times \$22.50)$	= $195.00
Stevens:	$(5 \times \$12.50) + (2 \times \$22.50) + (3 \times \$18.33)$	= $162.50

	Hansen	Kai	Patera	Stevens
Revenues, $65 × 10	$650	$650	$650	$650.00
Direct costs, $30 × 10	300	300	300	300.00
Indirect costs	125	135	195	162.50
Total costs	425	435	495	462.50
Operating income	$225	$215	$155	$187.50

2b.   Using annual-based indirect job-cost rates, all four customers will have the same operating income:

Revenues, $65 × 10 hours	$650
Direct costs, $30 × 10 hours	300
Indirect costs, $15 × 10 hours	150
Total costs	450
Operating income	$200

3.   All four jobs use 10 hours of professional labor time. Using the quarterly-based indirect-cost rates, there are four different operating incomes because the work done on them is completed in different quarters. In contrast, using the annual indirect-cost rate, all four customers show the same operating income. All these different operating income figures for jobs with the same number of professional labor-hours are due to the allocation of fixed indirect costs.

4-22 (Cont'd.)

An overview of the Tax Assist job-costing system is:

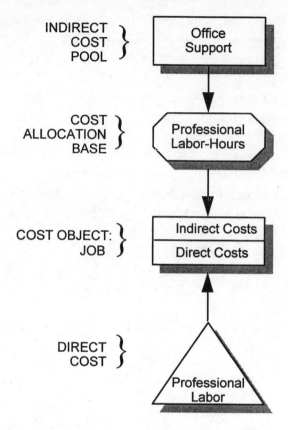

4-24 (35 – 45 min.) **Job costing, journal entries.**

Some instructors may also want to assign Exercise 4-25. It demonstrates the relationships of the general ledger to the underlying subsidiary ledgers and source documents.

1.   An overview of the product costing system is:

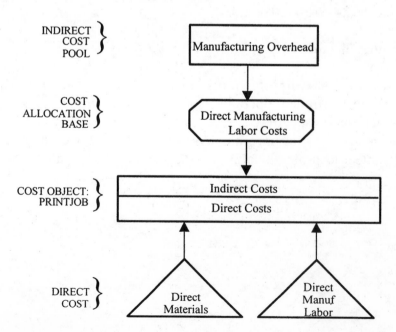

4-24 (Cont'd.)

2. & 3.

This answer assumes COGS given of $4,020 does not include the writeoff of overallocated manufacturing overhead.

2.	(1)	Materials Control	800	800
		Accounts Payable Control		
	(2)	Work-in-Process Control	710	
		Materials Control		710
	(3)	Manufacturing Overhead Control	100	
		Materials Control		100
	(4)	Work-in-Process Control	1,300	
		Manufacturing Overhead Control	900	
		Wages Payable Control		2,200
	(5)	Manufacturing Overhead Control	400	
		Accumulated Depreciation—buildings and		
		manufacturing equipment		400
	(6)	Manufacturing Overhead Control	550	
		Miscellaneous accounts		550
	(7)	Work-in-Process Control	2,080	
		Manufacturing Overhead Allocated		2,080
		(1.60 × $1,300 = $2,080)		
	(8)	Finished Goods Control	4,120	
		Work-in-Process Control		4,120
	(9)	Accounts Receivable Control (or Cash)	8,000	
		Revenues		8,000
	(10)	Cost of Goods Sold	4,020	
		Finished Goods Control		4,020
	(11)	Manufacturing Overhead Allocated	2,080	
		Manufacturing Overhead Control		1,950
		Cost of Goods Sold		130

3.

Materials Control

Bal. 12/31/2003	100	(2)	Issues		710
(1) Purchases	800	(3)	Issues		100
Bal. 12/31/2004	90				

Work-in-Process Control

Bal. 12/31/2003	60	(8)	Goods completed	4,120
(2) Direct materials	710			
(4) Direct manuf. labor	1,300			
(7) Manuf. overhead				
allocated	2,080			
Bal. 12/31/2004	30			

4-24 (Cont'd.)

Finished Goods Control

Bal. 12/31/2003	500	(10) Goods sold	4,020
(8) Goods completed	4,120		
Bal. 12/31/2004	600		

Cost of Goods Sold

(10) Goods sold	4,020	(11) Adjust for over-allocation	130
Bal. 12/31/2004	3,890		

Manufacturing Overhead Control

(3) Indirect materials	100	(11) To close	1,950
(4) Indirect manuf. labor	900		
(5) Depreciation	400		
(6) Miscellaneous	550		
Bal.	0		

Manufacturing Overhead Allocated

(11) To close	2,080	(7) Manuf. overhead allocated	2,080
		Bal.	0

4-26   (45 min.)   Job costing, journal entries.

Some instructors may wish to assign Problem 4-24. It demonstrates the relationships of journal entries, general ledger, subsidiary ledgers, and source documents.

1.   An overview of the product-costing system is:

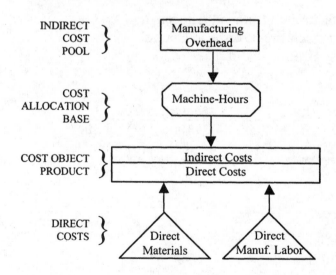

4-26 (Cont'd.)

2. Amounts in millions.

(1)	Materials Control		150	
	Accounts Payable Control			150
(2)	Work-in-Process Control		145	
	Materials Control			145
(3)	Manufacturing Department Overhead Control		10	
	Materials Control			10
(4)	Work-in-Process Control		90	
	Wages Payable Control			90
(5)	Manufacturing Department Overhead Control		30	
	Wages Payable Control			30
(6)	Manufacturing Department Overhead Control		19	
	Accumulated Depreciation			19
(7)	Manufacturing Department Overhead Control		9	
	Various liabilities			9
(8)	Work-in-Process Control		63	
	Manufacturing Overhead Allocated			63
(9)	Finished Goods Control		294	
	Work-in-Process Control			294
(10a)	Cost of Goods Sold		292	
	Finished Goods Control			292
(10b)	Accounts Receivable Control (or Cash)		400	
	Revenues			400

The posting of entries to T-accounts is:

Materials Control

Bal.	12	(2)	145
(1)	150	(3)	10

Work-in-Process Control

Bal.	2	(9)	294
(2)	145		
(4)	90		
(8)	63		
Bal.	6		

Finished Goods Control

Bal.	6	(10a)	292
(9)	294		

Cost of Goods Sold

(10a)	292		
(11)	5		

Manufacturing Department
Overhead Control

(3)	10	(11)	68
(5)	30		
(6)	19		
(7)	9		

Manufacturing Overhead Allocated

(11)	63	(8)	63

4-26 (Cont'd.)

Accounts Payable Control		
	(1)	150

Wages Payable Control		
	(4)	90
	(5)	30

Accumulated Depreciation		
	(6)	19

Various Liabilities		
	(7)	9

Accounts Receivable Control	
(10b) 400	

Revenues		
	(10b)	400

The ending balance of Work-in-Process Control is $6.

3. (11) Manufacturing Overhead Allocated   63
         Cost of Goods Sold   5
             Manufacturing Department Overhead Control   68

4-28 (20–30 min.) Job costing; actual, normal, and variation of normal costing.

1. Actual direct cost rate for professional labor   = $58 per professional labor-hour

    Actual indirect cost rate $\dfrac{\$744,000}{15,500 \text{ hours}}$ = $48 per professional labor-hour

    Budgeted direct cost rate
    for professional labor $\dfrac{\$960,000}{16,000 \text{ hours}}$ = $60 per professional labor-hour

    Budgeted indirect cost rate $\dfrac{\$720,000}{16,000 \text{ hours}}$ = $45 per professional labor-hour

	(a) Actual Costing	(b) Normal Costing	(c) Variation of Normal Costing
Direct-Cost Rate	$58 (Actual rate)	$58 (Actual rate)	$60 (Budgeted rate)
Indirect-Cost Rate	$48 (Actual rate)	$45 (Budgeted rate)	$45 (Budgeted rate)

4-28 (Cont'd.)

2.

	(a) Actual Costing	(b) Normal Costing	(c) Variation of Normal Costing
Direct Costs	$58 × 120 = $ 6,960	$58 × 120 = $ 6,960	$60 × 120 = $ 7,200
Indirect Costs	48 × 120 = 5,760	45 × 120 = 5,400	45 × 120 = 5,400
Total Job Costs	$12,720	$12,360	$12,600

All three costing systems use the actual professional labor time of 120 hours. The budgeted 110 hours for the Pierre Enterprises audit job is not used in job costing. However, Chirac may have used the 110 hour number in bidding for the audit.

The actual costing figure of $12,720 exceeds the normal costing figure of $12,360, because the actual indirect-cost rate ($48) exceeds the budgeted indirect-cost rate ($45). The normal costing figure of $12,360 is less than the variation of normal costing (based on budgeted rates for direct costs) figure of $12,600, because the actual direct-cost rate ($58) is less than the budgeted direct-cost rate ($60).

Although not required, the following overview diagram summarizes Chirac's job-costing system.

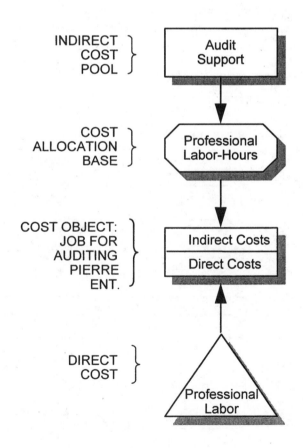

4-28 Excel Application

Job Costing
Chirac & Partners

Original Data

Budget for 2001

Professional labor comp.	$960,000
Audit support dept. costs	$720,000
Professional labor-hours billed	16,000

Actual Results for 2001

Audit support dept. costs	$744,000
Professional labor-hours billed	15,500
Actual professional labor cost rate	$58

Problem 1	Actual costing	Normal costing	Variation from normal costing
Direct cost rate	$58	$58	$60
Indirect cost rate	$48	$45	$45

Problem 2

Direct Costs:	Actual Costing	Normal costing	Variation from normal costing
Professional labor	$ 6,960	$ 6,960	$ 7,200
Indirect Costs:			
Audit support	$ 5,760	$ 5,400	$ 5,400
Total job cost	$12,720	$12,360	$12,600

4-30 (20–30 min) Job costing, accounting for manufacturing overhead, budgeted rates.

1. An overview of the job-costing system is:

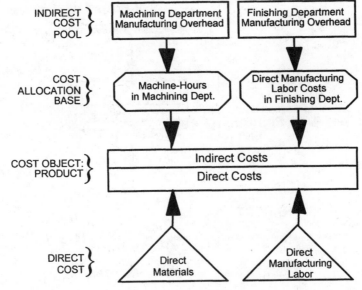

4-30 (Cont'd.)

2. Budgeted manufacturing overhead divided by allocation base:
   a. Machining Department:

   $$\frac{\$10,000,000}{200,000} = \$50 \text{ per machine-hour}$$

   b. Finishing Department:

   $$\frac{\$8,000,000}{\$4,000,000} = 200\% \text{ of direct manufacturing labor costs}$$

3.
Machining Department overhead, $50 × 130 hours	$6,500
Finishing Department overhead, 200% of $1,250	2,500
Total manufacturing overhead allocated	$9,000

4. Total costs of Job 431:

Direct costs:		
Direct materials—Machining Department	$14,000	
—Finishing Department	3,000	
Direct manufacturing labor —Machining Department	600	
—Finishing Department	1,250	$18,850
Indirect costs:		
Machining Department overhead, $50 × 130	$6,500	
Finishing Department overhead, 200% of $1,250	2,500	9,000
Total costs		$27,850

The per-unit product cost of Job 431 is $27,850 ÷ 200 units = $139.25 per unit

The point of this part is (a) to get the definitions straight and (b) to underscore that overhead is allocated by multiplying the actual amount of the allocation base by the budgeted rate.

5.

	Machining	Finishing
Manufacturing overhead incurred (actual)	$11,200,000	$7,900,000
Manufacturing overhead allocated		
220,000 hrs. × $50	11,000,000	
200% of $4,100,000		8,200,000
Underallocated manufacturing overhead	$ 200,000	
Overallocated manufacturing overhead		$ 300,000

Total overallocated overhead = $300,000 – $200,000 = $100,000

6. A homogeneous cost pool is one where all costs have the same or a similar cause-and-effect or benefits-received relationship with the cost-allocation base. Solomon likely assumes that all its manufacturing overhead cost items are not homogeneous. Specifically, those in the Machining Department have a cause-and-effect relationship with machine-hours, while those in the Finishing Department have a cause-and-effect relationship with direct manufacturing labor costs. Solomon believes that the benefits of using two cost pools (more accurate product costs and better ability to manage costs) exceeds the costs of implementing a more complex system.

4-32   (25-30 min.) **Service industry, job costing, two direct and indirect cost categories, law firm (continuation of 4-31).**

Although not required, the following overview diagram is helpful to understand Keating's job-costing system.

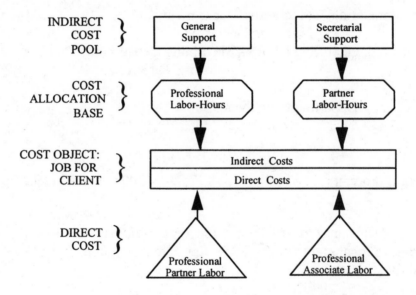

4-32 (Cont'd.)

1.

	Professional Partner Labor	Professional Associate Labor
Budgeted compensation per professional	$ 200,000	$80,000
Divided by budgeted hours of billable time per professional	÷1,600	÷1,600
Budgeted direct-cost rate	$125 per hour*	$50 per hour†

*Can also be calculated as $\dfrac{\text{Total budgeted partner labor costs}}{\text{Total budgeted partner labor - hours}} = \dfrac{\$200,000 \times 5}{1,600 \times 5} = \dfrac{\$1,000,000}{8,000} = \$125$

†Can also be calculated as $\dfrac{\text{Total budgeted associate labor costs}}{\text{Total budgeted associate labor - hours}} = \dfrac{\$80,000 \times 20}{1,600 \times 20} = \dfrac{\$1,600,000}{32,000} = \$ 50$

2.

	General Support	Secretarial Support
Budgeted total costs	$1,800,000	$400,000
Divided by budgeted quantity of allocation base	÷40,000 hours	÷8,000 hours
Budgeted indirect cost rate	$45 per hour	$50 per hour

3.

	Richardson		Punch	
Direct costs:				
Professional partners, $125 × 60; $125 × 30	$7,500		$3,750	
Professional associates, $50 × 40; $50 × 120	2,000		6,000	
Direct costs		$ 9,500		$ 9,750
Indirect costs:				
General support, $45 × 100; $45 × 150	4,500		6,750	
Secretarial support, $50 × 60; $50 × 30	3,000		1,500	
Indirect costs		7,500		8,250
Total costs		$17,000		$18,000

4.

	Richardson	Punch
Single direct - Single indirect (from Prob. 4-31)	$12,000	$18,000
Multiple direct – Multiple indirect (from requirement 3 of Prob. 4-32)	17,000	18,000
Difference	$5,000 undercosted	no change

The Richardson and Punch jobs differ in their use of resources. The Richardson job has a mix of 60% partners and 40% associates, while Punch has a mix of 20% partners and 80% associates. Thus, the Richardson job is a relatively high user of the more costly partner-related resources (both direct partner costs and indirect partner secretarial support). The refined-costing system in Problem 4-32 increases the reported cost in Problem 4-31 for the Richardson job by 41.7% (from $12,000 to $17,000).

4-34   (15 min.)   **Normal costing, overhead allocation, working backwards.**

1. Manufacturing overhead allocated = 200% × Direct manufacturing labor costs
    $3,600,000 = 2 × Direct manufacturing labor costs

    Direct manufacturing labor costs $= \dfrac{\$3,600,000}{2} = \$1,800,000$

2.
$$\text{Total manufacturing costs} = \text{Direct material used} + \text{Direct manufacturing labor costs} + \text{Manufacturing overhead allocated}$$

    $8,000,000   = Direct material used + $1,800,000 + $3,600,000

    Direct material used = $2,600,000

3.
$$\text{Work in Process on 1/1/2004} + \text{Total manufacturing costs} = \text{Cost of goods manufactured} + \text{Work in Process on 12/31/2004}$$

    Denote Work in Process on 12/31/2004 by X

    $320,000 + $8,000,000 = $7,920,000 + X

    X = $400,000

4-36   (35 min.)   **General ledger relationships, under- and overallocation.**

The solution assumes all materials used are <u>direct</u> materials. A summary of the T-accounts for Needham Company before adjusting for under- or overallocation of overhead follows:

Direct Materials Control				Work-in-Process Control		
1-1-2003	30,000	Material used for		1-1-2003	20,000	Transferred to
Purchases	400,000	manufacturing 380,000		Direct materials	380,000	finished goods 940,000
12-31-2003	50,000			Direct manuf.		
				Labor	360,000	
				Manuf. overhead		
				Allocated	480,000	
				12-31-2003	300,000	

Finished Goods Control				Cost of Goods Sold		
1-1-2003	10,000	Cost of goods		Finished goods		
Transferred in		sold 900,000		Sold	900,000	
from WIP	940,000					
12-31-2003	50,000					

Manufacturing Overhead Control				Manufacturing Overhead Allocated		
Manufacturing				Manufacturing		
Overhead				overhead		
Costs	540,000			allocated to		
				work in		
				process		480,000

4-36 (Cont'd.)

1. From Direct Materials Control T-account,
   Direct materials issued to production = $380,000 that appears as a credit.

2. Direct manufacturing labor-hours $= \dfrac{\text{Direct manufacturing labor costs}}{\text{Direct manufacturing wage rate per hour}}$

   $= \dfrac{\$360,000}{\$15 \text{ per hour}} = 24,000 \text{ hours}$

   $\dfrac{\text{Manufacturing overhead}}{\text{allocated}} = \dfrac{\text{Direct manufacturing}}{\text{labor hours}} \times \dfrac{\text{Manufacturing}}{\text{overhead rate}}$

   $= 24,000 \text{ hours} \times \$20 = \$480,000$

3. From the debit entry to Finished Goods T-account,
   Cost of jobs completed and transferred from WIP = $940,000

4. From Work-in-Process T-account,

   $\begin{aligned}\text{Work in process inventory} \\ \text{on } 12/31/2003\end{aligned}$ = $20,000 + $380,000 + $360,000 + $480,000 – $940,000

   = $300,000

5. From the credit entry to Finished Goods Control T-account,

   Cost of goods sold (before proration) = $900,000

6. $\dfrac{\text{Manufacturing overhead}}{\text{underallocated}} = \dfrac{\text{Debits to Manufacturing}}{\text{Overhead Control}} - \dfrac{\text{Credit to Manufacturing}}{\text{Overhead Allocated}}$

   = $540,000 – $480,000
   = $60,000 underallocated

7. a. Write-off to Cost of Goods Sold will increase (debit) Cost of Goods Sold by $60,000.
   Hence, Cost of Goods Sold = $900,000 + $60,000 = $960,000.

   b. Proration based on ending balances (before proration) in Work in Process, Finished Goods, and Cost of Goods Sold.

   Account balances in each account after proration follows.

Account (1)	Account Balance (Before Proration) (2)		Proration of $60,000 Underallocated Manufacturing Overhead (3)	Account Balance (After Proration) (4)=(2)+(3)
Work in Process	$ 300,000	(24%)	0.24 × $60,000 = $14,400	$ 314,400
Finished Goods	50,000	(4%)	0.04 × $60,000 = 2,400	52,400
Cost of Goods Sold	900,000	(72%)	0.72 × $60,000 = 43,200	943,200
	$1,250,000	100%	$60,000	$1,310,000

8.   Needham's operating income under the write-off to Cost of Goods Sold and Proration based on ending balances (before proration) follows

	Write-off to Cost of Goods Sold	Proration Based on Ending Balances
Revenues	$1,090,000	$1,090,000
Cost of goods sold	960,000	943,200
Gross margin	130,000	146,800
Marketing and distribution costs	140,000	140,000
Operating income/(loss)	$ (10,000)	$ 6,800

9.   If the purpose is to report the most accurate inventory and cost of goods sold figures, the preferred method is to prorate based on the manufacturing overhead allocated component in the inventory and cost of goods sold accounts. Proration based on the balances in Work in Process, Finished Goods, and Cost of Goods Sold will equal the proration based on the manufacturing overhead allocated component if the proportions of direct costs to manufacturing overhead costs are constant in the Work in Process, Finished Goods and Cost of Goods Sold accounts. Even if this is not the case, the prorations based on Work in Process, Finished Goods, and Cost of Goods Sold will better approximate the results if actual cost rates had been used rather than the write-off to Cost of Goods Sold method.

Another consideration in Needham's decision about how to dispose of underallocated manufacturing overhead is the effects on operating income. The write-off to Cost of Goods Sold will lead to an operating loss. Proration based on the balances in Work in Process, Finished Goods, and Cost of Goods Sold will help Needham avoid the loss and show an operating income.

The main merit of the write-off to Cost of Goods Sold method is its simplicity. However, accuracy and the effect on operating income favor the preferred and recommended proration approach.

4-38 (15 min.) **General ledger relationships, under- and overallocation, service industry.**

1.

   1.   Jobs-in-Process Control   150,000
          Cash Control   150,000

   2.   Direct Professional Labor Control   1,500,000
          Cash Control   1,500,000

   3.   Jobs-in-Process Control   1,450,000
          Direct Professional Labor Allocated   1,450,000

   4.   Engineering Support Overhead Control   1,180,000
          Cash Control   1,180,000

   5.   Jobs-in-Process Control   1,200,000
          Engineering Support Overhead Allocated   1,200,000

   6.   Cost of Jobs Billed   2,500,000
          Jobs-in-Process Control   2,500,000

2.   Direct Professional Labor Allocated   1,450,000
    Engineering Support Overhead Allocated   1,200,000
    Cost of Jobs Billed   30,000
          Direct Professional Labor Control   1,500,000
          Engineering Support Overhead Control   1,180,000

4-40 (20 min.)   **Job costing, contracting, ethics.**

1.   Direct manufacturing costs:

Direct materials	$25,000	
Direct manufacturing labor	6,000	$31,000
Indirect manufacturing costs,		
150% × $6,000		9,000
Total manufacturing costs		$40,000

Aerospace bills the Navy $52,000 ($40,000 × 130%) for 100 X7 seats or $520 ($52,000 ÷ 100) per X7 seat.

2.   Direct manufacturing costs:

Direct materials	$25,000	
Direct manufacturing labor[a]	5,000	$30,000
Indirect manufacturing costs,		
150% × $5,000		7,500
Total manufacturing costs		$37,500

[a]$6,000 − $400 ($25 × 16) setup − $600 ($50 × 12) design

Aerospace should have billed the Navy $48,750 ($37,500 × 130%) for 100 X7 seats or $487.50 ($48,750 ÷ 100) per X7 seat.

3.   The problems the letter highlights (assuming it is correct) include:

    a.   Costs included that should be excluded (design costs),
    b.   Costs double-counted (setup included as both a direct cost and in an indirect cost pool), and
    c.   Possible conflict of interest in Aerospace Comfort purchasing materials from a family-related company.

Steps the Navy could undertake include:
    (i)   Use only contractors with a reputation for ethical behavior as well as quality products or services.
    (ii)   Issue guidelines detailing acceptable and unacceptable billing practices by contractors. For example, prohibiting the use of double-counting cost allocation methods by contractors.
    (iii) Issue guidelines detailing acceptable and unacceptable procurement practices by contractors. For example, if a contractor purchases from a family-related company, require that the contractor obtain quotes from at least two other bidders.
    (iv) Employ auditors who aggressively monitor the bills submitted by contractors.
    (v)   Ask contractors for details regarding determination of costs.

CHAPTER 5
ACTIVITY-BASED COSTING AND ACTIVITY-BASED MANAGEMENT

5-2   Overcosting may result in competitors entering a market and taking market share for products that a company erroneously believes are low-margin or even unprofitable.

Undercosting may result in companies selling products on which they are in fact losing money, when they erroneously believe them to be profitable.

5-4   An activity-based approach refines a costing system by focusing on individual activities as the fundamental cost objects. It uses the cost of these activities as the basis for assigning costs to other cost objects such as products or services.

5-6   The purpose for computing a product cost will determine whether unit costs should be based on total manufacturing costs in all or only some levels of the cost hierarchy. Inventory valuation for financial reporting requires *total* manufacturing costs (all levels of the hierarchy) to be expressed on a per output-unit basis. In contrast, for cost management purposes, the cost hierarchy need not be unitized, as the units of output is not the cost driver at each level in the hierarchy.

5-8   Four decisions for which ABC information is useful are:
1.   pricing and product mix decisions,
2.   cost reduction and process improvement decisions,
3.   product design decisions, and
4.   planning and managing activities.

5-10   "Tell-tale" signs that indicate when ABC systems are likely to provide the most benefits are:
1.   Significant amounts of indirect costs are allocated using only one or two cost pools.
2.   All or most indirect costs are identified as output-unit-level costs (i.e., few indirect costs are described as batch-level, product-sustaining, or facility-sustaining costs).
3.   Products make diverse demands on resources because of differences in volume, process steps, batch size, or complexity.
4.   Products that a company is well suited to make and sell show small profits, whereas products that a company is less suited to produce and sell show large profits.
5.   Operations staff have significant disagreements with the accounting staff about the costs of manufacturing and marketing products and services

5-12   No, ABC systems apply equally well to service companies such as banks, railroads, hospitals, and accounting firms, as well merchandising companies such as retailers and distributors.

5-14   Increasing the number of indirect-cost pools does NOT guarantee increased accuracy of product or service costs. If the existing cost pool is already homogeneous, increasing the number of cost pools will not increase accuracy. If the existing cost pool is not homogeneous, accuracy will increase only if the increased cost pools themselves increase in homogeneity vis-a-vis the single cost pool.

5-16 (30 min.) **Cost smoothing or peanut-butter costing, cross-subsidization.**

1.   Cost smoothing or peanut-butter costing is a costing approach that uniformly assigns the cost of resources to customers when the individual customers use those resources in a nonuniform way. The reunion dinner averages the costs across all five people. These five people differ sizably in what they consume.

2.

Diner	Entree	Dessert	Drinks	Total
Armstrong	$27	$8	$24	$59
Gonzales	24	3	0	27
King	21	6	13	40
Poffo	31	6	12	49
Young	15	4	6	25
Average	$23.60	$5.40	$11.00	$40.00

The average-cost pricing will result in each person paying $40.

	Amount Over- or (Undercosted)
Accurately costed person	
• King, $40 – $40	$ 0
Undercosted people	
• Armstrong, $40 – $59	$(19)
• Poffo, $40 – $49	$(9)
Overcosted people	
• Gonzales, $40 – $27	$ 13
• Young, $40 – $25	$ 15

Yes, Young's complaint is justified. He is "overcharged" $15. He could point out likely negative behaviors with this approach to costing. These include:

a.   It can lead some people to order the most expensive items because others will "subsidize" their extravagance.

b.   It can lead to friction when those who dine economically are forced to subsidize those who dine extravagantly. At the limit, some people may decide not to attend the reunion dinners.

Likely benefits of this approach are:
a.   it is simple, and
b.   it (purportedly) promotes a group atmosphere at the dinner.

3.   Each one of the costs in the data is directly traceable to an individual diner. This makes it straightforward to compute the individual cost per diner. Examples where this is not possible include:
•   A plate of hors d'oeuvres is shared by two or more diners
•   A loaf of garlic bread is shared by two or more diners
•   A bottle of mineral water or wine is shared by two or more diners

Each of these items cannot be directly traced to only one diner.

5-16 (Cont'd.)

Some possible behaviors if each person pays for his or her own bill are:

a.   Some people may reduce their ordering of more expensive items because they will not be subsidized by other diners.
b.   May encourage some potential diners to attend who otherwise would have stayed away.
c.   May encourage a person "trying to impress others with his or her success" to order the most expensive items.

5-18 (25 min.) ABC, distribution.

1. Total distribution costs (given), $2,130,000

$$\text{Distribution cost per case under existing system} = \frac{\text{Total distribution costs}}{\text{Total cases of premium and regular wine shipped}} = \frac{\$2,130,000}{200,000} = \$10.65 \text{ per case}$$

	Regular Per Case		Premium Per Case	
	Total (1)	(2) = (1) ÷ 120,000	Total (3)	(4) = (3) ÷ 80,000
Distribution costs $10.65 × 120,000; $10.65 × 80,000	$1,278,000	$10.65	$852,000	$10.65

2.

	Regular Per Case		Premium Per Case	
	Total (1)	(2) = (1) ÷ 120,000	Total (3)	(4) = (3) ÷ 80,000
Delivery costs				
$8 × 120,000 cases	$ 960,000	$8.00		
$8 × 80,000 cases			$ 640,000	$ 8.00
Ordering costs				
$300 × 10 orders/year × 10 distr.	30,000	0.25		
$300 × 20 orders/year × 30 distr.			180,000	2.25
Promotion costs				
$8,000 × 10 distributors	80,000	0.67		
$8,000 × 30 distributors			240,000	3.00
Total costs	$1,070,000	$8.92	$1,060,000	$13.25

5-18 (Cont'd.)

3. The existing costing system uses cases shipped as the only cost allocation base for distribution costs. As a result, the distribution cost per case is the same for premium and regular wines ($10.65). In fact, premium wine uses distribution resources more intensively than regular wine: (a) Sonoma spends $8,000 on promotional costs at each distributor independent of cases sold. Premium wine distributors sell fewer cases a year than regular wine distributors. As a result the promotional cost per case of wine sold is higher for premium wine than for regular wine. (b) Sonoma's cost per order is $300 regardless of the number of cases sold in each order. Because premium wine distributors order fewer cases per order, the ordering costs per case are higher for premium wines than for regular wines.

The existing costing system undercosts distribution costs per case for premium wine and overcosts distribution costs per case for regular wine.

Sonoma's management can use the information from the ABC system to make better pricing and product mix decisions, to reduce costs by eliminating processes and activities that do not add value, to reduce the costs of doing various activities, and to plan and manage activities.

5-20 (15 min.) Alternative allocation bases for a professional services firm.

1.

| | Direct Professional Time | | | Support Services | | Amount |
Client (1)	Rate per Hour (2)	Number of Hours (3)	Total (4) = (2) × (3)	Rate (5)	Total (6) = (4) × (5)	Billed to Client (7) = (4) + (6)
SEATTLE DOMINION						
Wolfson	$500	15	$7,500	30%	$2,250	$ 9,750
Brown	120	3	360	30	108	468
Anderson	80	22	1,760	30	528	2,288
						$12,506
TOKYO ENTERPRISES						
Wolfson	$500	2	$1,000	30%	$300	$1,300
Brown	120	8	960	30	288	1,248
Anderson	80	30	2,400	30	720	3,120
						$5,668

5-20 (Cont'd.)

2.

Client	Direct Professional Time			Support Services		Amount Billed to Client
	Rate per Hour	Number of Hours	Total	Rate per Hour	Total	
(1)	(2)	(3)	(4) = (2) × (3)	(5)	(6) = (3) × (5)	(7) = (4)+(6)
SEATTLE DOMINION						
Wolfson	$500	15	$7,500	$50	$ 750	$ 8,250
Brown	120	3	360	50	150	510
Anderson	80	22	1,760	50	1,100	2,860
						$11,620
TOKYO ENTERPRISES						
Wolfson	$500	2	$1,000	$50	$ 100	$1,100
Brown	120	8	960	50	400	1,360
Anderson	80	30	2,400	50	1,500	3,900
						$6,360

	Requirement 1	Requirement 2
Seattle Dominion	$12,506	$11,620
Tokyo Enterprises	5,668	6,360
	$18,174	$17,980

Both clients use 40 hours of professional labor time. However, Seattle Dominion uses a higher proportion of Wolfson's time (15 hours), which is more costly. This attracts the highest support-services charge when allocated on the basis of direct professional labor costs.

3.   Assume that the Wolfson Group uses a cause-and-effect criterion when choosing the allocation base for support services. You could use several pieces of evidence to determine whether professional labor costs or hours is the driver of support-service costs:

a.   *Interviews with personnel.* For example, staff in the major cost categories in support services could be interviewed to determine whether Wolfson requires more support per hour than, say, Anderson. The professional labor costs allocation base implies that an hour of Wolfson's time requires 6.25 ($500 ÷ $80) times more support-service dollars than does an hour of Anderson's time.

b.   *Analysis of tasks undertaken for selected clients.* For example, if computer-related costs are a sizable part of support costs, you could determine if there was a systematic relationship between the percentage involvement of professionals with high billing rates on cases and the computer resources consumed for those cases.

5-22 (30 min.) **Department indirect-cost rates as activity rates (continuation of 5-21).**

1.

	2004 Variable MOH Costs	Total Driver Units	Rate
Design-CAD	$ 39,000	390	$100 per design-hour
Engineering	29,600	370	$ 80 per engineer-hour
Production	240,000	4,000	$ 60 per machine

2.

	United Motors	Holden Motors	Leland Vehicle
Design			
$100 × 110; $100 × 200; $100 × 80	$11,000	$ 20,000	$ 8,000
Engineering			
$80 × 70; $80 × 60; $80 × 240	5,600	4,800	19,200
Production			
$60 × 120; $60 × 2,800; $60 × 1,080	7,200	168,000	64,800
Total	$23,800	$192,800	$92,000

3.

		United Motors	Holden Motors	Leland Vehicle
a.	Department rate (Exercise 5-22)	$23,800	$192,800	$92,000
b.	Plantwide rate (Exercise 5-21)	9,258	216,020	83,322
Ratio of (a) ÷ (b)		2.57	0.89	1.10

The three contracts differ sizably in the way they use the resources of the three departments. The percentage of total driver units in each department used by the contract companies is:

Department	United Motors	Holden Motors	Leland Vehicle
Design	28%	51%	21%
Engineering	19	16	65
Production	3	70	27

The United Motors contract uses only 3% of total machines-hours in 2004, yet uses 28% of CAD design-hours and 19% of engineering hours. The result is that the plantwide rate, based on machine-hours, will greatly underestimate the cost of resources used on the United Motors contract. Hence, the 257% increase in indirect costs assigned to the United Motors contract when department rates are used.

In contrast, the Holden Motors contract uses less of design (51%) and engineering (16%) than of machine-hours (70%). Hence, the use of department rates will report lower indirect costs for Holden Motors than does a plantwide rate.

5-24 (30 min.) ABC, retail product-line profitability.

1.   The previous costing system (Panel A of Solution Exhibit 5-24) reports the following:

	Baked Goods	Milk & Fruit Juice	Frozen Products	Total
Revenues	$57,000	$63,000	$52,000	$172,000
Costs				
Cost of goods sold	38,000	47,000	35,000	120,000
Store support (30% of COGS)	11,400	14,100	10,500	36,000
Total costs	49,400	61,100	45,500	156,000
Operating income	$ 7,600	$ 1,900	$ 6,500	$ 16,000
Operating income ÷ Revenues	13.33%	3.02%	12.50%	9.30%

2.   The ABC system (Panel B of Solution Exhibit 5-24) reports the following:

	Baked Goods	Milk & Fruit Juice	Frozen Products	Total
Revenues	$57,000	$63,000	$52,000	$172,000
Costs				
Cost of goods sold	38,000	47,000	35,000	120,000
Ordering ($100 × 30; 25; 13)	3,000	2,500	1,300	6,800
Delivery ($80 × 98; 36; 28)	7,840	2,880	2,240	12,960
Shelf-stocking ($20 × 183; 166; 24)	3,660	3,320	480	7,460
Customer support				
($0.20 × 15,500; 20,500; 7,900)	3,100	4,100	1,580	8,780
Total costs	55,600	59,800	40,600	156,000
Operating income	$ 1,400	$ 3,200	$11,400	$ 16,000
Operating income ÷ Revenues	2.46%	5.08%	21.92%	9.30%

These activity costs are based on the following:

Activity	Cost Allocation Rate	Baked Goods	Milk & Fruit Juice	Frozen Products
Ordering	$100 per purchase order	30	25	13
Delivery	$80 per delivery	98	36	28
Shelf-stocking	$20 per hour	183	166	24
Customer support	$0.20 per item sold	15,500	20,500	7,900

The rankings of products in terms of relative profitability are:

Previous Costing System			ABC System	
1.	Baked goods	13.33%	Frozen products	21.92%
2.	Frozen products	12.50	Milk & fruit juice	5.08
3.	Milk & fruit juice	3.02	Baked goods	2.46

The percentage revenue, COGS, and activity costs for each product line are:

	Baked Goods	Milk & Fruit Juice	Frozen Products	Total
Revenues	33.14	36.63	30.23	100.00
COGS	31.67	39.17	29.16	100.00
Activity areas:				
Ordering	44.12	36.76	19.12	100.00
Delivery	60.49	22.22	17.29	100.00
Shelf-stocking	49.06	44.50	6.44	100.00
Customer support	35.31	46.70	17.99	100.00

3.   The baked goods line drops sizably in profitability when ABC is used.   Although it constitutes 31.67% of COGS, it uses a higher percentage of total resources in each activity area, especially the high cost delivery activity area. In contrast, frozen products draws a much lower percentage of total resources used in each activity area than its percentage of total COGS. Hence, under ABC, frozen products is much more profitable.

Family Supermarkets may want to explore ways to increase sales of frozen products. It may also want to explore price increases on baked goods.

5-26 (50 min.) **ABC, activity area cost-driver rates, product cross-subsidization.**

1.
Direct costs

Direct materials	$ 150,000
Indirect costs	
Product support	983,000
Total costs	$1,133,000

$$\text{Cost per pound of potato cuts} = \frac{\$1,133,000}{1,000,000} = \$1.133$$

2.

Cost Pool	Costs in Pool	Number of Driver Units	Costs per Driver Unit
Cleaning	$120,000	1,200,000 raw pounds	$ 0.10
Cutting	$231,000	3,850 hours*	$60.00
Packaging	$444,000	37,000 hours**	$12.00

*(900,000 ÷ 250) + (100,000 ÷ 400) = 3,600 + 250 = 3,850
**(900,000 ÷ 25) + (100,000 ÷ 100) = 36,000 + 1,000 = 37,000

3.

	Retail Potato Cuts		Institutional Potato Cuts	
Direct costs				
Direct materials	$135,000		$15,000	
Packaging	180,000	$ 315,000	8,000	$23,000
Indirect costs				
Cleaning				
$0.10 × 90% × 1,200,000	108,000			
$0.10 × 10% × 1,200,000			12,000	
Cutting				
$60 × 3,600 hours	216,000			
$60 × 250 hours			15,000	
Packaging				
$12 × 36,000	432,000			
$12 × 1,000		756,000	12,000	39,000
Total costs		$1,071,000		$62,000
Pounds produced		900,000		100,000
Costs per pound		$1.19		$0.62

Note: The total costs of $1,133,000 ($1,071,000 + $62,000) are the same as those in Requirement 1.

4.   There is much evidence of product-cost cross-subsidization.

Cost per Pound	Retail	Institutional
Current system	$1.133	$1.133
ABC system	$1.190	$0.620

Assuming the ABC numbers are more accurate, potato cuts sold to the retail market are undercosted while potato cuts sold to the institutional market are overcosted.

5-26 (Cont'd.)

The current system assumes each product uses all the activity areas in a homogeneous way. This is not the case. Institutional sales use sizably less resources in the cutting area and the packaging area. The percentage of total costs for each cost category are:

	Retail	Institutional	Total
Direct costs			
Direct materials	90.0%	10.0%	100.0%
Packaging	95.7	4.3	100.0
Indirect costs			
Cleaning	90.0	10.0	100.0
Cutting	93.5	6.5	100.0
Packaging	97.3	2.7	100.0
Units produced	90.0%	10.0%	100.0%

Idaho can use the revised cost information for a variety of purposes:

a. *Pricing/product emphasis decisions*. The sizable drop in the reported cost of potatoes sold in the institutional market makes it possible that Idaho was overpricing potato products in this market. It lost the bid for a large institutional contract with a bid 30% above the winning bid. With its revised product cost dropping from $1.133 to $0.620, Idaho could have bid much lower and still made a profit. An increased emphasis on the institutional market appears warranted.

b. *Product design decisions*. ABC provides a road map as to how to reduce the costs of individual products. The relative components of costs are:

	Retail	Institutional
Direct costs		
Direct materials	12.6%	24.20%
Packaging	16.8	12.90
Indirect costs		
Cleaning	10.1	19.35
Cutting	20.2	24.20
Packaging	40.3	19.35
Total costs	100.0%	100.00%

Packaging-related costs constitute 57.1% (16.8% + 40.3%) of total costs of the retail product line. Design efforts that reduce packaging costs can have a big impact on reducing total unit costs for retail.

c. *Process improvements*. Each activity area is now highlighted as a separate cost. The three indirect cost areas comprise over 60% of total costs for each product, indicating the upside from improvements in the efficiency of processes in these activity areas.

5-28 (30 min.) **ABC, product-costing at banks, cross-subsidization.**

1.

	Robinson	Skerrett	Farrel	Total
Revenues				
Spread revenue on annual basis				
(3% × ; $1,100, $800, $25,000)	$ 33	$ 24	$750.0	$ 807.0
Monthly fee charges				
($20 ×; 0, 12, 0)	0	240	0.0	240.0
Total revenues	33	264	750.0	1,047.0
Costs				
Deposit/withdrawal with teller				
$2.50 × 40; 50; 5	100	125	12.5	237.5
Deposit/withdrawal with ATM				
$0.80 × 10; 20; 16	8	16	12.8	36.8
Deposit/withdrawal on prearranged basis:				
$0.50 × 0; 12; 60	0	6	30.0	36.0
Bank checks written				
$8.00 × 9; 3; 2	72	24	16.0	112.0
Foreign currency drafts				
$12.00 × 4; 1; 6	48	12	72.0	132.0
Inquiries				
$1.50 × 10; 18; 9	15	27	13.5	55.5
Total costs	243	210	156.8	609.8
Operating income (loss)	$(210)	$ 54	$593.2	$ 437.2

The assumption that the Robinson and Farrel accounts exceed $1,000 every month and the Skerrett account is less than $1,000 each month means the monthly charges apply only to Skerrett.

One student with a banking background noted that in this solution 100% of the spread is attributed to the "depositor side of the bank." He noted that often the spread is divided between the "depositor side" and the "lending side" of the bank.

2. Cross-subsidization across individual Premier Accounts occurs when profits made on some accounts are offset by losses on other accounts. The aggregate profitability on the three customers is $437.20. The Farrel account is highly profitable ($593.20), while the Robinson account is sizably unprofitable. The Skerrett account shows a small profit but only because of the $240 monthly fees. It is unlikely that Skerrett will keep paying these high fees and that FIB would want Skerret to pay such high fees from a customer relationship standpoint.

The facts also suggest that the customers do not use the bank services uniformly. For example, Robinson and Skerret have a lot of transactions with the teller or ATM, and also inquire about their account balances more often than Farrell. This suggests cross-subsidization. FIB should be very concerned about the cross-subsidization. Competition likely would "understand" that high-balance low-activity type accounts (such as Farrel) are highly profitable. Offering free services to these customers is not likely to retain these accounts if other banks offer higher interest rates. Competition likely will reduce the interest rate spread FIB can earn on the high-balance low-activity accounts they are able to retain.

3.   Possible changes FIB could make are:

a.   Offer higher interest rates on high-balance accounts to increase FIB's competitiveness in attracting and retaining these accounts.

a.   Introduce charges for individual services. The ABC study reports the cost of each service. FIB has to decide if it wants to price each service at cost, below cost, or above cost. If it prices above cost, it may use advertising and other means to encourage additional use of those services by customers. Of course, in determining its pricing strategy, FIB would need to consider how other competing banks are pricing their products and services.

5-30 (20-25 min.) Job costing with multiple direct-cost categories, single indirect-cost pool, law firm (continuation of 5-29).

1.   Indirect costs = $7,000
Total professional labor-hours = 200 hours (104 hours on Widnes Coal + 96 hours on St. Helen's Glass)

Indirect cost allocated per professional labor-hour = $7,000 ÷ 200 = $35 per hour

2.

	Widnes Coal	St. Helen's Glass	Total
Direct costs:			
Direct professional labor,			
$70 × 104; $70 × 96	$ 7,280	$ 6,720	$14,000
Research support labor	1,600	3,400	5,000
Computer time	500	1,300	1,800
Travel and allowances	600	4,400	5,000
Telephones/faxes	200	1,000	1,200
Photocopying	250	750	1,000
Total direct costs	10,430	17,570	28,000
Indirect costs allocated,			
$35 × 104; $35 × 96	3,640	3,360	7,000
Total costs to be billed	$14,070	$20,930	$35,000

3.

	Widnes Coal	St. Helen's Glass	Total
Problem 5-29	$18,200	$16,800	$35,000
Problem 5-30	14,070	20,930	35,000

The Problem 5-30 approach directly traces to the individual jobs $14,000 that is allocated in the Problem 5-29 approach on the basis of direct professional labor-hours. The averaging assumption implicit in the Problem 5-29 approach appears incorrect—for example, the St. Helen's Glass job has travel costs over seven times higher than the Widnes Coal case despite having lower direct professional labor-hours.

5-32 (30 min.) **Plantwide, department, and activity-cost rates.**

1. Budgeted manufacturing overhead rates:

    i. Plantwide rate:

    $$\frac{\$340,000}{20,000} = \$17.00 \text{ per direct manufacturing labor-hour}$$

    ii. Departmental rates:

    Department 1: $\$240,000 \div 10,000 = \$24.00$ per direct manufacturing labor-hour
    Department 2: $\$100,000 \div 10,000 = \$10.00$ per direct manufacturing labor-hour

    Manufacturing overhead portion of ending inventories:

    i. Using plantwide overhead rate:
    800 units × 5 hours × $17.00 $68,000

    ii. Using department overhead rates:

    Product A: $200 \times [(4 \times \$24.00) + (1 \times \$10.00)] =$ $21,200
    Product B: $600 \times [(1 \times \$24.00) + (4 \times \$10.00)] =$ 38,400
                                                                                  $59,600

    The difference in inventory costs due to the different methods of allocating manufacturing overhead is $8,400 ($68,000 − $59,600).

2. *Product A*

	Plantwide Overhead Rate	Department Overhead Rates
Direct materials	$120.00	$120.00
Direct manufacturing labor	80.00	80.00
Manufacturing overhead:		
$17 × 5	85.00	—
($24 × 4) + ($10 × 1)	—	106.00
Total manufacturing costs	285.00	306.00
Markup		
($285 × 120%; $306 × 120%)	342.00	367.20
Selling price	$627.00	$673.20

5-32 (Cont'd.)

Product B

	Plantwide Overhead Rate	Department Overhead Rate
Direct materials	$150.00	$150.00
Direct manufacturing labor	80.00	80.00
Manufacturing overhead:		
$17 × 5	85.00	—
($24 × 1) + ($10 × 4)	—	64.00
Total manufacturing costs	315.00	294.00
Markup		
($315 × 120%; $294 × 120%)	378.00	352.80
Selling price	$693.00	$646.80

3. Sayther Company should use budgeted department manufacturing overhead rates because:
a. The two manufacturing departments differ sizably in their overhead cost structures, despite having the same budgeted direct manufacturing labor-hours. Department 1 has $240,000 budgeted overhead, and Department 2 has $100,000 budgeted overhead.
b. The two products use resources in the two manufacturing departments quite differently. The direct manufacturing labor-hours used in each department are:

Department	Product A	Product B
1	4	1
2	1	4

Differences a. and b. mean that more refined product costs will be calculated with budgeted department manufacturing overhead rates.

4. Sayther should further subdivide the department cost pools into activity-cost pools if (a) significant costs are incurred on *different* activities within the department, (b) the different activities have different cost-allocation bases, and (c) different products use the different activities in different proportions.

5-34 (30-40 min.)   **Activity-based costing, merchandising.**

1.

	General Supermarket Chains	Drugstore Chains	Ma and Pa Single Stores	Total
Revenues[a]	$3,708,000	$3,150,000	$1,980,000	$8,838,000
Cost of goods sold[b]	3,600,000	3,000,000	1,800,000	8,400,000
Gross margin	$ 108,000	$ 150,000	$ 180,000	438,000
Other operating costs				301,080
Operating income				$ 136,920
Gross margin %	2.91%	4.76%	9.09%	

[a]($30,900 × 120); ($10,500 × 300); ($1,980 × 1,000)
[b]($30,000 × 120); ($10,000 × 300); ($1,800 × 1,000)

The gross margin of Figure Four Inc. was 4.96% ($438,000 ÷ $8,838,000). The operating income margin of Figure Four Inc. was 1.55% ($136,920 ÷ $8,838,000).

2.   The per-unit cost driver rates are:

1.   Customer purchase order processing, $80,000 ÷ 2,000 orders   = $40 per order
2.   Line item ordering, $63,840 ÷ 21,280 line items   = $ 3 per line item
3.   Store delivery, $71,000 ÷ 1,420 deliveries   = $50 per delivery
4.   Cartons shipped, $76,000 ÷ 76,000 cartons   = $ 1 per carton
5.   Shelf-stocking, $10,240 ÷ 640 hours   = $16 per hour

3.   The activity-based costing of each distribution market for August 2002 is:

		General Supermarket Chains	Drugstore Chains	Ma and Pa Single Stores
1.	Customer purchase order processing, ($40 × 140; 360; 1,500)	$ 5,600	$14,400	$ 60,000
2.	Line item ordering, ($3 × (140 × 14; 360 × 12; 1,500 × 10))	5,880	12,960	45,000
3.	Store delivery, ($50 × 120, 300, 1,000)	6,000	15,000	50,000
4.	Cartons shipped, ($1 × (120 × 300; 300 ×80; 1,000 × 16))	36,000	24,000	16,000
5.	Shelf-stocking, ($16 × (120 × 3; 300 × 0.6; 1,000 × 0.1))	5,760	2,880	1,600
		$59,240	$69,240	$172,600

5-34 (Cont'd.)

The revised operating income statement is:

	General Supermarket Chains	Drugstore Chains	Ma and Pa Single Stores	Total
Revenues	$3,708,000	$3,150,000	$1,980,000	$8,838,000
Cost of goods sold	3,600,000	3,000,000	1,800,000	8,400,000
Gross margin	108,000	150,000	180,000	438,000
Operating costs	59,240	69,240	172,600	301,080
Operating income	$ 48,760	$ 80,760	$ 7,400	$ 136,920
Operating income margin	1.31%	2.56%	0.37%	1.55%

The ranking of the three markets are:

Using Gross Margin		Using Operating Income	
1. Ma and Pa Single Stores	9.09%	1. Drugstore Chains	2.56%
2. Drugstore Chains	4.76%	2. General Supermarket Chains	1.31%
3. General Supermarket Chains	2.91%	3. Ma and Pa Single Stores	0.37%

The activity-based analysis of costs highlights how the Ma and Pa Single Stores use a larger amount of Figure Four resources per revenue dollar than do the other two markets. The ratio of the operating costs to revenues across the three markets is:

General Supermarket Chains	1.60%	($59,240 ÷ $3,708,000)
Drugstore Chains	2.20%	($69,240 ÷ $3,150,000)
Ma and Pa Single Stores	8.72%	($172,600 ÷ $1,980,000)

This is a classic illustration of the maxim that "all revenue dollars are not created equal." The analysis indicates that the Ma and Pa Single Stores are the least profitable market. Figure Four should work to increase profits in this market through: (1) a possible surcharge, (2) decreasing the number of orders, (3) offering discounts for quantity purchases etc.

4.   a. *Choosing the appropriate cost drivers for each area.* The problem gives a cost driver for each chosen activity area. However, it is likely that over time further refinements in cost drivers would occur. For example, not all store deliveries are equally easy to make, depending on parking availability, accessibility of the storage/shelf space to the delivery point, etc. Similarly, not all cartons are equally easy to deliver—their weight, size, or likely breakage component are factors that can vary across carton types.

　　　　b. *Developing a reliable data base on the chosen cost drivers.* For some items, such as the number of orders and the number of line items, this information likely would be available in machine readable form at a high level of accuracy. Unless the delivery personnel have hand-held computers that they use in a systematic way, estimates of shelf-stocking time are likely to be unreliable. Advances in information technology likely will reduce problems in this area over time.

　　　　c. *Deciding how to handle costs that may be common across several activities.* For example, (3) store delivery and (4) cartons shipped to stores have the common cost of the same trip. Some organizations may treat (3) as the primary activity and attribute only incremental costs to (4). Similarly, (1) order processing and (2) line item ordering may have common costs.

d. *Choice of the time period to compute cost rates per cost driver.* Flair calculates driver rates on a monthly basis (August 2002). He may want to consider using longer time periods that may be less affected by seasonal or random variations in demand.

e. *Behavioral factors are likely to be a challenge to Flair.* He must now tell those salespeople who specialize in Ma and Pa accounts that they have been less profitable than previously thought.

5-34 Excel Application

Activity-Based Costing
Figure Four, Inc.

Financial Data

	General Supermarket	Drugstore Chains	Ma and Pa Stores
Average Rev. Per Delivery	$30,900	$10,500	$1,980
Average Cogs. Per Delivery	$30,000	$10,000	$1,800
Number of Deliveries	120	300	1000

Cost-Allocation Data

Activity Area	Total Costs Aug. 1999	Units of Cost-Allocation Base Used Aug. 1999	Rate per unit of Cost-Allocation Base	
Order Processing	$80,000	2,000	$40	per order
Line Item Ordering	63,840	21,280	$3	per line item per order
Store Deliveries	71,000	1,420	$50	per delivery
Cartons Shipped	76,000	76,000	$1	per carton per delivery
Shelf-Stocking	10,240	640	$16	per hour per delivery
	$301,080			

Activity Data

	General Supermarket	Drugstore Chains	Ma and Pa Stores
Total Orders	140	360	1500
Average line items per order	14	12	10
Total deliveries	120	300	1000
Average number of cartons per delivery	300	80	16
Average hours shelf-stocking per delivery	3	0.6	0.1

5-34 (Cont'd.)

Profitability Analysis

	General Supermarket	Drugstore Chains	Ma and Pa Stores	Figure Four Inc.
Revenue	$3,708,000	$3,150,000	$1,980,000	$8,838,000
Cost of Goods Sold	3,600,000	3,000,000	1,800,000	$8,400,000
Gross Profits	108,000	150,000	180,000	438,000
Gross Margin Percentage	2.9%	4.8%	9.1%	5.0%
Order Processing Cost	5,600	14,400	60,000	
Line Item Ordering Cost	5,880	12,960	45,000	
Delivery Cost	6,000	15,000	50,000	
Cost of Cartons	36,000	24,000	16,000	
Shelf Stocking Cost	5,760	2,880	1,600	
Total Operating Costs	59,240	69,240	172,600	301,080
Operating Income	$ 48,760	$ 80,760	$ 7,400	$ 136,920
Operating Margin Percentage	1.3%	2.6%	0.4%	1.5%

5-36 (40 min.) ABC, health care.

1a. Medical supplies rate $= \dfrac{\text{Medical supplies costs}}{\text{Total number of patient - years}} = \dfrac{\$300,000}{150} = \$2,000/\text{patient-year}$

$\dfrac{\text{Rent and clinic}}{\text{maintenance rate}} = \dfrac{\text{Rent and clinic maint. costs}}{\text{Total amount of square feet of space}} = \dfrac{\$180,000}{30,000} = \$6 \text{ per square foot}$

$\dfrac{\text{Admin. cost rate for}}{\substack{\text{patient-charts}\\ \text{food}\\ \text{and laundry}}} = \dfrac{\substack{\text{Admin. costs to manage patient}\\ \text{charts, food, laundry}}}{\text{Total number of patient - years}} = \dfrac{\$600,000}{150} = \$4,000/\text{patient-year}$

Laboratory services rate $= \dfrac{\text{Laboratory services costs}}{\text{Total number of laboratory tests}} = \dfrac{\$100,000}{2,500} = \$40 \text{ per test}$

These cost drivers are chosen as the ones that best match the descriptions of why the costs arise. Other answers are acceptable, provided clear explanations are given.

1b. Activity-based costs for each program and cost per patient-year of the alcohol and drug program follow:

	Alcohol	Drug	After-Care
Direct labor			
Physicians at $150,000 × 0; 4; 0	—	$ 600,000	—
Psychologists at $75,000 × 6; 4; 8	$450,000	300,000	$ 600,000
Nurses at $30,000 × 4; 6; 10	120,000	180,000	300,000
Direct labor costs	570,000	1,080,000	900,000
Medical supplies[1] $2,000 × 40; 50; 60	80,000	100,000	120,000
Rent and clinic maintenance[2]			
$6 × 9,000; 9,000; 12,000	54,000	54,000	72,000
Administrative costs to manage patient charts, food, and laundry[3]			
$4,000 × 40; 50; 60	160,000	200,000	240,000
Laboratory services[4] $40 × 400; 1,400; 700	16,000	56,000	28,000
Total costs	$880,000	$1,490,000	$1,360,000

	Alcohol	Drug
Cost per patient-year	$\dfrac{\$880,000}{40} = \$22,000$	$\dfrac{\$1,490,000}{50} = \$29,800$

[1]Allocated using patient-years
[2]Allocated using square feet of space
[3]Allocated using patient-years
[4]Allocated using number of laboratory tests

1c. The ABC system more accurately allocates costs because it identifies better cost drivers. The ABC system chooses cost drivers for overhead costs that have a cause-and-effect relationship between the cost drivers and the costs. Of course, Clayton should continue to evaluate if better cost drivers can be found than the ones they have identified so far.

By implementing the ABC system, Clayton can gain a more detailed understanding of costs and cost drivers. This is valuable information from a cost management perspective. The system can yield insight into the efficiencies with which various activities are performed. Clayton can then examine if redundant activities can be eliminated. Clayton can study trends and work toward improving the efficiency of the activities.

In addition, the ABC system will help Clayton determine which programs are the most costly to operate. This will be useful in making long-run decisions as to which programs to offer or emphasize. The ABC system will also assist Clayton in setting prices for the programs that more accurately reflect the costs of each program.

2. The concern with using costs per patient-year as the rule to allocate resources among its programs is that it emphasizes "input" to the exclusion of "outputs" or effectiveness of the programs. After-all, Clayton's goal is to cure patients while controlling costs, not minimize costs per-patient year. The problem, of course, is measuring outputs.

Unlike many manufacturing companies, where the outputs are obvious because they are tangible and measurable, the outputs of service organizations are more difficult to measure. Examples are "cured" patients as distinguished from "processed" or "discharged" patients, "educated" as distinguished from "partially educated" students, and so on.

5-38 (40–50 min.) **Activity-based job costing, unit-cost comparisons.**

An overview of the product-costing system is:

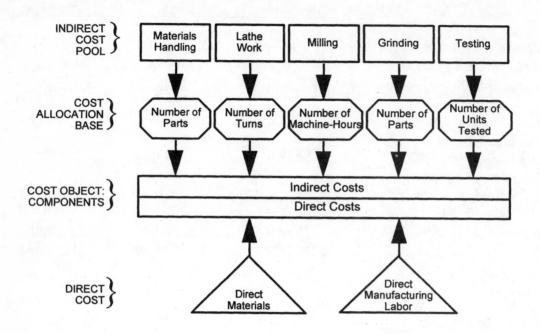

1.

	Job Order 410		Job Order 411	
Direct manufacturing costs:				
Direct materials	$9,700		$59,900	
Direct manufacturing labor				
$30 × 25; $30 × 375	750	$10,450	11,250	$ 71,150
Indirect manufacturing costs				
$115 × 25; $115 × 375		2,875		43,125
Total manufacturing costs		$13,325		$114,275
Number of units		÷ 10		÷ 200
Manufacturing costs per unit		$ 1,332.50		$ 571.375

5-38 (Cont'd.)

2.

	Job Order 410		Job Order 411	
Direct manufacturing costs:				
Direct materials	$9,700		$59,900	
Direct manufacturing labor				
$30 × 25; $30 × 375	750	$10,450	11,250	$ 71,150
Indirect manufacturing costs:				
Materials handling				
$0.40 × 500; $0.40 × 2,000	200		800	
Lathe work				
$0.20 × 20,000; $0.20 × 60,000	4,000		12,000	
Milling				
$20.00 × 150; $20.00 × 1,050	3,000		21,000	
Grinding				
$0.80 × 500; $0.80 × 2,000	400		1,600	
Testing				
$15.00 × 10; $15.00 × 200	150	7,750	3,000	38,400
Total manufacturing costs		$18,200		$109,550
Number of units per job		÷ 10		÷ 200
Unit manufacturing cost per job		$ 1,820		$ 547.75

3.

	Job Order 410	Job Order 411
Number of units in job	10	200
Costs per unit with prior costing system	$1,332.50	$571.375
Costs per unit with activity-based costing	$1,820.00	$547.75

Job order 410 has an increase in reported unit cost of 36.6% [($1,820 – $1,332.50) ÷ $1,332.50], while job order 411 has a decrease in reported unit cost of 4.1% [($547.75 – $571.375) ÷ $571.375].

A common finding when activity-based costing is implemented is that low-volume products have increases in their reported costs while high-volume products have decreases in their reported cost. This result is also found in requirements 1 and 2 of this problem. Costs such as materials-handling costs vary with the number of parts handled (a function of batches and complexity of products) rather than with direct manufacturing labor-hours, an output-unit level cost driver, which was the only cost driver in the previous job-costing system.

The product cost figures computed in requirements 1 and 2 differ because:
a.   the job orders differ in the way they use each of five activity areas, and
b.   the activity areas differ in their indirect cost allocation bases (specifically, each area does not use the direct manufacturing labor-hours indirect cost allocation base).

The following table documents how the two job orders differ in the way they use each of the five activity areas included in indirect manufacturing costs:

5-38 (Cont'd.)

Activity Area	Usage Based on Analysis of Activity Area Cost Drivers		Usage Assumed with Direct Manuf. Labor-Hours as Application Base	
	Job Order 410	Job Order 411	Job Order 410	Job Order 411
Materials handling	20.0%	80.0%	6.25%	93.75%
Lathe work	25.0	75.0	6.25	93.75
Milling	12.5	87.5	6.25	93.75
Grinding	20.0	80.0	6.25	93.75
Testing	4.8	95.2	6.25	93.75

The differences in product cost figures might be important to Tracy Corporation for product pricing and product emphasis decisions. The activity-based accounting approach indicates that job order 410 is being undercosted while job order 411 is being overcosted. Tracy Corporation may erroneously push job order 410 and deemphasize job order 411. Moreover, by its actions, Tracy Corporation may encourage a competitor to enter the market for job order 411 and take market share away from it.

4. Information from the ABC system can also help Tracy manage its business better in several ways.

a. *Product design*. Product designers at Tracy Corporation likely will find the numbers in the activity-based costing approach more believable and credible than those in the existing system. In a machine-paced manufacturing environment, it is unlikely that direct labor-hours would be the major cost driver. Activity-based costing provides more credible signals to product designers about the ways the costs of a product can be reduced—for example, use fewer parts, require fewer turns on the lathe, and reduce the number of machine-hours in the milling area.

b. *Cost management*. Tracy can reduce the cost of jobs both by making process improvements that reduce the activities that need to be done to complete jobs and by reducing the costs of doing the activities.

c. *Cost planning*. ABC provides a more refined model to forecast costs and to explain why actual costs differ from budgeted costs.

5-40 (40-60 min.) **Activity-based costing, cost hierarchy.**

This solution is adapted from the CMA suggested solution.

1a.   Budgeted manufacturing overhead rate $= \dfrac{\text{Budgeted manufacturing overhead}}{\text{Budgeted direct labor cost}}$

$= \dfrac{\$3,000,000}{\$600,000}$

$= \$5$ per direct labor-dollar

1b.

	Mauna Loa	**Malaysian**
Direct costs		
Direct materials	$4.20	$3.20
Direct labor	0.30	0.30
	4.50	3.50
Indirect costs		
Manufacturing overhead		
(0.30 × $5.00)	1.50	1.50
Total costs	$6.00	$5.00

Budgeted selling prices per pound:
    Mauna Loa ($6.00 × 1.30)   = $7.80
    Malaysian ($5.00 × 1.30)   = $6.50

2.   The total budgeted unit costs per pound are:

Mauna Loa Coffee			**Malaysian Coffee**		
Direct costs per unit			Direct costs per unit		
Direct materials	$4.20		Direct materials	$3.20	
Direct labor	0.30	$4.50	Direct labor	0.30	$3.50
Indirect costs per unit			Indirect costs per unit		
Purchase orders			Purchase orders		
(4 orders × $500 ÷ 100,000 lbs.)	0.02		(4 orders × $500 ÷ 2,000 lbs.)	1.00	
Material handling			Material handling		
(30 setups × $400 ÷ 100,000 lbs.)	0.12		(12 setups × $400 ÷ 2,000 lbs.)	2.40	
Quality control			Quality control		
(10 batches × $240 ÷ 100,000 lbs.)	0.02		(4 batches × $240 ÷ 2,000 lbs.)	0.48	
Roasting			Roasting		
(1,000 hours × $10 ÷ 100,000 lbs.)	0.10		(20 hours × $10 ÷ 2,000 lbs.)	0.10	
Blending			Blending		
(500 hours × $10 ÷ 100,000 lbs.)	0.05		(10 hours × $10 ÷ 2,000 lbs.)	0.05	
Packaging			Packaging		
(100 hours × $10 ÷ 100,000 lbs.)	0.01	0.32	(2 hours × $10 ÷ 2,000 lbs.)	0.01	4.04
Total cost per unit		$4.82	Total cost unit		$7.54

5-40 (Cont'd.)

The comparative cost numbers are:

	Mauna Loa	Malaysian
Requirement 1	$6.00	$5.00
Requirement 2	4.82	7.54

The ABC system in requirement 2 reports a decreased cost for the high-volume Mauna Loa and an increased cost for the low-volume Malaysian.

3.   The traditional costing approach leads to cross-subsidization between the two products. With the traditional approach, the high-volume Mauna Loa is overcosted, while the low-volume Malaysian is undercosted. The ABC system indicates that Mauna Loa is profitable and should be emphasized.

      Pricing of Mauna Loa can be reduced to make it more competitive. In contrast, Malaysian should be priced at a much higher level if the strategy is to cover the current period's cost. Coffee Bean may wish to have lower margins with its low-volume products in an attempt to build up volume.

CHAPTER 6
MASTER BUDGET AND RESPONSIBILITY ACCOUNTING

6-2 The *master budget* expresses management's operating and financial plans for a specified period (usually a year) and comprises a set of budgeted financial statements. It is the initial plan of what the company intends to accomplish in the period.

6-4 Budgeted performance is better than past performance for judging managers. Why? Mainly because inefficiencies included in past results can be detected and eliminated in budgeting. Also, future conditions may be expected to differ from the past.

6-6 A company that shares its own internal budget information with other companies can gain multiple benefits. One benefit is better coordination with suppliers, which can reduce the likelihood of supply shortages. Better coordination with customers can result in increased sales as demand by customers is less likely to exceed supply. Better coordination across the whole supply chain can also help a company reduce inventories and thus reduce the costs of holding inventories. In addition, a company can gain information about competitors that will be useful in strategic planning and benchmarking.

6-8 A *rolling budget,* also called a *continuous budget,* is a budget or plan that is always available for a specified future period, by adding a period (month, quarter, or year) in the future as the period just ended is dropped. A four-quarter rolling budget for 2004 is superceded by a four-quarter rolling budget for April 2004 to March 2005, and so on.

6-10 The sales forecast is typically the cornerstone for budgeting, because production (and, hence, costs) and inventory levels generally depend on the forecasted level of sales.

6-12 Factors reducing the effectiveness of budgeting of companies include:
1. Lack of a well-defined strategy,
2. Lack of a clear linkage of strategy to operational plans,
3. Lack of individual accountability for results, and
4. Lack of meaningful performance measures.

6-14 Nonoutput-based cost drivers can be incorporated into budgeting by the use of activity-based budgeting (ABB). ABB focuses on the budgeted cost of activities necessary to produce and sell products and services. Nonoutput-based cost drivers, such as the number of part numbers, number of batches, and number of new products can be used with ABB.

6-16 (15 min.) **Advantages of budgeting.**

(a) Budgets compel strategic planning and facilitate implementation of plans. An organization's strategy, plans, and budgets are interrelated. Formulation of budgets is necessary for implementation of plans which, in turn, is necessary for the organization's strategy. Sometimes the feedback from budgets may result in a revision of strategic plans.

(b) Budgets provide a framework for judging performance. Budgeted performance measures are preferable to using past performance for evaluating actual results for two reasons. First, past performance may have been mediocre and not suitable to serve as a benchmark. Secondly, due to globalization and the advances in information technology, communication technology, and distribution technology, the future environment may be expected to be very different from the past. Budgeted performance measures take into account anticipated changes and improvements.

(c) Budgets motivate managers and employees.

(d) Budgets promote coordination and communication within the organization. Coordination compels managers to think of interdependencies and interrelationships. Communication helps all employees understand and accept the organizational objectives.

6-18 (5 min.) **Direct materials purchases budget.**

Direct materials to be used in production (bottles)	1,500,000
Add target ending direct materials inventory (bottles)	50,000
Total requirements (bottles)	1,550,000
Deduct beginning direct materials inventory (bottles)	20,000
Direct materials to be purchased (bottles)	1,530,000

6-20 (30 min.) **Sales and production budget.**

1.

	Selling Price	Units Sold	Total Revenues
12-ounce bottles	$0.25	4,800,000[a]	$1,200,000
4-gallon units	1.50	1,200,000[b]	1,800,000
			$3,000,000

[a] 400,000 × 12 months = 4,800,000
[b] 100,000 × 12 months = 1,200,000

2.

Budgeted unit sales (12-ounce bottles)	4,800,000
Add target ending finished goods inventory	600,000
Total requirements	5,400,000
Deduct beginning finished goods inventory	900,000
Units to be produced	4,500,000

3.

$$\frac{\text{Beginning}}{\text{inventory}} = \frac{\text{Budgeted}}{\text{sales}} + \frac{\text{Target}}{\text{ending inventory}} - \frac{\text{Budgeted}}{\text{production}}$$

$$= 1,200,000 + 200,000 - 1,300,000$$
$$= 100,000 \text{ 4-gallon units}$$

6-22 (15-20 min.) Revenue, production, and purchases budget.

1. 800,000 motorcycles × 400,000 yen = 320,000,000,000 yen

2.
Budgeted sales (units)	800,000
Add target ending finished goods inventory	100,000
Total requirements	900,000
Deduct beginning finished goods inventory	120,000
Units to be produced	780,000

3.
Direct materials to be used in production, 780,000 × 2	1,560,000
Add target ending direct materials inventory	30,000
Total requirements	1,590,000
Deduct beginning direct materials inventory	20,000
Direct materials to be purchased (units)	1,570,000
Cost per wheel in yen	16,000
Direct materials purchase cost in yen	25,120,000,000

Note the relatively small inventory of wheels. In Japan, suppliers tend to be located very close to the major manufacturer. Inventories are controlled by just-in-time and similar systems. Indeed, some direct materials inventories are almost nonexistent.

6-24 (20-30 min.) Activity-based budgeting.

1. This question links to the ABC example used in the Problem for Self-Study in Chapter 5 and to Question 5-24 (ABC, retail product-line profitability).

Activity	Cost Hierarchy	Soft Drinks	Fresh Produce	Packaged Food	Total
Ordering					
$90 × 14; 24; 14	Batch-level	$1,260	$ 2,160	$1,260	$ 4,680
Delivery					
$82 × 12; 62; 19	Batch-level	984	5,084	1,558	7,626
Shelf-stocking	Output-unit-level				
$21 × 16; 172; 94		336	3,612	1,974	5,922
Customer support	Output-unit-level				
$0.18 × 4,600; 34,200; 10,750		828	6,156	1,935	8,919
Total budgeted costs		$3,408	$17,012	$6,727	$27,147

2.   An ABB approach recognizes how different products require different mixes of support activities. The relative percentage of how each product area uses the cost driver at each activity area is:

Activity	Cost Hierarchy	Soft Drinks	Fresh Produce	Packaged Food	Total
Ordering	Batch–level	26.9	46.2	26.9	100.0%
Delivery	Batch–level	12.9	66.7	20.4	100.0
Shelf–stocking	Output–unit–level	5.7	61.0	33.3	100.0
Customer support	Output–unit–level	9.3	69.0	21.7	100.0

By recognizing these differences, FS managers are better able to budget for different unit sales levels and different mixes of individual product–line items sold. Using a single cost driver (such as COGS) assumes homogeneity in the use of indirect costs (support activities) across product lines which does not occur at FS. Other benefits cited by managers include: (1) better identification of resource needs, (2) clearer linking of costs with staff responsibilities, and (3) identification of budgetary slack.

6-26 (15 min.) Responsibility and controllability.

1. (a) Purchasing agent
    (b) Purchasing agent

2. (a) Purchasing agent
    (b) Supplier

3. (a) Production department supervisor
    (b) Purchasing agent

4. (a) Production department supervisor
    (b) Production department supervisor

5. (a) Production department supervisor
    (b) Maintenance department supervisor

6. (a) New division manager
    (b) Former division manager

7. (a) *Production department supervisor
    (b) Plant superintendent / Bottleneck department supervisor

*The production department here refers to the one operating below capacity, and not the next, bottleneck, production department.

6-28 (40 min.) Budget schedules for a manufacturer.

a. Revenues Budget

	Executive Line	Chairman Line	Total
Units sold	740	390	
Selling price	$ 1,020	$ 1,600	
Budgeted revenues	$754,800	$624,000	$1,378,800

b. Production Budget in Units

	Executive Line	Chairman Line
Budgeted unit sales	740	390
Add budgeted ending fin. goods inventory	30	15
Total requirements	770	405
Deduct beginning fin. goods. inventory	20	5
Budgeted production	750	400

c. Direct Materials Usage Budget (units):

	Oak	Red Oak	Oak Legs	Red Oak Legs	Total
Executive Line:					
1. Budgeted input per f.g. unit	16	–	4	–	
2. Budgeted production	750	–	750	–	
3. Budgeted usage (1 × 2)	12,000	–	3,000	–	
Chairman Line:					
4. Budgeted input per f.g. unit	–	25	–	4	
5. Budgeted production	–	400	–	400	
6. Budgeted usage (4 × 5)	–	10,000	–	1,600	
7. Total direct materials usage (3 + 6)	12,000	10,000	3,000	1,600	

Direct Materials Cost Budget

	Oak	Red Oak	Oak Legs	Red Oak Legs	Total
8. Beginning inventory	320	150	100	40	
9. Unit price (FIFO)	$18	$23	$11	$17	
10. Cost of DM used from beginning inventory (8 × 9)	$5,760	$3,450	$1,100	$680	$10,990
11. Materials to be used from purchases (7 – 8)	11,680	9,850	2,900	1,560	
12. Cost of DM in March	$20	$25	$12	$18	
13. Cost of DM purchased and used in March (11 × 12)	$233,600	$246,250	$34,800	$28,080	542,730
14. Direct materials to be used (10 +13)	$239,360	$249,700	$35,900	$28,760	$553,720

6-5

6-28 (Cont'd.)

Direct Materials Purchases Budget:

	Oak	Red Oak	Oak Legs	Red Oak Legs	Total
Budgeted usage (from line 7)	12,000	10,000	3,000	1,600	
Add target ending inventory	192	200	80	44	
Total requirements	12,192	10,200	3,080	1,644	
Deduct beginning inventory	320	150	100	40	
Total DM purchases	11,872	10,050	2,980	1,604	
Purchase price (March)	$20	$25	$12	$18	
Total purchases	$237,440	$251,250	$35,760	$28,872	$553,322

d. Direct manufacturing labor budget

	Output Units Produced	Direct Manu. Labor-Hours per Output Unit	Total Hours	Hourly Rate	Total
Executive Line	750	3	2,250	$30	$ 67,500
Chairman Line	400	5	2,000	$30	60,000
			4,250		$127,500

e. Manufacturing overhead budget
   Variable manufacturing overhead costs
   (4,250 × $35) $148,750
   Fixed manufacturing overhead costs 42,500
   Total manufacturing overhead costs $191,250
   Total manufacturing overhead cost per hour

   $$\frac{\$191,250}{4,250} = \$45 \text{ per direct manufacturing labor-hour}$$

   Fixed manufacturing overhead cost per hour

   $$\frac{\$42,500}{4,250} = \$10 \text{ per direct manufacturing labor-hour}$$

f. Computation of unit costs of ending inventory of finished goods:

	Executive Line	Chairman Line
Direct materials		
Oak top ($20 × 16, 0)	$320	$ 0
Red oak ($25 × 0, 25)	0	625
Oak legs ($12 × 4, 0)	48	0
Red oak legs ($18 × 0, 4)	0	72
Direct manufacturing labor ($30 × 3, 5)	90	150
Manufacturing overhead		
Variable ($35 × 3, 5)	105	175
Fixed ($10 × 3, 5)	30	50
Total manufacturing cost	$593	$1,072

6-28 (Cont'd.)

Ending Inventories Budget

	Cost per Unit	Units	Total
Direct Materials			
Oak top	$ 20	192	$ 3,840
Red oak top	25	200	5,000
Oak legs	12	80	960
Red oak legs	18	44	792
			10,592
Finished Goods			
Executive	593	30	17,790
Chairman	1,072	15	16,080
			33,870
Total			$44,462

g. Cost of goods sold budget

Budgeted finished goods inventory, March 1, 2005 ($10,480 + $4,850)		$ 15,330
Direct materials used (from Dir. materials cost budget)	$553,720	
Direct manufacturing labor (Dir. manuf. labor budget)	127,500	
Manufacturing overhead (Manuf. overhead budget)	191,250	
Cost of goods manufactured		872,470
Cost of goods available for sale		887,800
Deduct ending finished goods inventory, March 31, 2002 (Inventories budget)		33,870
Cost of goods sold		$853,930

2.   Areas where continuous improvement might be incorporated into the budgeting process:

(a)   Direct materials. Either an improvement in usage or price could be budgeted. For example, the budgeted usage amounts could be related to the maximum improvement (current usage – minimum possible usage) of 1 square foot for either desk:

- Executive: 16 square feet – 15 square feet minimum = 1 square foot
- Chairman: 25 square feet – 24 square feet minimum = 1 square foot

Thus, a 1% reduction target per month could be:

- Executive: 15 square feet + (0.99 × 1) = 15.99
- Chairman: 24 square feet + (0.99 × 1) = 24.99

Some students suggested the 1% be applied to the 16 and 25 square-foot amounts. This can be done so long as after several improvement cycles, the budgeted amount is not less than the minimum desk requirements.

(b)   Direct manufacturing labor. The budgeted usage of 3 hours/5 hours could be continuously revised on a monthly basis. Similarly, the manufacturing labor cost per hour of $30 could be continuously revised down. The former appears more feasible than the latter.

(c)   Variable manufacturing overhead. By budgeting more efficient use of the allocation base, a signal is given for continuous improvement. A second approach is to budget continuous improvement in the budgeted variable overhead cost per unit of the allocation base.

(d)   Fixed manufacturing overhead. The approach here is to budget for reductions in the year-to-year amounts of fixed overhead. If these costs are appropriately classified as fixed, then they are more difficult to adjust down on a monthly basis.

6-30 (30–40 min.) **Revenue and production budgets.**

This is a routine budgeting problem. The key to its solution is to compute the correct *quantities* of finished goods and direct materials. Use the following general formula:

$$\begin{pmatrix} \text{Budgeted} \\ \text{production} \\ \text{or purchases} \end{pmatrix} = \begin{pmatrix} \text{Target} \\ \text{ending} \\ \text{inventory} \end{pmatrix} + \begin{pmatrix} \text{Budgeted} \\ \text{sales or} \\ \text{materials used} \end{pmatrix} - \begin{pmatrix} \text{Beginning} \\ \text{inventory} \end{pmatrix}$$

1.

Scarborough Corporation
Revenue Budget for 2006

	Units	Price	Total
Thingone	60,000	$165	$ 9,900,000
Thingtwo	40,000	250	10,000,000
Budgeted revenues			$19,900,000

2.

Scarborough Corporation
Production Budget (in units) for 2006

	Thingone	Thingtwo
Budgeted sales in units	60,000	40,000
Add target finished goods inventories, December 31, 2006	25,000	9,000
Total requirements	85,000	49,000
Deduct finished goods inventories, January 1, 2006	20,000	8,000
Units to be produced	65,000	41,000

3.

Scarborough Corporation
Direct Materials Purchases Budget (in quantities) for 2006

	Direct Materials		
	A	B	C
Direct materials to be used in production			
• Thingone (budgeted production of 65,000 units times 4 lbs. of A, 2 lbs. of B)	260,000	130,000	--
• Thingtwo (budgeted production of 41,000 units times 5 lbs. of A, 3 lbs. of B, 1 lb. of C)	205,000	123,000	41,000
Total	465,000	253,000	41,000
Add target ending inventories, December 31, 2006	36,000	32,000	7,000
Total requirements in units	501,000	285,000	48,000
Deduct beginning inventories, January 1, 2006	32,000	29,000	6,000
Direct materials to be purchased (units)	469,000	256,000	42,000

6-30 (Cont'd.)

4.

Scarborough Corporation
Direct Materials Purchases Budget (in dollars) for 2006

	Budgeted Purchases (Units)	Expected Purchase Price per unit	Total
Direct material A	469,000	$12	$5,628,000
Direct material B	256,000	5	1,280,000
Direct material C	42,000	3	126,000
Budgeted purchases			$7,034,000

5.

Scarborough Corporation
Direct Manufacturing Labor Budget (in dollars) for 2006

	Budgeted Production (Units)	Direct Manufacturing Labor-Hours per Unit	Total Hours	Rate per Hour	Total
Thingone	65,000	2	130,000	$12	$1,560,000
Thingtwo	41,000	3	123,000	16	1,968,000
Total					$3,528,000

6.

Scarborough Corporation
Budgeted Finished Goods Inventory
At December 31, 2006

Thingone:
    Direct materials costs:
      A, 4 pounds × $12 $48
      B, 2 pounds × $5   10 $ 58
    Direct manufacturing labor costs,
      2 hours × $12   24
    Manufacturing overhead costs at $20 per direct
      manufacturing labor-hour (2 hours × $20)   40
    Budgeted manufacturing costs per unit $122
    Finished goods inventory of Thingone
      $122 × 25,000 units $3,050,000

Thingtwo:
    Direct materials costs:
      A, 5 pounds × $12 $60
      B, 3 pounds × $5   15
      C, 1 each × $3   3 $ 78
    Direct manufacturing labor costs,
      3 hours × $16   48
    Manufacturing overhead costs at $20 per direct
      manufacturing labor-hour (3 hours × $20)   60
    Budgeted manufacturing costs per unit $186
    Finished goods inventory of Thingtwo
      $186 × 9,000 units   1,674,000
  Budgeted finished goods inventory, December 31, 2006 $4,724,000

6-32 (15 min.) **Responsibility of purchasing agent.**

The time lost in the plant should be charged to the purchasing department. The plant manager probably should not be asked to underwrite a loss due to failure of delivery over which he had no supervision. Although the purchasing agent may feel that he has done everything he possibly could, he must realize that, in the whole organization, he is *the one* who is in the best position to evaluate the situation. He receives an assignment. He may accept it or reject it. But if he accepts, he must perform. If he fails, the damage is evaluated. Everybody makes mistakes. The important point is to avoid making too many mistakes and also to understand fully that the extensive control reflected in responsibility accounting is the necessary balance to the great freedom of action that individual executives are given.

Discussions of this problem have again and again revealed a tendency among students (and among accountants and managers) to "fix the blame"—as if the variances arising from a responsibility accounting system should pinpoint misbehavior and provide answers. The point is that no accounting system or variances can provide answers. However, variances can lead to questions. In this case, in deciding where the penalty should be assigned, the student might inquire who should be asked—not who should be blamed.

Classroom discussions have also raised the following diverse points:

(a) Is the railroad company liable?

(b) Costs of idle time are usually routinely charged to the production department. Should the information system be fine-tuned to reallocate such costs to the purchasing department?

(c) How will the purchasing managers behave in the future regarding willingness to take risks?

The text emphasizes the following: Beware of overemphasis on controllability. For example, a time-honored theme of management is that responsibility should not be given without accompanying authority. Such a guide is a useful first step, but responsibility accounting is more far-reaching. The basic focus should be on information or knowledge, not on control. The key question is: Who is the best informed? Put another way, "Who is the person who can tell us the most about the specific item, regardless of ability to exert personal control?"

6-34 (60 min.) **Comprehensive operating budget, budgeted balance sheet.**

1. **Schedule 1: Revenues Budget**
   For the Year Ended December 31, 2004

	Units	Selling Price	Total Revenues
Snowboards	1,000	$450	$450,000

2. **Schedule 2: Production Budget (in Units)**
   for the Year Ended December 31, 2004

	Snowboards
Budgeted unit sales (Schedule 1)	1,000
Add target ending finished goods inventory	200
Total requirements	1,200
Deduct beginning finished goods inventory	100
Units to be produced	1,100

3. **Schedule 3A: Direct Materials Usage Budget**
   For the Year Ended December 31, 2004

	Wood	Fiberglass	Total
Physical Units Budget			
Wood: 1,100 × 5.00 b.f.	5,500		
Fiberglass: 1,100 × 6.00 yards		6,600	
To be used in production	5,500	6,600	
Cost Budget			
Available from beginning inventory			
Wood: 2,000 b.f. × $28.00	56,000		
Fiberglass: 1,000 b.f. × 4.80		4,800	
To be used from purchases this period			
Wood: (5,500 – 2,000) × $30.00	105,000		
Fiberglass: (6,600 – 1,000) × $5.00		28,000	
Total cost of direct materials to be used	$161,000	$32,800	$193,800

Schedule 3B: Direct Materials Purchases Budget
For the Year Ended December 31, 2004

	Wood	Fiberglass	Total
Physical Units Budget			
Production usage (from Schedule 3A)	5,500	6,600	
Add target ending inventory	1,500	2,000	
Total requirements	7,000	8,600	
Deduct beginning inventory	2,000	1,000	
Purchases	5,000	7,600	

6-34 (Cont'd.)

        Cost Budget

Wood: 5,000 × $30.00	$150,000		
Fiberglass: 7,600 × $5.00)		$38,000	
Purchases	$150,000	$38,000	$188,000

4. **Schedule 4: Direct Manufacturing Labor Budget**
   For the Year Ended December 31, 2004

Labor Category	Cost Driver Units	DML Hours per Driver Unit	Total Hours	Wage Rate	Total
Manufacturing Labor	1,100	5.00	5,500	$25.00	$137,500

5. **Schedule 5: Manufacturing Overhead Budget**
   For the Year Ended December 31, 2004

	At Budgeted Level of 5,500 Direct Manufacturing Labor-Hours
Variable manufacturing overhead costs ($7.00 × 5,500)	$ 38,500
Fixed manufacturing overhead costs	66,000
Total manufacturing overhead costs	$104,500

6. Budgeted manufacturing overhead rate: $\dfrac{\$104,500}{5,500} = \$19.00$ per hour

7. Budgeted manufacturing overhead cost per output unit: $\dfrac{\$104,500}{1,100} = \$95.00$ per output unit

8. Schedule 6A: Computation of Unit Costs of Manufacturing Finished Goods in 2004

	Cost per Unit of Input[a]	Inputs[b]	Total
Direct materials			
Wood	$30.00	5.00	$150.00
Fiberglass	5.00	6.00	30.00
Direct manufacturing labor	25.00	5.00	125.00
Total manufacturing overhead			95.00
			$400.00

[a]cost is per board foot, yard or per hour
[b]inputs is the amount of each input per board

9. **Schedule 6B: Ending Inventories Budget**
   December 31, 2004

	Units	Cost per Unit	Total
Direct materials			
Wood	1,500	$ 30.00	$ 45,000
Fiberglass	2,000	5.00	10,000
Finished goods			
Snowboards	200	400.00	80,000
Total Ending Inventory			$135,000

6-34 (Cont'd.)

10. **Schedule 7: Cost of Goods Sold Budget**
    For the Year Ended December 31, 2004

	From Schedule		Total
Beginning finished goods inventory January 1, 2004, $374.80 × 100	Given		$ 37,480
Direct materials used	3A	$193,800	
Direct manufacturing labor	4	137,500	
Manufacturing overhead	5	104,500	
Cost of goods manufactured			435,800
Cost of goods available for sale			473,280
Deduct ending finished goods inventory, December 31, 2004	6B		80,000
Cost of goods sold			$393,280

11. **Budgeted Income Statement for Slopes**
    For the Year Ended December 31, 2004

Revenues	Schedule 1		$450,000
Cost of goods sold	Schedule 7		393,280
Gross margin			56,720
Operating costs			
Variable marketing costs ($250 × 30)		$ 7,500	
Fixed nonmanufacturing costs		30,000	37,500
Operating income			$ 19,220

12. **Budgeted Balance Sheet for Slopes**
    as of December 31, 2004

Cash		$ 10,000
Inventory	Schedule 6B	135,000
Property, plant, and equipment (net)		850,000
Total assets		$995,000
Current liabilities		$ 17,000
Long-term liabilities		178,000
Stockholders' equity		800,000
Total liabilities and stockholders' equity		$995,000

6-36 (30 min.) Cash budget, fill in the blanks, chapter appendix.

	I	Quarters II	III	IV	Year as a Whole
Cash balance, beginning	$ 15,000	$ 32,000	$ 15,000	$ 50,000	$ 15,000
Add receipts					
Collections from customers	385,000	315,000	295,000	365,000	1,360,000
Total cash available for needs	400,000	347,000	310,000	415,000	1,375,000
Deduct disbursements					
Direct materials	175,000	125,000	110,000	155,000	565,000
Payroll	125,000	110,000	95,000	118,000	448,000
Other costs	50,000	45,000	40,000	49,000	184,000
Interest costs (bond)	3,000	3,000	3,000	3,000	12,000
Machinery purchase	0	85,000	0	0	85,000
Income taxes	15,000	14,000	12,000	20,000	61,000
Total disbursements	368,000	382,000	260,000	345,000	1,355,000
Minimum cash balance desired	15,000	15,000	15,000	15,000	15,000
Total cash needed	383,000	397,000	275,000	360,000	1,370,000
Cash excess (deficiency)	17,000	(50,000)	35,000	55,000	5,000
Financing					
Borrowing (at beginning)	0	50,000	0	0	50,000
Repayment (at end)	0	0	0	(50,000)	(50,000)
Interest (at 12% per annum)	0	0	0	(4,500)	(4,500)
Total effects of financing	0	50,000	0	(54,500)	(4,500)
Cash balance, ending	$ 32,000	$ 15,000	$ 50,000	$ 15,500	$ 15,500

Note that the short-term loan is only repaid when it can be paid in full and after maintaining the minimum balance. The interest on the loan is only paid at the time the loan is repaid.

6-38 (60-75 min.) **Comprehensive budget; fill in schedules.**

1. Schedule A: Budgeted Monthly Cash Receipts

Item	September	October	November	December
Total sales	$40,000*	$48,000*	$60,000*	$80,000*
Credit sales (25%)	10,000*	12,000*	15,000	20,000
Cash sales (75%)	$30,000	$36,000	$45,000	$60,000
Receipts:				
Cash sales		$36,000*	$45,000	$60,000
Collections on accounts receivable		10,000*	12,000	15,000
Total		$46,000*	$57,000	$75,000

*Given.

2. Schedule B: Budgeted Monthly Cash Disbursements for Purchases

Item	October	November	December	4th Quarter
Purchases	$42,000*	$56,000	$25,200	$123,200
Deduct 2% cash discount	840*	1,120	504	2,464
Disbursements	$41,160*	$54,880	$24,696	$120,736

*Given. Note that purchases are 70.0% of next month's sales given a gross margin of 30%.

3. Schedule C: Budgeted Monthly Cash Disbursements for Operating Costs

Item	October	November	December	4th Quarter
Salaries and wages (15% of sales)	$ 7,200*	$ 9,000	$12,000	$28,200
Rent (5% of sales)	2,400*	3,000	4,000	9,400
Other cash operating costs (4% of sales)	1,920*	2,400	3,200	7,520
Total	$11,520*	$14,400	$19,200	$45,120

*Given.

4. Schedule D: Budgeted Total Monthly Cash Disbursements

Item	October	November	December	4th Quarter
Purchases	$41,160*	$54,880	$24,696	$120,736
Cash operating costs	11,520*	14,400	19,200	45,120
Light fixtures	600*	400	--	1,000
Total	$53,280*	$69,680	$43,896	$166,856

*Given.

5. Schedule E: Budgeted Cash Receipts and Disbursements

Item	October	November	December	4th Quarter
Receipts	$46,000*	$57,000	$75,000	$178,000
Disbursements	53,280*	69,680	43,896	166,856
Net cash increase			$31,104	$ 11,144
Net cash decrease	$ 7,280*	$12,680		

*Given

6. Schedule F: Financing Required

Item	October	November	December	4th Quarter
Beginning cash balance	$12,000*	$ 8,720*	$ 8,040	$12,000
Net cash increase			31,104	11,144
Net cash decrease	7,280*	12,680		
Cash position before borrowing (a)	4,720*	(3,960)	39,144	23,144
Minimum cash balance required	8,000*	8,000	8,000	8,000
Excess (Deficiency)	(3,280)*	(11,960)	31,144	15,144
Borrowing required (b)	4,000*	12,000		16,000
Interest payments (c)			540	540
Borrowing repaid (d)			16,000	16,000
Ending cash balance (a+b–c–d)	$ 8,720*	$ 8,040	$22,604	$22,604

*Given.

Interest computation:

$ 4,000 @ 18% for 3 months	=	$180
$12,000 @ 18% for 2 months	=	360
Total interest expense		$540

7. Short-term, self-liquidating financing is best. The schedules clearly demonstrate the mechanics of a self-liquidating loan. The need for such a loan arises because of the seasonal nature of many businesses. When sales soar, the payroll and suppliers must be paid in cash. The basic source of cash is proceeds from sales. However, the credit extended to customers creates a lag between the sale and the collection of cash. When the cash is collected, it in turn may be used to repay the loan. The amount of the loan and the timing of the repayment are heavily dependent on the credit terms that pertain to both the purchasing and selling functions of the business. Somewhat strangely, in seasonal businesses, the squeeze on cash is often heaviest in the months of peak sales and is lightest in the months of low sales.

6-38 (Cont'd.)

8.

Newport Stationery Store
Budgeted Income Statement
For the Quarter Ending December 31, 2004

Revenues—Schedule A		$188,000
Cost of goods sold (70% of sales)		131,600*
Gross margin		56,400
Operating costs		
Salaries and wages—Schedule C	$28,200	
Rent—Schedule C	9,400	
Other cash operating costs—Schedule C	7,520	
Depreciation ($1,000 × 3 months)	3,000	48,120
Operating income		8,280
Deduct interest expense— Schedule F		540
Add purchase discounts— Schedule B		2,464
Net income (before taxes)		$ 10,204
*Note: Ending inventory and proof of cost of goods sold:		
Inventory, September 30	$ 63,600	
Add purchases—Schedule B	123,200	$186,800
Deduct inventory, December 31:		
Basic inventory	30,000	
December purchases—Schedule B	25,200	55,200
Cost of goods sold		$131,600

6-38 (Cont'd.)

Newport Stationery Store
Budgeted Balance Sheet
December 31, 2004

Assets:
  Current assets:

Cash—Schedule F		$ 22,604
Accounts receivable		
December credit sales—Schedule A		20,000
Inventory (see Note above)		55,200
Total current assets		97,804
Equipment and fixtures:		
Equipment—net ($100,000 – $3,000 depreciation)	$97,000	
Fixtures—Schedule D	1,000	98,000
Total		$195,804
Liabilities and Owners' Equity:		
Liabilities		None
Owners' equity		$195,804*
Total		$195,804

*Owners' equity, September 30:

$12,000 + $63,600 + $10,000 + $100,000 (Given)	$185,600
Net income, quarter ended December 31	10,204
Owners' equity, December 31	$195,804

9.   All of the transactions have been simplified--for example, no bad debts are considered. Also, many businesses face wide fluctuation of cash flows within a month. For example, perhaps customer receipts lag and are bunched together near the end of a month, and disbursements are due evenly throughout the month, or are bunched near the beginning of the month. Cash needs would then need to be evaluated on a weekly and, perhaps, daily basis rather than on a monthly basis.

6-40   (60 min.) **Comprehensive review of budgeting, cash budgeting, chapter appendix.**

a.   **Schedule 1: Revenues Budget**
For the Year Ended December 31, 2005

	Units (Lots)	Selling Price	Total Sales
Lemonade	1,080	$9,000	$ 9,720,000
Diet Lemonade	540	8,500	4,590,000
Total			$14,310,000

b.   **Schedule 2: Production Budget in Units**
For the Year Ended December 31, 2005

	Products	
	Lemonade	Diet Lemonade
Budgeted unit sales (Schedule 1)	1,080	540
Add target ending finished goods inventory	20	10
Total requirements	1,100	550
Deduct beginning finished goods inventory	100	50
Units to be produced	1,000	500

6-40 (Cont'd.)

c. Schedule 3A: Direct Materials Usage Budget in Units and Dollars
For the Year Ended December 31, 2005

	Syrup-Lemon.	Syrup-Diet Lem.	Containers	Packaging	Total
Units of direct materials to be used for production of Lemonade (1,000 lots × 1)	1,000		1,000	1,000	
Units of direct materials to be used for production of Diet Lemonade (500 lots × 1)		500	500	500	
Total direct materials to be used (in units)	1,000	500	1,500	1,500	
Units of direct materials to be used from beginning inventory (under FIFO)	80	70	200	400	
Multiply by cost per unit of beginning inventory	$ 1,100	$ 1,000	$ 950	$ 900	
Cost of direct materials to be used from beginning inventory (a)	$ 88,000	$ 70,000	$ 190,000	$ 360,000	$ 708,000
Units of direct materials to be used from purchases (1,000 – 80; 500 – 70; 1,500 – 200; 1,500 – 400)	920	430	1,300	1,100	
Multiply by cost per unit of purchased materials	$ 1,200	$ 1,100	$ 1,000	$ 800	
Cost of direct materials to be used from purchases (b)	$1,104,000	$473,000	$1,300,000	$ 880,000	3,757,000
Total cost of direct materials to be used (a + b)	$1,192,000	$543,000	$1,490,000	$1,240,000	$4,465,000

d. Schedule 3B: Direct Materials Purchases Budget in Units and Dollars
For the Year Ended December 31, 2005

	Syrup-Lemon.	Syrup-Diet Lem.	Containers	Packaging	Total
Direct materials to be used in production (in units) from Schedule 3A	1,000	500	1,500	1,500	
Add target ending direct materials inventory in units	30	20	100	200	
Total requirements in units	1,030	520	1,600	1,700	
Deduct beginning direct materials inventory in units	80	70	200	400	
Units of direct materials to be purchased	950	450	1,400	1,300	
Multiply by cost/unit of purchased materials	$ 1,200	$ 1,100	$ 1,000	$ 800	
Direct materials purchase costs	$1,140,000	$495,000	$1,400,000	$1,040,000	$4,075,000

6-40 (Cont'd.)

e. **Schedule 4: Direct Manufacturing Labor Budget**
   For the Year Ended December 31, 2005

	Output Units Produced (Schedule 2)	Direct Manufacturing Labor Hours per Unit	Total Hours	Hourly Rate	Total
Lemonade	1,000	20	20,000	$25	$500,000
Diet Lemonade	500	20	10,000	25	250,000
Total			30,000		$750,000

f. **Schedule 5: Manufacturing Overhead Costs Budget**
   for the Year Ended December 31, 2005

Variable manufacturing overhead costs:

Lemonade [$600 × 2 hours per lot × 1,000 lots (Schedule 2)]	$1,200,000
Diet Lemonade [$600 × 2 hours per lot × 500 lots (Schedule 2)]	600,000
Variable manufacturing overhead costs	1,800,000
Fixed manufacturing overhead costs	1,200,000
Total manufacturing overhead costs	$3,000,000

Fixed manufacturing overhead per bottling hour = $1,200,000 ÷ 3,000 = $400. Note that the total number of bottling hours is 3,000 hours: 2,000 hours for Lemonade (2 hours per lot × 1,000 lots) plus 1,000 hours for Diet Lemonade (2 hours per lot × 500 lots).

g. **Schedule 6A: Ending Finished Goods Inventory Budget**
   as of December 31, 2005

	Units (Lots)	Cost per Unit (Lot)		Total
Direct materials:				
Syrup for Lemonade	30	$1,200	$ 36,000	
Syrup for Diet Lemonade	20	1,100	22,000	
Containers	100	1,000	100,000	
Packaging	200	800	160,000	$318,000

	Units	Cost per Unit		
Finished goods:				
Lemonade	20	$5,500*	$110,000	
Diet Lemonade	10	5,400*	54,000	164,000
Total ending inventory				$482,000

*From Schedule 6B

6-40 (Cont'd.)

Schedule 6B: Computation of Unit Costs of Manufacturing Finished Goods
For the Year Ended December 31, 2005

	Cost per Unit (Lot) or Hour of Input	Lemonade Inputs in Units (Lots) or Hours	Amount	Diet Lemonade Inputs in Units (Lots) or Hours	Amount
Syrup			$1,200		$1,100
Containers			1,000		1,000
Packaging			800		800
Direct manufacturing labor	$ 25	20	500	20	500
Variable manufacturing overhead*	600	2	1,200	2	1,200
Fixed manufacturing overhead*	400	2	800		800
Total			$5,500		$5,400

*Variable manufacturing overhead varies with bottling hours (2 hours per lot for both Lemonade and Diet Lemonade). Fixed manufacturing overhead is allocated on the basis of bottling hours at the rate of $400 per bottling hour calculated in Schedule 5.

h. **Schedule 7: Cost of Goods Sold Budget**
   For the Year Ended December 31, 2005

	From Schedule		Total
Beginning finished goods inventory, January 1, 2005	Given*		$ 790,000
Direct materials used	3A	$4,465,000	
Direct manufacturing labor	4	750,000	
Manufacturing overhead	5	3,000,000	
Cost of goods manufactured			8,215,000
Cost of goods available for sale			9,005,000
Deduct ending finished goods inventory, December 31, 2005	6		164,000
Cost of goods sold			$8,841,000

*Given in description of basic data and requirements (Lemonade, $5,300 × 100; diet Lemonade, $5,200 × 50)

i. **Schedule 8: Marketing Costs Budget**
   For the Year Ended December 31, 2005
   Marketing costs, 12% × Revenues, $14,310,000 $1,717,200

j. **Schedule 9: Distribution Costs Budget**
   For the Year Ended December 31, 2005
   Distribution costs, 8% × Revenues, $14,310,000 $1,144,800

6-40 (Cont'd.)

k. **Schedule 10: Administration Costs Budget**
For the Year Ended December 31, 2005
Administration costs, 10% × Cost of goods
manufactured, $8,215,000 $ 821,500

l. **Budgeted Income Statement**
For the Year Ended December 31, 2005

Sales	Schedule 1		$14,310,000
Cost of goods sold	Schedule 7		8,841,000
Gross margin			5,469,000
Operating costs:			
Marketing costs	Schedule 8	$1,717,200	
Distribution costs	Schedule 9	1,144,800	
Administration costs	Schedule 10	821,500	
Total operating costs			3,683,500
Operating income			1,785,500
Income tax expense			625,000
Net income			$ 1,160,500

Schedule 11: Collections from Customers

Budgeted Revenue for 2005	Schedule 1	$14,310,000
Add collections from beginning		
accounts receivable balance	Given	550,000
		14,860,000
Deduct ending accounts receivable		
balance	Given	600,000
Collections from customers		$14,260,000

Schedule 12: Direct Materials Disbursements

Budgeted direct material purchase		
costs for 2005	Schedule 3B	$ 4,075,000
Add payment for beginning accounts		
payable balance	Given	300,000
		4,375,000
Deduct ending accounts payable		
balance	Given	400,000
Disbursements for direct materials		$ 3,975,000

Schedule 13: Variable Manufacturing Overhead Disbursements

Variable Manufacturing Overhead:		
Lemonade (1,000 × $600 × 2)	Schedule 5	$ 1,200,000
Diet Lemonade (500 × $600 × 2)	Schedule 5	600,000
Total		$ 1,800,000

6-40 (Cont'd.)

Schedule 14: Fixed Manufacturing Overhead Disbursements

Budgeted fixed manufacturing overhead	Schedule 5	$ 1,200,000
Deduct depreciation	Given	400,000
Cash disbursements for fixed overhead		$ 800,000

m.

Cash Budget
December 31, 2005

Cash balance, beginning	Given	$ 100,000
Add receipts		
Collections from customers	Schedule 11	14,260,000
Total cash available for needs		$14,360,000
Deduct disbursements		
Direct materials	Schedule 12	$ 3,975,000
Direct manufacturing labor	Schedule 4	750,000
Variable manufacturing overhead	Schedule 13	1,800,000
Fixed manufacturing overhead	Schedule 14	800,000
Equipment purchase	Given	1,350,000
Marketing costs	Schedule 8	1,717,200
Distribution costs	Schedule 9	1,144,800
Administration costs	Schedule 10	821,500
Income tax expense	Given	625,000
Total disbursements		$12,983,500
Cash excess (deficiency)		$ 1,376,500
Financing		
Borrowing		0
Repayment		0
Interest		0
Total effects of financing		0
Cash balance ending		$ 1,376,500

CHAPTER 7
FLEXIBLE BUDGETS, VARIANCES, AND
MANAGEMENT CONTROL: I

7-2   Two sources of information about budgeted amounts are (a) past amounts and (b) detailed engineering studies.

7-4   The key difference is the output level used to set the budget. A *static budget* is based on the level of output planned at the *start of the budget period*. A *flexible budget* is developed using budgeted revenues or cost amounts based on the actual output level in the budget period. The actual level of output is not known until the *end of the budget period*.

7-6   The steps in developing a flexible budget are:

Step 1:   Identify the actual quantity of output.

Step 2:   Calculate the flexible budget for revenues based on budgeted selling price and actual quantity of output.

Step 3:   Calculate the flexible budget for costs based on budgeted variable costs per output unit, actual quantity of output, and budgeted fixed costs.

7-8   A manager should subdivide the flexible-budget variance for direct materials into a price variance (that reflects the difference between actual and budgeted prices of direct materials) and an efficiency variance (that reflects the difference between the actual and budgeted quantities of direct materials used to produce actual output). The individual causes of these variances can then be investigated, recognizing possible interdependencies across these individual causes.

7-10   Direct materials price variances are often computed at the time of purchase of materials, while direct materials efficiency variances are often computed at the time of usage of materials. Purchasing managers are typically responsible for price variances, while production managers are typically responsible for usage variances.

7-12   An individual business function, such as production, is interdependent with other business functions. Factors outside of production can explain why variances arise in the production area. For example:
- poor design of products or processes can lead to a sizable number of defects,
- marketing personnel making promises for delivery times that require a large number of rush orders can create production-scheduling difficulties, and
- purchase of poor-quality materials by the purchasing manager can result in defects and waste.

7-14   Variances can be calculated at the activity level as well as at the company level. For example, a price variance and an efficiency variance can be computed for an activity area.

7-16 (20-30 min.) **Flexible budget.**

	Actual Results (1)	Flexible-Budget Variances (2) = (1) – (3)	Flexible Budget (3)	Sales-Volume Variances (4) =(3)–(5)	Static Budget (5)
Units sold	2,800[G]	0	2,800	200 U	3,000[G]
Revenues	$313,600[a]	$ 5,600 F	$ 308,000[b]	$22,000 U	$330,000[c]
Variable costs	229,600[d]	22,400 U	207,200[e]	14,800 F	222,000[f]
Contribution margin	84,000	16,800 U	100,800	7,200 U	108,000
Fixed costs	50,000[G]	4,000 F	54,000[G]	0	54,000[G]
Operating income	$ 34,000	$12,800 U	$ 46,800	$ 7,200 U	$ 54,000

$12,800 U
Total flexible-budget variance $ 7,200 U
Total sales-volume variance

$20,000 U
Total static-budget variance

[a] $112 × 2,800 = $313,600
[b] $110 × 2,800 = $308,000
[c] $110 × 3,000 = $330,000
[d] Given. Unit variable cost = $229,600 ÷ 2,800 = $82 per tire
[e] $74 × 2,800 = $207,200
[f] $74 × 3,000 = $222,000
[G] Given

2.   The key information items are:

	Actual	Budgeted
Units	2,800	3,000
Unit selling price	$ 112	$ 110
Unit variable cost	$ 82	$ 74
Fixed costs	$50,000	$54,000

The total static-budget variance in operating income is $20,000 U. There is both an unfavorable total flexible-budget variance ($12,800) and an unfavorable sales-volume variance ($7,200).

The unfavorable sales-volume variance arises solely because actual units manufactured and sold were 200 less than the budgeted 3,000 units. The unfavorable flexible-budget variance of $12,800 in operating income is due primarily to the $8 increase in unit variable costs. This increase in unit variable costs is only partially offset by the $2 increase in unit selling price and the $4,000 decrease in fixed costs.

7-18 (10 min.) **Flexible budget.**

1.

Total static-budget variance	=	Actual results	–	Static-budget amount
	=	$6,556,000	–	$3,150,000
	=	$3,406,000 F		

2.

Total flexible-budget variance	=	Actual results	–	Flexible-budget amount
	=	$6,556,000	–	$6,930,000
	=	$374,000 U		

Total sales-volume variance	=	Flexible-budget amount	–	Static-budget amount
	=	$6,930,000	–	$3,150,000
	=	$3,780,000 F		

3.

```
  Actual Results          Flexible Budget            Static Budget
    $6,556,000               $6,930,000                $3,150,000
        ▲                        ▲                         ▲
        |    $374,000 U          |      $3,780,000 F       |
        |_____|_____|
     Total flexible-budget variance   Total sales-volume variance
        ▲                                                  ▲
        |                                                  |
        |_____$3,406,000 F_____|
                       Total static-budget variance
```

The total flexible-budget variance is $374,000 unfavorable. This arises because for the actual output level: (a) selling prices were lower than budgeted, or (b) variable costs were higher than budgeted, or (c) fixed costs were higher than budgeted, or (d) some combination of (a), (b), and (c).

7-20 (15 min.) **Materials and manufacturing labor variances.**

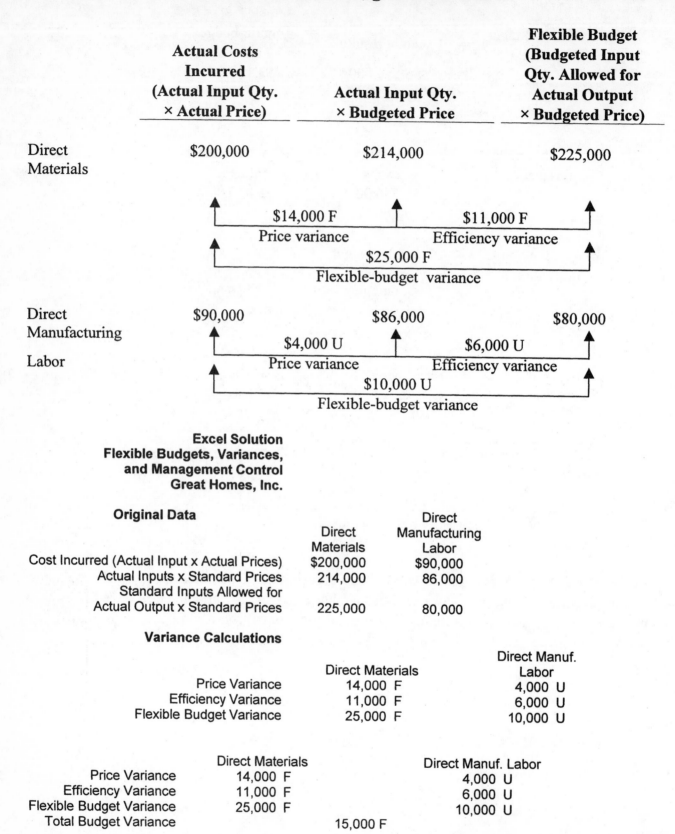

	Actual Costs Incurred (Actual Input Qty. × Actual Price)	Actual Input Qty. × Budgeted Price	Flexible Budget (Budgeted Input Qty. Allowed for Actual Output × Budgeted Price)
Direct Materials	$200,000	$214,000	$225,000

$14,000 F Price variance $11,000 F Efficiency variance

$25,000 F Flexible-budget variance

Direct Manufacturing Labor	$90,000	$86,000	$80,000

$4,000 U Price variance $6,000 U Efficiency variance

$10,000 U Flexible-budget variance

Excel Solution
Flexible Budgets, Variances,
and Management Control
Great Homes, Inc.

Original Data

	Direct Materials	Direct Manufacturing Labor
Cost Incurred (Actual Input x Actual Prices)	$200,000	$90,000
Actual Inputs x Standard Prices	214,000	86,000
Standard Inputs Allowed for Actual Output x Standard Prices	225,000	80,000

Variance Calculations

	Direct Materials	Direct Manuf. Labor
Price Variance	14,000 F	4,000 U
Efficiency Variance	11,000 F	6,000 U
Flexible Budget Variance	25,000 F	10,000 U

	Direct Materials	Direct Manuf. Labor
Price Variance	14,000 F	4,000 U
Efficiency Variance	11,000 F	6,000 U
Flexible Budget Variance	25,000 F	10,000 U
Total Budget Variance	15,000 F	

7-22 (30-40 min.) Flexible budgets, variance analysis.

1.   Variance Analysis of Flanagan Company for May

Level 0 Analysis

Actual operating income (see calculations below)	$ 49,000
Budgeted operating income (see calculations below)	100,000
Static-budget variance of operating income	$ 51,000 U

Level 1 Analysis

	Actual Results (1)	Static-Budget Variances (2) = (1) – (3)	Static Budget (3)
Units sold	23,000	3,000 F	20,000
Revenues	$874,000	$ 74,000 F	$800,000[a]
Variable costs	630,000	130,000 U	500,000[b]
Contribution margin	244,000	56,000 U	300,000
Fixed costs	195,000	5,000 F	200,000
Operating income	$ 49,000	$ 51,000 U	$100,000

$51,000 U
Total static-budget variance

Level 2 Analysis

	Actual Results (1)	Flexible-Budget Variances (2) = (1) – (3)	Flexible Budget (3)	Sales-Volume Variances (4) = (3) – (5)	Static Budget (5)
Units sold	23,000	0	23,000	3,000 F	20,000
Revenue	$874,000	$ 46,000 U	$920,000[c]	$120,000 F	$800,000
Variable costs	630,000	55,000 U	575,000[d]	75,000 U	500,000
Contribution margin	244,000	101,000 U	345,000	45,000 F	300,000
Fixed costs	195,000	5,000 F	200,000	0	200,000
Operating income	$ 49,000	$ 96,000 U	$145,000	$ 45,000 F	$100,000

$96,000 U $45,000 F
Total flexible-budget   Total sales-volume
variance   variance

$51,000 U
Total static-budget variance

[a]$40 × 20,000 = $800,000

[b]$25 × 20,000 = $500,000

[c]$40 × 23,000 = $920,000

[d]$25 × 23,000 = $575,000

7-22 (Cont'd.)

2. Flexible budget variance for revenues, $46,000 U. Cause: The actual selling price per unit is $38 ($874,000 ÷ 23,000) compared to a budgeted $40 per unit. This reduction in selling price may explain the 15% increase in unit sales (23,000 versus the budgeted 20,000).
    Flexible budget variance for variable costs, $55,000 U. Reason: Variable costs may have exceeded the budget for many reasons, including individual price increases in materials and supplies and possible inefficiencies because of the 15% spurt in production.
    Flexible budget variance for fixed costs, $5,000 F. Reason: Fixed cost could be less than the budget because of delays in planned salary increases, adjustments in insurance coverage, or other reasons.

7-24 (30 min.) Flexible budget, working backward.

1.

	Actual Results (1)	Flexible-Budget Variances (2)=(1)–(3)	Flexible Budget (3)	Sales-Volume Variances (4)=(3)–(5)	Static Budget (5)
Units Sold	650,000	0	650,000	50,000 F	600,000
Revenues	$3,575,000	$1,300,000 F	$2,275,000[a]	$175,000 F	$2,100,000
Variable costs	2,575,000	1,275,000 U	1,300,000[b]	100,000 U	1,200,000
Contribution margin	1,000,000	25,000 F	975,000	75,000 F	900,000
Fixed costs	700,000	100,000 U	600,000	0	600,000
Operating income	$ 300,000	$ 75,000 U	$ 375,000	$ 75,000 F	$ 300,000

$75,000 U
Total flexible-budget variance

$75,000 F
Total sales volume variance

$0
Total static-budget variance

[a] 650,000 × $3.50 = $2,275,000
[b] 650,000 × $2.00 = 1,300,000

2.

Actual selling price:	$3,575,000 ÷ 650,000	=	$5.50
Budgeted selling price:	2,100,000 ÷ 600,000	=	3.50
Actual variable cost per unit:	2,575,000 ÷ 650,000	=	3.96
Budgeted variable cost per unit:	1,200,000 ÷ 600,000	=	2.00

3.   The CEO's reaction was inappropriate. A zero total static-budget variance may be due to offsetting total flexible-budget and total sales-volume variances. In this case, these two variances exactly offset each other:

Total flexible-budget variance $75,000 Unfavorable
Total sales-volume variance $75,000 Favorable

A closer look at the variance components reveals some major deviations from plan. Actual variable costs increased from $2.00 to $3.96, causing an unfavorable flexible-budget

7-24 (Cont'd.)

in platinum prices. Specialty Balls was able to pass most of the increase in costs onto their customers – average selling price went up about 57%, bringing about an offsetting favorable flexible-budget revenue variance in the amount of $1,300,000. An increase in the actual number of units sold also contributed to more favorable results. Although such an increase in quantity in the face of a price increase may appear counter-intuitive, customers may have forecast higher future platinum prices and therefore decided to stock up.

4.   The most important lesson learned here is that a superficial examination of summary level data (Levels 0 and 1) may be insufficient. It is imperative to scrutinize data at a more detailed level (Level 2). Had Specialty Balls not been able to pass costs on to customers, losses would have been considerable.

7-26   (20 min.) Continuous improvement. (continuation of 7-25)

1.   Standard quantity input amounts per output unit are:

	Direct Materials (pounds)	Direct Manufacturing Labor (hours)
January	10.0000	0.5000
February (Jan. × 0.997)	9.9700	0.4985
March (Feb. × 0.997)	9.9400	0.4970

2.   The answer to requirement 1 of Question 7-25 is identical except for the flexible- budget amount.

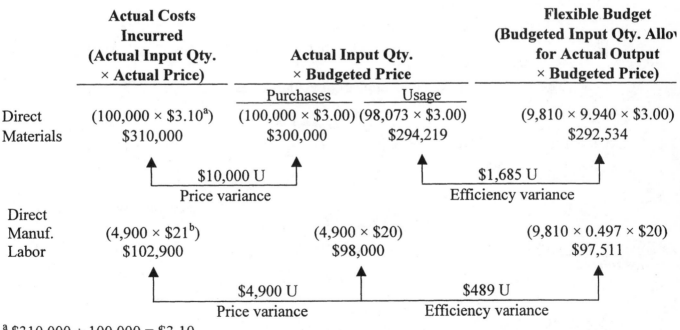

^{a} $310,000 ÷ 100,000 = $3.10
^{b} $102,900 ÷ 4,900 = $21

7-26 (Cont'd.)

Using continuous improvement standards sets a tougher benchmark. The efficiency variances for January (from Exercise 7-25) and March (from Exercise 7-26) are:

	January	March
Direct materials	$ 81 F	$1,685 U
Direct manufacturing labor	$100 F	$ 489 U

Note that the question assumes the continuous improvement applies only to quantity inputs. An alternative approach is to have continuous improvement apply to budgeted input cost per output unit ($30 for direct materials in January and $10 for direct manufacturing labor in January). This approach is more difficult to incorporate in a Level 2 variance analysis, as Level 2 requires separate amounts for quantity inputs and the cost per input.

7-28 (15–25 min.) **Journal entries and T-accounts (continuation of 7-27).**

a.	Work-in-Process Control	400,000	
	Direct Materials Price Variance	7,400	
	Accounts Payable Control		377,400
	To record purchase of direct materials.		

b.	Work-in-Process Control	400,000	
	Direct Materials Efficiency Variance		30,000
	Materials Control		377,400
	To record direct materials used.		

b.	Work-in-Process Control	200,000	
	Direct Manufacturing Labor Price Variance		3,600
	Direct Manufacturing Labor Efficiency Variance		20,000
	Wages Payable Control		176,400
	To record liability and allocation of direct labor costs.		

Materials Control		Direct Materials Price Variance		Direct Materials Efficiency Variance	
(a) 377,400		(a) 7,400			(a) 30,000

Work-in-Process Control		Direct Manufacturing Labor Price Variance		Direct Manufacturing Labor Efficiency Variance	
(b) 400,000			(b) 3,600		(b) 20,000
(c) 200,000					

Wages Payable Control		Accounts Payable Control	
	(b) 176,400		377,400 (a)

7-28 (Cont'd.)

Requirement 2 from Exercise 7-27:

The following journal entries pertain to the measurement of price variances when materials of 600,000 are purchased:

a1.	Materials Control	600,000	
	Direct Materials Price Variance	12,000	
	Accounts Payable Control		612,000
	To record direct materials purchased.		

a2.	Work-in-Process Control	400,000	
	Materials Control		370,000
	Direct Materials Efficiency Variance		30,000
	To record direct materials used.		

Materials Control	
(a1) 600,000	(a2) 370,000

Direct Materials Price Variance	
(a1) 12,000	

Accounts Payable Control	
	(a1) 612,000

Work-in-Process Control	
(a2) 400,000	

Direct Materials Efficiency Variance	
	(a2) 30,000

The difference between standard costing and normal costing for direct cost items is:

	Standard Costs	Normal Costs
Direct Costs	Standard price(s) × Standard input allowed for actual outputs achieved	Actual price(s) × Actual input

These journal entries differ from the *normal costing* entries because Work-in-Process Control is no longer carried at "actual" costs. Furthermore, Materials Control can also be carried at standard unit prices rather than actual unit prices. Finally, variances appear for direct materials and direct manufacturing labor under *standard costing* but not under *normal costing*.

7-30 (45-50 min.) **Activity-based costing, flexible-budget variances for finance function activities.**

1. *Receivables*
   Receivables is an output unit level activity. Its flexible-budget variance can be calculated as follows:

$$\text{Flexible-budget variance} = \text{Actual costs} - \text{Flexible-budget costs}$$

$$= (\$0.75 \times 948{,}000) - (\$0.639 \times 948{,}000)$$
$$= \$711{,}000 - \$605{,}772$$
$$= \$105{,}228 \text{ U}$$

Payables
Payables is a batch level activity.

		Static-budget Amounts	Actual Amounts
a.	Number of deliveries	1,000,000	948,000
b.	Batch size (units per batch)	5	4.468
c.	Number of batches (a ÷ b)	200,000	212,175
d.	Cost per batch	$2.90	$2.80
e.	Total payables activity cost (c × d)	$580,000	$594,090

Step 1: The number of batches in which payables should have been processed = 948,000 actual units ÷ 5 budgeted units per batch = 189,600 batches

Step 2: The flexible-budget amount for payables
   = 189,600 batches × $2.90 budgeted cost per batch
   = $549,840

The flexible-budget variance can be computed as follows:

$$\text{Flexible-budget variance} = \text{Actual costs} - \text{Flexible-budget costs}$$

$$= (212{,}175 \times \$2.80) - (189{,}600 \times \$2.90)$$

$$= \$594{,}090 - \$549{,}840 = \$44{,}250 \text{ U}$$

Travel expenses
Travel expenses is a batch level activity.

		Static-Budget Amounts	Actual Amounts
a.	Number of deliveries	1,000,000	948,000
b.	Batch size (units per batch)	500	501.587
c.	Number of batches (a ÷ b)	2,000	1,890
d.	Cost per batch	$7.60	$7.40
e.	Total travel expenses activity cost (c × d)	$15,200	$13,986

7-30 (Cont'd.)

Step 1: The number of batches in which the travel expense should have been processed = 948,000 actual units ÷ 500 budgeted units per batch = 1,896 batches

Step 2: The flexible-budget amount for travel expenses
= 1,896 batches × $7.60 budgeted cost per batch
= $14,410

The flexible budget variance can be calculated as follows:

Flexible budget variance = Actual costs – Flexible-budget costs
= (1,890 × $7.40) – (1,896 × $7.60)
= $13,986 – $14,410 = $424 F

2.   The flexible budget variances can be subdivided into price and efficiency variances.

$$\text{Price variance} = \left[\begin{array}{c} \text{Actual price} \\ \text{of input} \end{array} - \begin{array}{c} \text{Budgeted price} \\ \text{of input} \end{array} \right] \times \begin{array}{c} \text{Actual quantity} \\ \text{of input} \end{array}$$

$$\text{Efficiency variance} = \left[\begin{array}{c} \text{Actual quantity} \\ \text{of input used} \end{array} - \begin{array}{c} \text{Budgeted quantity of} \\ \text{input allowed for} \\ \text{actual output} \end{array} \right] \times \begin{array}{c} \text{Budgeted price} \\ \text{of input} \end{array}$$

Receivables

Price Variance   = ($0.750 – $0.639) × 948,000
                            = $105,228 U
Efficiency variance = (948,000 – 948,000) × $0.639
                            = $0

Payables
Price variance   = ($2.80 – $2.90) × 212,175
                            = $21,218 F
Efficiency variance = (212,175 – 189,600) × $2.90
                            = $65,468 U

Travel expenses
Price variance   = ($7.40 – $7.60) × 1,890
                            = $378 F
Efficiency variance = (1,890 – 1,896) × $7.60
                            = $46 F

7-32 (30 min.) **Flexible budget, direct materials and direct manufacturing labor variances.**

1.

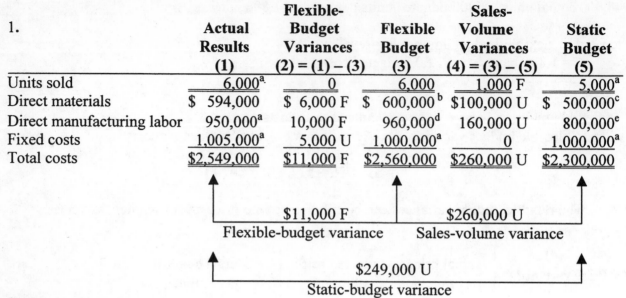

	Actual Results (1)	Flexible-Budget Variances (2) = (1) – (3)	Flexible Budget (3)	Sales-Volume Variances (4) = (3) – (5)	Static Budget (5)
Units sold	6,000[a]	0	6,000	1,000 F	5,000[a]
Direct materials	$ 594,000	$ 6,000 F	$ 600,000[b]	$100,000 U	$ 500,000[c]
Direct manufacturing labor	950,000[a]	10,000 F	960,000[d]	160,000 U	800,000[e]
Fixed costs	1,005,000[a]	5,000 U	1,000,000[a]	0	1,000,000[a]
Total costs	$2,549,000	$11,000 F	$2,560,000	$260,000 U	$2,300,000

$11,000 F $260,000 U
Flexible-budget variance   Sales-volume variance

$249,000 U
Static-budget variance

[a] Given
[b] $100 × 6,000 = $600,000
[c] $100 × 5,000 = $500,000
[d] $160 × 6,000 = $960,000
[e] $160 × 5,000 = $800,000

7-32 (Cont'd.)

2.

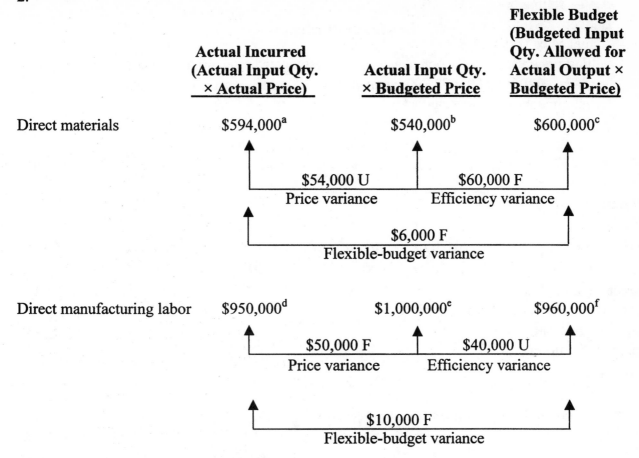

	Actual Incurred (Actual Input Qty. × Actual Price)	Actual Input Qty. × Budgeted Price	Flexible Budget (Budgeted Input Qty. Allowed for Actual Output × Budgeted Price)
Direct materials	$594,000[a]	$540,000[b]	$600,000[c]

$54,000 U $60,000 F
Price variance   Efficiency variance

$6,000 F
Flexible-budget variance

Direct manufacturing labor	$950,000[d]	$1,000,000[e]	$960,000[f]

$50,000 F $40,000 U
Price variance   Efficiency variance

$10,000 F
Flexible-budget variance

[a] 54,000 pounds × $11/pound = $594,000
[b] 54,000 pounds × $10/pound = $540,000
[c] 6,000 statues × 10 pounds/statue ×$10/pound = 60,000 pounds × $10/pound = $600,000
[d] 25,000 pounds × $38/pound = $950,000
[e] 25,000 pounds × $40/pound = $1,000,000
[f] 6,000 statues × 4 hours/statue × $40/hour = 24,000 hours × $40/hour = $960,000

7-34 (60 min.) **Comprehensive variance analysis, responsibility issues.**

1a. Actual selling price = $82.00
   Budgeted selling price = $80.00
   Actual sales volume = 4,850 units
   Selling price variance = (Actual sales price – Budgeted sales price) × Actual units
   = ($82 – $80) × 4,850 = $9,700 Favorable

1b. Development of Flexible Budget

	Budgeted Unit Amounts	Actual Volume	Flexible Budget Amount
Revenues	$80.00	4,850	$388,000
Variable costs			
DM–Frames	$2.20/oz. × 3.00 oz.	6.60[a] 4,850	32,010
DM–Lenses	$3.10/oz. × 6.00 oz.	18.60[b] 4,850	90,210
Direct manuf. labor	$15.00/hr. × 1.20 hrs.	18.00[c] 4,850	87,300
Total variable manufacturing costs			$209,520
Fixed manufacturing costs			75,000
Total manufacturing cost			284,520
Gross margin			$103,480

[a]$33,000 ÷ 5,000 units; [b]$93,000 ÷ 5,000 units; [c]$90,000 ÷ 5,000 units

	Actual Results (1)	Flexible-Budget Variances (2)=(1)-(3)	Flexible Budget (3)	Sales - Volume Variance (4)=(3)-(5)	Static Budget (5)
Units sold	4,850		4,850		5,000
Revenues	$397,700	$ 9,700 F	$388,000	$ 12,000 U	$400,000
Variable costs					
DM–frames	37,248	5,238 U	32,010	990 F	33,000
DM–lens	100,492	10,282 U	90,210	2,790 F	93,000
Direct labor	96,903	9,603 U	87,300	2,700 F	90,000
Total variable costs	234,643	25,123 U	209,520	6,480 F	216,000
Fixed manuf. costs	72,265	2,735 F	75,000	0	75,000
Total costs	306,908	22,388 U	284,520	6,480 F	291,000
Gross margin	$ 90,792	$12,688 U	$103,480	$ 5,520 U	$109,000

7-34 (Cont'd.)

1c.   **Price and Efficiency Variances**

DM–Frames–Actual ounces used = 3.20 per unit × 4,850 units = 15,520 oz.
Price per oz = $37,248/15,520 = $2.40
DM–Lenses–Actual ounces used = 7.00 per unit × 4,850 units = 33,950 oz.
Price per oz = $100,492/33,950 = $2.96
Direct Labor–Actual labor hours = $96,903/14.80 = 6,547.5 hours
Labor hours per unit = 6,547.5/4,850 units = 1.35 hours per unit

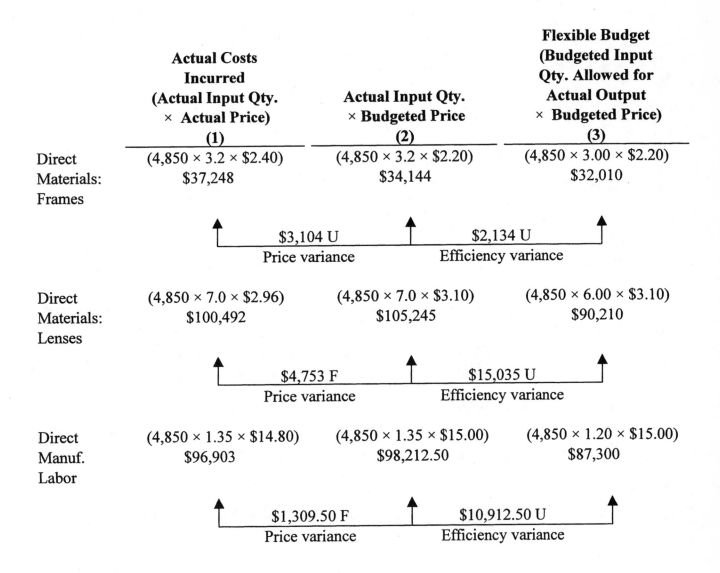

	Actual Costs Incurred (Actual Input Qty. × Actual Price) (1)	Actual Input Qty. × Budgeted Price (2)	Flexible Budget (Budgeted Input Qty. Allowed for Actual Output × Budgeted Price) (3)
Direct Materials: Frames	(4,850 × 3.2 × $2.40) $37,248	(4,850 × 3.2 × $2.20) $34,144	(4,850 × 3.00 × $2.20) $32,010
	$3,104 U Price variance	$2,134 U Efficiency variance	
Direct Materials: Lenses	(4,850 × 7.0 × $2.96) $100,492	(4,850 × 7.0 × $3.10) $105,245	(4,850 × 6.00 × $3.10) $90,210
	$4,753 F Price variance	$15,035 U Efficiency variance	
Direct Manuf. Labor	(4,850 × 1.35 × $14.80) $96,903	(4,850 × 1.35 × $15.00) $98,212.50	(4,850 × 1.20 × $15.00) $87,300
	$1,309.50 F Price variance	$10,912.50 U Efficiency variance	

7-34 (Cont'd.)

Possible explanations for price variances are:

    (a) Purchasing and labor negotiations.

    (b) Quality of frames and lenses purchased.

    (c) Standards set incorrectly.

Possible explanations for efficiency variance are:

    (a) Higher materials usage due to lower quality frames and lenses purchased at lower price.

    (b) Lesser trained workers hired at lower rates result in higher materials usage and lower labor efficiency.

    (c) Standards set incorrectly.

7-36 (30 min.) Level 2 variance analysis, solve for unknowns.

1. Budgeted selling price $= \dfrac{\$4,800,000}{600,000} = \$\ 8.00$ per cap

   Actual selling price $= \dfrac{\$5,000,000}{500,000} = \$10.00$ per cap

2. Budgeted variable cost per unit $= \dfrac{\$1,800,000}{600,000} = \$3.00$ per unit

   Actual variable cost per unit $= \dfrac{\$1,400,000}{500,000} = \$2.80$ per unit

3., 4., 5. and 6.

	Actual Results (1)	Flexible-Budget Variances (2)=(1)–(3)	Flexible Budget (3)	Sales - Volume Variance (4)=(3)–(5)	Static Budget (5)
Units sold	500,000	0	500,000	100,000 U	600,000
Revenues (sales)	$5,000,000	$1,000,000 F	$4,000,000	$800,000 U	$4,800,000
Variable costs	1,400,000	100,000 F	1,500,000	300,000 F	1,800,000
Contribution margin	3,600,000	1,100,000 F	2,500,000	500,000 U	3,000,000
Fixed costs	1,150,000	150,000 U	1,000,000	0	1,000,000
Operating income	$2,450,000	$ 950,000 F	$1,500,000	$500,000 U	$2,000,000

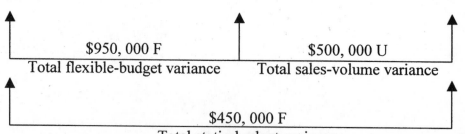

$950, 000 F $500, 000 U

Total flexible-budget variance   Total sales-volume variance

$450, 000 F

Total static-budget variance

7-36 (Cont'd.)

3. Flexible-budget operating income = $1,500,000

4. Total flexible-budget variance = $950,000 F

5. Total sales-volume variance = $500,000 U

6. Total static-budget variance = $450,000 F

7-38 (60 min.) Comprehensive variance analysis review.

1. **Actual Results**

Units sold (80% × 1,500,000)	1,200,000
Selling price per unit	$3.70
Revenues (1,200,000 × $3.70)	$4,440,000
Direct materials purchased and used:	
Direct materials per unit	$0.80
Total direct materials cost (1,200,000 × $0.80)	$960,000
Direct manufacturing labor:	
Actual manufacturing rate per hour	$ 15
Labor productivity per hour in units	250
Manufacturing labor-hours of input (1,200,000 ÷ 250)	4,800
Total direct manufacturing labor costs (4,800 × $15)	$72,000
Direct marketing costs:	
Direct marketing cost per unit	$0.30
Total direct marketing costs (1,200,000 × $0.30)	$360,000
Fixed costs ($900,000 – $30,000)	$870,000

Static Budgeted Amounts

Units sold	1,500,000
Selling price per unit	$4.00
Revenues (1,500,000 × $4.00)	$6,000,000
Direct materials purchased and used:	
Direct materials per unit	$0.85
Total direct materials costs (1,500,000 × $0.85)	$1,275,000
Direct manufacturing labor:	
Direct manufacturing rate per hour	$15.00
Labor productivity per hour in units	300
Manufacturing labor-hours of input (1,500,000 ÷ 300)	5,000
Total direct manufacturing labor cost (5,000 × $15.00)	$75,000
Direct marketing costs:	
Direct marketing cost per unit	$0.30
Total direct marketing cost (1,500,000 × $0.30)	$450,000
Fixed costs	$900,000

7-38 (Cont'd.)

	Actual Results	Static-Budget Amounts
Revenues	$4,440,000	$6,000,000
Variable costs		
Direct materials	960,000	1,275,000
Direct manufacturing labor	72,000	75,000
Direct marketing costs	360,000	450,000
Total variable costs	1,392,000	1,800,000
Contribution margin	3,048,000	4,200,000
Fixed costs	870,000	900,000
Operating income	$2,178,000	$3,300,000

2. Actual operating income $2,178,000
    Static-budget operating income   3,300,000
    Total static-budget variance $1,122,000 U

3., 4., 5. and 6.

	Actual Results	Flexible-Budget Variances	Flexible Budget	Sales-Volume Variances	Static Budget
Units sold	1,200,000	0	1,200,000	300,000	1,500,000
Revenues	$4,440,000	$360,000 U	$4,800,000	$1,200,000 U	$6,000,000
Variable costs					
Direct materials	960,000	60,000 F	1,020,000	255,000 F	1,275,000
Direct manuf. labor	72,000	12,000 U	60,000	15,000 F	75,000
Direct marketing costs	360,000	0	360,000	90,000 F	450,000
Total variable costs	1,392,000	48,000 F	1,440,000	360,000 F	1,800,000
Contribution margin	3,048,000	312,000 U	3,360,000	840,000 U	4,200,000
Fixed costs	870,000	30,000 F	900,000		900,000
Operating income	$2,178,000	$282,000 U	$2,460,000	$ 840,000 U	$3,300,000

                         $282, 000 U $840, 000 U
                   Total flexible-budget   Total sales-volume
                      variance   variance

                                    $1,122,000 U
                            Total static-budget variance

7-38 (Cont'd.)

7. and 8.

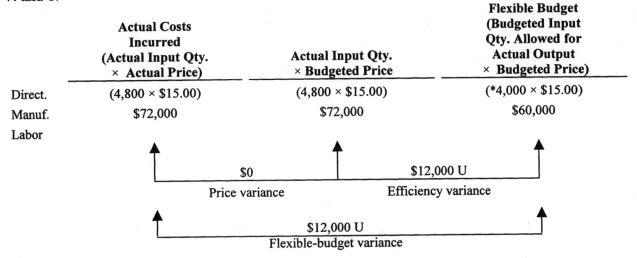

	Actual Costs Incurred (Actual Input Qty. × Actual Price)	Actual Input Qty. × Budgeted Price	Flexible Budget (Budgeted Input Qty. Allowed for Actual Output × Budgeted Price)
Direct. Manuf. Labor	(4,800 × $15.00) $72,000	(4,800 × $15.00) $72,000	(*4,000 × $15.00) $60,000

$0
Price variance

$12,000 U
Efficiency variance

$12,000 U
Flexible-budget variance

* 1,200,000 units ÷ 300 direct manufacturing labor standard productivity rate per hour.

7-40 (30 min.) Comprehensive variance analysis.

1.   Computing unit selling prices and unit costs of inputs:

Actual selling price = $3,555,000 ÷ 450,000
= $7.90

Budgeting selling price = $3,200,000 ÷ 400,000
= $8.00

Selling-price variance = $\left(\begin{array}{c}\text{Actual} \\ \text{selling price}\end{array} - \begin{array}{c}\text{Budgeted} \\ \text{selling price}\end{array}\right) \times \begin{array}{c}\text{Actual} \\ \text{units sold}\end{array}$
= ($7.90/unit − $8.00/unit) × 450,000 units
= $45,000 U

2., 3., and 4.

The actual and budgeted unit costs are:

	Actual	Budgeted
Direct materials		
Cookie mix	$0.02 ($93,000 ÷ 4,650,000)	$0.02
Milk chocolate	0.20 ($532,000 ÷ 2,660,000)	0.15
Almonds	0.50 ($240,000 ÷ 480,000)	0.50
Direct manuf. labor		
Mixing	14.40 ($108,000 ÷ 450,000 × 60)	14.40
Baking	18.00 ($240,000 ÷ 800,000 × 60)	18.00

The actual output achieved is 450,000 pounds of chocolate nut supreme.

7-40 (Cont'd.)

The direct cost price and efficiency variances are:

	Actual Costs Incurred (Actual Input Qty. × Actual Price) (1)	Price Variance (2)=(1)–(3)	Actual Input Qty. × Budgeted Price (3)	Efficiency Variance (4)=(3)–(5)	Flex. Budget (Budgeted Input Qty. Allowed for Actual Output × Budgeted Price) (5)
Direct materials					
Cookie mix	$ 93,000	$ 0	$ 93,000[a]	$ 3,000 U	$ 90,000[h]
Milk chocolate	532,000	133,000 U	399,000[b]	61,500 U	337,500[i]
Almonds	240,000	0	240,000[c]	15,000 U	225,000[j]
	$865,000	$133,000 U	$732,000	$79,500 U	$652,500
Direct manuf. labor costs					
Mixing	$108,000	$ 0	$108,000[d]	$ 0	$108,000[k]
Baking	240,000	0	240,000[e]	30,000 F	270,000[l]
	$348,000	$ 0	$348,000	$30,000 F	$378,000

[a] $0.02 × 4,650,000 = $93,000

[b] $0.15 × 2,660,000 = $399,000

[c] $0.50 × 480,000 = $240,000

[d] $14.40 × (450,000 ÷ 60) = $108,000

[e] $18.00 × (800,000 ÷ 60) = $240,000

[h] $0.02 × 10 × 450,000 = $90,000

[i] $0.15 × 5 × 450,000 = $337,500

[j] $0.50 × 1 × 450,000 = $225,000

[k] $14.40 × (450,000 ÷ 60) = $108,000

[l] $18.00 × (450,000 ÷ 30) = $270,000

Comments on the variances include:

- Selling price variance. This may arise from a proactive decision to reduce price to expand market share or from a reaction to a price reduction by a competitor. It could also arise from unplanned price discounting by salespeople.

- Material price variance. The $0.05 increase in the price per ounce of milk chocolate could arise from uncontrollable market factors or from poor contract negotiations by Aunt Molly's.

- Material efficiency variance. For all three material inputs, usage is greater than budgeted. Possible reasons include lower quality inputs, use of lower quality workers, and the mixing and baking equipment not being maintained in a fully operational mode.

- Labor efficiency variance. The favorable efficiency variance for baking could be due to workers eliminating nonvalue-added steps in production.

7-42 (30 min.) **Flexible budgeting, activity-based costing, variance analysis.**

		Static-budget Amounts	Actual Amounts
1.	a. Units of cakes produced and sold	240,000	330,000
	b. Average batch size (cakes per batch)	6,000	10,000
	c. Number of batches (a ÷ b)	40	33
	d. Changeover labor-hours per batch	20	24
	e. Total changeover labor-hours (c × d)	800	792
	f. Cost per changeover labor-hours	$20	$21
	g. Total changeover labor cost (e × f)	$16,000	$16,632

Step 1: The number of batches in which the actual output units should have been produced:
  330,000 actual units of output ÷ 6,000 budgeted batch size = 55 batches

Step 2: The number of changeover labor-hours that should have been used:

  20 budgeted changeover-hours x 55 batches = 1,100 changeover-hours.

Step 3: The flexible-budget amount for changeover hours:

  1,100 changeover-hours × $20 budgeted cost per changeover-hour = $22,000.

Flexible-budget variance = Actual costs – Flexible-budget costs
  = (792 × $21) – (1,100 × $20)
  = $16,632 – $22,000 = $5,368 F

2. Price variance = $\left[\begin{array}{c} \text{Actual price} \\ \text{of input} \end{array} - \begin{array}{c} \text{Budgeted price} \\ \text{of input} \end{array} \right] \times \begin{array}{c} \text{Actual quantity} \\ \text{of input} \end{array}$

  = ($21 – $20) × 792 = $1 × 792 = $792 U

Efficiency variance = $\left[\begin{array}{c} \text{Actual quantity} \\ \text{of input used} \end{array} - \begin{array}{c} \text{Budgeted quantity of} \\ \text{input allowed for} \\ \text{actual output} \end{array} \right] \times \begin{array}{c} \text{Budgeted price} \\ \text{of input used} \end{array}$

  = (792 – 1,100) × $20 = 308 × $20 = $6,160 F

The favorable flexible-budget variance of $5,368 is comprised of two offsetting amounts:

• Price variance of $792 U due to actual changeover labor cost of $21 per hour exceeding the $20 budgeted rate.
• Efficiency variance of $6,160 F due to the actual batch size of 10,000 being *sizably* above the budgeted batch size of 6,000. Efficiency variance is favorable because less batches were required to produce 330,000 cakes even though actual changeover labor-hours of 24 per batch were higher than the budgeted changeover-hours per batch of 20 hours.

7-42 (Cont'd.)

3. Explanations for the price variance of $792 U include:

- More highly trained workers hired to make changeovers.
- Change in labor market required unexpected increase in labor rates to retain workers.
- Budgeted amounts were set without adequate analysis.

Explanations for the efficiency variance of $6,160 F include:

- More highly trained workers were able to produce larger batch sizes.
- More automated machinery was acquired.
- Budgeted amounts were set without adequate analysis.

7-44 (30 min.) Price and efficiency variances, problems in standard setting, benchmarking.

1. Budgeted direct materials input per shirt = 400 rolls ÷ 4,000 shirts= 0.10 roll of cloth
Budgeted direct manuf. labor-hours per shirt (1,000 hours ÷ 4,000 shirts) = 0.25 hours
Budgeted direct materials cost ($20,000 ÷ 400) = $50 per roll
Budgeted direct manufacturing labor cost per hour ($18,000 ÷ 1,000) = $18 per hour
Actual output achieved = 4,488 shirts

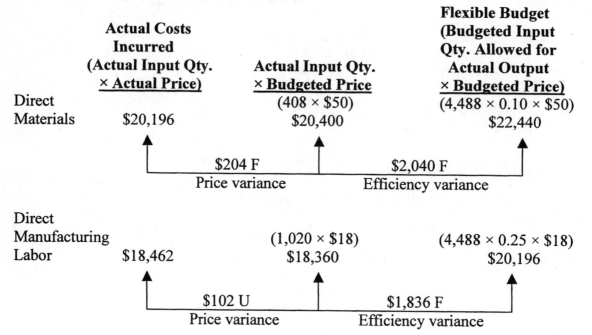

2. Actions employees may have taken include:
    (a) Adding steps that are not necessary in working on a shirt.
    (b) Taking more time on each step than is necessary.
    (c) Creating problem situations so that the budgeted amount of average downtime will be overstated.
    (d) Creating defects in shirts so that the budgeted amount of average rework will be overstated.

Employees may take these actions for several possible reasons.
    (a) They may be paid on a piece-rate basis with incentives for above-budgeted production.
    (b) They may want to create a relaxed work atmosphere, and less demanding standard can reduce stress.
    (c) They have a "them vs. us" mentality rather than a partnership perspective.
    (d) They may want to gain all the benefits that ensue from superior performance (job security, wage rate increases) without putting in the extra effort required.

This behavior is unethical if it is deliberately designed to undermine the credibility of the standards used at Savannah Fashions.

3. Savannah could use Benchmarking Clearing House information in several ways:
    (a) For pricing and product emphasis purposes. Savannah should avoid getting into a pricing war with a competitor who has a sizably lower cost structure.
    (b) As indicators of areas where Savannah is either highly cost-competitive or highly cost-noncompetitive.
    (c) As performance targets for motivating and evaluating managers and workers.

4. Main pros of Benchmarking Clearing House information:
    (a) Highlights to Savannah in a direct way how it may or may not be cost-competitive.
    (b) Provides a "reality check" to many internal positions about efficiency or effectiveness.

Main cons are:
    (a) Savannah may not be comparable to companies in the database.
    (b) Cost data about other companies may not be reliable.
    (c) Cost of Benchmarking Clearing House reports.

CHAPTER 8
FLEXIBLE BUDGETS, VARIANCES,
AND MANAGEMENT CONTROL: II

8-2   At the start of an accounting period, a larger percentage of fixed overhead costs are locked-in than is the case with variable overhead costs. When planning fixed overhead costs, a company must choose the appropriate level of capacity or investment that will benefit the company over a long time. This is a strategic decision.

8-4   Steps in developing a budgeted variable-overhead cost rate are:
1.   Choose the period to be used for the budget,
2.   Select the cost-allocation bases to use in allocating variable overhead costs to the output produced,
3.   Identify the variable overhead costs associated with each cost-allocation base, and
4.   Compute the rate per unit of each cost-allocation base used to allocate variable overhead costs to output produced.

8-6   Reasons for a $25,000 favorable variable-overhead efficiency variance are:
- Workers more skillful in using machines than budgeted,
- Production scheduler was able to schedule jobs better than budgeted, resulting in lower-than-budgeted machine-hours,
- Machines operated with fewer slowdowns than budgeted, and
- Machine time standards set with padding built in by machine workers.

8-8   Steps in developing a budgeted fixed-overhead rate are:
1.   Choose the period to use for the budget,
2.   Select the cost-allocation base to use in allocating fixed overhead costs to output produced,
3.   Identify the fixed-overhead costs associated with each cost-allocation base, and
4.   Compute the rate per unit of each cost-allocation base used to allocate fixed overhead costs to output produced.

8-10   An important caveat is what change in selling price might have been necessary to attain the level of sales assumed in the denominator of the fixed manufacturing overhead rate. For example, the entry of a new low-price competitor may have reduced demand below the denominator level if the budgeted selling price was maintained. An unfavorable production-volume variance may be small relative to the selling-price variance had prices been dropped to attain the denominator level of unit sales.

8-12   Fixed manufacturing costs represent resources sacrificed in acquiring capacity that cannot be decreased if the resources needed are less than the resources acquired. A lump-sum amount of fixed costs will be unaffected by the degree of operating efficiency in a given budget period.

8-14 For planning and control purposes, fixed overhead costs are a lump sum amount that is not controlled on a per-unit basis. In contrast, for inventory costing purposes, fixed overhead costs are allocated to products on a per-unit basis.

8-16 (20 min.) **Variable manufacturing overhead, variance analysis.**

1.

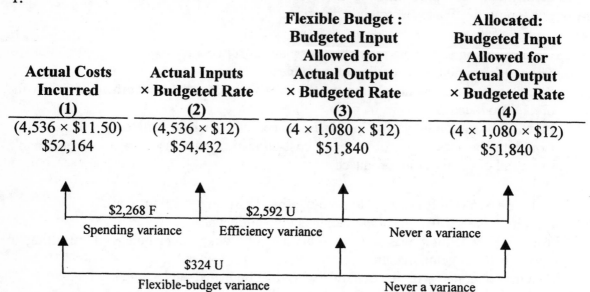

Actual Costs Incurred (1)	Actual Inputs × Budgeted Rate (2)	Flexible Budget : Budgeted Input Allowed for Actual Output × Budgeted Rate (3)	Allocated: Budgeted Input Allowed for Actual Output × Budgeted Rate (4)
(4,536 × $11.50)	(4,536 × $12)	(4 × 1,080 × $12)	(4 × 1,080 × $12)
$52,164	$54,432	$51,840	$51,840

$2,268 F $2,592 U
Spending variance   Efficiency variance   Never a variance

$324 U
Flexible-budget variance   Never a variance

2. Esquire had a favorable spending variance of $2,268 because the actual variable overhead rate was $11.50 per direct manufacturing labor-hour versus $12 budgeted. It had an unfavorable efficiency variance of $2,592 U because each suit averaged 4.2 labor-hours (4,536 hours ÷ 1,080 suits) versus 4.0 budgeted.

8-18 (30 min.) **Variable manufacturing overhead variance analysis.**

1. Denominator level= (3,200,000 × 0.02 hours) = 64,000 hours

2.

	Actual Results	Flexible Budget Amount
1. Output units (baguettes)	2,800,000	2,800,000
2. Direct manufacturing labor-hours	50,400	56,000[a]
3. Labor-hours per output unit (2 ÷ 1)	0.018	0.020
4. Variable MOH costs	$680,400	$560,000
5. Variable MOH per labor-hour (4 ÷ 2)	$13.50	$10
6. Variable MOH per output unit (4 ÷ 1)	$0.243	$0.200

a. 2,800,000 x 0.020= 56,000 hours

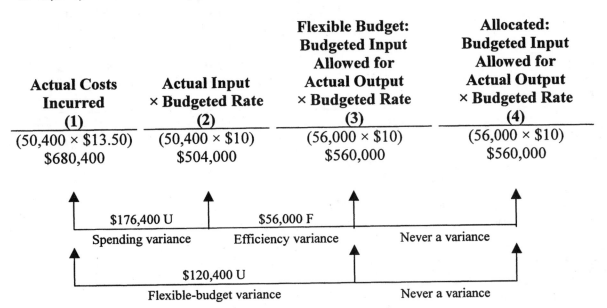

Actual Costs Incurred (1)	Actual Input × Budgeted Rate (2)	Flexible Budget: Budgeted Input Allowed for Actual Output × Budgeted Rate (3)	Allocated: Budgeted Input Allowed for Actual Output × Budgeted Rate (4)
(50,400 × $13.50) $680,400	(50,400 × $10) $504,000	(56,000 × $10) $560,000	(56,000 × $10) $560,000

$176,400 U — Spending variance

$56,000 F — Efficiency variance

Never a variance

$120,400 U — Flexible-budget variance

Never a variance

3.   Spending variance of $176,400 U. It is unfavorable because variable manufacturing overhead was 35% higher than planned. A possible explanation could be an increase in energy rates relative to the rate per standard labor-hour assumed in the flexible budget.

Efficiency variance of $56,000 F. It is favorable because the actual number of direct manufacturing labor-hours required was lower than the number of hours in the flexible budget. Labor was more efficient in producing the baguettes than management had anticipated in the budget. This could occur because of improved morale in the company, which could result from an increase in wages or an improvement in the compensation scheme.

Flexible-budget variance.   It is unfavorable because the favorable efficiency variance was not large enough to compensate for the large unfavorable spending variance.

8-20 (30-40 min.) **Manufacturing overhead, variance analysis.**

1.   The summary analysis is:

	Spending Variance	Efficiency Variance	Production-Volume Variance
Variable Manufacturing Overhead	$40,700 F	$59,200 U	Never a variance
Fixed Manufacturing Overhead	$23,420 U	Never a variance	$36,000 U

Variable Manufacturing Overhead

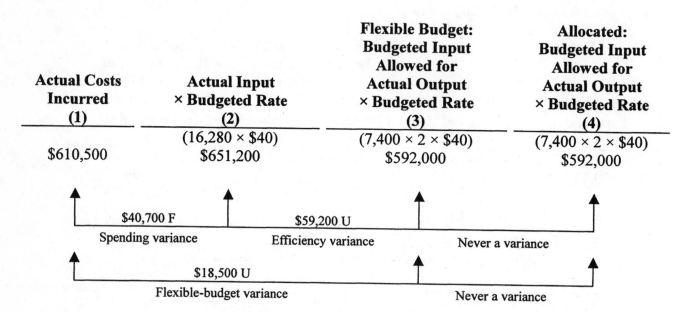

Fixed-Manufacturing Overhead

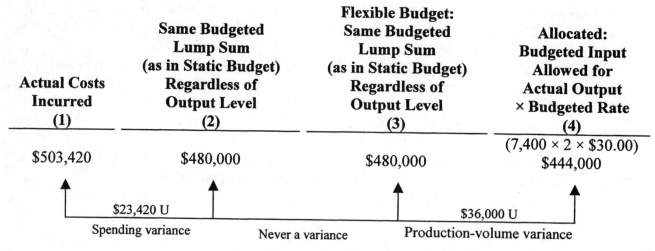

8-20 (Cont.d')

Summary information is:

	Actual	Flexible Budget
Output units	7,400	7,400
Allocation base (hours)	16,280	14,800[a]
Allocation base per output unit	2.20	2.00
Variable MOH	$610,500	$592,000[b]
Variable MOH per hour	$37.50[c]	$40.00
Fixed MOH	$503,420	$480,000
Fixed MOH per hour	$30.92[d]	–

[a] $7,400 \times 2.00 = 14,800$

[b] $7,400 \times 2 \times \$40 = \$592,000$

[c] $\$610,500 \div 16,280 \text{ hours} = \$37.50 \text{ per hour}$

[d] $\$503,420 \div 16,280 \text{ hours} \cong \$30.92 \text{ per hour}$

The budgeted fixed manufacturing overhead rate is $30.00 per assembly-hour:

$$\frac{\$480,000}{8,000 \times 2 \text{ hours}} = \$30.00 \text{ per assembly-hour}$$

2.   Zyton produced 600 less CardioX units than were budgeted. The variable manufacturing overhead cost efficiency variance of $59,200 U arises because more assembly-time-hours per output unit ($16,280 \div 7,400 = 2.2$ hours) were used than the budgeted 2.0 hours per unit. The variable manufacturing overhead cost spending variance of $40,700 F indicates one or more of the following probably occurred—(i) actual prices of individual items included in variable overhead differ from their budgeted prices, or (ii) actual usage of individual items included in variable overhead differs from their budgeted usage.

The fixed manufacturing overhead cost spending variance of $23,420 U means fixed overhead was above that budgeted. For example, it could be due to an unexpected increase in plant leasing costs. The unfavorable production-volume variance of $36,000 arises because actual output of 7,400 units is below the 8,000 units used in determining the $30.00 per assembly-hour budgeted rate.

3.   Planning and control of *variable* manufacturing overhead costs has both a long-run and a short-run focus. It involves Zyton planning to undertake only value-added overhead activities (a long-run view) and then managing the cost drivers of those activities in the most efficient way (a short-run view). Planning and control of *fixed* manufacturing overhead costs at Zyton have primarily a long-run focus. It involves undertaking only value-added fixed-overhead activities for a budgeted level of output. Zyton makes most of the key decisions that determine the level of fixed-overhead costs at the start of the accounting period.

8-22 (20-30 min.) **Straightforward 4-variance overhead analysis.**

1.   The budget for fixed manufacturing overhead is $4,000 \times 6 \times \$15 = \$360,000$.

An overview of the 4-variance analysis is:

4-Variance Analysis	Spending Variance	Efficiency Variance	Production-Volume Variance
Variable Manufacturing Overhead	$17,800 U	$16,000 U	Never a Variance
Fixed Manufacturing Overhead	$13,000 U	Never a Variance	$36,000 F

Solution Exhibit 8-22 has details of these variances.
A detailed comparison of actual and flexible budgeted amounts is:

	Actual	Flexible Budget
Output units (auto parts)	4,400	4,400
Allocation base (machine-hours)	28,400	26,400[a]
Allocation base per output unit	6.45[b]	6.00
Variable MOH	$245,000	$211,200[c]
Variable MOH per hour	$8.63[d]	$8.00
Fixed MOH	$373,000	$360,000[e]
Fixed MOH per hour	$13.13[f]	—

[a] 4,400 units $\times$ 6.00 machine-hours/unit = 26,400 machine-hours

[b] 28,400 $\div$ 4,400 = 6.45 machine-hours per unit

[c] 4,400 units $\times$ 6.00 machine-hours per unit $\times$ $8.00 per machine-hour = $211,200

[d] $245,000 $\div$ 28,400 = $8.63

[e] 4,000 units $\times$ 6.00 machine-hours per unit $\times$ $15 per machine-hour = $360,000

[f] $373,000 $\div$ 28,400 = $13.13

2.   Variable Manufacturing Overhead Control   245,000
      Accounts Payable Control and other accounts   245,000

     Work-in-Process Control   211,200
      Variable Manufacturing Overhead Allocated   211,200

     Variable Manufacturing Overhead Allocated   211,200
     Variable Manufacturing Overhead Spending Variance   17,800
     Variable Manufacturing Overhead Efficiency Variance   16,000
      Variable Manufacturing Overhead Control   245,000

     Fixed Manufacturing Overhead Control   373,000
      Wages Payable Control, Accumulated Depreciation
        Control, etc.   373,000

     Work-in-Process Control   396,000
      Fixed Manufacturing Overhead Allocated   396,000

     Fixed Manufacturing Overhead Allocated   396,000
     Fixed Manufacturing Overhead Spending Variance   13,000
      Fixed Manufacturing Overhead Production-Volume Variance   36,000
      Fixed Manufacturing Overhead Control   373,000

3.   The control of variable manufacturing overhead requires the identification of the cost drivers for such items as energy, supplies, and repairs. Control often entails monitoring nonfinancial measures that affect each cost item, one by one. Examples are kilowatts used, quantities of lubricants used, and repair parts and hours used. The most convincing way to discover why overhead performance did not agree with a budget is to investigate possible causes, line item by line item.

    Individual fixed manufacturing overhead items are not usually affected very much by day-to-day control. Instead, they are controlled periodically through planning decisions and budgeting procedures that may sometimes have horizons covering six months or a year (for example, management salaries) and sometimes covering many years (for example, long-term leases and depreciation on plant and equipment).

8-22 (Cont'd.)

SOLUTION EXHIBIT 8-22

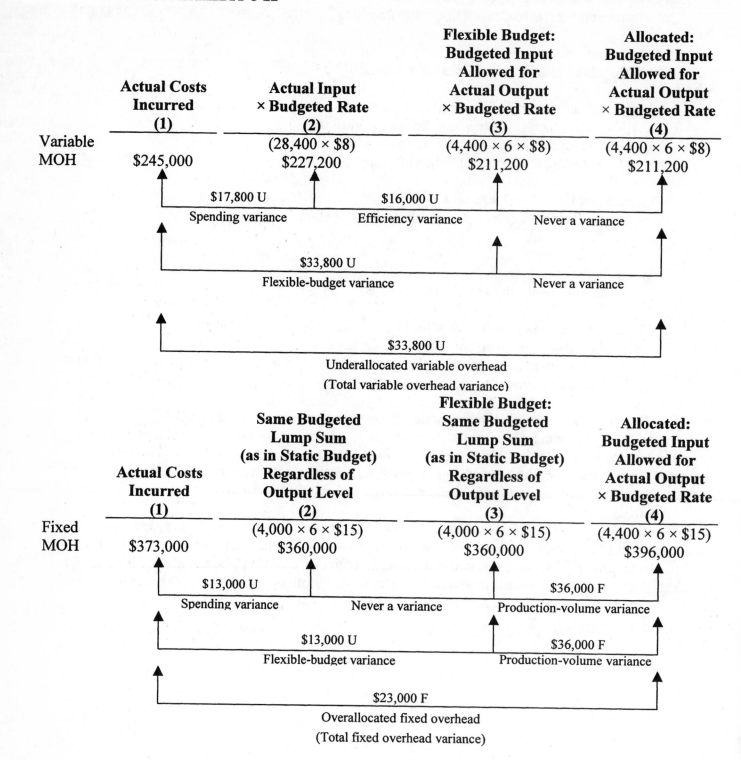

	Actual Costs Incurred (1)	Actual Input × Budgeted Rate (2)	Flexible Budget: Budgeted Input Allowed for Actual Output × Budgeted Rate (3)	Allocated: Budgeted Input Allowed for Actual Output × Budgeted Rate (4)
Variable MOH	$245,000	(28,400 × $8) $227,200	(4,400 × 6 × $8) $211,200	(4,400 × 6 × $8) $211,200

$17,800 U — Spending variance $16,000 U — Efficiency variance   Never a variance

$33,800 U — Flexible-budget variance   Never a variance

$33,800 U — Underallocated variable overhead

(Total variable overhead variance)

	Actual Costs Incurred (1)	Same Budgeted Lump Sum (as in Static Budget) Regardless of Output Level (2)	Flexible Budget: Same Budgeted Lump Sum (as in Static Budget) Regardless of Output Level (3)	Allocated: Budgeted Input Allowed for Actual Output × Budgeted Rate (4)
Fixed MOH	$373,000	(4,000 × 6 × $15) $360,000	(4,000 × 6 × $15) $360,000	(4,400 × 6 × $15) $396,000

$13,000 U — Spending variance   Never a variance $36,000 F — Production-volume variance

$13,000 U — Flexible-budget variance $36,000 F — Production-volume variance

$23,000 F — Overallocated fixed overhead

(Total fixed overhead variance)

8-24 (20-25 min.) **Spending and efficiency overhead variances, service sector.**

1. and 2.   Budgeted variable overhead rate = \$2 per hour of home delivery time

$$\text{Budgeted fixed overhead rate} = \frac{\$24,000}{8,000 \times 0.80} = \frac{\$24,000}{6,400 \text{ hours}}$$

$$= \$3.75 \text{ per hour of home delivery time}$$

A detailed comparison of actual and flexible budgeted amounts is:

	Actual	Flexible Budget
Output units (deliveries)	7,460	7,460
Allocation base (hours)	5,595	5,968[a]
Allocation base per output unit	0.75[b]	0.80
Variable MOH	\$14,174	\$11,936[c]
Variable MOH per hour	\$2.53[d]	\$2.00
Fixed MOH	\$27,600	\$24,000
Fixed MOH per hour	\$4.93[e]	–

[a] $7,460 \times 0.80 = 5,968$

[b] $5,595 \div 7,460 = 0.75$

[c] $7,460 \times 0.80 \times \$2.00 = \$11,936$

[d] $\$14,174 \div 5,595 = \$2.53$

[e] $\$27,600 \div 5,595 = \$4.93$

The required variances are:

	Spending Variance	Efficiency Variance
Variable overhead	\$2,984 U	\$ 746 F
Fixed overhead	\$3,600 U	—

These variances are computed as follows:

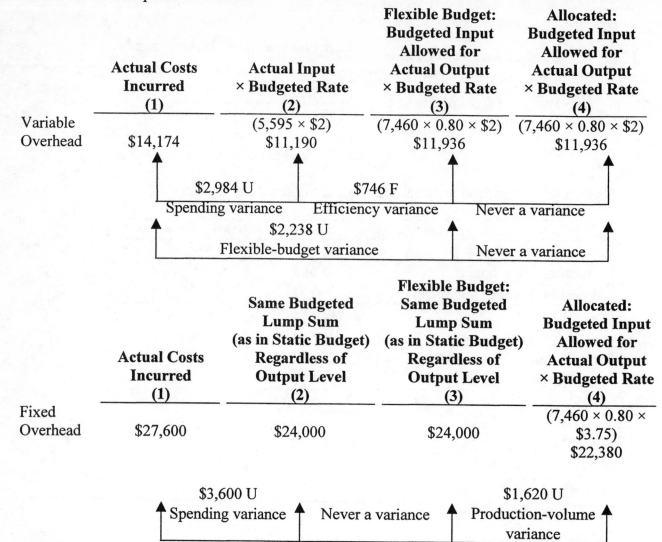

	Actual Costs Incurred (1)	Actual Input × Budgeted Rate (2)	Flexible Budget: Budgeted Input Allowed for Actual Output × Budgeted Rate (3)	Allocated: Budgeted Input Allowed for Actual Output × Budgeted Rate (4)
Variable Overhead	$14,174	(5,595 × $2) $11,190	(7,460 × 0.80 × $2) $11,936	(7,460 × 0.80 × $2) $11,936

$2,984 U — Spending variance $746 F — Efficiency variance Never a variance

$2,238 U — Flexible-budget variance Never a variance

	Actual Costs Incurred (1)	Same Budgeted Lump Sum (as in Static Budget) Regardless of Output Level (2)	Flexible Budget: Same Budgeted Lump Sum (as in Static Budget) Regardless of Output Level (3)	Allocated: Budgeted Input Allowed for Actual Output × Budgeted Rate (4)
Fixed Overhead	$27,600	$24,000	$24,000	(7,460 × 0.80 × $3.75) $22,380

$3,600 U — Spending variance Never a variance $1,620 U — Production-volume variance

The spending variances for variable and fixed overhead are both unfavorable. This means that MOW had increases over budget in either or both the cost of individual items (such as telephone calls and gasoline) in the overhead cost pools, or the usage of these individual items per unit of the allocation base (delivery time). The favorable efficiency variance for variable overhead costs results from more efficient use of the cost allocation base—each delivery takes 0.75 hours versus a budgeted 0.80 hours.

3.   MOW best manages its fixed overhead costs by long-term planning of capacity rather than day-to-day decisions. This involves planning to undertake only value-added fixed-overhead activities and then determining the appropriate level for those activities. Most fixed overhead costs are committed well before they are incurred. In contrast, for variable overhead, a mix of long-run planning and daily monitoring of the use of individual items is required to manage costs efficiently. MOW plans to undertake only value-added variable-overhead activities (a long-run focus) and then manage the cost drivers of those activities in the most efficient way (a short-run focus).

8-24 (Cont'd.)

8-24 Excel Application

Flexible Budgets, Variances, and Management Control
Meals on Wheels

Original Data

	Actual Results	Flexible-Budget Amounts
Output Units (# Deliveries)	7,460	8,000
Hours of Delivery Time	5,595	6,400
Hours per Delivery	0.75	0.80
Variable Overhead Costs	$14,174	$12,800
Variable Overhead Costs per Hour of Delivery Time	$2.53	$2.00
Fixed Overhead Costs	$27,600	$24,000

Variance Calculations

Actual Costs Incurred (1)	$14,174
Actual Input x Budgeted Rate (2)	$11,190
Budgeted Input Allowed for Actual Output x Budgeted Rate (3)	$11,936
Spending Variance (1)-(2)	$2,984 U
Efficiency Variance (2)-(3)	$746 F
Fixed Overhead Spending Variance	$3,600 U

8-24 (Cont.d')

Flexible Budgets, Variances, and Management Control
Meals on Wheels

Cost Item/Allocation Base	Actual Results	Flexible-Budget Amount
Variable Overhead Costs	$14,174	$12,800
Fixed Overhead Costs	$27,600	$24,000
Time per Delivery (hours)	0.75	0.80
Number of Home Deliveries	7,460	8,000
Hours of Delivery time	5,595	6,400
Variable Overhead Cost per Delivery	$1.90	$1.60
Variable Overhead Cost per hour of Delivery Time	$2.53	$2.00

Problem 1

Actual Costs Incurred (1)	Actual Input x Budgeted Rate (2)	Budgeted Input Allowed for Actual Output x Budgeted Rate (3)
$14,174	$11,190	$11,936

Spending Variance $2,984 U   Efficiency Variance $746 F

Problem 2

Fixed Overhead Spending Variance $3,600 U

8-26 (30 min.) **Overhead variances, missing information.**

1.

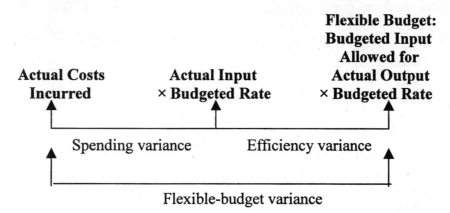

Actual input × Budgeted rate (9,800 × $5)	$49,000
Spending variance	250 U
Actual costs incurred	$49,250
Flexible budget (9,900 × $5)	$49,500
Actual input × Budgeted rate (9,800 × $5)	49,000
Efficiency variance	$ 500 F
Flexible budget variance (250 U + 500 F)	$ 250 F

Variable overhead is overallocated in the amount of $250 (the same amount as favorable flexible-budget variance).

2.

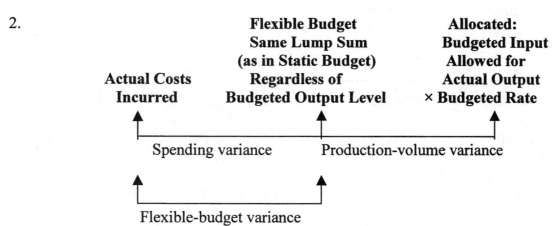

8-26 (Cont.d')

Actual total overhead costs incurred	$80,000
Actual variable overhead costs incurred	49,250
Actual fixed overhead costs incurred	$30,750
Spending variance (fixed overhead)	750 U
Flexible budget	$30,000
Flexible budget	$30,000
Divide by denominator volume in machine-hours	÷10,000
Budgeted rate per machine-hour	$ 3
Allocated ($3 × 9,900 machine-hours)	$29,700
Flexible budget	30,000
Production-volume variance	300 U
Flexible-budget variance = spending variance	$ 750 U
Underallocated amount ($300 U + $750 U)	$ 1,050

Total Operating Overhead	$47,000 F	$17,000 U

8-28 (40 min.) Flexible-budget variances, review of Chapters 7 and 8.

1.   A summary of the variances for the four categories of cost is:

Flexible-Budget Variances

Direct materials	$32,640 U
Direct labor	2,112 U
Variable indirect	64 F
Fixed indirect	7,000 U

Price-Spending Variances		*Efficiency Variances*	
Direct materials	$17,280 U	Direct materials	$15,360 U
Direct labor	1,728 F	Direct labor	3,840 U
Variable indirect	5,184 F	Variable indirect	5,120 U
Fixed indirect	7,000 U	Fixed indirect	–

In addition, there is a production-volume variance of $6,000 F for fixed indirect costs.

Direct Cost Variances

The key items for computing the flexible-budget, price, and efficiency for direct cost items are:

	Actual Quantity of Inputs (1)	Actual Unit Cost of Inputs (2)	Actual Cost of Inputs (3) = (1) × (2)	Budgeted Unit Cost of Inputs (4)	Actual Inputs × Budgeted Cost per Inputs (5) = (1) × (4)
Direct materials	17,280,000 pages	$ 0.0130[b]	$224,640	$ 0.0120[d]	$207,360
Direct labor costs	1,728 hours[a]	$29.00[c]	$ 50,112	$30.00[e]	$ 51,840

[a] $17,280,000 \div 10,000 = 1,728$ hours

[b] $224,640 \div 17,280,000 = \$0.0130$ per page

[c] $50,112 \div 1,728 = \$29.00$ per hour

[d] $180,000 \div 15,000,000$ (300,000 copies × 50 pages) = $0.0120 per page

[e] $45,000 \div 1,500(15,000,000 \div 10,000) = \$30.00$ per hour

	Budgeted Inputs Allowed per Output Unit (1)	Actual Output Achieved (2)	Budgeted Unit Cost of Inputs (3)	Flexible Budget (4) = (1) x (2) × (3)
Direct materials	50	320,000	$ 0.0120	$192,000
Direct labor costs	.005[f]	320,000	$30.00	48,000

[f] Budgeted 10,000 pages produced per labor-hour yields budgeted output of 200 newspapers (50 pages each) per hour. Thus, each output unit is budgeted to require 0.005 (1 ÷ 200) direct labor-hours.

The price and efficiency variances for direct materials and direct labor are:

	Actual Costs Incurred (Actual Input × Actual Price)	Price Variance	Actual Inputs × Budgeted Prices	Efficiency Variance	Flexible Budget: Budgeted Input Allowed for Actual Output × Budgeted Price
Direct materials	$224,640	$17,280 U	$207,360	$15,360 U	$192,000
Direct labor costs	50,112	1,728 F	51,840	3,840 U	48,000

8-28 (Cont.d')

Indirect Cost Variances

A summary of the information is:

	Actual	Flexible Budget
Output units (papers)	320,000	320,000
Allocation base (printed paper)	17,280,000	16,000,000 [a]
Allocation base per output unit	54	50
Variable MOH	$63,936	$64,000 [b]
Variable MOH per printed page	$0.0037	$0.0040 [d]
Fixed MOH	$97,000	$90,000
Fixed MOH per printed page	$0.0056 [c]	–

[a] $320,000 \times 50 = 16,000,000$

[b] $\$320,000 \times 50 \times \$0.0040 = \$64,000$

[c] $\$97,000 \div 17,280,000 = \$0.0056$ per printed page

[d] $\$60,000 \div (50 \times 300,000)$ pages $= \$0.004$ per page

The spending and efficiency variances for variable indirect costs are:

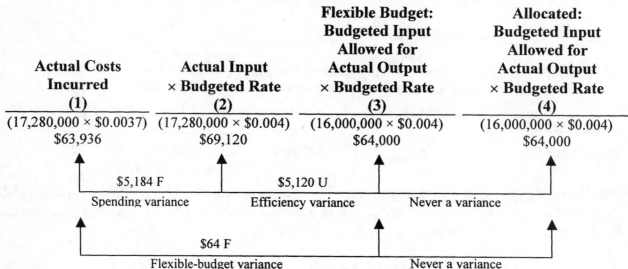

Actual Costs Incurred (1)	Actual Input × Budgeted Rate (2)	Flexible Budget: Budgeted Input Allowed for Actual Output × Budgeted Rate (3)	Allocated: Budgeted Input Allowed for Actual Output × Budgeted Rate (4)
(17,280,000 × $0.0037) $63,936	(17,280,000 × $0.004) $69,120	(16,000,000 × $0.004) $64,000	(16,000,000 × $0.004) $64,000

$5,184 F Spending variance | $5,120 U Efficiency variance | Never a variance

$64 F Flexible-budget variance | Never a variance

Fixed MOH allocated per page = $90,000 ÷ (50 × 300,000) pages = $0.006 per page
The spending and production-volume variances for fixed indirect costs are:

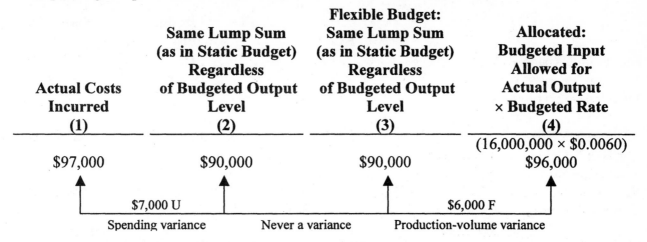

Actual Costs Incurred (1)	Same Lump Sum (as in Static Budget) Regardless of Budgeted Output Level (2)	Flexible Budget: Same Lump Sum (as in Static Budget) Regardless of Budgeted Output Level (3)	Allocated: Budgeted Input Allowed for Actual Output × Budgeted Rate (4)
			(16,000,000 × $0.0060)
$97,000	$90,000	$90,000	$96,000
	$7,000 U		$6,000 F
	Spending variance	Never a variance	Production-volume variance

2.   The largest individual variance category is for direct materials—comprising a $17,280 U price variance (the actual cost per page of $0.013 exceeds the budgeted $0.012 per page) and a $15,360 U efficiency variance (the 1,280,000 unusable pages × $0.012 budgeted cost).

The direct labor price variance ($1,728 F) is due to the actual labor rate being $29.00 per hour compared to the budgeted $30.00 per hour.

The spending variance for variable indirect costs of $5,184 F is due to the actual variable overhead costs being less than budgeted.

The unfavorable variable indirect costs efficiency variance of $5,120 U is due to 1,280,000 extra pages being used (the cost allocation base) over that budgeted.

The labor efficiency variance is $3,840 U due to the use of more labor hours than budgeted.

The spending variance for fixed indirect costs is due to actual costs being $7,000 above the budgeted $90,000. An analysis of the line items in this budget would help assist in determining the causes of this variance.

The production-volume variance of $6,000 F arises because the denominator used to allocate the $90,000 of fixed indirect costs is 16,000,000 printed pages rather than the 15,000,000 budgeted. This increase arises due to an increase in the production run (320,000 newspapers vs. 300,000 budgeted).

8-30 (60 min.) **Journal entries** (continuation of 8-29).

1. Key information underlying the computation of variances is:

	Actual Results	Flexible Budget Amount	Static-Budget Amount
1. Output units (panels)	19,200	19,200	17,760
2. Machine-hours	36,480	38,400	35,520
3. Machine-hours per panel	1.90	2.00	2.00
4. Variable MOH costs	$1,532,160	$1,536,000	$1,420,800
5. Variable MOH costs per machine-hour (Row 4 ÷Row 2)	$42.00	$40.00	$40.00
6. Variable MOH costs per unit (Row 4 ÷ Row 1))	$79.80	$80.00	$80.00
7. Fixed MOH costs	$7,004,160	$6,961,920	$6,961,920
8. Fixed MOH costs per machine-hour (Row 7 ÷ Row 2))	$192.00	$181.30	$196.00
9. Fixed MOH costs per unit (7 ÷ 1)	$364.80	$362.60	$392.00

Solution Exhibit 8-30 shows the computation of the variances.

Journal entries for variable MOH, year ended December 31, 2003:

Variable MOH Control	1,532,160	
Accounts Payable Control and Other Accounts		1,532,160
Work-in-Process Control	1,536,000	
Variable MOH Allocated		1,536,000
Variable MOH Allocated	1,536,000	
Variable MOH Spending Variance	72,960	
Variable MOH Control		1,532,160
Variable MOH Efficiency Variance		76,800

8-30 (Cont.d')

Journal entries for fixed MOH, year ended December 31, 2003:

Fixed MOH Control	7,004,160	
Wages Payable, Accumulated Depreciation, etc.		7,004,160
Work-in-Process Control	7,526,400	
Fixed MOH Allocated		7,526,400
Fixed MOH Allocated	7,526,400	
Fixed MOH Spending Variance	42,240	
Fixed MOH Control		7,004,160
Fixed MOH Production-Volume Variance		564,480

2. **Adjustment of COGS**

Variable MOH Efficiency Variance	76,800	
Fixed MOH Production-Volume Variance	564,480	
Variable MOH Spending Variance		72,960
Fixed MOH Spending Variance		42,240
Cost of Goods Sold		526,080

8-30 (Cont'd.)

SOLUTION EXHIBIT 8-30

Variable Manufacturing Overhead

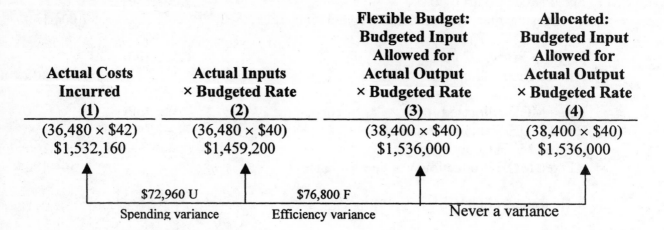

Actual Costs Incurred (1)	Actual Inputs × Budgeted Rate (2)	Flexible Budget: Budgeted Input Allowed for Actual Output × Budgeted Rate (3)	Allocated: Budgeted Input Allowed for Actual Output × Budgeted Rate (4)
(36,480 × $42) $1,532,160	(36,480 × $40) $1,459,200	(38,400 × $40) $1,536,000	(38,400 × $40) $1,536,000

$72,960 U   Spending variance $76,800 F   Efficiency variance   Never a variance

Fixed Manufacturing Overhead

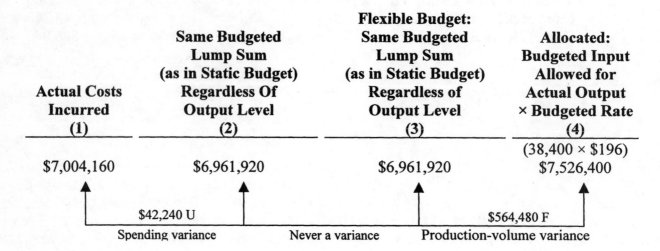

Actual Costs Incurred (1)	Same Budgeted Lump Sum (as in Static Budget) Regardless Of Output Level (2)	Flexible Budget: Same Budgeted Lump Sum (as in Static Budget) Regardless of Output Level (3)	Allocated: Budgeted Input Allowed for Actual Output × Budgeted Rate (4)
$7,004,160	$6,961,920	$6,961,920	(38,400 × $196) $7,526,400

$42,240 U   Spending variance   Never a variance $564,480 F   Production-volume variance

8-32 (30-40 min.) **Variance analysis, graphs.**

1. $\dfrac{\text{Variable MOH}}{\text{budgeted rate}} = \dfrac{\$1{,}000{,}000 \text{ Budgeted cost}}{10{,}000 \text{ Budgeted machine - hours}} = \$100 \text{ per machine-hour}$

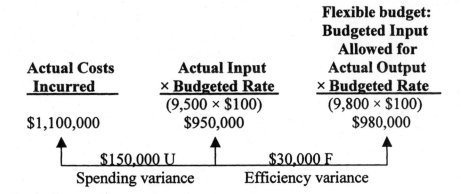

Actual Costs Incurred	Actual Input × Budgeted Rate (9,500 × \$100)	Flexible budget: Budgeted Input Allowed for Actual Output × Budgeted Rate (9,800 × \$100)
\$1,100,000	\$950,000	\$980,000

\$150,000 U   Spending variance   \$30,000 F   Efficiency variance

2. $\dfrac{\text{Fixed MOH}}{\text{budgeted rate}} = \dfrac{\$600{,}000 \text{ Budgeted cost}}{10{,}000 \text{ Budgeted machine - hours}} = \$60 \text{ per machine-hour}$

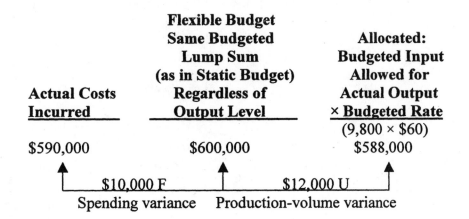

Actual Costs Incurred	Flexible Budget Same Budgeted Lump Sum (as in Static Budget) Regardless of Output Level	Allocated: Budgeted Input Allowed for Actual Output × Budgeted Rate (9,800 × \$60)
\$590,000	\$600,000	\$588,000

\$10,000 F   Spending variance   \$12,000 U   Production-volume variance

8-32 (Cont.d')

3.   Panel A: Variable Manufacturing Overhead Costs

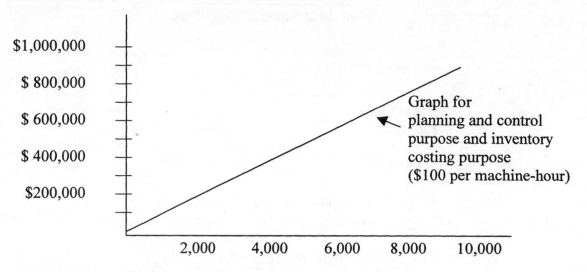

Panel B: Fixed Manufacturing Overhead Costs

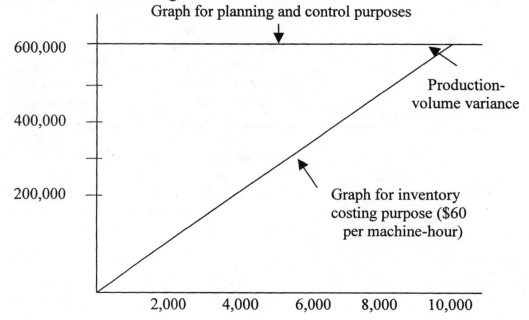

8-34 (15–25 min.) **Flexible budgets, 4-variance analysis.**

1. $$\text{Budgeted hours allowed per unit of output} = \frac{\text{Budgeted DLH}}{\text{Budgeted actual output}}$$

    $$\frac{3,600,000}{720,000} = 5 \text{ hours per unit}$$

    Budgeted DLH allowed for May output = 66,000 units × 5 hrs./unit = 330,000 hrs.

            Allocated total MOH = 330,000 × Total MOH rate per hour

                                      = 330,000 × $1.20 = $396,000

2, 3, 4, 5. See Solution Exhibit 8-34

                Variable overhead rate per DLH = $0.25 + $0.34 = $0.59

                Fixed overhead rate per DLH = $0.18 + $0.15 + $0.28 = $0.61

                Fixed overhead budget for May = ($648,000 + $540,000 + $1,008,000) ÷ 12

                                         = $2,196,000 ÷ 12 = $183,000

Using the format of Exhibit 8-3 for variable overhead and then fixed overhead:

Actual variable overhead: $75,000 + $111,000 = $186,000

Actual fixed overhead: $51,000 + $54,000 + $84,000 = $189,000

An overview of the 4-variance analysis using the block format of the text is:

4-Variance Analysis	Spending Variance	Efficiency Variance	Production-Volume Variance
Variable Manufacturing Overhead	$150 U	$8,850 F	Never a variance
Fixed Manufacturing Overhead	$6,000 U	Never a variance	$18,300 F

8-34 (Cont'd.)

SOLUTION EXHIBIT 8-34
Variable Manufacturing Overhead

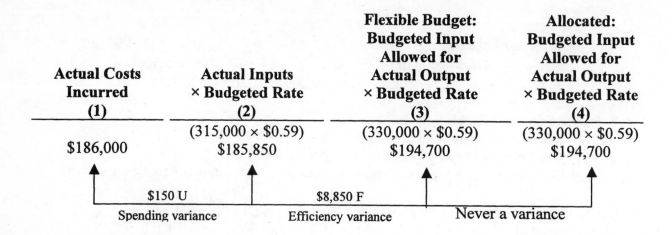

Actual Costs Incurred (1)	Actual Inputs × Budgeted Rate (2)	Flexible Budget: Budgeted Input Allowed for Actual Output × Budgeted Rate (3)	Allocated: Budgeted Input Allowed for Actual Output × Budgeted Rate (4)
$186,000	(315,000 × $0.59) $185,850	(330,000 × $0.59) $194,700	(330,000 × $0.59) $194,700

$150 U
Spending variance

$8,850 F
Efficiency variance

Never a variance

Fixed Manufacturing Overhead

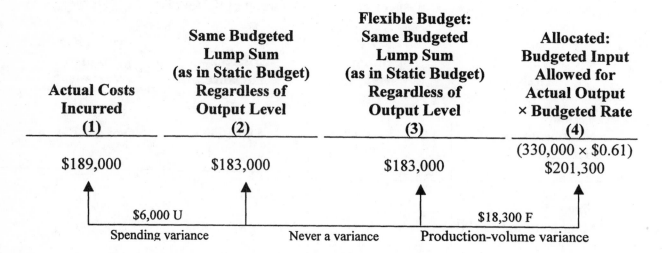

Actual Costs Incurred (1)	Same Budgeted Lump Sum (as in Static Budget) Regardless of Output Level (2)	Flexible Budget: Same Budgeted Lump Sum (as in Static Budget) Regardless of Output Level (3)	Allocated: Budgeted Input Allowed for Actual Output × Budgeted Rate (4)
$189,000	$183,000	$183,000	(330,000 × $0.61) $201,300

$6,000 U
Spending variance

Never a variance

$18,300 F
Production-volume variance

Alternate computation of the production volume variance:

$$= \left[\left(\begin{array}{c} \text{Budgeted hours} \\ \text{allowed for actual} \\ \text{output achieved} \end{array} \right) - \left(\begin{array}{c} \text{Denominator} \\ \text{hours} \end{array} \right) \right] \times \left[\begin{array}{c} \text{Budgeted} \\ \text{fixed} \\ \text{overhead} \\ \text{rate} \end{array} \right]$$

$$= \left[(330,000) - \left(\frac{3,600,000}{12} \right) \right] \times \$0.61$$

$$= (330,000 - 300,000) \times \$0.61 = \$18,300 \text{ F}$$

8-36 (25 min.) **Sales-volume variance, production-volume variance.**

1.
Budgeted selling price		$100
Budgeted variable cost per unit	$40	
Budgeted fixed cost per unit ($5,000,000 ÷ 20,000)	25	
Budgeted cost per unit		65
Budgeted profit per unit		$ 35

Operating income based on budgeted profit per unit
$35 per unit × 22,000 units $770,000

Flexible-budget operating income is	
Revenues $100 × 22,000	$2,200,000
Variable costs $40 × 22,000	880,000
Fixed costs	500,000
Operating income	$ 820,000

Static-budget operating income is	
Revenues $100 × 20,000	$2,000,000
Variable costs $40 × 20,000	800,000
Fixed costs	500,000
Operating income	$ 700,000

2.   The sales-volume variance recognizes that when Morano sells 22,000 units instead of the budgeted 20,000, only the revenue and the variable costs are affected. Fixed costs remain unchanged.

$$\text{Sales volume variance} = \left[\text{Budgeted selling price} - \text{Budgeted variable cost per unit} \right] \times \text{Difference in quantity of units sold relative to the static budget}$$

$$= \ (\$100 - \$40) \times 2,000 = \$60 \times 2,000 = \$120,000 \ F$$

$$\text{Production-volume variance} = \text{Budgeted fixed overhead cost per unit} \times \text{Difference in quantity of units sold relative to the static budget}$$

$$= \frac{\$500,000}{20,000} \times 2,000 = \$25 \times 2,000 = \$50,000 \ F$$

8-36 (Cont.d')

Compare the sales-volume variance and the production-volume variance. The $120,000 F sales-volume variance explains the difference between the static-budget operating income and the flexible-budget operating income:

Static-budget operating income	$700,000
Sales-volume variance	$120,000 F
Flexible-budget operating income	$820,000

The $50,000 F production-volume variance explains the difference between operating income based on the budgeted profit per unit and the flexible-budget operating income:

Operating income based on budgeted profit per unit	$770,000
Production-volume variance	50,000 F
Flexible-budget operating income	$820,000

8-38 (40 min.) Activity-based costing, variance analysis.

1.

		Static-Budget Amounts	Actual Amounts
a.	Units of SFA produced and sold	21,000	22,000
b.	Batch size	500	550
c.	Number of batches (a ÷ b)	42	40
d.	Testing-hours per batch	5.5	5.4
e.	Total testing-hours (c × d)	231	216
f.	Variable overhead cost per testing-hour	$40	$42
g.	Variable testing overhead costs (e × f)	$9,240	$9,072
h.	Total fixed testing overhead costs	$28,875	$27,216
i.	Fixed overhead cost per testing-hour (h ÷ e)	$125	$126

The flexible budget is based on the budgeted number of testing-hours for the actual output achieved, 22,000 units ÷ 500 units per batch = 44 batches

Computation of variable testing overhead cost variances follows:

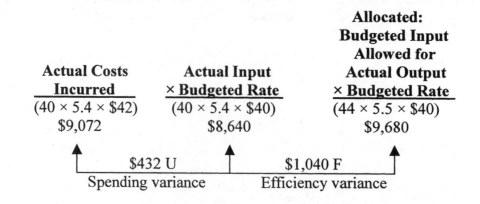

8-38 (Cont.d')

The unfavorable spending variance is due to the actual variable overhead cost per testing-hour increasing from the budgeted $40 per hour to the actual rate of $42 per hour. The favorable efficiency variance is due to the actual output of 22,000 units (1) requiring fewer batches, 40, than the budgeted amount of 42 and (2) each batch taking less time, 5.4 hours, than the budgeted time of 5.5 hours.

2. Computation of the fixed testing overhead cost variances follows:

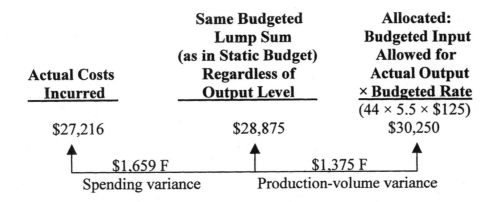

Actual Costs Incurred	Same Budgeted Lump Sum (as in Static Budget) Regardless of Output Level	Allocated: Budgeted Input Allowed for Actual Output × Budgeted Rate (44 × 5.5 × $125)
$27,216	$28,875	$30,250

$1,659 F
Spending variance

$1,375 F
Production-volume variance

The fixed testing overhead cost spending variance is $1,659 F because the amount of actual costs was lower than the budgeted amount of $28,875. The production-volume variance is $1,375 F because the actual number of SFA produced and sold required more budgeted testing-hours than the budgeted testing-hour capacity available.

8-40 (30–50 min.) Review of Chapters 7 and 8, 3—variance analysis.

1. Total standard production costs are based on 7,800 units of output.

Direct materials, 7,800 × $15.00	
(or 7,800 × 3 lbs. × $5.00 or 23,400 lbs. × $5.00)	$ 117,000
Direct manufacturing labor, 7,800 × $75.00	
(or 7,800 × 5 hrs. × $15.00 or 39,000 hrs. × $15.00)	585,000
Manufacturing overhead:	
Variable, 7,800 × $30.00 (or 39,000 hrs. × $6.00)	234,000
Fixed, 7,800 × $40.00 (or 39,000 hrs. × $8.00)	312,000
Total	$1,248,000

The following is for later use:
Fixed manufacturing overhead, a lump-sum budget $320,000*

$$*\text{Fixed manufacturing overhead rate} = \frac{\text{Budgeted fixed manufacturing overhead}}{\text{Denominator level}}$$

$$\$8.00 = \frac{\text{Budget}}{40,000 \text{ hrs.}}$$

$$\text{Budget} = 40,000 \text{ hours} \times \$8.00 = \$320,000$$

8-40 (Cont.d')

2.   Solution Exhibit 8-40 presents a columnar presentation of the variances. An overview of the 3-variance analysis using the block format of the text is:

3-Variance Analysis	Spending Variance	Efficiency Variance	Production Volume Variance
Total Manufacturing Overhead	$39,400 U	$6,600 U	$8,000 U

SOLUTION EXHIBIT 8-40

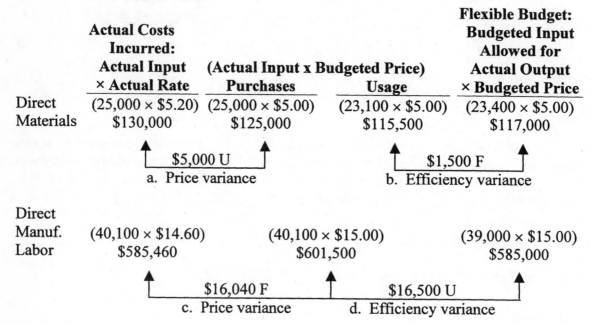

	Actual Costs Incurred	Actual Input × Budgeted Rate	Flexible Budget: Budgeted Input Allowed for Actual Output × Budgeted Rate	Allocated: (Budgeted Input Allowed for Actual Output × Budgeted Rate)
Variable Manufacturing Overhead	(not given)	(40,100 × $6.00) $240,600	(39,000 × $6.00) $234,000	(39,000 × $6.00) $234,000

```
              ↑ ——— $6,600 U ——— ↑                    ↑
                Efficiency variance        Never a variance
```

	Actual Costs Incurred	Actual Input × Budgeted Rate	Flexible Budget: Budgeted Input Allowed for Actual Output × Budgeted Rate	Allocated: (Budgeted Input Allowed for Actual Output × Budgeted Rate)
Fixed Manufacturing Overhead	(not given)	$320,000	$320,000	(39,000 × $8.00) $312,000

```
              ↑ ——— Never a variance ——— ↑ ——— $8,000 U* ——— ↑
                                          Prodn. volume variance
```

	Actual Costs Incurred	Actual Input × Budgeted Rate	Flexible Budget: Budgeted Input Allowed for Actual Output × Budgeted Rate	Allocated: (Budgeted Input Allowed for Actual Output × Budgeted Rate)
Total Manufacturing Overhead	(given) $600,000	($240,600 + $320,000) $560,600	($234,000 + $320,000) $554,000	($234,000 + $312,000) $546,000

```
   ↑ ——— $39,400 U ——— ↑ ——— $6,600 U ——— ↑ ——— $8,000 U ——— ↑
    e. Spending variance  f. Efficiency variance   g. Prodn. volume variance
```

*Denominator level in hours   40,000
Production volume in standard hours allowed   <u>39,000</u>
Production-volume variance   <u>1,000</u> hours x $8.00 = $8,000 U

CHAPTER 9
INVENTORY COSTING AND CAPACITY ANALYSIS

9-2   The term direct costing is a misnomer for variable costing for two reasons:

a.   Variable costing does not include all direct costs as inventoriable costs. Only variable direct manufacturing costs are included. Any fixed direct manufacturing costs, and any direct nonmanufacturing costs, (either variable or fixed) are excluded from inventoriable costs.

b.   Variable costing includes as inventoriable costs not only direct manufacturing costs but also some indirect costs (variable indirect manufacturing costs).

9-4   The main issue between variable costing and absorption costing is the proper timing of the release of fixed manufacturing costs as costs of the period:

    a. at the time of incurrence, or

    b. at the time the finished units to which the fixed overhead relates are sold.

Variable costing uses (a) and absorption costing uses (b).

9-6   Variable costing does not view fixed costs as unimportant or irrelevant, but it maintains that the distinction between behaviors of different costs is crucial for certain decisions. The planning and management of fixed costs is critical, irrespective of what inventory costing method is used.

9-8   (a) The factors that affect the breakeven point under variable costing are:

    1.   Fixed costs,

    2.   Contribution margin per unit.

    (b) The factors that affect the breakeven point under absorption costing are:

    1.   Fixed costs,

    2.   Contribution margin per unit,

    3.   Production level in units in excess of breakeven sales in units.

    4.   Denominator level chosen to set the fixed manufacturing cost rate.

9-10 Approaches used to reduce the negative aspects associated with using absorption costing include:

a.   Change the accounting system:

    • Adopt either variable or throughput costing, both of which reduce the incentives of managers to produce for inventory.

    • Adopt an inventory holding charge for managers who tie up funds in inventory.

b.   Extend the time period used to evaluate performance. By evaluating performance over a longer time period (say, 3 to 5 years), the incentive to take short-run actions that reduce long-term income is lessened.

c.   Include nonfinancial as well as financial variables in the measures used to evaluate performance.

9-12 The *downward demand spiral* is the continuing reduction in demand for its product that occurs when the prices of competitors' products are not met and (as demand drops further), higher and higher unit costs result in more and more reluctance to meet competitors' prices. Pricing decisions need to consider competitors and customers as well as costs.

9-14 For tax reporting in the U.S., the IRS requires companies to use the practical capacity concept. At year end, proration of any variances between inventories and cost of goods sold is required (unless the variance is immaterial in amount).

9-16 (30 min.) Variable and absorption costing, explaining operating income differences.

1. Key inputs for income statement computations are:

	April	May
Beginning inventory	0	150
Production	500	400
Goods available for sale	500	550
Units sold	350	520
Ending inventory	150	30

The fixed cost per unit and total manufacturing costs per unit under absorption costing are:

		April	May
(a)	Fixed manufacturing costs	$2,000,000	$2,000,000
(b)	Units produced	500	400
(c)=(a)÷(b)	Fixed manufacturing costs per unit	$4,000	$5,000
(d)	Variable manufacturing costs per unit	$10,000	$10,000
(e)=(c)+(d)	Total manufacturing costs per unit	$14,000	$15,000

9-16 (Cont'd.)

(a) Variable costing

	April 2003		May 2003	
Revenues[a]		$8,400,000		$12,480,000
Variable costs				
Beginning inventory	$ 0		$1,500,000	
Variable manufacturing costs[b]	5,000,000		4,000,000	
Cost of goods available for sale	5,000,000		5,500,000	
Deduct ending inventory[c]	1,500,000		300,000	
Variable cost of goods sold	3,500,000		5,200,000	
Variable operating costs[d]	1,050,000		1,560,000	
Total variable costs		4,550,000		6,760,000
Contribution margin		3,850,000		5,720,000
Fixed costs				
Fixed manufacturing costs	2,000,000		2,000,000	
Fixed operating costs	600,000		600,000	
Total fixed costs		2,600,000		2,600,000
Operating income		$1,250,000		$ 3,120,000

[a] $24,000 × 350; $24,000 × 520
[b] $10,000 × 500; $10,000 × 400
[c] $10,000 × 150; $10,000 × 30
[d] $3,000 × 350; $3,000 × 520

(b) Absorption costing

	April 2003		May 2003	
Revenues[a]		$8,400,000		$12,480,000
Cost of goods sold				
Beginning inventory	$ 0		$2,100,000	
Variable manufacturing costs[b]	5,000,000		4,000,000	
Fixed manufacturing costs[c]	2,000,000		2,000,000	
Cost of goods available for sale	7,000,000		8,100,000	
Deduct ending inventory[d]	2,100,000		450,000	
Cost of goods sold		4,900,000		7,650,000
Gross margin		3,500,000		4,830,000
Operating costs				
Variable operating costs[e]	1,050,000		1,560,000	
Fixed operating costs	600,000		600,000	
Total operating costs		1,650,000		2,160,000
Operating income		$1,850,000		$ 2,670,000

[a] $24,000 × 350; $24,000 × 520
[b] $10,000 × 500; $10,000 × 400
[c] ($4,000 × 500); ($5,000 × 400)
[d] ($14,000 × 150; $15,000 × 30)
[e] ($3,000 × 350; $3,000 × 520)

9-16 (Cont'd.)

2. $\left(\begin{array}{c}\text{Absorption-costing}\\\text{operating income}\end{array}\right) - \left(\begin{array}{c}\text{Variable-costing}\\\text{operating income}\end{array}\right) = \left(\begin{array}{c}\text{Fixed manufacturing}\\\text{costs in}\\\text{ending inventory}\end{array}\right) - \left(\begin{array}{c}\text{Fixed manufacturing}\\\text{costs in}\\\text{beginning inventory}\end{array}\right)$

April:

$$\$1,850,000 - \$1,250,000 = (\$4,000 \times 150) - (\$0)$$
$$\$600,000 = \$600,000$$

May:

$$\$2,670,000 - \$3,120,000 = (\$5,000 \times 30) - (\$4,000 \times 150)$$
$$- \$450,000 = \$150,000 - \$600,000$$
$$- \$450,000 = - \$450,000$$

The difference between absorption and variable costing is due solely to moving fixed manufacturing costs into inventories as inventories increase (as in April) and out of inventories as they decrease (as in May).

9-16 Excel Application

Inventory Costing and Capacity Analysis
Nascar Motors

Original Data

Unit Data	April	May
Beginning Inventory	0	150
Production	500	400
Sales	350	520
Ending Inventory	150	30

Revenue and Cost Data		
Selling Price	$24,000	$24,000
Variable Costs		
Manufacturing Costs per Unit Produced	$10,000	$10,000
Operating Costs per Unit Sold	3,000	3,000
Fixed Costs		
Manufacturing Costs	$2,000,000	$2,000,000
Operating Costs	600,000	600,000

Inventoriable Costs	Variable Costing	Absorption Costing
Variable Manufacturing Costs	$10,000	$10,000
Fixed Indirect Manufacturing Costs	4,000	5,000
Total Inventoriable Costs	$10,000	$14,000

9-4

Excel Solution 9-16 (Cont'd)

Problem 1

Panel A: Variable Costing

	April	May
Revenues (350 x $24,000; 520 x $24,000)	$8,400,000	$12,480,000
Variable Costs		
Beginning Inventory ($10,000 x 0; 150)	-	1,500,000
Variable Manufacturing Costs ($10,000 x 500; 400)	$5,000,000	4,000,000
Cost of Goods Available for Sale	5,000,000	5,500,000
Ending Inventory ($10,000 x 150; 30)	1,500,000	300,000
Variable Cost of Goods Sold	3,500,000	5,200,000
Variable Operating Costs ($3,000 x 350; 520)	1,050,000	1,560,000
Total Variable Costs	4,550,000	6,760,000
Contribution Margin	3,850,000	5,720,000
Fixed Costs		
Fixed Manufacturing Costs	2,000,000	2,000,000
Fixed Operating Costs	600,000	600,000
Total Fixed Costs	2,600,000	2,600,000
Operating Income	$1,250,000	$3,120,000

Panel B: Absorption Costing

	April	May
Revenues	$8,400,000	$12,480,000
Cost of Goods Sold		
Beginning Inventory ($14,000 x 0; 150)	-	2,100,000
Variable Manufacturing Costs ($10,000 x 500; 400)	$5,000,000	4,000,000
Fixed Manuf. Costs ($4000 x 500; $5000 x 400)	2,000,000	2,000,000
Cost of Goods Available for Sale	7,000,000	8,100,000
Ending Inventory ($14,000 x 150; $15,000 x 30)	2,100,000	450,000
Cost of Goods Sold	4,900,000	7,650,000
Gross Margin	3,500,000	4,830,000
Operating Costs		
Variable Operating Costs ($3,000 x 350; 520)	1,050,000	1,560,000
Fixed Operating Costs	600,000	600,000
Total Operating Costs	1,650,000	2,160,000
Operating Income	$1,850,000	$2,670,000

9-18 (40 min.) **Variable and absorption costing, explaining operating income differences.**

1. Key inputs for income statement computations are:

	January	February	March
Beginning inventory	0	300	300
Production	1,000	800	1,250
Goods available for sale	1,000	1,100	1,550
Units sold	700	800	1,500
Ending inventory	300	300	50

The fixed manufacturing costs per unit and total manufacturing costs per unit under absorption costing are:

		January	February	March
(a)	Fixed manufacturing costs	$400,000	$400,000	$400,000
(b)	Units produced	1,000	800	1,250
(c)=(a)÷(b)	Fixed manufacturing costs per unit	$400	$500	$320
(d)	Variable manufacturing costs per unit	$900	$900	$900
(e)=(c)+(d)	Total manufacturing costs per unit	$1,300	$1,400	$1,220

9-18 (Cont'd.)

(a) Variable Costing

	January 2004		February 2004		March 2004	
Revenues[a]		$1,750,000		$2,000,000		$3,750,000
Variable costs						
Beginning inventory[b]	$ 0		$270,000		$ 270,000	
Variable manufacturing costs[c]	900,000		720,000		1,125,000	
Cost of goods available for sale	900,000		990,000		1,395,000	
Ending inventory[d]	270,000		270,000		45,000	
Variable cost of goods sold	630,000		720,000		1,350,000	
Variable operating costs[e]	420,000		480,000		900,000	
Total variable costs		1,050,000		1,200,000		2,250,000
Contribution margin		700,000		800,000		1,500,000
Fixed costs						
Fixed manufacturing costs	400,000		400,000		400,000	
Fixed operating costs	140,000		140,000		140,000	
Total fixed costs		540,000		540,000		540,000
Operating income		$ 160,000		$ 260,000		$ 960,000

a $2,500 × 700; $2,500 × 800; $2,500 × 1,500
b $? × 0; $900 × 300; $900 × 300
c $900 × 1,000; $900 × 800; $900 × 1,250
d $900 × 300; $900 × 300; $900 × 50
e $600 × 700; $600 × 800; $600 × 1,500

9-18 (Cont'd.)

(b)   Absorption Costing

	January 2004		February 2004		March 2004	
Revenues[a]		$1,750,000		$2,000,000		$3,750,000
Cost of goods sold						
Beginning inventory[b]	$ 0		$ 390,000		$ 420,000	
Variable manufacturing costs[c]	900,000		720,000		1,125,000	
Fixed manufacturing costs[d]	400,000		400,000		400,000	
Cost of goods available for sale	1,300,000		1,510,000		1,945,000	
Deduct ending inventory[e]	390,000		420,000		61,000	
Cost of goods sold		910,000		1,090,000		1,884,000
Gross margin		840,000		910,000		1,866,000
Operating costs						
Variable operating costs[f]	420,000		480,000		900,000	
Fixed operating costs	140,000		140,000		140,000	
Total operating costs		560,000		620,000		1,040,000
Operating income		$ 280,000		$ 290,000		$ 826,000

[a] $2,500 × 700; $2,500 × 800; $2,500 × 1,500
[b] ($? × 0; $1,300 × 300; $1,400 × 300)
[c] $900 × 1,000; $900 × 800, $900 × 1,250
[d] ($400 × 1,000); ($500 × 800); ($320 × 1,250)
[e] ($1,300 × 300); ($1,400 × 300); ($1,220 × 50)
[f] $600 × 700; $600 × 800; $600 × 1,500

9-18 (Cont'd.)

2.

$$\left(\begin{array}{c}\text{Absorption-costing}\\\text{operating income}\end{array}\right) - \left(\begin{array}{c}\text{Variable costing}\\\text{operating income}\end{array}\right) = \left(\begin{array}{c}\text{Fixed manufacturing}\\\text{costs in}\\\text{ending inventory}\end{array}\right) - \left(\begin{array}{c}\text{Fixed manufacturing}\\\text{costs in}\\\text{beginning inventory}\end{array}\right)$$

January: $280,000   – $160,000   =   ($400 × 300)   – $0
$120,000 = $120,000

February: $290,000   – $260,000   =   ($500 × 300)   –   ($400 × 300)
$30,000 = $30,000

March: $826,000   – $960,000   =   ($320 × 50)   –   ($500 × 300)
– $134,000 = – $134,000

The difference between absorption and variable costing is due solely to moving fixed manufacturing costs into inventories as inventories increase (as in January) and out of inventories as they decrease (as in March).

9-20 (40 min) Variable vs. absorption costing.

1.

Income Statement for the Zwatch Company, Variable Costing
For the Year Ended December 31, 2004

Revenues: $22 × 345,400		$7,598,800
Variable costs		
Beginning inventory: $5.10 × 85,000	$ 433,500	
Variable manufacturing costs: $5.10 × 294,900	1,503,990	
Cost of goods available for sale	1,937,490	
Deduct ending inventory: $5.10 × 34,500	175,950	
Variable cost of goods sold	1,761,540	
Variable operating costs: $1.10 × 345,400	379,940	
Total variable costs (at standard costs)	2,141,480	
Adjustment for variances	0	
Total variable costs		2,141,480
Contribution margin		5,457,320
Fixed costs		
Fixed manufacturing overhead costs	1,440,000	
Fixed operating costs	1,080,000	
Adjustment for fixed cost variances	0	
Total fixed costs		2,520,000
Operating income		$2,937,320

9-20 (Cont'd.)

Absorption Costing Data

Fixed manufacturing overhead allocation rate =
Fixed manufacturing overhead/Denominator level machine-hours = $1,440,000/6,000
= $240 per machine-hour

Fixed manufacturing overhead allocation rate per unit =
Fixed manufacturing overhead allocation rate/standard production rate = $240/50
= $4.80 per unit

Income Statement for the Zwatch Company, Absorption Costing
For the Year Ended December 31, 2004

Revenues: $22 × 345,400		$7,598,800
Cost of goods sold		
Beginning inventory ($5.10 + $4.80) × 85,000	$ 841,500	
Variable manuf. costs: $5.10 × 294,900	1,503,990	
Fixed manuf. costs: $4.80 × 294,900	1,415,520	
Cost of goods available for sale	3,761,010	
Deduct ending inventory: ($5.10 + $4.80) × 34,500	(341,550)	
Adjust for manuf. variances ($4.80 × 5,100)[a]	24,480	
Cost of goods sold		3,443,940
Gross margin		4,154,860
Operating costs		
Variable operating costs: $1.10 × 345,400	$ 379,940	
Fixed operating costs	1,080,000	
Adjust for operating cost variances	0	
Total operating costs		1,459,940
Operating income		$2,694,920

[a] Production volume variance
= [(6,000 hours × 50) – 294,900) × $4.80
= (300,000 – 294,900) × $4.80
= $24,480

2. Zwatch's pre-tax profit margins –

Under variable costing:

Revenues	$7,598,800
Operating income	2,937,320
Pre-tax profit margin	38.7%

Under absorption costing:

Revenues	$7,598,800
Operating income	2,694,920
Pre-tax profit margin	35.5%

9-20 (Cont'd.)

3. Operating income using variable costing is about 9% higher than operating income calculated using absorption costing.

Variable costing operating income – Absorption costing operating income =
$2,937,320 – $2,694,920 = $242,400

Fixed manufacturing costs in beginning inventory under absorption costing –
Fixed manufacturing costs in ending inventory under absorption costing =
($4.80 × 85,000) – ($4.80 × 34,500) = $242,400

4. The factors the CFO should consider include:
   (a) Effect on managerial behavior, and
   (b) Effect on external users of financial statements.

Absorption costing has many critics. However, the dysfunctional aspects associated with absorption costing can be reduced by:

- Careful budgeting and inventory planning,
- Adding a capital charge to reduce the incentives to build up inventory, and
- Monitoring nonfinancial performance measures.

9-22 (40 min) Absorption vs. variable costing.

1. The number of Mimic™ pills sold in 2004 is:
    44,800 × 365 × 3 = 49,056,000 pills

Ending inventory on December 31, 2004, is 5,694,000 pills:

Unit data

Beginning inventory	0
Production	54,750,000
Sales	49,056,000
Ending inventory	5,694,000

Variable cost data
  Manufacturing costs per pill produced

Direct materials	$0.05
Direct manufacturing labor	0.04
Manufacturing overhead	0.11
Total variable manufacturing costs	$0.20

Fixed cost data

Manufacturing costs	$ 7,358,400
R&D	4,905,600
SG&A	19,622,400

Wholesale selling price per pill	$1.20

Fixed manufacturing costs allocation rate per pill	$0.15 (Given)
(7,358,400 ÷ 54,750,000)	

2. Variable costing:

Revenues: $1.20 × 49,056,000		$58,867,200
Variable costs		
Beginning inventory	$ 0	
Variable manuf. cost: $0.20 × 54,750,000	10,950,000	
Cost of goods available for sale	10,950,000	
Deduct ending inventory: $0.20 × 5,694,000	1,138,800	
Variable cost of goods sold	9,811,200	
Variable marketing costs: $0.07 × 49,056,000	3,433,920	
Adjust for variable-cost variance	0	
Total variable costs		13,245,120
Contribution margin		45,622,080
Fixed costs		
Fixed manufacturing costs	7,358,400	
Fixed R&D	4,905,600	
Fixed marketing	19,622,400	
Total fixed costs		31,886,400
Operating income		$13,735,680

9–22 (Cont'd.)

Absorption costing:

Revenues: $1.20 × 49,056,000		$58,867,200
Costs of goods sold		
Beginning inventory	$ 0	
Variable manuf. cost: $0.20 × 54,750,000	10,950,000	
Fixed manuf. costs: $0.15 × 54,750,000	8,212,500	
Cost of goods available for sale	19,162,500	
Deduct ending inventory: $0.35 × 5,694,000	(1,992,900)	
Adjust for manuf. variances [a]	(854,100)	
Cost of goods sold		16,315,500
Gross margin		42,551,700
Operating costs		
Variable marketing costs: $0.07 × 49,056,000	3,433,920	
Fixed R&D	4,905,600	
Fixed marketing	19,622,400	
Adjustment for operating cost variances	0	
Total operating costs		27,961,920
Operating income		$14,589,780

[a] Production - volume variance = (0.15 × 54,750,000 units) – $7,358,4000 = $854,100F

3. The difference of $854,100 is due to:

$$= \left(\begin{array}{c} \text{Fixed manufacturing} \\ \text{costs in ending inventory} \\ \text{under absorption costing} \end{array} \right) - \left(\begin{array}{c} \text{Fixed manufacturing} \\ \text{costs in beginning inventory} \\ \text{under absorption costing} \end{array} \right)$$

$$= (\$0.15 \times 5,694,000) - \$0$$
$$= \$854,100$$

9-24 (10 min.) **Capacity management, denominator-level capacity concepts.**

1. d
2. c, d
3. d
4. a
5. c
6. a, b
7. a
8. b
9. c, d
10. b
11. a, b

9-26 (30 min.) **Variable and absorption costing and breakeven points.**

1. Production = Sales + Ending Inventory - Beginning Inventory
   $$= 242,400 + 24,800 - 32,600$$
   $$= 234,600 \text{ cases}$$

2. Breakeven point in cases:
   a. Variable Costing:

   $$QT = \frac{\text{Total Fixed Costs} + \text{Target Operating Income}}{\text{Contribution Margin Per Unit}}$$

   $$QT = \frac{(\$3,753,600 + \$6,568,800) + \$0}{\$94 - (\$16 + \$10 + \$6 + \$14 + \$2)}$$

   $$QT = \frac{\$10,322,400}{\$46}$$

   $$QT = 224,400 \text{ cases}$$

9-26 (Cont'd.)

b. Absorption costing:

Fixed manuf. cost rate = $3,753,600 \div 234,600 = \$16$ per case

$$QT = \frac{\begin{array}{c}\text{Total Fixed} \\ \text{Cost}\end{array} + \begin{array}{c}\text{Target} \\ \text{OI}\end{array} + \left[\begin{array}{c}\text{Fixed Manuf.} \\ \text{Cost Rate}\end{array} \times \left(\begin{array}{c}\text{Breakeven} \\ \text{Sales in Units}\end{array} - \begin{array}{c}\text{Units} \\ \text{Produced}\end{array}\right)\right]}{\text{Contribution Margin Per Unit}}$$

$$QT = \frac{\$10,322,400 + [\$16\,(QT - 234,600)]}{\$46}$$

$$QT = \frac{\$10,322,400 + 16\,QT - 3,753,600}{\$46}$$

$$QT = \frac{\$6,568,800 + \$16\,QT}{\$46}$$

$46\,QT - 16\,QT = \$6,568,800$

$30\,QT \qquad = \$6,568,800$

$QT \qquad = 218,960$ cases.

3. If grape prices increase by 25%, the cost of grapes per case will increase from \$16 in 2004 to \$20 in 2005. This will decrease the unit contribution margin from \$46 in 2004 to \$42 in 2005.

a. Variable Costing:

$$QT = \frac{\$10,322,400}{\$42}$$

$$= 245,772 \text{ cases (rounded up)}$$

b. Absorption Costing:

$$QT = \frac{\$6,568,800 + \$16\,QT}{\$42}$$

$\$42\,QT = \$6,568,800 + \$16\,QT$

$\$26\,QT = \$6,568,800$

$QT = 252,647$ cases (rounded up)

9-28 (15 min.) **ABC and capacity usage.**

1.

Activity	Rate per Unit of Cost Driver
Power	$200,000 activity costs ÷ 50,000 kilowatt hours = $4 per kilowatt hour
Quality inspection	$300,000 activity costs ÷ 10,000 inspections = $30 per inspection

Cost allocation:

Power
Tulsa (10,000 kilowatt hours × $4)	$ 40,000
Okla (35,000 kilowatt hours × $4)	140,000
Total power costs allocation	$180,000

Quality inspection
Tulsa (5,000 inspections × $30)	$150,000
Okla (4,000 inspections × $30)	120,000
Total quality inspection costs allocation	$270,000

2. Cost of unused capacity:

Power ($200,000 – $180,000)	$ 20,000
Quality inspection ($300,000 – $270,000)	30,000
Total cost of unused capacity	$ 50,000

9-30 (40 min.) **Variable costing versus absorption costing.**

1. Absorption Costing:

Mavis Company Income Statement
For the Year Ended December 31, 2004

Revenues (540,000 × $5.00)		$2,700,000
Cost of goods sold:		
Beginning inventory (30,000 × $3.70[a])	$ 111,000	
Variable manufacturing costs (550,000 × $3.00)	1,650,000	
Fixed manuf. costs (550,000 × $0.70)	385,000	
Cost of goods available for sale	2,146,000	
Deduct ending inventory (40,000 × $3.70)	148,000	
Cost of goods sold (at std. costs)		1,998,000
Gross margin (at standard costs)		702,000
Deduct adjustment for variances (50,000[b] × $0.70)		35,000
Gross margin		667,000
Operating costs:		
Variable operating costs (540,000 × $1)	540,000	
Fixed operating costs	120,000	
Adjustment for variances	0	
Total operating costs		660,000
Operating income		$ 7,000

[a] $3.00 + ($7.00 ÷ 10) = $3.00 + $0.70 = $3.70
[b] [(10 × 60,000) − 550,000)] = 50,000 units

2. Variable Costing:

Mavis Company Income Statement
For the Year Ended December 31, 2004

Revenues		$2,700,000
Variable costs:		
Beginning inventory (30,000 × $3.00)	$ 90,000	
Variable manufacturing costs		
(550,000 × $3.00)	1,650,000	
Cost of goods available for sale	1,740,000	
Deduct ending inventory (40,000 × $3.00)	120,000	
Variable manufacturing cost of goods sold	1,620,000	
Variable operating costs	540,000	
Total variable costs (at std. cost)	2,160,000	
Adjustment for variances	0	
Total variable costs		2,160,000
Contribution margin		540,000
Fixed costs:		
Fixed manufacturing overhead costs	420,000	
Fixed operating costs	120,000	
Adjustment for fixed cost variances	0	
Total fixed costs		540,000
Operating income		$ 0

3.   The difference in operating income between the two costing methods is:

$$\begin{pmatrix} \text{Absorption-} \\ \text{costing} \\ \text{operating} \\ \text{income} \end{pmatrix} - \begin{pmatrix} \text{Variable-} \\ \text{costing} \\ \text{operating} \\ \text{income} \end{pmatrix} = \begin{pmatrix} \text{Fixed} \\ \text{manuf. costs} \\ \text{in ending} \\ \text{inventory} \end{pmatrix} - \begin{pmatrix} \text{Fixed} \\ \text{manuf. costs} \\ \text{in beginning} \\ \text{inventory} \end{pmatrix}$$

$7,000 − $0	=	[(40,000 × $0.70) − (30,000 × $0.70)]
$7,000	=	$28,000 − $21,000
$7,000	=	$7,000

The absorption-costing operating income exceeds the variable costing figure by $7,000 because of the increase of $7,000 during 2004 of the amount of fixed manufacturing costs in ending inventory vis-a-vis beginning inventory.

4.

Total fixed
manufacturing
costs

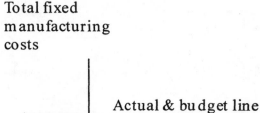

$420,000

$385,000

Actual & budget line

Underallocated

Allocated line
@$7.00

55,000   60,000

Machine-hours

5.   Absorption costing is more likely to lead to buildups of inventory than does variable costing. Absorption costing enables managers to increase reported operating income by building up inventory which reduces the amount of fixed manufacturing overhead included in the current period's cost of goods sold.

        Ways to reduce this incentive include:
(a) Careful budgeting and inventory planning,
(b) Change the accounting system to variable costing or throughput costing,
(c) Incorporate a carrying charge for carrying inventory,
(d) Use a longer time period to evaluate performance than a quarter or a year, and
(e) Include nonfinancial as well as financial measures when evaluating management performance.

9-32 (40 min.) The All-Fixed Company in 2004.

This problem always generates active classroom discussion.

1.   The treatment of fixed manufacturing overhead in absorption costing is affected primarily by what denominator level is selected as a base for allocating fixed manufacturing costs to units produced. In this case, is 10,000 tons per year, 20,000 tons, or some other denominator level the most appropriate base?

   We usually place the following possibilities on the board or overhead projector and then ask the students to indicate by vote how many used one denominator level versus another. Incidentally, discussion tends to move more clearly if variable-costing income statements are discussed first, because there is little disagreement as to computations under variable costing.

a.   Variable-Costing Income Statement:

		2003	2004	Together
Revenues (and contribution margin)		$300,000	$300,000	$600,000
Fixed costs:				
Manufacturing costs	$280,000			
Operating costs	40,000	320,000	320,000	640,000
Operating income		$ (20,000)	$ (20,000)	$ (40,000)

b.   Absorption-Costing Income Statement:

The ambiguity about the 10,000- or 20,000-unit denominator level is intentional. IF YOU WISH, THE AMBIGUITY MAY BE AVOIDED BY GIVING THE STUDENTS A SPECIFIC DENOMINATOR LEVEL IN ADVANCE.

Alternative 1.   Use 20,000 units as a denominator; fixed manufacturing overhead per unit is $280,000 ÷ 20,000 = $14.

	2003	2004	Together
Revenues	$300,000	$ 300,000	$600,000
Manufacturing costs at $14	280,000	--	280,000
Deduct ending inventory	140,000	--	--
Cost of goods sold	140,000	140,000*	280,000
Underallocated manuf. overhead-- output level variance	--	280,000	280,000
Operating costs	40,000	40,000	80,000
Total costs	180,000	460,000	640,000
Operating income	$120,000	$(160,000)	$(40,000)

* Inventory carried forward from 2003 and sold in 2004.

Alternative 2. Use 10,000 units as a denominator; fixed manufacturing overhead per unit is $280,000 ÷10,000 = $28.

	2003	2004	Together
Revenues	$300,000	$300,000	$600,000
Manufacturing costs at $28	560,000	--	560,000
Deduct ending inventory	280,000	--	--
Cost of goods sold	280,000	280,000*	560,000
Underallocated manuf. overhead-- output level variance	--	280,000	--
Overallocated manuf. overhead -- output level variance	(280,000)	--	--
Operating costs	40,000	40,000	80,000
Total costs	40,000	600,000	640,000
Operating income	$260,000	$(300,000)	$ (40,000)

*Inventory carried forward from 2003 and sold in 2004.

Note that operating income under variable costing follows sales and is not affected by inventory changes.

Note also that students will understand the variable-costing presentation much more easily than the alternatives presented under absorption costing.

2.
$$\text{Breakeven point under variable costing} = \frac{\text{Fixed costs}}{\text{Contribution margin per ton}} = \frac{\$320,000}{\$30}$$

$$= 10,667 \text{ tons per year or } 21,333 \text{ for two years.}$$

9-32 (Cont'd.)

    If the company could sell 667 more tons per year at $30 each, it could get the extra $20,000 contribution margin needed to break even.

    Most students will say that the breakeven point is 10,667 tons per year under both absorption costing and variable costing. The logical question to ask a student who answers 10,667 tons for variable costing is: "What operating income do you show for 2003 under absorption costing?" If a student answers $120,000 (alternative 1 above), or $260,000 (alternative 2 above), ask: "But you say your breakeven point is 10,667 tons. How can you show an operating income on only 10,000 tons sold during 2003?"

    The answer to the above dilemma lies in the fact that operating income is affected by both sales and production under absorption costing.

    Given that sales would be 10,000 tons in 2003, solve for the production level that will provide a breakeven level of zero operating income. Using the formula in the chapter, sales of 10,000 units, and a fixed manufacturing overhead rate of $14 (based on $280,000 ÷ 20,000 units denominator level = $14):

Let P = Production level

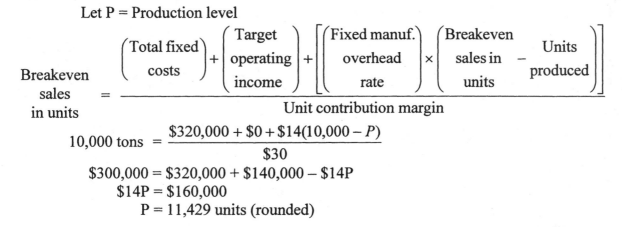

$$\text{10,000 tons} = \frac{\$320,000 + \$0 + \$14(10,000 - P)}{\$30}$$

$$\$300,000 = \$320,000 + \$140,000 - \$14P$$
$$\$14P = \$160,000$$
$$P = 11,429 \text{ units (rounded)}$$

Proof:

Gross margin, 10,000 × ($30 − $14)		$160,000
Output level variance,		
(20,000 − 11,429) × $14	$120,000	
Marketing and administrative costs	40,000	160,000
Operating income		$ 0

9-32 (Cont'd.)

Given that production would be 20,000 tons in 2003, solve for the breakeven unit sales level. Using the formula in the chapter and a fixed manufacturing overhead rate of $14 (based on a denominator level of 20,000 units):

Let N = Breakeven sales in units

$$N = \frac{\left(\begin{array}{c}\text{Total fixed}\\\text{costs}\end{array}\right) + \left(\begin{array}{c}\text{Target}\\\text{operating}\\\text{income}\end{array}\right) + \left[\left(\begin{array}{c}\text{Fixed manuf.}\\\text{overhead}\\\text{rate}\end{array}\right) \times \left(N - \begin{array}{c}\text{Units}\\\text{produced}\end{array}\right)\right]}{\text{Unit contribution margin}}$$

$$N = \frac{\$320,000 + \$0 + \$14(N - 20,000)}{\$30}$$

$30N = \$320,000 + \$14N - \$280,000$

$16N = \$40,000$

N   = 2,500 units

Proof:

Gross margin, 2,500 × ($30 – $14)		$40,000
Output level MOH variance	$ 0	
Marketing and administrative costs	40,000	40,000
Operating income		$ 0

We find it helpful to put the following comparisons on the board:

Variable costing breakeven　　= f(sales)
　　　　　　　　　　　　　　= 10,667 tons

Absorption costing breakeven　= f(sales and production)
　　　　　　　　　　　　　　= f(10,000 and 11,429)
　　　　　　　　　　　　　　= f(2,500 and 20,000)

3.   Absorption costing inventory cost: Either $140,000 or $280,000 at the end of 2003 and zero at the end of 2004.
    Variable costing: Zero at all times. This is a major criticism of variable costing and focuses on the issue of the definition of an asset.

3.   Operating income is affected by both production *and* sales under absorption costing. Hence, most managers would prefer absorption costing because their performance in any given reporting period, at least in the short run, is influenced by how much production is scheduled near the end of a period.

9-34 (25-30 min.) **Alternative denominator-level concepts.**

1.

Denominator-Level Concept	Budgeted Fixed Manufacturing Overhead per Period	Budgeted Denominator Level	Budgeted Fixed Manufacturing Overhead Cost Rate
Theoretical capacity	$42,000,000	5,256,000	$ 7.99
Practical capacity	42,000,000	3,500,000	12.00
Normal capacity utilization	42,000,000	2,800,000	15.00
Master-budget utilization			
(a) Jan.–June 2003	21,000,000	1,120,000	18.75
(b) July–Dec. 2003	21,000,000	1,680,000	12.50

The differences arise for several reasons:

a. The theoretical and practical capacity concepts emphasize supply factors, while normal capacity utilization and master-budget utilization emphasize demand factors.

b. The two separate six-month rates for the master-budget utilization concept differ because of seasonal differences in budgeted production.

2. Theoretical capacity is based on the production of output at maximum efficiency for 100% of the time.

Practical capacity--reduces theoretical capacity for unavoidable operating interruptions such as scheduled maintenance time, shutdowns for holidays and other days, and so on.

For each of the three determinants of capacity in Lucky Larger's plant, practical capacity is less than theoretical capacity:

	Barrels Per Hour (1)	Working Hours Per Day (2)	Working Days Per Year (3)	Capacity (4)=(1) × (2) × (3)
Theoretical capacity	600	24	365	5,256,000
Practical capacity	500	20	350	3,500,000

3. The smaller the denominator, the higher the amount of overhead costs capitalized for inventory units. Thus, if the plant manager wishes to be able to "adjust" plant operating income by building inventory, master-budget utilization or possibly normal capacity utilization would be preferred.

9-36 (20 min.) Downward demand spiral.

1.		
Budgeted variable manufacturing costs per unit	$200	
Allocated fixed manufacturing overhead costs per unit	100[a]	
Budgeted total manufacturing costs per unit	300	
Markup (100% × $300)	300	
Budgeted selling price	$600	

[a] $1,000,000 ÷ 10,000 units = $100 per unit

9-36 (Cont'd.)

2.

Budgeted variable manufacturing costs per unit	$200
Allocated fixed manufacturing overhead costs per unit	125[b]
Budgeted total manufacturing costs per unit	325
Markup (100% × $325)	325
Revised budgeted selling price	$650

[b] $1,000,000 ÷ 8,000 units = $125 per unit

3. Considering that the market is highly competitive, raising the selling price, in an attempt to recover fixed manufacturing overhead costs, will make Pismo Company less competitive. Pismo's higher selling price would likely make it lose its customers to the competitors. This is the classic syndrome of the start of a downward demand spiral. Pismo Company should use its practical capacity to allocate fixed manufacturing overhead costs. If an upturn is expected, Pismo should keep its excess capacity. Otherwise, it should either lease or get rid of the excess capacity in order to bring down its fixed manufacturing overhead costs to the demand level.

9-38 (30 min.) Denominator volume, production volume variance.

1.

Denominator-Level Capacity Concept (1)	Budgeted Fixed Manufacturing Overhead (2)	Budgeted Denominator Level (in Machine Hours) (3)	Budgeted Fixed Manufacturing Overhead Rate Per Machine-Hour (4) = (2) ÷ (3)
Theoretical capacity	$10,500,000	2,100,000	$5.0
Practical capacity	10,500,000	1,500,000	7.0
Normal capacity utilization	10,500,000	1,312,500	8.0
Master-budget capacity utilization	10,500,000	1,000,000	10.5

2.

$$\text{Production volume variance} = \left[\text{Denominator level} - \text{Budgeted inputs allowed for actual input} \right] \times \left[\text{Budgeted fixed manufacturing overhead rate per machine-hour} \right]$$

Theoretical capacity: Production volume variance = (2,100,000 – 1,100,000) × $5.0
= $5,000,000 U

Practical capacity: Production volume variance = (1,500,000 – 1,100,000) × $7.0
= $2,800,000 U

Normal capacity utilization: Production volume variance = (1,312,500 – 1,100,000) × $8
= $1,700,000 U

Master budget capacity utilization: Production volume variance = (1,000,000 – 1,100,000) × $10.5
= $1,050,000 F

9-40 (20 min.) **Cost allocation, budgeted rates, ethics** (continuation of Problem 9-39).

1.   Hospitals are charged a budgeted variable cost rate and an allocation of budgeted fixed costs. By overestimating budgeted meal counts, the denominator of the budgeted fixed cost rate is larger, and hence the amount charged to individual hospitals is lower. Consider 2004 where the budgeted fixed cost rate of $1.50 is computed as follows:

$$\frac{\$4,380,000}{2,920,000 \text{ meals}} = \$1.50 \text{ per meal}$$

Suppose in 2004, hospital administrators "inflated" their budgeted meal count by 20%: The budgeted fixed cost rate for 2004 rate would have been

$$\frac{\$4,380,000}{3,504,000 \text{ meals}} = \$1.25 \text{ per meal}$$

Hence, by deliberately overstating budgeted meal count demand, they could reduce the costs charged per meal in 2004. The use of budgeted meals as the denominator means the central food-catering facility bears the risk of demand overestimates.

2.   Evidence that could be collected include:

(a)   Budgeted meal-count estimates and actual meal-count figures each year for each hospital controller. Over an extended time period, there should be a sizable number of both underestimates and overestimates. Controllers could be ranked on both their percentage of overestimation and the frequency of their overestimation.

(b)   Look at the underlying demand estimates by patients at individual hospitals. Each hospital controller has other factors (such as hiring of nurses) that give insight into their expectations of future meal-count demands. If these factors are inconsistent with the meal-count demand figures provided to the central food-catering facility, explanations should be sought.

3.   (a)   Highlight the importance of a corporate culture of honesty and openness. WHM could institute a Code of Ethics that highlights the upside of individual hospitals providing honest estimates of demand (and the penalties for those who do not).
        (b)   Have individual hospitals contract in advance for their budgeted meal count. Unused amounts would be charged to each hospital at the end of the accounting period. This approach puts a penalty on hospital administrators who overestimate demand.
        (c)   Use an incentive scheme that has an explicit component for meal-count forecasting accuracy. Each meal-count "forecasting error" would reduce the bonus by $0.05. Thus, if a hospital bids for 292,000 meals and actually uses 200,000 meals, its bonus would be reduced by $0.05 × (292,000 – 200, 000) = $4,600.

CHAPTER 10
DETERMINING HOW COSTS BEHAVE

10-2   Three alternative linear cost functions are:
1.   Variable cost function—a cost function in which total costs change in proportion to the changes in the level of activity in the relevant range.
2.   Fixed cost function—a cost function in which total costs do not change with changes in the level of activity in the relevant range.
3.   Mixed cost function—a cost function that has both variable and fixed elements. Total costs change but not in proportion to the changes in the level of activity in the relevant range.

10-4   No. High correlation merely indicates that the two variables move together in the data examined. It is essential to also consider economic plausibility before making inferences about cause and effect. Without any economic plausibility for a relationship, it is less likely that a high level of correlation observed in one set of data will be similarly found in other sets of data.

10-6   The conference method estimates cost functions on the basis of analysis and opinions about costs and their drivers gathered from various departments of a company (purchasing, process engineering, manufacturing, employee relations, etc.). Advantages of the conference method include:
1.   The speed with which cost estimates can be developed.
2.   The pooling of knowledge from experts across functional areas.
3.   The improved credibility of the cost function to all personnel.

10-8   The six steps are:
1.   Choose the dependent variable (the variable to be predicted, which is some type of cost).
2.   Identify the independent variable or cost driver.
3.   Collect data on the dependent variable and the cost driver.
4.   Plot the data.
5.   Estimate the cost function.
6.   Evaluate the cost driver of the estimated cost function.

Step 3 typically is the most difficult for a cost analyst.

10-10   Criteria important when choosing among alternative cost functions are:
1.   Economic plausibility.
2.   Goodness of fit.
3.   Slope of the regression line.

10-12 Frequently encountered problems when collecting cost data on variables included in a cost function are:

1. The time period used to measure the dependent variable is not properly matched with the time period used to measure the cost driver(s).
2. Fixed costs are allocated as if they are variable.
3. Data are either not available for all observations or are not uniformly reliable.
4. Extreme values of observations occur.
5. A homogeneous relationship between the individual cost items in the dependent variable cost pool and the cost driver(s) does not exist.
6. The relationship between the cost and the cost driver is not stationary.
7. Inflation has occurred in a dependent variable, a cost driver, or both.

10-14 No. A cost driver is any factor whose change causes a change in the total cost of a related cost object. A cause-and-effect relationship underlies selection of a cost driver. Some users of regression analysis include numerous independent variables in a regression model in an attempt to maximize goodness of fit, irrespective of the economic plausibility of the independent variables included. Some of the independent variables included may not be cost drivers.

10-16 (10 min.) **Estimating a cost function**

1. $\text{Slope coefficient} = \dfrac{\text{Difference in costs}}{\text{Difference in machine-hours}}$

$$\dfrac{\$3,900 - \$3,000}{7,000 - 4,000}$$

$$= \dfrac{\$900}{3,000} = \$0.30 \text{ per machine-hour}$$

$\text{Constant} = \text{Total cost} - (\text{Slope coefficient} \times \text{Quantity of cost driver})$
$= \$3,900 - (\$0.30 \times 7,000) = \$1,800$
$= \$3,000 - (\$0.30 \times 4,000) = \$1,800$

The cost function based on the two observations is:

$\text{Maintenance costs} = \$1,800 + \$0.30 \times \text{Machine-hours}$

2. The cost function in requirement 1 is an estimate of how costs behave within the relevant range, not at cost levels outside the relevant range. If there are no months with zero machine-hours represented in the maintenance account, data in that account cannot be used to estimate the fixed costs at the zero machine-hours level. Rather, the constant component of the cost function provides the best available starting point for a straight line that approximates how a cost behaves within the relevant range.

10-18 (20 min.) **Various cost-behavior patterns.**

1. K
2. B
3. G
4. J   Note that A is incorrect because, although the cost per pound eventually equals a constant at $9.20, the total dollars of cost increases linearly from that point onward.
5. I   The total costs will be the same regardless of the volume level.
6. L
7. F   This is a classic step-cost function.
8. K
9. C

10-20 (15 min.) **Account analysis method.**

1. Variable costs:

Car wash labor	$240,000
Soap, cloth, and supplies	32,000
Water	28,000
Electric power to move conveyor belt	72,000
Total variable costs	$372,000

Fixed costs:

Depreciation	$ 64,000
Salaries	46,000
Total fixed costs	$110,000

Costs are classified as variable because the *total* costs in these categories change in proportion to the number of cars washed in Lorenzo's operation. Costs are classified as fixed because the *total* costs in these categories do not vary with the number of cars washed. If the conveyor belt moves regardless of the number of cars on it, the electricity costs to power the conveyor belt would be a fixed cost.

2. Variable costs per car = $\dfrac{\$372,000}{80,000}$ = $4.65 per car

Total costs estimated for 90,000 cars = $110,000 + ($4.65 × 90,000) = $528,500

10-22 (20 min.) **Estimating a cost function, high-low method.**

1. See Solution Exhibit 10-22. There is a positive relationship between the number of service reports (a cost driver) and the customer-service department costs. This relationship is economically plausible.

2.

	Number of Service Reports	Customer-Service Department Costs
Highest observation of cost driver	436	$21,890
Lowest observation of cost driver	122	12,941
Difference	314	$ 8,949

Customer-service department costs = $a + b$ (number of service reports)

$$\text{Slope coefficient } (b) = \frac{\$8,949}{314} = \$28.50 \text{ per service report}$$

$$\text{Constant } (a) = \$21,890 - \$28.50\,(436) = \$9,464$$
$$= \$12,941 - \$28.50\,(122) = \$9,464$$

Customer-service
department costs   = $9,464 + $28.50 (number of service reports)

3. Other possible cost drivers of customer-service department costs are:
   a. Number of products replaced with a new product (and the dollar value of the new products charged to the customer-service department).
   b. Number of products repaired and the time and cost of repairs.

SOLUTION EXHIBIT 10-22
Plot of Number of Service Reports versus Customer-Service Dept. Costs for Capitol Products

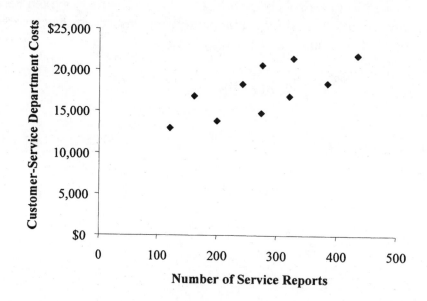

10-24 (20 min.) **Cost-volume-profit and regression analysis**.

1a. $\text{Average cost of manufacturing} = \dfrac{\text{Total manufacturing costs}}{\text{Number of bicycle frames}}$

$= \dfrac{\$900,000}{30,000} = \$30 \text{ per frame}$

This cost is greater than the $28.50 per frame that Ryan has quoted.

1b. Garvin cannot take the average manufacturing cost in 2002 of $30 per frame and multiply it by 36,000 bicycle frames to determine the total cost of manufacturing 36,000 bicycle frames. The reason is that some of the $900,000 (or equivalently the $30 cost per frame) are fixed costs and some are variable costs. Without distinguishing fixed from variable costs, Garvin cannot determine the cost of manufacturing 36,000 frames. For example, if all costs are fixed, the manufacturing costs of 36,000 frames will continue to be $900,000. If, however, all costs are variable, the cost of manufacturing 36,000 frames would be $30 × 36,000 = $1,080,000. If some costs are fixed and some are variable, the cost of manufacturing 36,000 frames will be somewhere between $900,000 and $1,080,000.

Some students could argue that another reason for not being able to determine the cost of manufacturing 36,000 bicycle frames is that not all costs are output unit-level costs. If some costs are, for example, batch-level costs, more information would be needed on the number of batches in which the 36,000 bicycle frames would be produced, in order to determine the cost of manufacturing 36,000 bicycle frames.

2. $\begin{array}{l}\text{Expected cost to make} \\ \text{36,000 bicycle frames}\end{array} = \$432,000 + \$15 \times 36,000$

$= \$432,000 + \$540,000 = \$972,000$

Purchasing bicycle frames from Ryan will cost $28.50 × 36,000 = $1,026,000. Hence it will cost Garvin $1,026,000 − $972,000 = $54,000 more to purchase the frames from Garvin rather than manufacture them in-house.

3. Garvin would need to consider several factors before being confident that the equation in requirement 2 accurately predicts the cost of manufacturing bicycle frames.

    a. Is the relationship between total manufacturing costs and quantity of bicycle frames economically plausible? For example, is the quantity of bicycles made the only cost driver or are there other cost-drivers (for example batch-level costs of setups, production-orders or material handling) that affect manufacturing costs?

    b. How good is the goodness of fit? That is, how well does the estimated line fit the data?

    c. Is the relationship between the number of bicycle frames produced and total manufacturing costs linear?

    d. Does the slope of the regression line indicate that a strong relationship exists between manufacturing costs and the number of bicycle frames produced?

    e. Are there any data problems such as, for example, errors in measuring costs, trends in prices of materials, labor or overheads that might affect variable or fixed costs over time, extreme values of observations, or a nonstationary relationship over time between total manufacturing costs and the quantity of bicycles produced?

    f. How is inflation expected to affect costs?

    g. Will Ryan supply high-quality bicycle frames on time?

10-26   (30 min.)   **Regression analysis, activity-based costing, choosing cost drivers.**

1a.   Solution Exhibit 10-26A presents the plots and regression line of number of packaged units moved on distribution costs.

SOLUTION EXHIBIT 10-26A
Plots and Regression Line of Number of Packaged Units Moved on Distribution Costs

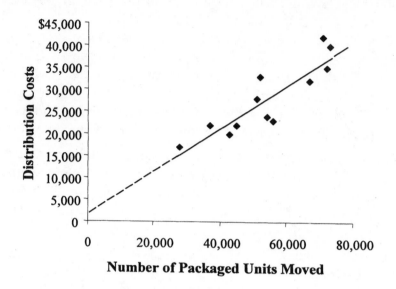

1b.   Solution Exhibit 10-26B presents the plots and regression line of number of shipments made on distribution costs.

SOLUTION EXHIBIT 10-26B
Plots and Regression Line of Number of Shipments Made on Distribution Costs

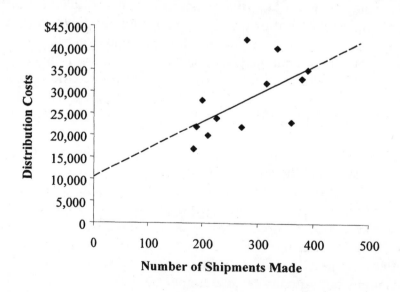

10-26 (Cont'd.)

Number of packaged units moved appears to be a better cost driver of distribution costs for the following reasons:

(i)   *Economic plausibility.*   Both number of packaged units moved and number of shipments are economically plausible cost drivers. Because the product is heavy, however, costs of freight are likely to be a sizable component of distribution costs. Thus, number of packaged units moved will affect distribution costs significantly because freight costs are largely a function of the number of units transported.

(ii) *Goodness of fit.* Compare Solution Exhibits 10-26A and 10-26B. Number of packaged units moved has a better goodness of fit with distribution costs than do number of shipments made. That is, the vertical differences between actual and predicted distribution costs are smaller for the number of packaged units moved regression than for the number of shipments made regression.

(iii) *Slope of regression line.* Again, compare Solution Exhibits 10-26A and 10-26B. The number of packaged units moved regression line has a relatively steep slope and a small scatter of observations around the regression lines indicating a strong relationship between number of packaged units moved and distribution costs. On average, distribution costs increase with the number of packaged units moved. The number of shipments made regression line is flatter and has more scatter of observations about the line indicating a weak relationship between the number of shipments made and distribution costs. On average, the number of shipments made has a smaller effect on distribution costs.

2.   Using the preferred cost function,
Distribution costs = $1,349 + ($0.496 × Number of packaged units moved),
Flaherty would budget distribution costs of
$$\$1,349 + (\$0.496 \times 40,000) = \$1,349 + \$19,840 = \$21,189$$

10-28 (20 min.) Learning curve, incremental unit-time learning model.

1.   The direct manufacturing labor-hours (DMLH) required to produce the first 2, 3, and 4 units, given the assumption of an incremental unit-time learning curve of 90%, is as follows:

Cumulative Number of Units (1)	Individual Unit Time for Xth Unit (2)	Cumulative Total Time (3)
1	3,000	3,000
2	2,700 (3,000 × 0.90)	5,700
3	2,539	8,239
4	2,430 (2,700 × 0.90)	10,669

Values in column 2 are calculated using the formula $y = aX^b$
where $a = 3,000$, $X = 2$, 3, or 4, and $b = -0.1520$, which gives

when $X = 2$, $y = 3,000 \times 2^{-0.1520} = 2,700$

when $X = 3$, $y = 3,000 \times 3^{-0.1520} = 2,539$

when $X = 4$, $y = 3,000 \times 4^{-0.1520} = 2,430$

10-28 (Cont'd.)

	Variable Costs of Producing		
	2 Units	3 Units	4 Units
Direct materials $80,000 × 2; 3; 4	$160,000	$240,000	$ 320,000
Direct manufacturing labor			
$25 × 5,700; 8,239; 10,669	142,500	205,975	266,725
Variable manufacturing overhead			
$15 × 5,700; 8,239; 10,669	85,500	123,585	160,035
Total variable costs	$388,000	$569,560	$746,760

2.

	Variable Costs of Producing	
	2 Units	4 Units
Incremental unit-time learning model		
(from requirement 1)	$388,000	$746,760
Cumulative average-time learning model		
(from Exercise 10-27)	376,000	708,800
Difference	$ 12,000	$ 37,960

Total variable costs for manufacturing 2 and 4 units are lower under the cumulative average-time learning curve relative to the incremental unit-time learning curve. Direct manufacturing labor-hours required to make additional units decline more slowly in the incremental unit-time learning curve relative to the cumulative average-time learning curve when the same 90% factor is used for both curves. The reason is that, in the incremental unit-time learning curve, as the number of units double, only the last unit produced has a cost of 90% of the initial cost. In the cumulative average-time learning model, doubling the number of units causes the average cost of *all* the additional units produced (not just the last unit) to be 90% of the initial cost.

10-30 (30–40 min.) **High-low method versus regression analysis.**

1.   Solution Exhibit 10-30 presents the plots of advertising costs on revenues.
SOLUTION EXHIBIT 10-30
Plot and Regression Line of Advertising Costs on Revenues

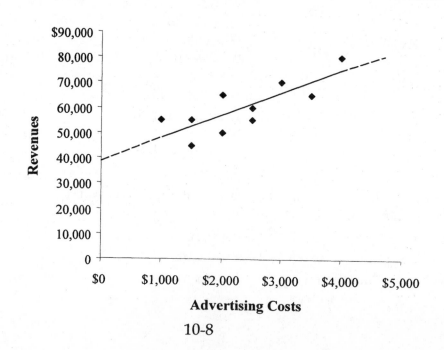

10-30 (Cont'd.)

2.   Solution Exhibit 10-30 also shows the regression line of advertising costs on revenues. We evaluate the estimated regression equation using the criteria of economic plausibility, goodness of fit, and slope of the regression line.

Economic plausibility.   Advertising costs appears to be a plausible cost driver of revenues. Restaurants frequently use newspaper advertising to promote their restaurants and increase their patronage.

Goodness of fit.   The vertical differences between actual and predicted revenues appears to be reasonably small. This indicates that advertising costs are related to restaurant revenues.

Slope of regression line.   The slope of the regression line appears to be relatively steep. Given the small scatter of the observations around the line, the steep slope indicates that, on average, restaurant revenues increase with newspaper advertising.

3.   The high-low method would estimate the cost function as follows:

	Advertising Costs	Revenues
Highest observation of cost driver	$4,000	$80,000
Lowest observation of cost driver	1,000	55,000
Difference	$3,000	$25,000

$$\text{Revenues} = a + (b \times \text{advertising costs})$$

$$\text{Slope coefficient } (b) = \frac{\$25,000}{\$3,000} = 8.333$$

$$\text{Constant } (a) = \$80,000 - (\$4,000 \times 8.333)$$
$$= \$80,000 - 33,332 = \$46,668$$

$$\text{or} \quad \text{Constant } (a) = \$55,000 - (\$1,000 \times 8.333)$$
$$= \$55,000 - 8,333 = \$46,667$$

$$\text{Revenues} = \$46,667 + (8.333 \times \text{Advertising costs})$$

4.   The increase in revenues for each $1,000 spent on advertising within the relevant range is
    a.   Using the regression equation, $8.723 \times \$1,000 = \$8,723$
    b.   Using the high-low equation, $8.333 \times \$1,000 = \$8,333$

The high-low equation does fairly well in estimating the relationship between advertising costs and revenues. However, Martinez and Brown should use the regression equation. The reason is that the regression equation uses information from all observations whereas the high-low method relies only on the observations that have the highest and lowest values of the cost driver. These observations are generally not representative of all the data.

10-32 (10-15 min.) Time lag consideration in interpreting regression results.

The relationship between machine-hours and maintenance costs is negative because Aza Company schedules maintenance during slow production periods. There is a time lag between heavy machine usage during peak production months, and maintenance in later months when the production volume is low. To correctly understand the relationship between machine-hours and maintenance costs, Aza should estimate the regression equation of maintenance costs on lagged machine-hours (that is, machine-hours in prior months).

The explanation for the relationship between sales revenue and advertising costs is that the result of advertising is often not instantaneous. Generally advertising generates increased sales revenue in subsequent month(s), so Aza should estimate the relationship between advertising costs in a particular period and sales in future periods. Another explanation is that Aza increases its advertising costs during periods of declining sales in an attempt to increase sales volume of the clothing lines that will soon be out of season. For example, Aza may increase its advertising on winter clothing during late winter before the customers start purchasing spring clothes.

10-34 (20–30 min.) Cost estimation, incremental unit-time learning model.

1.   Cost to Produce the Second through the Eighth Boats:

Direct materials, 7 × $100,000	$ 700,000
Direct manufacturing labor, 49,356* × $30	1,480,680
Variable overhead, 49,356 × $20	987,120
Other overhead, 25% of $1,480,680	370,170
Total costs	$3,537,970

*The direct labor hours to produce the second through the eighth boats can be calculated via a table format, given the assumption of an incremental unit-time learning curve of 85%:

Cumulative Number of Units	Individual Unit Time for Xth Unit (m)*	Cumulative Total Time
1	10,000	10,000
2	8,500	18,500
3	7,729	26,229
4	7,225	33,454
5	6,856	40,310
6	6,569	46,879
7	6,336	53,215
8	6,141	59,356

*Calculated as $m = pX^q$ where $p = 10,000$, $q = -0.2345$, and $X = 1, 2, 3,\ldots, 8$.

10-34 (Cont'd.)

The direct manufacturing labor-hours to produce the second through the eighth boat is 59,356 – 10,000 = 49,356 hours.

2. Difference in total costs to manufacture the second through the eighth boat under the incremental unit-time learning model and the cumulative average-time learning model is $3,537,970 (calculated in requirement 1 of this problem) – $2,949,975 (from requirement 1 of Problem 10-33) = $587,995.

The incremental unit-time learning curve has a slower decline in the reduction in time required to produce successive units than does the cumulative average-time learning curve (see Problem 10-33, requirement 1). Assuming the same 85% factor is used for both curves:

	Estimated Cumulative Direct Manufacturing Labor-Hours	
Cumulative Number of Units	Cumulative Average-Time Learning Model	Incremental Unit-Time Learning Model
1	10,000	10,000
2	17,000	18,500
4	28,900	33,454
8	49,130	59,356

The reason is that, in the incremental unit-time learning model, as the number of units double, only the last unit produced has a cost of 85% of the initial cost. In the cumulative average-time learning model, doubling the number of units causes the average cost of *all* the additional units produced (not just the last unit) to be 85% of the initial cost.

Nautilus should examine its own internal records on past jobs and seek information from engineers, plant managers, and workers when deciding which learning curve better describes the behavior of direct manufacturing labor-hours on the production of the PT109 boats.

10-36 (30 min.) Evaluating multiple regression models, nonprofit (continuation of Problem 10-35).

1. It is economically plausible that the correct form of the model of overhead costs includes both number of academic programs and number of enrolled students as cost drivers. The findings in Problem 10-35 indicate that each of the independent variables affects overhead costs. (Each regression has a significant r^2 and t-value on the independent variable.) Hanks could choose to divide overhead costs into two cost pools, (i) those overhead costs that are more closely related to number of academic program and (ii) those overhead costs more closely related to number of enrolled students, and rerun the simple regression analysis on each overhead cost pool. Alternatively, Hanks could run a multiple regression analysis with total overhead costs as the dependent variable and the number of academic programs and number of enrolled students as the two independent variables.

2. Solution Exhibit 10-36 evaluates the multiple regression model using the format of Exhibit 10-19. Hanks should use the multiple regression model over the two simple regression models of Problem 10-35. The multiple regression model appears economically plausible, and the regression model performs very well when estimating overhead costs. It has an excellent goodness of fit, significant t-values on both independent variables, and meets all the specification assumptions for ordinary least-squares regression.

There is some correlation between the two independent variables but multicollinearity does not appear to be a problem here. The significance of both independent variables (despite some correlation between them) suggests that each variable is a driver of overhead cost. Of course, as the chapter describes, even if the independent variables exhibited multicollinearity, Hanks should still prefer to use the multiple regression model over the simple regression models of Problem 10-35. Omitting any one of the variables will cause the estimated coefficient of the independent variable, included in the model, to be biased away from its true value.

3. Possible uses for the multiple regression results include:

    a. Planning and budgeting at Southwestern University. The regression analysis indicates the variables (number of academic programs and number of enrolled students) that help predict changes in overhead costs.

    b. Cost control and performance evaluation. Hanks could compare actual performance with budgeted or expected numbers and seek ways to improve the efficiency of the University operations, and evaluate the performance of managers responsible for controlling overhead costs.

    c. Cost management. If cost pressures increase, the University might save costs by closing down academic programs that have few students enrolled.

SOLUTION EXHIBIT 10-36

Evaluation of Cost Function for Overhead Costs Estimated with Multiple Regression for Southwestern University

Criterion	Number of Academic Programs and Number of Enrolled Students as Independent Variables
1. Economic Plausibility	A positive relationship between overhead costs and number of academic programs and number of enrolled students is economically plausible at Southwestern University.
2. Goodness of Fit	$r^2 = 0.81$. Excellent goodness of fit.
3. Significance of Independent Variable(s)	t-values of 3.46 on number of academic programs and 2.03 on number of enrolled students are both significant.
4. Specification Analysis of Estimation Assumptions	The assumptions of linearity, constant variance, and normality of residuals hold, but inferences drawn from only 12 observations are not reliable; the Durbin-Watson statistic = 1.84 indicates that independence of residuals holds.

10-38 (30–40 min.)   **Purchasing Department cost drivers, multiple regression analysis (Continuation of 10-37).**

The problem reports the exact *t*-values from the computer runs of the data. Because the coefficients and standard errors given in the problem are rounded to three decimal places, dividing the coefficient by the standard error may yield slightly different *t*-values.

1.   Regression 4 is a well-specified regression model:

Economic plausibility: Both independent variables are plausible and are supported by the findings of the Couture Fabrics study.

Goodness of fit: The r^2 of 0.63 indicates an excellent goodness of fit.

Significance of independent variables: The *t*-value on # of POs is 2.14 while the *t*-value on # of Ss is 2.00. These *t*-values are either significant or border on significance.

Specification analysis: Results are available to examine the independence of residuals assumption. The Durbin-Watson statistic of 1.90 indicates that the assumption of independence is not rejected.

Regression 4 is consistent with the findings in Problem 10-37 that both the number of purchase orders and the number of suppliers are drivers of purchasing department costs. Regressions 2, 3, and 4 all satisfy the four criteria outlined in the text. Regression 4 has the best goodness of fit (0.63 for Regression 4 compared to 0.42 and 0.39 for Regressions 2 and 3, respectively). Most importantly, it is economically plausible that both the number of purchase orders and the number of suppliers drive purchasing department costs. We would recommend that Lee use Regression 4 over Regressions 2 and 3.

2.   Regression 5 adds an additional independent variable (MP$) to the two independent variables in Regression 4. This additional variable (MP$) has a *t*-value of –0.07, implying its slope coefficient is insignificantly different from zero. The r^2 in Regression 5 (0.63) is the same as that in Regression 4 (0.63), implying the addition of this third independent variable adds close to zero explanatory power. In summary, Regression 5 adds very little to Regression 4. We would recommend that Lee use Regression 4 over Regression 5.

3.   Budgeted purchasing department costs for the Baltimore store next year are:

$$\$485,384 + (\$123.22 \times 3,900) + (\$2,952 \times 110) = \$1,290,662$$

4.   Multicollinearity is a frequently encountered problem in cost accounting; it does not arise in simple regression because there is only one independent variable in a simple regression. One consequence of multicollinearity is an increase in the standard errors of the coefficients of the individual variables. This frequently shows up in reduced *t*-values for the independent variables in the multiple regression relative to their *t*-values in the simple regression:

Variables	*t*-value in Multiple Regression	*t*-value from Simple Regressions in Problem 10-37
Regression 4:		
# of POs	2.14	2.43
# of Ss	2.00	2.28
Regression 5:		
# of POs	1.95	2.43
# of Ss	1.84	2.28
MP$	−0.07	0.84

The decline in the *t*-values in the multiple regressions is consistent with some (but not very high) collinearity among the independent variables. Pairwise correlations between the independent variables are:

	Correlation
# of POs / # of Ss	0.29
# of POs / MP$	0.27
# of Ss / MP$	0.34

There is no evidence of difficulties due to multicollinearity in Regressions 4 and 5.

5.   Decisions in which the regression results in Problems 10-37 and 10-38 could be useful are:

Cost management decisions: Fashion Flair could restructure relationships with the suppliers so that fewer separate purchase orders are made. Alternatively, it may aggressively reduce the number of existing suppliers.

Purchasing policy decisions: Fashion Flair could set up an internal charge system for individual retail departments within each store. Separate charges to each department could be made for each purchase order and each new supplier added to the existing ones. These internal charges would signal to each department ways in which their own decisions affect the total costs of Fashion Flair.

Accounting system design decisions: Fashion Flair may want to discontinue allocating purchasing department costs on the basis of the dollar value of merchandise purchased. Allocation bases better capturing cause-and-effect relations at Fashion Flair are the number of purchase orders and the number of suppliers.

10-40 (40 min.) **High-low method, alternative regression functions, accrual accounting adjustments.**

1. Solution Exhibit 10-40A presents the two data plots. The plot of engineering support reported costs and machine-hours shows two separate groups of data, each of which may be approximated by a separate cost function. The problem arises because the plant records materials and parts costs on an "as purchased," rather than an "as used," basis. The plot of engineering support restated costs and machine-hours shows a high positive correlation between the two variables (the coefficient of determination is 0.94); a single linear cost function provides a good fit to the data. Better estimates of the cost relation result because Kennedy adjusts the materials and parts costs to an accrual accounting basis.

2.

	Cost Driver Machine-Hours	Reported Engineering Support Costs
Highest observation of cost driver (August)	73	$ 617
Lowest observation of cost driver (September)	19	1,066
Difference	54	$ (449)

$$\text{Slope coefficient, } b = \frac{\text{Difference between costs associated with highest and lowest observations of the cost driver}}{\text{Difference between highest and lowest observations of the cost driver}}$$

$$= \frac{-\$449}{54} = -\$8.31 \text{ per machine-hour}$$

Constant (at highest observation of cost driver) $= \$ 617 - (-\$8.31 \times 73) = \$1,224$
Constant (at lowest observation of cost driver) $= \$1,066 - (-\$8.31 \times 19) = \$1,224$

The estimated cost function is $y = \$1,224 - \$8.31X$

	Cost Driver Machine-Hours	Restated Engineering Support Costs
Highest observation of cost driver (August)	73	$966
Lowest observation of cost driver (September)	19	370
Difference	54	$596

$$\text{Slope coefficient, } b = \frac{\text{Difference between costs associated with highest and lowest observations of the cost driver}}{\text{Difference between highest and lowest observations of the cost driver}}$$

$$= \frac{\$596}{54} = \$11.04 \text{ per machine-hour}$$

10-40 (Cont'd.)

Constant (at highest observation of cost driver) = $\$ \ 966 - (\$11.04 \times 73) = \$160$
Constant (at lowest observation of cost driver) = $\$ \ 370 - (\$11.04 \times 19) = \$160$

The estimated cost function is $y = \$160 + \$11.04 \ X$

3. The cost function estimated with engineering support restated costs better approximates the regression analysis assumptions. See Solution Exhibit 10-40B for a comparison of the two regressions.

4. Of all the cost functions estimated in requirements 2 and 3, Kennedy should choose Regression 2 using engineering support restated costs as best representing the relationship between engineering support costs and machine-hours. The cost functions estimated using engineering support reported costs are mis-specified and not-economically plausible because materials and parts costs are reported on an "as-purchased," rather than on an "as-used," basis. With respect to engineering support restated costs, the high-low and regression approaches yield roughly similar estimates. The regression approach is technically superior because it determines the line that best fits all observations. In contrast, the high-low method considers only two points (observations with the highest and lowest cost drivers) when estimating the cost function. Solution Exhibit 10-40B shows that the cost function estimated using the regression approach has excellent goodness of fit ($r^2 = 0.94$) and appears to be well specified.

5. Problems Kennedy might encounter include:
    a. A perpetual inventory system may not be used in this case; the amounts requisitioned likely will not permit an accurate matching of costs with the independent variable on a month-by-month basis.
    b. Quality of the source records for usage by engineers may be relatively low; e.g., engineers may requisition materials and parts in batches, but not use them immediately.
    c. Records may not distinguish materials and parts for maintenance from materials and parts used for repairs and breakdowns; separate cost functions may be appropriate for the two categories of materials and parts.
    d. Year-end accounting adjustments to inventory may mask errors that gradually accumulate month-by-month.

6. Picking the correct cost function is important for cost prediction, cost management, and performance evaluation. For example, had United Packaging used Regression 1 (engineering support reported costs) to estimate the cost function, it would erroneously conclude that engineering support costs decrease with machine-hours. In a month with 60 machine-hours, Regression 1 would predict costs of $\$1,393.20 - (\$14.23 \times 60) = \$539.40$. If actual costs turn out to be $800, management would conclude that changes should be made to reduce costs. In fact, on the basis of the preferred Regression 2, support overhead costs are lower than the predicted amount of $\$176.38 + (\$11.44 \times 60) = \$862.78$—a performance that management should seek to replicate, not change.

10-40 (Cont'd.)

On the other hand, if machine-hours worked in a month were low, say 25 hours, Regression 1 would erroneously predict support overhead costs of $1,393.20 – ($14.23 × 25) = $1,037.45. If actual costs are $700, management would conclude that its performance has been very good. In fact, compared to the costs predicted by the preferred Regression 2 of $176.38 + ($11.44 × 25) = $462.38, the actual performance is rather poor. Using Regression 1, management may feel costs are being managed very well when in fact they are much higher than what they should be and need to be managed "down."

SOLUTION EXHIBIT 10-40A
Plots and Regression Lines for Engineering Support
Reported Costs and Engineering Support Restated Costs

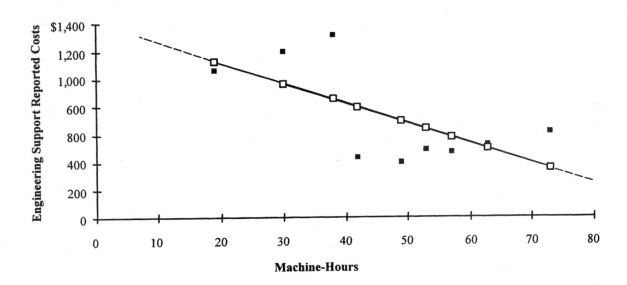

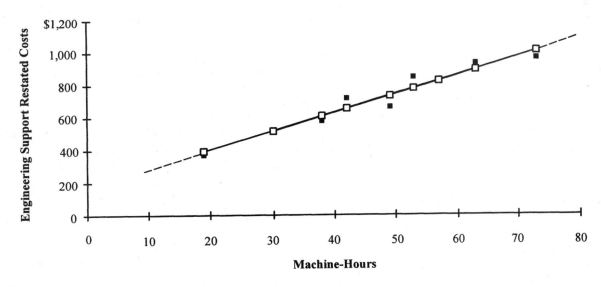

10-40 (Cont'd.)

SOLUTION EXHIBIT 10-40B
Comparison of Alternative Cost Functions for Engineering Support Costs at United Packaging

CRITERION	Regression 1 Dependent Variable: Engineering Support Reported Costs	Regression 2 Dependent Variable: Engineering Support Restated Costs
1. Economic Plausibility	Negative slope relationship is economically implausible over the long run.	Positive slope relationship is economically plausible.
2. Goodness of Fit	$r^2 = 0.43$. Moderate goodness of fit.	$r^2 = 0.94$. Excellent goodness of fit.
3. Significance of Independent Variables	t-statistic on machine-hours is statistically significant ($t = -2.31$), albeit economically implausible.	t-statistic on machine-hours is highly statistically significant ($t=10.59$).
4. Specification Analysis:		
A. Linearity	Linearity does not describe data very well.	Linearity describes data very well.
B. Constant variance of residuals	Appears questionable, although 12 observations do not facilitate the drawing of reliable inferences.	Appears reasonable, although 12 observations do not facilitate the drawing of reliable inferences.
C. Independence of residuals	Durbin-Watson = 2.26. Residuals serially uncorrelated.	Durbin-Watson = 1.31. Some evidence of serial correlation in the residuals.
D. Normality of residuals	Database too small to make reliable inferences.	Database too small to make reliable inferences.

CHAPTER 11
DECISION MAKING AND RELEVANT INFORMATION

11-2 Relevant costs are expected future costs that differ among the alternative courses of action being considered. Historical costs are irrelevant because they are past costs and, therefore, cannot differ among alternative future courses of action.

11-4 Quantitative factors are outcomes that are measured in numerical terms. Some quantitative factors are financial—that is, they can be easily expressed in monetary terms. Direct materials is an example of a quantitative financial factor. Qualitative factors are outcomes that are difficult to measure accurately in numerical terms. An example is employee morale.

11-6 No. Some variable costs may not differ among the alternatives under consideration and, hence, will be irrelevant. Some fixed costs may differ among the alternatives and, hence, will be relevant.

11-8 Opportunity cost is the contribution to income that is forgone (rejected) by not using a limited resource in its next-best alternative use.

11-10 No. Managers should aim to get the highest contribution margin per unit of the constraining (that is, scarce, limiting, or critical) factor. The constraining factor is what restricts or limits the production or sale of a given product (for example, availability of machine-hours).

11-12 Cost written off as depreciation is irrelevant when it pertains to a past cost. But the purchase cost of new equipment to be acquired in the future that will then be written off as depreciation is often relevant.

11-14 The three steps in solving a linear programming problem are:
1. Determine the objective function.
2. Specify the constraints.
3. Compute the optimal solution.

11-16 (20 min.) **Disposal of assets.**

1. This is an unfortunate situation, yet the $80,000 costs are irrelevant regarding the decision to remachine or scrap. The only relevant factors are the future revenues and future costs. By ignoring the accumulated costs and deciding on the basis of expected future costs, operating income will be maximized (or losses minimized). The difference in favor of remachining is $3,000:

	(a) Remachine	(b) Scrap
Future revenues	$35,000	$2,000
Deduct future costs	30,000	–
Operating income	$ 5,000	$2,000
	↑ $3,000 ↑	
Difference in favor of remachining		

2.   This, too, is an unfortunate situation. But the $100,000 original cost is irrelevant to this decision. The difference in relevant costs in favor of rebuilding is $7,000 as follows:

	(a) Replace	(b) Rebuild
New truck	$102,000	–
Deduct current disposal price of existing truck	10,000	–
Rebuild existing truck	–	$85,000
	$ 92,000	$85,000

Difference in favor of rebuilding $7,000

Note, here, that the current disposal price of $10,000 is relevant, but the original cost (or book value, if the truck were not brand new) is irrelevant.

11-18 (15 min.) **Multiple choice.**

1. (b)

Special order price per unit	$6.00
Variable manufacturing cost per unit	4.50
Contribution margin per unit	$1.50

Effect on operating income   = $1.50 × 20,000 units
                                             = $30,000 increase

2. (b)

Costs of purchases, 20,000 units × $60		$1,200,000
Total relevant costs of making:		
Variable manufacturing costs, $64 – $16	$48	
Fixed costs eliminated	9	
Costs saved by not making	$57	
Multiply by 20,000 units, so total costs saved are $57 × 20,000		1,140,000
Extra costs of purchasing outside		60,000
Minimum overall savings for Reno		25,000
Necessary relevant costs that would have to be saved in manufacturing Part No. 575		$ 85,000

11-20 (30 min.) Make versus buy, activity-based costing.

1. The expected manufacturing cost per unit of CMCBs in 2004 is as follows:

	Total Manufacturing Costs of CMCB (1)	Manufacturing Cost per Unit (2) = (1) ÷ 10,000
Direct materials, $170 × 10,000	$1,700,000	$170
Direct manufacturing labor, $45 × 10,000	450,000	45
Variable batch manufacturing costs, $1,500 × 80	120,000	12
Fixed manufacturing costs		
Avoidable fixed manufacturing costs	320,000	32
Unavoidable fixed manufacturing costs	800,000	80
Total manufacturing costs	$3,390,000	$339

2. The following table identifies the incremental costs in 2004 if Svenson (a) made CMCBs and (b) purchased CMCBs from Minton.

Incremental Items	Total Incremental Costs Make	Total Incremental Costs Buy	Per-Unit Incremental Costs Make	Per-Unit Incremental Costs Buy
Cost of purchasing CMCBs from Minton		$ 3,000,000		$300
Direct materials	$1,700,000		$170	
Direct manufacturing labor	450,000		45	
Variable batch manufacturing costs	120,000		12	
Avoidable fixed manufacturing costs	320,000		32	
Total incremental costs	$2,590,000	$3,000,000	$259	$300
Difference in favor of making	↑ $410,000 ↑		↑ $41 ↑	

Note that the opportunity cost of using capacity to make CMCBs is zero since Svenson would keep this capacity idle if it purchases CMCBs from Minton.

Svenson should continue to manufacture the CMCBs internally since the incremental costs to manufacture are $259 per unit compared to the $300 per unit that Minton has quoted. Note that the unavoidable fixed manufacturing costs of $800,000 ($80 per unit) will continue to be incurred whether Svenson makes or buys CMCBs. These are not incremental costs under either the make or the buy alternative and are, hence, irrelevant.

3. Svenson should continue to make CMCBs. The simplest way to analyze this problem is to recognize that Svenson would prefer to keep any excess capacity idle rather than use it to make CB3s. Why? Because expected incremental future revenues from CB3s, $2,000,000 are *less* than expected incremental future costs, $2,150,000. If Svenson keeps its capacity idle, we know from requirement 2 that it should make CMCBs rather than buy them.

11-20 (Cont'd.)

An important point to note is that, because Svenson forgoes no contribution by not being able to make and sell CB3s, the opportunity cost of using its facilities to make CMCBs is zero. It is, therefore, not forgoing any profits by using the capacity to manufacture CMCBs. If it does not manufacture CMCBs, rather than lose money on CB3s, Svenson will keep capacity idle.

A longer and more detailed approach is to use the total alternatives or opportunity cost analyses shown in Exhibit 11-7 of the chapter.

	Choices for Svenson		
Relevant Items	Make CMCBs and Do Not Make CB3s	Buy CMCBs and Do Not Make CB3s	Buy CMCBs and Make CB3s
TOTAL-ALTERNATIVES APPROACH TO MAKE-OR-BUY DECISIONS			
Total incremental costs of making/buying CMCBs (from requirement 2)	$2,590,000	$3,000,000	$3,000,000
Excess of future costs over future revenues from CB3s	0	0	150,000
Total relevant costs	$2,590,000	$3,000,000	$3,150,000

Svenson will minimize manufacturing costs by making CMCBs.

OPPORTUNITY-COST APPROACH TO MAKE-OR-BUY DECISIONS			
Total incremental costs of making/buying CMCBs (from requirement 2)	$2,590,000	$3,000,000	$3,000,000
Opportunity cost: profit contribution forgone because capacity will not be used to make CB3s	0*	0*	0
Total relevant costs	$2,590,000	$3,000,000	$3,000,000

*Opportunity cost is 0 because Svenson does not give up anything by not making CB3s. Svenson is best off leaving the capacity idle (rather than manufacturing and selling CB3s).

11-22 (20–25 min.) **Relevant costs, contribution margin, product emphasis.**

1.

	Cola	Lemonade	Punch	Natural Orange Juice
Selling price	$18.00	$19.20	$26.40	$38.40
Deduct variable cost per case	13.50	15.20	20.10	30.20
Contribution margin per case	$ 4.50	$ 4.00	$ 6.30	$ 8.20

2.   The argument fails to recognize that shelf space is the constraining factor. There are only 12 feet of front shelf space to be devoted to drinks. Sexton should aim to get the highest daily contribution margin per foot of front shelf space:

	Cola	Lemonade	Punch	Natural Orange Juice
Contribution margin per case	$ 4.50	$ 4.00	$ 6.30	$ 8.20
Sales (number of cases) per foot of shelf space per day	× 25	× 24	× 4	× 5
Daily contribution per foot of front shelf space	$112.50	$96.00	$25.20	$41.00

3.   The allocation that maximizes the daily contribution from soft drink sales is:

	Feet of Shelf Space	Daily Contribution per Foot of Front Shelf Space	Total Contribution Margin per Day
Cola	6	$112.50	$ 675.00
Lemonade	4	96.00	384.00
Natural Orange Juice	1	41.00	41.00
Punch	1	25.20	25.20
			$1,125.20

The maximum of six feet of front shelf space will be devoted to Cola because it has the highest contribution margin per unit of the constraining factor. Four feet of front shelf space will be devoted to Lemonade, which has the second highest contribution margin per unit of the constraining factor. No more shelf space can be devoted to Lemonade since each of the remaining two products, Natural Orange Juice and Punch (that have the second lowest and lowest contribution margins per unit of the constraining factor) must each be given at least one foot of front shelf space.

11-24 (20 min.) **Which base to close, relevant-cost analysis, opportunity costs.**

The future outlay operating costs will be $400 million regardless of which base is closed, given the additional $100 million in costs at Everett if Alameda is closed. Further, one of the bases will permanently remain open while the other will be shut down. The only relevant revenue and cost comparisons are:

a. $500 million from sale of the Alameda base. Note that the historical cost of building the Alameda base ($100 million) is irrelevant. Note, also, that future increases in the value of the land at the Alameda base is also irrelevant. One of the bases must be kept open, so if it is decided to keep the Alameda base open, the Defense Department will not be able to sell this land at a future date.

b. $60 million in savings in fixed income note if the Everett base is closed. Again, the historical cost of building the Everett base ($150 million) is irrelevant.

The relevant costs and benefits analysis favors closing the Alameda base despite the objections raised by the California delegation in Congress. The net benefit equals $440 ($500 – $60) million.

11-26 (20 min.) **Choosing customers.**

If Broadway accepts the additional business from Kelly, it would take an additional 500 machine-hours. If Broadway accepts all of Kelly's and Taylor's business for February, it would require 2,500 machine-hours (1,500 hours for Taylor and 1,000 hours for Kelly). Broadway has only 2,000 hours of machine capacity. It must, therefore, choose how much of the Taylor or Kelly business to accept.

To maximize operating income, Broadway should maximize contribution margin per unit of the constrained resource. (Fixed costs will remain unchanged at $100,000 regardless of the business Broadway chooses to accept in February, and is, therefore, irrelevant.) The contribution margin per unit of the constrained resource for each customer in January is:

	Taylor Corporation	Kelly Corporation
Contribution margin per machine-hour	$\dfrac{\$78,000}{1,500} = \$52$	$\dfrac{\$32,000}{500} = \$64$

Since the $80,000 of additional Kelly business in February is identical to jobs done in January, it will also have a contribution margin of $64 per machine-hour, which is greater than the contribution margin of $52 per machine-hour from Taylor. To maximize operating income, Broadway should first allocate all the capacity needed to take the Kelly Corporation business (1,000 machine-hours) and then allocate the remaining 1,000 (2,000 – 1,000) machine-hours to Taylor.

	Taylor Corporation	Kelly Corporation	Total
Contribution margin per machine-hour	$52	$64	
Machine-hours to be worked	× 1,000	× 1,000	
Contribution margin	$52,000	$64,000	$116,000
Fixed costs			100,000
Operating income			$ 16,000

11-28 (30 min.) **Equipment upgrade versus replacement** (A. Spero, adapted).

1. Solution Exhibit 11-28 presents a cost comparison of the upgrade and replacement alternatives for the three years taken together. It indicates that Pacifica Corporation should replace the production line because it is better off by $180,000 by replacing rather than upgrading.

SOLUTION EXHIBIT 11-28
Comparing Upgrade and Replace Alternatives

	Three Years Together		
	Upgrade (1)	Replace (2)	Difference (3) = (1) – (2)
Cash-operating costs, $12; $9 × 180,000	$2,160,000	$1,620,000	$ 540,000
Current disposal price		(90,000)	90,000
One-time capital costs, written off periodically as depreciation	300,000	750,000	(450,000)
Total relevant costs	$2,460,000	$2,280,000	$ 180,000

Note that sales and book value of the existing machine are the same under both alternatives and, hence, are irrelevant.

2a. Suppose the capital expenditure to replace the production line is $X. Using data from Solution Exhibit 11-28, the cost of replacing the production line is equal to $1,620,000 – $90,000 + $X. Using data from Solution Exhibit 11-28, the cost of upgrading the production line is equal to $2,160,000 + $300,000 = $2,460,000. We want to find $X such that

$$\$1,620,000 - \$90,000 + \$X = \$2,460,000$$
that is, $\qquad \$1,530,000 + \$X = \$2,460,000$
that is, $\qquad \$X = \$2,460,000 - \$1,530,000$
or $\qquad \$X = \$ 930,000$

Pacifica would prefer replacing, rather than upgrading, the existing line if the replacement cost of the new line does not exceed $930,000. Note that the $930,000 can also be obtained by adding the $180,000 calculated in requirement 1 to the replacement cost of $750,000 for the new machine assumed in requirement 1 ($750,000 + $180,000 = $930,000).

2b. Suppose the units produced and sold each year equal y. Using data from Solution Exhibit 11-28, the cost of replacing the production line is $9y – $90,000 + $750,000, while the cost of upgrading is $12y + $300,000. We solve for the y at which the two costs are the same.

$$\$9y - \$90,000 + \$750,000 = \$12y + \$300,000$$
$$\$9y + \$660,000 = \$12y + \$300,000$$
$$\$3y = \$360,000$$
$$y = 120,000 \text{ units}$$

For expected production and sales of less than 120,000 units over 3 years (40,000 units per year), the upgrade alternative is cheaper. When production and sales are low, the higher operating costs of upgrading are more than offset by the significant savings in capital costs when upgrading relative to replacing. For expected production and sales exceeding 120,000 units over 3 years, the replace alternative is cheaper. For high output, the benefits of the lower operating costs of replacing, relative to upgrading, exceed the higher capital costs.

11-28 (Cont'd.)

3. Operating income for the first year under the upgrade and replace alternatives are as follows:

	Upgrade	Replace
Revenues $25 × 60,000	$1,500,000	$1,500,000
Cash-operating costs $12 × 60,000, $9 × 60,000	720,000	540,000
Depreciation	220,000[a]	250,000[b]
Loss on disposal of old production line	—	270,000[c]
Total costs	940,000	1,060,000
Operating income	$ 560,000	$ 440,000

[a]($360,000 + $300,000) ÷ 3 = $220,000   [b]$750,000 ÷ 3 = $250,000
[c]Book value – current disposal price = $360,000 – $90,000 = $270,000

First-year operating income is higher by $120,000 under the upgrade alternative. If first year's operating income is an important component of Azinger's bonus, he would prefer the upgrade over the replace alternative even though the decision model (in requirement 1) prefers the replace to the upgrade alternative. This exercise illustrates the conflict between the decision model and the performance evaluation model.

11-30 (30 min.) Relevant costs, opportunity costs.

1. Easyspread 2.0 has a higher relevant operating income than Easyspread 1.0. Based on this analysis, Easyspread 2.0 should be introduced immediately:

	Easyspread 1.0	Easyspread 2.0
Relevant revenues	$150	$185
Relevant costs:		
Manuals, diskettes, compact discs	$ 0	$25
Total relevant costs	0	25
Relevant operating income	$150	$160

Reasons for other cost items being irrelevant are:
Easyspread 1.0
• Manuals, diskettes—already incurred
• Development costs—already incurred
• Marketing and administrative—fixed costs of period
Easyspread 2.0
• Development costs—already incurred
• Marketing and administration—fixed costs of period
Note that total marketing and administration costs will not change whether Easyspread 2.0 is introduced on July 1, 2003, or on October 1, 2003.

2. Other factors to be considered:
   a. Customer satisfaction. If 2.0 is significantly better than 1.0 for its customers, a customer driven organization would immediately introduce it unless other factors offset this bias towards "do what is best for the customer."
   b. Quality level of Easyspread 2.0. It is critical for new software products to be fully debugged. Easyspread 2.0 must be error-free. Consider an immediate release only if 2.0 passes all quality tests and can be fully supported by the salesforce.

11-30 (Cont'd.)

c. Importance of being perceived to be a market leader. Being first in the market with a new product can give Basil Software a "first-mover advantage," e.g., capturing an initial large share of the market that, in itself, causes future potential customers to lean towards purchasing Easyspread 2.0. Moreover, by introducing 2.0 earlier, Basil can get quick feedback from users about ways to further refine the software while its competitors are still working on their own first versions. Moreover, by locking in early customers, Basil may increase the likelihood of these customers also buying future upgrades of Easyspread 2.0.

d. Morale of developers. These are key people at Basil Software. Delaying introduction of a new product can hurt their morale, especially if a competitor then preempts Basil from being viewed as a market leader.

11-32   (30-40 min.)   **Product mix, relevant costs** (N. Melumad, adapted).

	R3	HP6
Selling price	$100	$150
Variable manufacturing cost per unit	60	100
Variable marketing cost per unit	15	35
Total variable costs per unit	75	135
Contribution margin per unit	$ 25	$ 15
Contribution margin per hour of the constrained resource (the regular machine)	$\dfrac{\$25}{1}=\$25$	$\dfrac{\$15}{0.5}=\$30$
Total contribution margin from selling only R3 or only HP6 R3: $25 × 50,000; HP6: $30 × 50,000	$1,250,000	$1,500,000
Less Lease costs of high-precision machine to produce and sell HP6	–	300,000
Net relevant benefit	$1,250,000	$1,200,000

Even though HP6 has the higher contribution margin per unit of the constrained resource, the fact that Pendleton must incur additional costs of $300,000 to achieve this higher contribution margin means that Pendleton is better off using its entire 50,000-hour capacity on the regular machine to produce and sell 50,000 units (50,000 hours ÷ 1 hour per unit) of R3. The additional contribution from selling HP6 rather than R3 is $250,000 ($1,500,000 – $1,250,000), which is not enough to cover the additional costs of leasing the high-precision machine. Note that, all other overhead costs are fixed and cannot be changed; they are irrelevant for the decision.

2.   If capacity of the regular machines is increased by 15,000 machine-hours to 65,000 machine-hours (50,000 originally + 15,000 new), the net relevant benefit from producing R3 and HP6 is as follows:

	R3	HP6
Total contribution margin from selling only R3 or only HP6 R3: $25 × 65,000; HP6: $30 × 65,000	$1,625,000	$1,950,000
Less Lease costs of high-precision machine that would be incurred if HP6 is produced and sold	—	300,000
Less Cost of increasing capacity by 15,000 hours on regular machine	150,000	150,000
Net relevant benefit	$1,475,000	$1,500,000

Investing in the additional capacity increases Pendleton's operating income by $250,000 ($1,500,000 calculated in requirement 2 *minus* $1,250,000 calculated in requirement 1), so Pendleton should add 15,000 hours to the regular machine. With the extra capacity available to it, Pendleton should use its entire capacity to produce HP6. Using all 65,000 hours of capacity to produce HP6 rather than to produce R3 generates additional contribution margin of $325,000 ($1,950,000 – $1,625,000) which is more than the additional cost of $300,000 to lease the high-precision machine. Pendleton should therefore produce and sell 130,000 units of HP6 (65,000 hours ÷ 0.5 hours per unit of HP6) and zero units of R3.

3.

	R3	HP6	S3
Selling price	$100	$150	$120
Variable manufacturing costs per unit	60	100	70
Variable marketing costs per unit	15	35	15
Total variable costs per unit	75	135	85
Contribution margin per unit	$ 25	$ 15	$ 35
Contribution margin per hour of the constrained resource (the regular machine)	$\frac{\$25}{1}=\$25$	$\frac{\$15}{0.5}=\$30$	$\frac{\$35}{1}=\$35$

The first step is to compare the operating profits that Pendleton could earn if it accepted the Carter Corporation offer for 20,000 units with the operating profits Pendleton is currently earning. S3 has the highest contribution margin per hour on the regular machine and requires no additional investment such as leasing a high-precision machine. To produce the 20,000 units of S3 requested by Carter Corporation, Pendleton would require 20,000 hours on the regular machine resulting in contribution margin of $35 × 20,000 = $700,000.

Pendleton now has 45,000 hours available on the regular machine to produce R3 or HP6.

	R3	HP6
Total contribution margin from selling only R3 or only HP6 R3: $25 × 45,000; HP6: $30 × 45,000	$1,125,000	$1,350,000
Less Lease costs of high-precision machine to produce and sell HP 6	–	300,000
Net relevant benefit	$1,125,000	$1,050,000

Pendleton should use all the 45,000 hours of available capacity to produce 45,000 units of R3. Thus, the product mix that maximizes operating income is 20,000 units of S3, 45,000 units of R3, and zero units of HP6. This optimal mix results in a contribution margin of $1,825,000 ($700,000 from S3 and $1,125,000 from R3). Relative to requirement 2, operating income increases by $325,000 ($1,825,000 minus $1,500,000 calculated in requirement 2). Hence, Pendleton should accept the Carter Corporation business and supply 20,000 units of S3.

11-34 (30 min.) **Discontinuing or adding another division (continuation of 11-33).**

1.   Solution Exhibit 11-34, Column 1, presents the relevant loss of revenues and the relevant savings in costs from closing the Northern Division. As the calculations show, Grossman's operating income would decrease by $140,000 if it shut down the Northern Division (loss in revenues of $1,500,000 versus savings in costs of $1,360,000).

Grossman will save variable manufacturing costs, marketing and distribution costs, and division general administration costs by closing the Northern Division but equipment-related depreciation and corporate office allocations are irrelevant to the decision. Equipment-related costs are irrelevant because they are past costs (and the equipment has zero disposal price). Corporate office costs are irrelevant because Grossman will not save any actual corporate office costs by closing the Northern Division. The corporate office costs that used to be allocated to the Northern Division will be allocated to other divisions.

2.   The manager at corporate headquarters responsible for making the decision is evaluated on Northern Division's operating income after allocating corporate office costs. The manager will evaluate the options as follows: If the manager does not close the Northern Division in 2002, the division is expected to show an operating loss of $110,000 after allocating all corporate office costs. If the manager closes the Northern Division, the division would show an operating loss of $100,000 from the write off of equipment. It would show no revenues and, hence, would not attract any corporate office costs. It would also not incur any manufacturing, marketing and distribution, and general administration costs.

From the viewpoint of maximizing the operating income against which the manager is evaluated, the manager would prefer to shut down Northern Division (and show an operating loss of $100,000 instead of an operating loss of $110,000 by operating it). In fact, the manager might argue that even the $100,000 operating loss is more a consequence of accounting write offs rather than a "real" operating loss.

Recall from requirement 1 that the decision model favored keeping the Northern Division open. The performance evaluation model of the manager making the decision suggests that the Northern Division be closed. Hence, the performance evaluation model is inconsistent with the decision model.

3.   Solution Exhibit 11-34, Column 2, presents the relevant revenues and relevant costs of opening the Southern Division (a division whose revenues and costs are expected to be identical to the revenues and costs of the Northern Division). Grossman should open the Southern Division because it would increase operating income by $40,000 (increase in relevant revenues of $1,500,000 and increase in relevant costs of $1,460,000). The relevant costs include direct materials, direct manufacturing labor, marketing and distribution, equipment, and division general administration costs but not corporate office costs. Note, in particular, that the cost of equipment written off as depreciation is relevant because it is an expected future cost that Grossman will incur only if it opens the Southern Division. Corporate office costs are irrelevant because actual corporate office costs will not change if Grossman opens the Southern Division. The current corporate staff will be able to oversee the Southern Division's operations. Grossman will allocate some corporate office costs to the Southern Division but this allocation represents corporate office costs that are already currently being allocated to some other division. Because actual total corporate office costs do not change, they are irrelevant to the division.

11-34 (Cont'd.)

SOLUTION EXHIBIT 11-34
Relevant-Revenue and Relevant-Cost Analysis for Closing Northern Division and Opening Southern Division

	(Loss in Revenues) and Savings in Costs from Closing Northern Division (1)	Incremental Revenues and (Incremental Costs) from Opening Southern Division (2)
Revenues	$(1,500,000)	$1,500,000
Variable direct materials and direct manufacturing labor costs	825,000	(825,000)
Equipment cost written off as depreciation	0	(100,000)
Marketing and distribution costs	205,000	(205,000)
Division general administration costs	330,000	(330,000)
Corporate office costs	0	0
Total costs	(1,360,000)	(1,460,000)
Effect on operating income (loss)	$ (140,000)	$ 40,000

11-36 (30 min.) **Make versus buy, activity-based costing, opportunity costs**
(N. Melumad and S. Reichelstein, adapted).

1. Relevant costs under buy alternative:

Purchases, 10,000 × $8.20	$82,000

Relevant costs under make alternative:

Direct materials	$40,000
Direct manufacturing labor	20,000
Variable manufacturing overhead	15,000
Inspection, setup, materials handling	2,000
Machine rent	3,000
Total relevant costs under make alternative	$80,000

The allocated fixed plant administration, taxes, and insurance will not change if Ace makes or buys the chains. Hence, these costs are irrelevant to the make-or-buy decision. The analysis indicates that Ace should not buy the chains from the outside supplier.

2. Relevant costs under the make alternative:

Relevant costs (as computed in requirement 1)	$80,000

Relevant costs under the buy alternative:

Costs of purchases (10,000 × $8.20)	$82,000
Additional fixed costs	16,000
Additional contribution margin from using the space where the chains were made to upgrade the bicycles by adding mud flaps and reflector bars, 10,000 × ($20 – $18)	(20,000)
Total relevant costs under the buy alternative	$78,000

Ace should now buy the chains from an outside vendor and use its own capacity to upgrade its own bicycles.

3. In this requirement, the decision on mud flaps and reflectors is irrelevant to the analysis.

Cost of manufacturing chains:

Variable costs, ($4 + $2 + $1.50 = $7.50) × 6,200	$46,500
Batch costs, $200/batch[a] × 8 batches	1,600
Machine rent	3,000
	$51,100

Cost of buying chains, $8.20 × 6,200	$50,840

[a]$2,000 ÷ 10 batches

In this case, Ace should buy the chains from the outside vendor.

11-38 (15 min.) **Make or buy (continuation of 11-37).**

The maximum price Class Company should be willing to pay is $3.9417 per unit.

Expected unit production and sales of new product must be half of the old product (1/2 × 240,000 = 120,000) because the fixed manufacturing overhead rate for the new product is twice that of the fixed manufacturing overhead rate for the old product.

| | | Proposed | | |
| | | Make New | Old | |
	Present	Product	Product	Total
Revenues	$1,440,000	$1,080,000	$1,440,000	$2,520,000
Variable (or purchase) costs:				
Manufacturing	720,000	600,000	946,000*	1,546,000
Marketing and other	360,000	240,000	288,000	528,000
Total variable costs	1,080,000	840,000	1,234,000	2,074,000
Contribution margin	360,000	240,000	206,000	446,000
Fixed costs:				
Manufacturing	120,000	120,000		120,000
Marketing and other	216,000	60,000	216,000	276,000
Total fixed costs	336,000	180,000	216,000	396,000
Operating income	$ 24,000	$ 60,000	$ (10,000)	$ 50,000

*This is an example of opportunity costs, whereby subcontracting at a price well above the $3.50 current manufacturing (absorption) cost is still desirable because the old product will be displaced in manufacturing by a new product that is more profitable.

Because the new product promises an operating income of $60,000 (ignoring the irrelevant problems of how fixed marketing costs may be newly reallocated between products), the old product can sustain up to a $10,000 loss and still help accomplish management's overall objectives. Maximum costs that can be incurred on the old product are $1,440,000 plus the $10,000 loss, or $1,450,000. Maximum purchase cost: $1,450,000 – ($288,000 + $216,000) = $946,000. Maximum purchase cost per unit: $946,000 ÷ 240,000 units = $3.9417 per unit.

Alternative Computation

Operating income is $9.00 – $8.50 = $0.50 per unit		
for 120,000 new units		$60,000
Target operating income		50,000
Maximum loss allowed on old product		$10,000
Maximum loss per unit allowed on old product,		
$10,000 ÷ 240,000 =		$0.0417
Selling price of old product		$6.0000
Allowance for loss		0.0417
Total costs allowed per unit		6.0417
Continuing costs for old product other than purchase cost:		
Fixed manufacturing costs—all transferred to new product	$ –	
Variable marketing costs	1.20	
Fixed marketing costs	0.90	2.1000
Maximum purchase cost per unit		$3.9417

11-40 (30–40 min.) **Optimal product mix.**

1. Let D represent the batches of Della's Delight made and sold.
    Let C represent the batches of Cathy's Chocolate Chips made and sold.
The contribution margin per batch for Della's Delight is $525 – $175 = $350.
The contribution margin per batch for Cathy's Chocolate Chip is $335 – $85 = $250.

The LP formulation for the decision is:

Maximize $350D + $250 C
Subject to   30D + 15C ≤ 600 (Mixing Department constraint)
             10D + 15C ≤ 300 (Baking Department constraint)
             20D   ≤ 320 (Dipping Department constraint)

2. Solution Exhibit 11-40 presents a graphical summary of the relationships. The optimal corner is the point (15,10), 15 Della's Delights and 10 Cathy's Chocolate Chips.

SOLUTION EXHIBIT 11-40
Graphic Solution to Find Optimal Mix, Della Simpson, Inc.

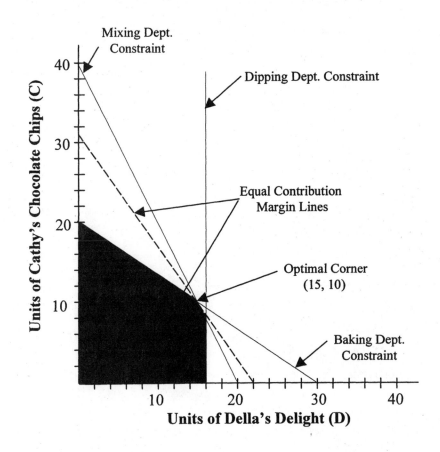

11-40 (Cont'd.)

We next calculate the optimal production mix using the trial-and-error method.

The corner point where the Mixing Dept. and Baking Dept. constraints meet can be calculated by solving:

$$30D + 15C = 600 \text{ (1) Mixing Dept. constraint}$$
$$10D + 15C = 300 \text{ (2) Baking Dept. constraint}$$

Substracting (2) from (1), we have

$$20D = 300$$
$$\text{or } D = 15$$

Substituting in (2)

$$10 \times 15 + 15C = 300$$
$$\text{that is,} \quad 15C = 300 - 150 = 150$$
$$\text{or} \quad C = 10$$

The corner point where the Mixing Dept. and Dipping Dept. constraints meet can be calculated by solving

$$30D + 15C = 600 \text{ (1) Mixing Dept. constraint}$$
$$20D = 320 \text{ (3) Dipping Dept. constraint}$$

From equation (3), $D = 320 \div 20 = 16$
Substituting in (1),

$$(30 \times 16) + 15C = 600$$
$$15C = 600 - 480 = 120$$
$$C = 8$$

We next use the trial-and-error method to check the contribution margins at each of the five corner points of the area of feasible solutions.

Trial	Corner (D,C)	Total Contribution Margin
1	(0,0)	($350 × 0) + ($250 × 0) = $0
2	(16,0)	($350 × 16) + ($250 × 0) = $5,600
3	(16,8)	($350 × 16) + ($250 × 8) = $7,600
4	(15,10)	($350 × 15) + ($250 × 10) = $7,750
5	(0,20)	($350 × 0) + ($250 × 20) = $5,000

The optimal solution that maximizes operating income is 15 Della's Delights and 10 Cathy's Chocolate Chips.

11-42 (40 min.) **Optimal product mix** (CMA, adapted).

In order to maximize OmniSport Inc.'s profitability, OmniSport should manufacture 12,000 snowboard bindings, manufacture 1,000 pairs of skates, and purchase 6,000 pairs of skates from Colcott Inc. This combination of manufactured and purchased goods maximizes the contribution margin per available machine-hour, which is the limiting resource.

Because snowboards have a higher contribution margin per machine-hour than in-line skates, OmniSport should manufacture the maximum number of snowboards. Because the contribution margin per manufactured pair of in-line skates is higher than the contribution margin from a purchased pair of in-line skates, total contribution margin will be maximized by using the remaining manufacturing capacity to produce in-line skates and then purchasing the remaining required skates. The calculations for the optimal combination follow:

	Purchased In-line Skates 6,000		Manufactured In-line Skates 1,000		Manufactured Snowboard Bindings 12,000		Total
	Per Unit	Total	Per Unit	Total	Per Unit	Total	
Selling price	$98	$588,000	$98	$98,000	$60	$720,000	$1,406,000
Variable costs							
Direct materials	75	450,000	20	20,000	20	240,000	710,000
Machine operating costs	–	–	24	24,000	8	96,000	120,000
Manufacturing overhead costs (1)	–	–	12	12,000	4	48,000	60,000
Markt. & admn. costs	4	24,000	9	9,000	8	96,000	129,000
Variable costs	79	474,000	65	65,000	40	480,000	1,019,000
Contribution margin	$19	$114,000	$33	$33,000	$20	$240,000	387,000
Fixed costs							
Manufacturing overhead							30,000
Marketing & administrative costs							60,000
Fixed costs							90,000
Operating income							$ 297,000
Machine-hours per unit	–		1.5		0.5		
Contribution per machine-hour	–		$22.0		$40.0		

Supporting calculations
(1) Manufacturing overhead

Manufactured in-line skates
Machine-hours	=	$24.00 per pair/$16.00 per hour = 1.5 hours per pair
Manufacturing capacity	=	5,000 pairs × 1.5 hours per pair = 7,500 hours
Overhead per machine-hour	=	$18.00 per pair/1.5 hours per pair = $12.00 per hour
Total overhead	=	7,500 hours × $12.00 per hour = $90,000
Total variable overhead	=	$90,000 (total) – $30,000 (fixed) = $60,000 (variable)
Variable overhead per machine-hour	=	$60,000/7,500 hours = $8.00 per hour
Fixed overhead per machine-hour	=	$30,000 fixed overhead/7,500 hours = $4.00 per hour
Variable overhead per pair of skates	=	1.5 hours × $8.00 per hour = $12.00 per pair
Fixed overhead per pair of skates	=	1.5 hours × $4.00 per hour = $6.00 per pair

Snowboard bindings
Machine-hours	=	$8 per board/$16.00 per hour = 0.5 hour per board
Variable overhead per snowboard	=	$8.00 per hour × 0.5 hour per board = $4.00 per board
Fixed overhead per snowboard	=	$4.00 per hour × 0.5 hour per board = $2.00 per board

11-42 (Cont'd.)

OmniSport Inc. Contribution Analysis

	Quantity (1)	Machine Hours per Unit (2)	Total Machine Hours Used (3) = (1) × (2)	Machine Hour Balance (4)	Unit Contribution (5)	Total Product Contribution (6) = (1) × (5)
Machine-hours available				7,500		
Snowboard bindings	12,000	0.5	6,000	1,500	$20	$240,000
In-line skates—manufacture	1,000	1.5	1,500	–	33	33,000
In-line skates—purchase	6,000	–	–	–	19	114,000
Total contribution						387,000
Less original contribution (5,000 pairs of skates × $33.00 per pair)						(165,000)
Improvement in contribution						$222,000

CHAPTER 12
PRICING DECISIONS AND COST MANAGEMENT

12-2 Not necessarily. For a one-time-only special order, the relevant costs are only those costs that will change as a result of accepting the order. In this case, full product costs will rarely be relevant. It is more likely that full product costs will be relevant costs for long-run pricing decisions.

12-4 Activity-based costing helps managers in pricing decisions in two ways.
1. It gives managers more accurate product-cost information for making pricing decisions.
2. It helps managers to manage costs during value engineering by identifying the cost impact of eliminating, reducing, or changing various activities.

12-6 A target cost per unit is the estimated long-run cost per unit of a product or service that enables the company to achieve its target operating income per unit when selling at the target price.

12-8 A value-added cost is a cost that customers perceive as adding value, or utility, to a product or service. Examples are costs of materials, direct labor, tools, and machinery. A nonvalue-added cost is a cost that customers do not perceive as adding value, or utility, to a product or service. Examples of nonvalue-added costs are costs of rework, scrap, expediting, and breakdown maintenance.

12-10 Cost-plus pricing is a pricing approach in which managers add a markup to cost in order to determine price.

12-12 Two examples where the difference in the costs of two products or services are much smaller than the differences in their prices follow:
1. The difference in prices charged for a telephone call, hotel room, or car rental during busy versus slack periods is often much greater than the difference in costs to provide these services.
2. The difference in costs for an airplane seat in coach class sold to a passenger traveling on business or a passenger traveling for pleasure is roughly the same. However, airline companies routinely charge business travelers—those who are likely to start and complete their travel during the same week excluding the weekend—a much higher price than pleasure travelers who generally stay at their destinations over at least one weekend.

12-14 Three benefits of using a product life-cycle reporting format are:
1. The full set of revenues and costs associated with each product becomes more visible.
2. Differences among products in the percentage of total costs committed at early stages in the life cycle are highlighted.
3. Interrelationships among business function cost categories are highlighted.

12-16 (20–30 min.) **Relevant-cost approach to pricing decisions, special order.**

1.

Relevant revenues, $3.80 × 1,000		$3,800
Relevant costs		
Direct materials, $1.50 × 1,000	$1,500	
Direct manufacturing labor, $0.80 × 1,000	800	
Variable manufacturing overhead, $0.70 × 1,000	700	
Variable selling costs, 0.05 × $3,800	190	
Total relevant costs		3,190
Increase in operating income		$ 610

This calculation assumes that:

a. The monthly fixed manufacturing overhead of $150,000 and monthly fixed marketing costs of $65,000 will be unchanged by acceptance of the 1,000 unit order.

b. The price charged and the volumes sold to other customers are not affected by the special order.

Chapter 12 uses the phrase "one-time-only special order" to describe this special case.

2. The president's reasoning is defective on at least two counts:

a. The inclusion of irrelevant costs—assuming the monthly fixed manufacturing overhead of $150,000 will be unchanged; it is irrelevant to the decision.

b. The exclusion of relevant costs—variable selling costs (5% of the selling price) are excluded when they should be included because they are relevant to the decision.

3. Key issues are:

a. Will the existing customer base demand price reductions? If this 1,000-tape order is not independent of other sales, reducing the price from $5.00 to $3.80 can have a large negative effect on total revenues.

b. Is the 1,000-tape order a one-time-only order, or is there the possibility of sales in subsequent months? The fact that the customer is not in Dill Company's "normal marketing channels" does not necessarily mean it is a one-time-only order. Indeed, the sale could well open a new marketing channel. Dill Company should be reluctant to consider only short-run variable costs for pricing long-run business.

12-18 (25 min.) **Short-run pricing, capacity constraints.**

1. With no constraints on availability of Pyrone or on plant capacity, Boutique would want to charge a minimum price for Seltium that would cover its incremental costs to manufacture Seltium. (Because there is excess capacity, there is no opportunity cost.) In this case, the incremental costs are the variable costs to manufacture a kilogram of Seltium:

Pyrone (2 kilograms × $4 per kilogram)	$ 8
Direct manufacturing labor	4
Variable manufacturing overhead costs	3
Total variable manufacturing costs	$15

Hence, the minimum price that Boutique should charge to manufacture Seltium is $15 per kilogram. For 3,000 kilograms of Seltium, it should charge a minimum of $45,000 ($15 × 3,000).

2. Now Pyrone is in short supply. Using it to make Seltium reduces the Bolzene that Boutique can make and sell. There is, therefore, an opportunity cost of manufacturing Seltium, the lost contribution from using the Pyrone to manufacture Bolzene. To make 3,000 kilograms of Seltium requires 6,000 (2 × 3,000) kilograms of Pyrone.

The 6,000 kilograms of Pyrone can be used to manufacture 4,000 (6,000 ÷ 1.5) kilograms of Bolzene, since each kilogram of Bolzene requires 1.5 kilograms of Pyrone.

The contribution margin from 4,000 kilograms of Bolzene is $24,000 ($6 per kilogram × 4,000 kilograms). This is the opportunity cost of using Pyrone to manufacture Seltium. The minimum price that Boutique should charge to manufacture Seltium should cover not only the incremental (variable) costs of manufacturing Seltium but also the opportunity cost:

	Costs of Manufacturing Seltium	
	Total for	
	3,000 Kilograms	**Per Kilogram**
Relevant Costs	**(1)**	**(2) = (1) ÷ 3,000**
Incremental (variable) costs of manufacturing Seltium	$45,000	$15
Opportunity cost of forgoing manufacture and sale of Bolzene	24,000	8
Minimum cost of order	$69,000	$23

For 3,000 kilograms of Seltium, Boutique should charge a minimum of $69,000. The minimum price per kilogram that Boutique should charge for Seltium is $23 per kilogram ($69,000 ÷ 3,000 kilograms).

12-20 (25–30 min.) **Target operating income, value-added costs, service company.**

1. The classification of total costs in 2004 into value-added, nonvalue-added, or in the gray area in between follows:

	Value Added (1)	Gray Area (2)	Nonvalue-added (3)	Total (4) = (1)+(2)+(3)
Doing calculations and preparing drawings 75% × $400,000	$300,000			$300,000
Checking calculations and drawings 4% × $400,000		$16,000		16,000
Correcting errors found in drawings 7% × $400,000			$28,000	28,000
Making changes in response to client requests 6% × $400,000	24,000			24,000
Correcting errors to meet government building code, 8% × $400,000			32,000	32,000
Total professional labor costs	324,000	16,000	60,000	400,000
Administrative and support costs at 40% ($160,000 ÷ $400,000) of professional labor costs	129,600	6,400	24,000	160,000
Travel	18,000	—	—	18,000
Total	$471,600	$22,400	$84,000	$578,000

Doing calculations and responding to client requests for changes are value-added costs because customers perceive these costs as necessary for the service of preparing architectural drawings. Costs incurred on correcting errors in drawings and making changes because they were inconsistent with building codes are nonvalue-added costs. Customers do not perceive these costs as necessary and would be unwilling to pay for them. Carasco should seek to eliminate these costs. Checking calculations and drawings is in the gray area (some, but not all, checking may be needed). There is room for disagreement on these classifications. For example, checking calculations may be regarded as value added.

2. Reduction in professional labor-hours by
   a. Correcting errors in drawings (7% × 8,000) — 560 hours
   b. Correcting errors to conform to building code (8% × 8,000) — 640 hours

   Total — 1,200 hours

   Cost savings in professional labor costs (1,200 hours × $50) — $ 60,000
   Cost savings in variable administrative and support costs (40% × $60,000) — 24,000
   Total cost savings — $ 84,000
   Current operating income in 2004 — $102,000
   Add cost savings from eliminating errors — 84,000
   Operating income in 2004 if errors eliminated — $186,000

3.   Currently 85% × 8,000 hours = 6,800 hours are billed to clients generating revenues of $680,000. The remaining 15% of professional labor-hours (15% × 8,000 = 1,200 hours) is lost in making corrections. Carasco bills clients at the rate of $680,000 ÷ 6,800 = $100 per professional labor-hour. If the 1,200 professional labor-hours, currently not being billed to clients, were billed to clients, Carasco's revenues would increase by 1,200 hours × $100 = $120,000 from $680,000 to $800,000.

Costs remain unchanged	
Professional salary costs	$400,000
Administrative and support (40% × $400,000)	160,000
Travel	18,000
Total costs	$578,000
Carasco's operating income would be	
Revenues	$800,000
Total costs	578,000
Operating income	$222,000

12-22 (20 min.) Target costs, effect of product-design changes on product costs.

1. and 2. Manufacturing costs of HJ6 in 2003 and 2004 are as follows:

	2003		2004	
	Total (1)	Per Unit (2) = (1) ÷ 3,500	Total (3)	Per Unit (4) = (3) ÷ 4,000
Direct materials, $1,200 × 3,500; $1,100 × 4,000	$4,200,000	$1,200	$4,400,000	$1,100
Batch-level costs, $8,000 × 70; $7,500 × 80	560,000	160	600,000	150
Manuf. operations costs, $55 × 21,000; $50 × 22,000	1,155,000	330	1,100,000	275
Engineering change costs, $12,000 × 14; $10,000 × 10	168,000	48	100,000	25
Total	$6,083,000	$1,738	$6,200,000	$1,550

3. $$\frac{\text{Target manufacturing cost}}{\text{per unit of HJ6 in 2004}} = \frac{\text{Manufacturing costs}}{\text{per unit in 2003}} \times 90\%$$
$$= \$1,738 \times 0.90 = \$1,564.20$$

Actual manufacturing cost per unit of HJ6 in 2004 was $1,550. Hence, Medical Instruments did achieve its target manufacturing cost per unit of $1,564.20

4. To reduce the manufacturing cost per unit in 2004, Medical Instruments reduces the cost per unit of activity in each of the four cost categories—direct materials costs, batch-level costs, manufacturing operations costs, and engineering change costs. It also reduced machine-hours and number of engineering changes made—the quantities of the cost drivers. In 2003, Medical Instruments used 6 machine-hours per unit of HJ6 (21,000 machine-hours ÷3,500 units). In 2004, Medical Instruments used 5.5 machine-hours per unit of HJ6 (22,000 machine-hours ÷ 4,000 units). Medical Instruments reduced engineering changes from 14 in 2003 to 10 in 2004. Medical Instruments achieved these gains through value engineering activities that retained only those product features that customers wanted while eliminating activities and their costs.

12-24 (20–25 min.) **Cost-plus and target pricing** (S. Sridhar, adapted).

1.

Investment	$1,800,000
Return on investment	20%
Operating income (20% × $1,800,000)	$360,000
Operating income per unit of RF17 ($360,000 ÷ 15,000)	$24
Full cost per unit of RF17	$200
Selling price ($200 + $24)	$224
Markup percentage on full cost ($24 ÷ $200)	12%

2. Selling price of RF17 = Variable costs per unit of RF17 × 1.40

Hence, Variable costs per unit of RF17 $= \dfrac{\text{Selling price of RF17}}{1.40} = \dfrac{\$224}{1.40} = \$160$

3. Fixed costs are $40 ($200 – $160) per unit × 15,000 units = $600,000

Revenues ($230 × 13,500)	$3,105,000
Variable costs ($160 × 13,500)	2,160,000
Contribution margin ($70 × 13,500)	945,000
Fixed costs	600,000
Operating income	$ 345,000

The operating income if Waterford increases the selling price of RF17 to $230 is $345,000. This is less than the $360,000 operating income Waterford earns by selling 15,000 units at a price of $224. The $6 ($230 – $224) increase in price causes demand to decrease by 1,500 units (15,000 – 13,500). The demand for RF17 is elastic—an increase in price causes a significant decrease in demand. Waterford should not increase the selling price to $230.

4.

Target investment in 2005	$1,650,000
Target return on investment	20%
Target operating income in 2005, 20% × $1,650,000	$330,000
Target revenues in 2005, $210 × 15,000	$3,150,000
Less target operating income in 2005	330,000
Target costs in 2005	$2,820,000
Target cost per unit in 2005, $2,820,000 ÷ 15,000	$188

12-26 (15 min.) Considerations other than cost in pricing.

1. No. We would expect the incremental costs of providing telephone services to be no different in peak versus off-peak hours. Most costs of maintaining and operating the telephone network are fixed costs that are the same in peak and off-peak periods. In fact, the *unit cost per telephone call* is likely to be higher during off-peak hours when fewer calls are made. Yet the prices charged for telephone calls during peak periods are higher than the prices charged for off-peak evenings, nights, and weekends.

12-26 (Cont'd.)

2. Charging higher prices for peak period calls is an example of price discrimination. Price discrimination occurs because calls made between 8 A.M. and 5 P.M. on working days are generally made by businesses that are relatively more price insensitive—they must make telephone calls to conduct their regular day-to-day business activities. Charging a higher price for calls during business hours maximizes the telephone company's operating income. Charging higher prices during business hours is also an example of peak-load pricing. Because the number of telephone calls that can be put through at any one time is limited, the telephone company raises prices to levels that the market will bear when demand is high.

Calls during evenings, nights, and weekends are generally made by individuals for personal or pleasure reasons. Because they pay for the calls themselves, individuals are much more sensitive to price than business callers—that is, their demand is more price-elastic. It is profitable for AT&T to charge low rates to stimulate demand for personal and pleasure calls.

12-28 (25 min.) Cost-plus and market-based pricing.

1. California Temps's full cost per hour of supplying contract labor is:

Variable costs	$12
Fixed costs ($240,000 ÷ 80,000 hours)	3
Full cost per hour	$15

Price per hour at full cost plus 20% = $15 × 1.20 = $18 per hour.

2. Contribution margins for different prices and demand realizations are as follows:

Price per Hour (1)	Variable Cost per Hour (2)	Contribution Margin per Hour (3)=(1)–(2)	Demand in Hours (4)	Total Contribution (5)=(3)×(4)
$16	$12	$4	120,000	$480,000
17	12	5	100,000	500,000
18	12	6	80,000	480,000
19	12	7	70,000	490,000
20	12	8	60,000	480,000

Fixed costs will remain the same regardless of the demand realizations. Fixed costs are, therefore, irrelevant since they do not differ among the alternatives.

The table above indicates that California Temps can maximize contribution margin and, hence, operating income by charging a price of $17 per hour.

3. The cost-plus approach to pricing in requirement 1 does not explicitly consider the effect of prices on demand. The approach in requirement 2 models the interaction between price and demand and determines the optimal level of profitability using concepts of relevant costs. The two different approaches lead to two different prices in requirements 1 and 2. As the chapter describes, pricing decisions should consider both demand or market considerations and supply or cost factors. The approach in requirement 2 is the more balanced approach. In most cases, of course, managers use the cost-plus method of requirement 1 as only a starting point. They then modify the cost-plus price on the basis of market considerations—anticipated customer reaction to alternative price levels and the prices charged by competitors for similar products.

12-30 (20–25 min.) Product costs, activity-based costing.

This problem assumes knowledge of activity-based costing systems as described in Chapter 5. The problem illustrates how both product designers and manufacturing personnel can play key roles in a company manufacturing competitively priced products. Solution Exhibit 12-30 presents an overview of the product costing system at Executive Power. The following table presents the manufacturing cost per unit for different cost categories for P-41 and P-63.

Cost Categories	P-41	P-63
Direct manufacturing product costs		
Direct materials	$407.50	$292.10
Indirect manufacturing product costs		
Materials handling		
(85 × $1.20; 46 × $1.20)	102.00	55.20
Assembly management		
(3.2 × $40; 1.9 × $40)	128.00	76.00
Machine insertion of parts		
(49 × $0.70; 31 × $0.70)	34.30	21.70
Manual insertion of parts		
(36 × $2.10; 15 × $2.10)	75.60	31.50
Quality testing		
(1.4 × $25; 1.1 × $25)	35.00	27.50
Total indirect manufacturing product costs	374.90	211.90
Total manufacturing product costs	$782.40	$504.00

SOLUTION EXHIBIT 12-30
Overview of Product Costing at Executive Power

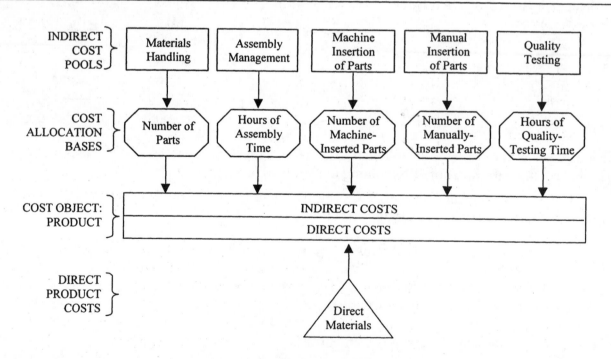

12-30 Excel Application

Pricing Decisions and Cost Management
Executive Power

Original Data

Indirect Manufacturing Cost Pool	Allocation Rate	
Materials Handling	$1.20	per part
Assembly Management	$40.00	per hour of assembly time
Machine Insertion of Parts	$0.70	per machine-inserted part
Manual Insertion of Parts	$2.10	per manually-inserted part
Quality Testing	$25.00	per testing-hour

Product Characteristics	P-41	P-63
Direct Materials Costs	$407.50	$292.10
Number of Parts	85	46
Hours of Assembly Time	3.2	1.9
Number of Machine-Inserted Parts	49	31
Number of Manually-Inserted Parts	36	15
Hours of Quality Testing	1.4	1.1

Manufacturing Cost Calculations

Cost Categories	P-41	P-63
Direct Manufacturing Costs		
Direct Materials	$407.50	$292.10
Indirect Manufacturing Costs		
Materials Handling	102.00	55.20
Assembly Management	128.00	76.00
Machine-Insertion of Parts	34.30	21.70
Manual-Insertion of Parts	75.60	31.50
Quality Testing	35.00	27.50
Total Indirect Manufacturing Costs	374.90	211.90
Total Manufacturing Product Costs	$782.40	$504.00

12-32 (40–45 min.) **Target prices, target costs, value engineering, cost incurrence, locked-in cost, activity-based costing.**

1.

	Old CE100	Cost Change	New CE100
Direct materials costs	$182,000	$2.20 × 7,000 = $15,400 less	$166,600
Direct manufacturing labor costs	28,000	$0.50 × 7,000 = $3,500 less	24,500
Machining costs	31,500	Unchanged because capacity same	31,500
Testing costs	35,000	(20% × 2.5 × 7,000) × $2 = $7,000 less	28,000
Rework costs	14,000	(See Note 1)	5,600
Ordering costs	3,360	(See Note 2)	2,100
Engineering costs	21,140	Unchanged because capacity same	21,140
Total manufacturing costs	$315,000		$279,440

Note 1:

10% of old CE100s are reworked. That is, 700 (10% of 7,000) CE100s made are reworked. Rework costs = $20 per unit reworked × 700 = $14,000. If rework falls to 4% of New CE100s manufactured, 280 (4% of 7,000) New CE100s manufactured will require rework. Rework costs = $20 per unit × 280 = $5,600.

Note 2 :

Ordering costs for New CE100 = 2 orders/month × 50 components × $21/order
$$= \$2,100$$

Unit manufacturing costs of New CE100 = $279,440 ÷ 7,000 = $39.92

2. Total manufacturing cost reductions based on new design
$$= \$315,000 - \$279,440$$
$$= \$35,560$$

Reduction in unit manufacturing costs based on new design
$$= \$35,560 \div 7,000$$
$$= \$5.08 \text{ per unit.}$$

The reduction in unit manufacturing costs based on the new design can also be calculated as:

Unit cost of old design, $45 ($315,000 ÷ 7,000 units) – Unit cost of new design, $39.92 = $5.08

Hence, the target cost reduction of $6 per unit is not achieved by the redesign.

3. Changes in design have a considerably larger impact on costs per unit relative to improvements in manufacturing efficiency ($5.08 versus $1.50). One explanation is that many costs are locked in once the design of the radio-cassette is completed. Improvements in manufacturing efficiency cannot reduce many of these costs. Design choices can influence many direct and overhead cost categories, for example, by reducing direct materials requirements, by reducing defects requiring rework, and by designing in fewer components that translate into fewer orders placed and lower ordering costs.

12-34 (30–40 min.)   Life-cycle product costing, product mix.

1. A life-cycle income statement traces revenue and costs of each individual software package from its initial research and development to its final customer servicing and support. The two main differences from a conventional income statement are:
   a. Costs incurred in different calendar periods are included in the same statement.
   b. Costs and revenue of each package are reported separately rather than aggregated into companywide categories.

   The benefits of using a product life-cycle report are:
   a. The full set of revenues and costs associated with each product becomes visible.
   b. Differences among products in the percentage of total costs committed at early stages in the life cycle are highlighted.

   c. Interrelationships among business function cost categories are highlighted. What is the effect, for example, of cutting back on R&D and product-design cost categories on customer-service costs in subsequent years?

2.

	EE-46		ME-83		IE-17	
Revenue ($000s)		$2,500		$1,500		$1,600
Costs ($000s)						
Research & development	$700		$450		$240	
Design	200		120		96	
Production	300		210		208	
Marketing	500		270		448	
Distribution	75		60		96	
Customer service	375	2,150	150	1,260	608	1,696
Operating income ($000s)		$ 350		$ 240		$ (96)

As emphasized in this chapter, the time value of money is not taken into account when summing life-cycle revenue or life-cycle costs. Chapter 21 discusses this topic in detail.

Rankings of the three packages on profitability (and relative profitability) are:

Operating income	$\dfrac{\text{Operating income}}{\text{Revenues}}$
1. EE-46: $350,000	1. ME-83: 16.0%
2. ME-83: $240,000	2. EE-46: 14.0%
3. IE-17: $ (96,000)	3. IE-17: (6.0%)

The EE-46 and ME-83 packages should be emphasized, and the IE-17 package should be de-emphasized. It is interesting that IE-17 had the lowest R&D costs but was the least profitable. DSS should evaluate whether reducing R&D costs contributed in any way to IE-17's poor performance.

3.   The cost structures of the three software packages are:

	EE-46	ME-83	IE-17
Research & development	32.5%	35.7%	14.1%
Design	9.3	9.5	5.7
Production	14.0	16.7	12.3
Marketing	23.3	21.4	26.4
Distribution	3.5	4.8	5.7
Customer service	17.4	11.9	35.8
	100.0%	100.0%	100.0%

The major differences are:
- a.   EE-46 and ME-83 have over 30% of their costs in the R&D/product design categories, compared to less than 15% (14.1%) for IE-17.
- b.   IE-17 has 35.8% of its costs in the customer-service category, compared to 17.4% for EE-46 and 11.9% for ME-83.

There are several explanations for these differences:
- a.   EE-46 and ME-83 differ sizably from IE-17 in their R&D/product design intensity. For example, EE-46 and ME-83 may require considerably (a) more interaction with users, and (b) more experimentation with software algorithms than does IE-17.
- b.   The software division should have invested more in the R&D/product design categories for IE-17. The high percentage for customer service costs could reflect the correcting of problems that should have been corrected prior to manufacture. Life-cycle reports highlight possible causal relationships among cost categories.

12-36 (30 min.) Airline pricing, considerations other than cost in pricing.

1.   If the fare is $2,000,
- a. Air Americo would expect to have 190 business and 20 pleasure travelers.
- b. Variable cost per passenger would be $180.
- c. Contribution margin per passenger = $2,000 – 180 = $1,820.

If the fare is $500,
- a. Air Americo would expect to have 200 business and 100 pleasure travelers.
- b. Variable cost per passenger would be $80.
- c. Contribution margin per passenger = $500 – $80 = $420.

Contribution margin from business travelers at prices of $500 and $2,000, respectively, follow:

At a price of $500: $420 × 200 passengers   = $ 84,000
At a price of $2,000: $1,820 × 190 passengers = $345,800

Air Americo would maximize contribution margin and operating income by charging business travelers a fare of $2,000.

12-36 (Cont'd.)

Contribution margin from pleasure travelers at prices of $500 and $2,000, respectively, follow:

At a price of $500: $420 × 100 passengers = $42,000
At a price of $2,000: $1,820 × 20 passengers = $36,400

Air Americo would maximize contribution margin and operating income by a price differentiation strategy, where business travelers are charged $2,000 and pleasure travelers $500. In deciding between the alternative prices, all other costs such as fuel costs, allocated annual lease costs, allocated ground services costs, and allocated flight crew salaries are irrelevant. That's because these costs will not change whatever prices Air America chooses.

2.   The elasticity of demand of the two classes of passengers drives the different demands of the travelers. Business travelers are relatively price insensitive because they must get to their destination during the week (exclusive of weekends) and their fares are paid by their companies. A 300% increase in fares from $500 to $2,000 will deter only 5% of the business passengers from flying with Air America.

In contrast, a similar fare increase will lead to an 80% drop in pleasure travelers who are paying for their own travel, unlike business travelers, and who may have alternative vacation plans they could pursue instead. Furthermore, lowering fares stimulates demand for pleasure travelers and results in higher contribution margins and operating incomes.

3.   Since business travelers often want to return within the same week, while pleasure travelers often stay over weekends, a requirement that a Saturday night stay is needed to qualify for the $500 discount fare would discriminate between the passenger categories. This price discrimination is legal because airlines are service companies rather than manufacturing companies and because these practices do not, nor are they intended to, destroy competition.

12-38 (40 min.) Target prices, target costs, value engineering.

1.   Activity-based allocation of overhead costs to Tvez are as follows:

	Units of Cost Drivers (1)	Cost Allocation (2) = (1) × Rate/Hour
Machine setup costs:		
$25 per setup-hour	100[a] × 12 = 1,200 hrs.	$ 30,000
Testing costs:		
$2 per testing-hour	50,000 × 2.5 = 125,000 hrs.	250,000
Engineering costs		170,000
Total ABC overhead allocation		$450,000

[a] 100 setups = 50,000 units ÷ 500 units per setup

12-38 (Cont'd.)

Activity-based full-product costs of Tvez are as follows:

Direct materials costs	$ 850,000
Direct manufacturing labor costs	300,000
Direct machine costs	150,000
Machine setup costs	30,000
Testing costs	250,000
Engineering costs	170,000
Total manufacturing and full product costs	$1,750,000
Number of units	50,000
Full product cost per unit	$35.00

2. Markup on full product cost per unit of Tvez $= \dfrac{\text{Selling price} - \text{Full product cost}}{\text{Full product cost}}$

$$= \frac{\$40.60 - \$35}{\$35} = \frac{\$5.60}{\$35} = 16\%$$

3. The target price for New Tvez is $34.80. Suppose the target cost per unit of New Tvez is $X

Then $\qquad X(1.16) = \$34.80$

That is $\qquad X = \dfrac{\$34.80}{1.16} = \$30$

4. Activity-based costs of New Tvez are as follows:

Direct materials ($17 – $3) × 50,000 units	$ 700,000
Direct manufacturing labor ($6 – $0.75) × 50,000 units	262,500
Direct machining	150,000
Machine setup costs	
(6 hours × 100 setups × $25 per setup-hour)	15,000
Testing costs (2.5 hours – 0.5 hours) × 50,000 × $2	200,000
Engineering costs (same as for Tvez)	170,000
Manufacturing and full costs of the product	$1,497,500
Number of units	50,000
Manufacturing and full costs per unit ($1,497,500 ÷ 50,000)	$29.95

The New Tvez design will reduce the manufacturing costs per unit by $5.05 ($35 – $29.95) more than the $5.00 ($35 – $30) necessary to reduce the cost of New Tvez to $30.00. Hence, New Tvez will achieve the targeted cost reductions.

5. Price of New Tvez using a 16% markup on full product cost of $29.95 = $29.95 × 1.16 = $34.74.

CHAPTER 13
STRATEGY, BALANCED SCORECARD, AND STRATEGIC PROFITABILITY ANALYSIS

13-2 The five key forces to consider in industry analysis are: (a) competitors, (b) potential entrants into the market, (c) equivalent products, (d) bargaining power of customers, and (e) bargaining power of input suppliers.

13-4 The four key perspectives in the balanced scorecard are: (1) Financial perspective—this perspective evaluates the profitability of the strategy, (2) Customer perspective—this perspective identifies the targeted market segments and measures the company's success in these segments, (3) Internal business process perspective—this perspective focuses on internal operations that further both the customer perspective by creating value for customers and the financial perspective by increasing shareholder wealth, and (4) Learning and growth perspective—this perspective identifies the capabilities in which the organization must excel in order to achieve superior internal processes that create value for customers and shareholders.

13-6 A good balanced scorecard design has several features:
1. It tells the story of a company's strategy by articulating a sequence of cause-and-effect relationships.
2. It helps to communicate the strategy to all members of the organization by translating the strategy into a coherent and linked set of understandable and measurable operational targets.
3. It places strong emphasis on financial objectives and measures in for-profit companies. Nonfinancial measures are regarded as part of a program to achieve future financial performance.
4. It limits the number of measures to only those that are critical to the implementation of strategy.
5. It highlights suboptimal tradeoffs that managers may make when they fail to consider operational and financial measures together.

13-8 Three key components in doing a strategic analysis of operating income are:
1. The growth component which measures the changes in revenues and costs attributable solely to an increase in the quantity of output sold from one year to the next.
2. The price-recovery component which measures the changes in revenues and costs attributable solely to changes in the prices of inputs and outputs from one year to the next.
3. The productivity component which measures the change in costs attributable to a change in the quantity and mix of inputs used in the current year relative to the quantity and mix of inputs that would have been used in the previous year to produce current year output.

13-10 Engineered costs result from a cause-and-effect relationship between the cost driver, output, and the (direct or indirect) resources used to produce that output. Discretionary costs arise from periodic (usually) annual decisions regarding the maximum amount to be incurred. There is no measurable cause-and-effect relationship between output and resources used.

13-12 Downsizing (also called rightsizing) is an integrated approach configuring processes, products, and people to match costs to the activities that need to be performed for operating effectively and efficiently in the present and future. Downsizing is an attempt to eliminate unused capacity.

13-14 Total factor productivity is the quantity of output produced divided by the costs of all inputs used, where the inputs are costed on the basis of current period prices.

13-16 (15 min.) Balanced scorecard.

1. La Quinta's 2004 strategy is a cost leadership strategy. La Quinta plans to grow by producing high-quality boxes at a low cost delivered to customers in a timely manner. La Quinta's boxes are not differentiated, and there are many other manufacturers who produce similar boxes. To succeed, La Quinta must achieve lower costs relative to competitors through productivity and efficiency improvements.

2. Measures that we would expect to see on a La Quinta's balanced scorecard for 2004 are

Financial Perspective
(1) Operating income from productivity gain, (2) operating income from growth, (3) cost reductions in key areas.
   These measures evaluate whether La Quinta has successfully reduced costs and generated growth through cost leadership.

Customer Perspective
(1) Market share, (2) new customers, (3) customer satisfaction index, (4) customer retention, (5) time taken to fulfill customer orders.
   The logic is that improvements in these customer measures are leading indicators of superior financial performance.

Internal Business Process Perspective
(1) Yield, (2) productivity, (3) order delivery time, (4) on-time delivery.
   Improvements in these measures are expected to lead to more satisfied customers and in turn to superior financial performance

Learning and Growth Perspective
(1) Percentage of employees trained in process and quality management, (2) employee satisfaction, (3) number of major process improvements.
   Improvements in these measures have a cause-and-effect relationship with improvements in internal business processes, which in turn lead to customer satisfaction and financial performance.

13-18 (20-30 min.) Balanced scorecard.

Perspectives	Strategic Objectives	Performance Measures
• Financial	• Increase shareholder value	• Earnings per share • Net income • Return on assets • Return on sales • Return on equity • Product cost per unit • Customer cost per unit
	• Increase profit generated by each salesperson	• Profit per salesperson
• Customer	• Acquire new customers • Retain customers • Develop profitable customers	• Number of new customers • Percentage of customers retained • Customer profitability
• Internal Business Processs	• Improve manufacturing quality • Introduce new products • Minimize invoice error rate • On-time delivery by suppliers • Increase proprietary products	• Percentage of defective product units • Percentage of error-free invoices • Percentage of on-time deliveries by suppliers • Number of patents
• Learning and Growth	• Increase information system capabilities • Enhance employee skills	• Percentage of processes with real-time feedback • Employee turnover rate • Average job-related training hours per employee

13-20 (15 min.) **Strategy, balanced scorecard.**

1.   Meredith Corporation follows a product differentiation strategy in 2003. Meredith's D4H machine is distinct from its competitors and generally regarded as superior to competitors' products. To succeed, Meredith must continue to differentiate its product and charge a premium price.

2.   Balanced Scorecard measures for 2003 follow:

Financial Perspective
(1) Increase in operating income from charging higher margins, (2) price premium earned on products.

These measures indicate whether Meredith has been able to charge premium prices and achieve operating income increases through product differentiation.

Customer Perspective
(1) Market share in high-end special-purpose textile machines, (2) customer satisfaction, (3) new customers.

Meredith's strategy should result in improvements in these customer measures which are leading indicators of superior financial performance.

Internal Business Process Perspective
(1) Manufacturing quality, (2) new product features added, (3) order delivery time.

Improvements in these measures are expected to result in more satisfied customers and in turn superior financial performance.

Learning and Growth Perspective
(1) Development time for designing new machines, (2) improvements in manufacturing processes, (3) employee education and skill levels, (4) employee satisfaction.

Improvements in these measures have a cause-and-effect relationship with improvements in internal business processes, which in turn lead to customer satisfaction and financial performance.

13-22 (20 min.) **Analysis of growth, price-recovery, and productivity components (continuation of 13-21).**

Effect of the industry-market-size factor

If the 10-unit increase in sales from 200 to 210 units, 3% or 6 (3% × 200) units is due to growth in market size, and 4 (10 − 6) units is due to an increase in market share.
The change in Meredith's operating income from the industry-market size factor rather than from specific strategic actions is:

$280,000 (the growth component in Exercise 13-21) $\times \dfrac{6}{10}$ $168,000 F

Effect of product differentiation
The change in operating income due to:

Increase in the selling price of D4H (revenue effect of price recovery)	$420,000 F
Increase in price of inputs (cost effect of price recovery)	184,500 U

Growth in market share due to product differentiation

$280,000 (the growth component in Exercise 13-21) $\times \dfrac{4}{10}$ 112,000 F

Change in operating income due to product differentiation $347,500 F

Effect of cost leadership
The change in operating income from cost leadership is:

Productivity component $92,000 F

The change in operating income between 2002 and 2003 can be summarized as follows:

Change due to industry-market-size	$168,000 F
Change due to product differentiation	347,500 F
Change due to cost leadership	92,000 F
Change in operating income	$607,500 F

Meredith has been successful in implementing its product differentiation strategy. Nearly 57% ($347,500 ÷ $607,500) of the increase in operating income during 2003 was due to product differentiation. Meredith's operating income increase in 2003 was also helped by a growth in the overall market and some productivity improvements.

13-24 (15 min.) **Strategy, balanced scorecard, service company.**

1.　　Snyder Corporation's strategy in 2003 is cost leadership. Snyder's consulting services for implementing sales management software is not distinct from its competitors. The market for these services is very competitive. To succeed, Snyder must deliver quality service at low cost. Improving productivity while maintaining quality is key.

2.　　Balanced Scorecard measures for 2003 follow:

Financial Perspective
(1) Increase operating income from productivity gains and growth, (2) revenues per employee, (3) cost reductions in key areas, for example, software implementation and overhead costs.

　　　These measures indicate whether Snyder has been able to reduce costs and achieve operating income increases through cost leadership.

Customer Perspective
(1) Market share, (2) new customers, (3) customer responsiveness, (4) customer satisfaction.

　　　Snyder's strategy should result in improvements in these customer measures, which are leading indicators of superior financial performance.

Internal Business Process Perspective
(1)　Time to complete customer jobs, (2) time lost due to errors, (3) quality of job (Is system running smoothly after job is completed?)

　　　Improvements in these measures are expected to lead to more satisfied customers, lower costs, and superior financial performance.

Learning and Growth Perspective

(1)　Time required to analyze and design implementation steps, (2) time taken to perform key steps implementing the software, (3) skill levels of employees, (4) hours of employee training, (5) employee satisfaction and motivation.

　　　Improvements in these measures have a cause-and-effect relationship with improvements in internal business processes, customer satisfaction, and financial performance.

13-26 (25 min.) **Analysis of growth, price-recovery and productivity components** (continuation of 13-25).

Effect of industry-market-size factors

Of the 10-unit increase in sales from 60 to 70 units, 5% or 3 units (5% × 60) is due to growth in market size, and 7 (10 – 3) units is due to an increase in market share.

The change in Snyder's operating income from the industry market-size factor rather than from specific strategic actions is:

$200,000 (the growth component in Exercise 13-25) × $\dfrac{3}{10}$ $60,000 F

Effect of product differentiation

Of the $2,000 decrease in selling price, 1% or $500 (1% × $50,000) is due to a general decline in prices, and the remaining decrease of $1,500 ($2,000 – $500) is due to a strategic decision by Snyder's management to implement its cost leadership strategy of lowering prices to stimulate demand.

The change in operating income due to a decline in selling price (other than the strategic reduction in price included in the cost leadership component) $500 × 70 units	$ 35,000 U
Increase in prices of inputs (cost effect of price recovery)	129,000 U
Change in operating income due to product differentiation	$164,000 U

Effect of cost leadership

Productivity component	$189,000 F
Effect of strategic decision to reduce selling price, $1,500 × 70	105,000 U

Growth in market share due to productivity improvement and strategic decision to reduce selling price

$200,000 (the growth component in Exercise 13-25) × $\dfrac{7}{10}$ 140,000 F

Change in operating income due to cost leadership $224,000 F

The change in operating income between 2002 and 2003 can then be summarized as

Change due to industry-market-size	$ 60,000 F
Change due to product differentiation	164,000 U
Change due to cost leadership	224,000 F
Change in operating income	$120,000 F

Snyder has been very successful in implementing its cost leadership strategy. Due to a lack of product differentiation, Snyder was unable to pass along increases in labor costs by increasing the selling price—in fact selling price declined by $2,000 per work unit. However, Snyder was able to take advantage of its productivity gains to reduce price, gain market share, and increase operating income.

13-28 (20 min.) **Balanced scorecard.**

1.   Caltex's strategy is to focus on "service-oriented customers" who are willing to pay a higher price for services. Even though its product is largely a commodity product, gasoline, Caltex wants to differentiate itself through the service it provides at its retailing stations.

Does the scorecard represent Caltex's strategy? By and large it does. The focus of the scorecard is on measures of process improvement, quality, market share, and financial success from product differentiation and charging higher prices for customer service. There are some deficiencies that the subsequent assignment questions raise but, abstracting from these concerns for the moment, the scorecard does focus on implementing a product differentiation strategy.

Having concluded that the scorecard has been reasonably well designed, how has Caltex performed relative to its strategy in 2004? It appears from the scorecard that Caltex was successful in implementing its strategy in 2004. It achieved all targets in the financial, internal business, and learning and growth perspectives. The only target it missed was the market share target in the customer perspective. At this stage, students may raise some questions about whether this is a good scorecard measure. Requirement 3 gets at this issue in more detail. The bottom line is that measuring "market share in the overall gasoline market" rather than in the "service-oriented customer" market segment is not a good scorecard measure, so not achieving this target may not be as big an issue as it may seem at first.

2.   Yes, Caltex should include some measure of employee satisfaction and employee training in the learning and growth perspective. Caltex's differentiation strategy and ability to charge a premium price is based on customer service. The key to good, fast, and friendly customer service is well trained and satisfied employees. Untrained and dissatisfied employees will have poor interactions with customers and cause the strategy to fail. Hence, training and employee satisfaction are very important to Caltex for implementing its strategy. These measures are leading indicators of whether Caltex will be able to successfully implement its strategy and, hence, should be measured on the balanced scorecard.

3.   Caltex's strategy is to focus on the 60% of gasoline consumers who are service-oriented not on the 40% price-shopper segment. To evaluate if it has been successful in implementing its strategy, Caltex needs to measure its market share in its targeted market segment, "service-oriented customer," not its market share in the overall market. Given Caltex's strategy, it should not be concerned if its market share in the price-shopper segment declines. In fact, charging premium prices will probably cause its market share in this segment to decline. Caltex should replace "market share in overall gasoline market" with "market share in the service-oriented customer segment" in its balanced scorecard customer measure. Caltex may also want to consider putting a customer satisfaction measure on the scorecard. This measure should capture an overall evaluation of customer reactions to the facility, the convenience store, employee interactions, and quick turnaround. The customer satisfaction measure would serve as a leading indicator of market share in the service-oriented customer segment.

13-28 (Cont'd.)

4.   Although there is a cause-and-effect link between internal business process measures and customer measures on the current scorecard, Caltex should add more measures to tighten this linkage. In particular, the current scorecard measures focus exclusively on refinery operations and not on gas station operations. Caltex should add measures of gas station performance such as cleanliness of the facility, turnaround time at the gas pumps, the shopping experience at the convenience store, and the service provided by employees. Many companies do random audits of their facilities to evaluate how well their branches and retail outlets are performing. These measures would serve as leading indicators of customer satisfaction and market share in Caltex's targeted segments.

5.   Caltex is correct in not measuring changes in operating income from productivity improvements on its scorecard under the financial perspective. Caltex's strategy is to grow by charging premium prices for customer service. The scorecard measures focus on Caltex's success in implementing this strategy. Productivity gains per se are not critical to Caltex's strategy and, hence, should not be measured on the scorecard.

13-30 (35 min.) Strategic analysis of operating income.

1.   Halsey is following a product differentiation strategy. Halsey offers a wide selection of clothes and excellent customer service. Halsey's strategy is to distinguish itself from its competitors and to charge a premium price.

2.   Operating income for each year is as follows:

	2004	2005
Revenues ($60 × 40,000; $59 × 40,000)	$2,400,000	$2,360,000
Costs		
Costs of goods sold ($40 × 40,000; $41 × 40,000)	1,600,000	1,640,000
Selling & customer service costs ($7 × 51,000); $6.90 × 43,000)	357,000	296,700
Purchasing & admin. costs ($250 × 980; $240 × 850)	245,000	204,000
Total costs	2,202,000	2,140,700
Operating income	$ 198,000	$ 219,300
Change in operating income	▲ $21,300 F ▲	

3.   **The Growth Component**

$$\begin{array}{l} \text{Revenue effect} \\ \text{of growth} \\ \text{component} \end{array} = \left(\begin{array}{c} \text{Actual units of} \\ \text{output sold} \\ \text{in 2005} \end{array} - \begin{array}{c} \text{Actual units of} \\ \text{output sold} \\ \text{in 2004} \end{array}\right) \times \begin{array}{c} \text{Output} \\ \text{price} \\ \text{in 2004} \end{array}$$

$$= (40,000 - 40,000) \times \$60 = \$0$$

13-30 (Cont'd.)

$$
\begin{array}{l}
\text{Cost effect} \\
\text{of growth} \\
\text{component}
\end{array}
=
\left(
\begin{array}{l}
\text{Actual units of input or} \\
\text{capacity that would} \\
\text{have been used to produce} \\
\text{year 2005 output assuming} \\
\text{the same input - output} \\
\text{relationship that existed in 2004}
\end{array}
-
\begin{array}{l}
\text{Actual units of} \\
\text{inputs or capacity} \\
\text{to produce} \\
\text{2004 output}
\end{array}
\right)
\times
\begin{array}{l}
\text{Input} \\
\text{prices} \\
\text{in 2004}
\end{array}
$$

Pieces of clothing that would be required to be purchased in 2005 would be the same as that required in 2004 because output is the same between 2004 and 2005. Purchasing and administrative costs and selling and customer-service costs will not change since adequate capacity exists in 2004 to support year 2005 output and customers.

The cost effects of growth component are:

Costs of goods sold	$(40,000 - 40,000)$	×	$40	= $0
Selling & cust.-serv. costs	$(51,000 - 51,000)$	×	$7	= 0
Purch. & admin. costs	$(980 - 980)$	×	$250	= 0
Cost effect of growth component				$0

In summary, the net effect on operating income as a result of the growth component equals:

Revenue effect of growth component	$0
Cost effect of growth component	0
Change in operating income due to growth component	$0

The Price-Recovery Component

$$
\begin{array}{l}
\text{Revenue effect of} \\
\text{price - recovery} \\
\text{component}
\end{array}
=
\left(
\begin{array}{l}
\text{Output price} \\
\text{in 2005}
\end{array}
-
\begin{array}{l}
\text{Output price} \\
\text{in 2004}
\end{array}
\right)
\times
\begin{array}{l}
\text{Actual units} \\
\text{of output} \\
\text{sold in 2005}
\end{array}
$$

$$
= (\$59 - \$60) \times 40,000 = \$40,000 \text{ U}
$$

$$\begin{matrix} \text{Cost effect of} \\ \text{price - recovery} \\ \text{component} \end{matrix} = \begin{pmatrix} \begin{matrix}\text{Input} \\ \text{prices in} \\ \text{year} \\ 2005 \end{matrix} & - & \begin{matrix}\text{Input} \\ \text{prices in} \\ \text{year} \\ 2004 \end{matrix} \end{pmatrix} \times \begin{matrix} \text{Actual units of inputs or capacity} \\ \text{that would have been used} \\ \text{to produce year 2005 output} \\ \text{assuming the same input - output} \\ \text{relationship that} \\ \text{existed in 2004} \end{matrix}$$

Costs of goods sold	($41 – $40)	×	40,000	=	$40,000 U
Selling & cust.-serv. costs	($6.90 – $7)	×	51,000	=	5,100 F
Purchas. & admin. costs	($240 – $250)	×	980	=	9,800 F
Total cost effect of price-recovery component					$25,100 U

In summary, the net decrease in operating income as a result of the price-recovery component equals:

Revenue effect of price-recovery component	$40,000 U
Cost effect of price-recovery component	25,100 U
Change in operating income due to price-recovery component	$65,100 U

The Productivity Component

$$\begin{matrix} \text{Productivity} \\ \text{component} \end{matrix} = \begin{pmatrix} \begin{matrix}\text{Actual units of} \\ \text{inputs or capacity} \\ \text{used to produce} \\ \text{year 2005 output} \end{matrix} & - & \begin{matrix}\text{Actual units of} \\ \text{inputs or capacity that} \\ \text{would have been used} \\ \text{to produce year 2005} \\ \text{output assuming the same} \\ \text{input - output relationship} \\ \text{that existed in 2004} \end{matrix} \end{pmatrix} \times \begin{matrix}\text{Input} \\ \text{prices in} \\ 2005 \end{matrix}$$

The productivity component of cost changes are:

Costs of goods sold	(40,000 – 40,000)	× $41	=	$ 0
Selling & cust.-serv. costs	(43,000 – 51,000)	× $6.90	=	55,200 F
Purchasing & admin. costs	(850 – 980)	× $240	=	31,200 F
Change in operating income due to productivity component				$86,400 F

13-30 (Cont'd.)

The change in operating income between 2004 and 2005 can be analyzed as follows:

	Income Statement Amounts in 2004 (1)	Revenue and Cost Effects of Growth Component in 2005 (2)	Revenue and Cost Effects of Price-Recovery Component in 2005 (3)	Cost Effect of Productivity Component in 2005 (4)	Income Statement Amounts in 2005 (5) = (1) + (2) + (3) + (4)
Revenues	$2,400,000	$0	$40,000 U	—	$2,360,000
Costs	2,202,000	0	25,100 U	$ 86,400 F	2,140,700
Operating income	$ 198,000	$0	$65,100 U	$ 86,400 F	$ 219,300

$21,300 F

Change in operating income

4.   The analysis of operating income indicates that a significant amount of the increase in operating income resulted from productivity gains rather than product differentiation. The company was unable to charge a premium price for its clothes. Thus, the strategic analysis of operating income indicates that Halsey has not been successful at implementing its premium price, product differentiation strategy, despite the fact that operating income increased by more than 10% between 2004 and 2005. Halsey could not pass on increases in purchase costs to its customers via higher prices. Halsey must either reconsider its product-differentiation strategy or focus managers on increasing margins and growing market share by offering better product variety and superb customer service.

13-30 Excel Application

Strategy, Balanced Scorecard, and Strategic Profitability Analysis

Halsey Company

Original Data

	2004	2005
Pieces of clothing purchased and sold	40,000	40,000
Average selling price	$60	$59
Average cost per piece of clothing	$40	$41
Selling and customer-service capacity	51,000	43,000
Selling and customer-service costs	$357,000	$296,700
Selling and customer-service capacity cost per customer	$7	$6.90

13-30 (Cont'd.)

Purchasing and administrative capacity	980	850
Purchasing and administrative costs	$245,000	$204,000
Purchasing and administrative capacity cost per distinct design	$250	$240
Revenues	$2,400,000	$2,360,000
Costs		
Direct materials costs	1,600,000	1,640,000
Selling and customer service costs	357,000	296,700
Purchasing and administrative costs	245,000	204,000
Total costs	2,202,000	2,140,700
Operating Income	$198,000	$219,300

Revenue and Cost Effects of Growth

Revenue effect of growth	-
Cost effect of growth	
Direct materials costs	-
Selling and customer service costs	-
Purchasing and administrative costs	-
Total cost-effect of growth	-

Price-Recovery Component

Revenue effect of price-recovery	$(40,000)	U
Cost effect of price-recovery		
Direct materials costs	40,000	U
Selling and customer service costs	(5,100)	F
Purchasing and administrative costs	(9,800)	F
Total cost-effect of price-recovery	25,100	U

Productivity Component

Direct materials costs	$0	
Selling and customer service costs	$(55,200.00)	F
Purchasing and administrative costs	$(31,200)	F
Cost effect of productivity component	$(86,400)	F

Strategic Analysis of Profitability

	Income Statement Amounts in 2004	Effects of Growth Component	Effects of Price-Recovery Component	Effects of Productivity Component	Income Statement Amounts in 2005
Revenues	$2,400,000	$-	$(40,000)	-	$2,360,000
Costs	2,202,000	-	25,100	$(86,400)	2,140,700
Operating Income	198,000	-	(65,100)	86,400	219,300

13-32 (20 min.)**Engineered and discretionary overhead costs, unused capacity, repairs and maintenance.**

1. Rowland's repair and maintenance costs are indirect engineered costs. The amount of repair and maintenance costs each year may not correlate directly to the quantity of gears produced. Over time, however, there is a clear cause-and-effect relationship between the output (quantity of gears produced) and repair and maintenance costs—the more gears that are produced, the greater the number of hours the machines will be run, and the greater the repairs and maintenance the machines will need.

2. (1) Available repair and maintenance capacity
   8 hours per day × 250 days × 4 workers — 8,000 hours
   (2) Repair and maintenance work actually done — 6,000 hours
   (3) = (1) – (2) Hours of unused repair and maintenance capacity — 2,000 hours
   (4) Repair and maintenance cost per hour, $40,000 ÷ 2,000 — $20 per hour
   (5) = (3) × (4) Cost of unused repair and maintenance capacity — $40,000

Reasons why Rowland might want to downsize its repair and maintenance capacity are:
   a. to reduce costs of carrying unused capacity
   b. to create a culture of streamlining processes and operating efficiently

Reasons why Rowland might not want to downsize its repair and maintenance capacity are:
   a. it projects greater demand for repairs and maintenance activity in the near future
   b. it would negatively affect employee morale
   c. it may want to use the expertise of the repairs and maintenance staff in other areas such as process improvements
   d. it does not regard the unused capacity as particularly excessive

3. If repair and maintenance costs are discretionary costs, calculating unused capacity is much more difficult. Repair and maintenance costs would be discretionary if repair and maintenance are mostly of a preventive type that management can choose when to do. In this case, the lack of a cause-and-effect relationship between output and repair and maintenance activity means that Rowland cannot determine the repair and maintenance resources used and, hence, the amount of unused capacity.

13-34 (20 min.) **Partial productivity measurement** (Chapter Appendix)

1.   Berkshire Corporation's partial productivity ratios in 2005 are as follows:

$$\frac{\text{Direct materials}}{\text{partial productivity}} = \frac{\text{Quantity of output produced in 2005}}{\text{Kilograms of direct materials used in 2005}} = \frac{525,000}{610,000} = 0.86 \text{ units per kg.}$$

$$\frac{\text{Direct manuf. labor}}{\text{partial productivity}} = \frac{\text{Quantity of output produced in 2005}}{\text{Direct manuf. labor - hours used in 2005}} = \frac{525,000}{9,500} = \frac{55.26 \text{ units}}{\text{per}}$$
$$\text{labor - hour}$$

$$\frac{\text{Manufacturing overhead}}{\text{partial productivity}} = \frac{\text{Quantity of output produced in 2005}}{\text{Units of manuf. capacity in 2005}} = \frac{525,000}{582,000} = \frac{0.90 \text{ units}}{\text{per unit of}}$$
$$\text{capacity}$$

To compare partial productivities in 2005 with partial productivities in 2004, we first calculate the inputs that would have been used in 2004 to produce year 2005's 525,000 units of output assuming the year 2004 relationship between inputs and outputs.

Direct materials $= 450,000 \text{ kg (2004)} \times \dfrac{525,000 \text{ output units in 2005}}{375,000 \text{ output units in 2004}}$

$= 450,000 \times 1.4 = 630,000 \text{ kg.}$

Direct manuf. labor $= 7,500 \text{ hours (2004)} \times \dfrac{525,000 \text{ output units in 2005}}{375,000 \text{ output units in 2004}}$

$= 7,500 \times 1.4 = 10,500 \text{ labor-hours}$

Manufacturing capacity = 600,000 units of capacity, because manufacturing capacity is fixed, and adequate capacity existed in 2004 to produce year 2005 output.

13-34 (Cont'd.)

Partial productivity calculations for 2004 based on year 2005 output (to make the partial productivities comparable across the two years)

$$\text{Direct materials partial productivity} = \frac{\text{Quantity of output produced in 2005}}{\substack{\text{Kilograms of direct materials that would}\\\text{have been used in 2004 to produce}\\\text{year 2005 output}}} = \frac{525{,}000}{630{,}000} = 0.83 \text{ units per kg}$$

$$\text{Direct manufac. labor partial productivity} = \frac{\text{Quantity of output produced in 2005}}{\substack{\text{Direct manuf. labor - hours that would}\\\text{have been used in 2004 to produce}\\\text{year 2005 output}}} = \frac{525{,}000}{10{,}500} = 50 \text{ units per labor - hour}$$

$$\text{Manufacturing overhead partial productivity} = \frac{\text{Quantity of output produced in 2005}}{\substack{\text{Units of manuf. capacity that would}\\\text{have been used in 2004 to produce}\\\text{year 2005 output}}} = \frac{525{,}000}{600{,}000} = 0.875 \text{ units per unit of capacity}$$

The calculations indicate that Berkshire improved the partial productivity of all its inputs between 2004 and 2005 via improvements in efficiency of direct materials and direct manufacturing labor and by reducing unused manufacturing capacity.

2.   All partial productivity ratios increase from 2004 to 2005. We can therefore, conclude that total factor productivity definitely increased from 2004 to 2005. Partial productivities cannot, however, tell us how much total factor productivity changed, because partial productivity measures cannot be aggregated over different inputs.

3.   Berkshire Corporation management can use the partial productivity measures to set targets for the next year. Partial productivity measures can easily be compared over multiple periods. For example, they may specify bonus payments if partial productivity of direct manufacturing labor increases to 60 units of output per direct manufacturing labor-hour and if partial productivity of direct materials improves to 0.90 units of output per kilogram of direct materials. A major advantage of partial productivity measures is that they focus on a single input; hence, they are simple to calculate and easy to understand at the operations level. Managers and operators can also examine these numbers to understand the reasons underlying productivity changes from one period to the next—better training of workers, lower absenteeism, lower labor turnover, better incentives, or improved methods. Management can then implement and sustain these factors in the future.

13-36 (25 min.) **Balanced scorecard, ethics.**

1. Yes, the Household Products Division (HPD) should include measures of employee satisfaction and customer satisfaction even if these measures are subjective. For a maker of kitchen dishwashers, employee and customer satisfaction are leading indicators of future financial performance. There is a cause-and-effect linkage between these measures and future financial performance. If HPD's strategy is correct and if the scorecard has been properly designed, employee and customer satisfaction information is very important in evaluating the implementation of HPD's strategy.

HPD should use employee and customer satisfaction measures even though these measures are subjective. One of the pitfalls to avoid when implementing a balanced scorecard is not to use only objective measures in the scorecard. Of course, HPD should guard against imprecision and potential for manipulation. Patricia Conley appears to be aware of this. She has tried to understand the reasons for the poor scores and has been able to relate these scores to other objective evidence such as employee dissatisfaction with the new work rules and customer unhappiness with missed delivery dates.

2. Incorrect reporting of employee and customer satisfaction ratings to make divisions performance look good is unethical. In assessing the situation, the specific "Standards of Ethical Conduct for Management Accountants" (described in Exhibit 1-7) that the management account should consider are listed below.

Competence
Clear reports using relevant and reliable information should be prepared. Preparing reports on the basis of incorrect employee and customer satisfaction ratings in order to make the division's performance look better than it is violates competence standards. It is unethical for Conley to change the employee and customer satisfaction ratings in order to make the division's performance look good.

Integrity
The management accountant has a responsibility to avoid actual or apparent conflicts of interest and advise all appropriate parties of any potential conflict. Conley may be tempted to report better employee and customer satisfaction ratings to please Emburey. This action, however, violates the responsibility for integrity. The Standards of Ethical Conduct require the management accountant to communicate favorable as well as unfavorable information.

Objectivity
The management accountant's standards of ethical conduct require that information should be fairly and objectively communicated and that all relevant information should be disclosed. From a management accountant's standpoint, modifying employee and customer satisfaction ratings to make division performance look good would violate the standard of objectivity.

Conley should indicate to Emburey that the employee and customer satisfaction ratings are, indeed, appropriate. If Emburey still insists on reporting better employee and customer satisfaction numbers, Conley should raise the matter with one of Emburey's superiors. If, after taking all these steps, there is continued pressure to overstate employee and customer satisfaction ratings, Conley should consider resigning from the company and not engage in unethical behavior.

CHAPTER 14
COST ALLOCATION, CUSTOMER-PROFITABILITY ANALYSIS, AND SALES-VARIANCE ANALYSIS

14-2   The salary of a plant security guard would be a direct cost when the cost object is the security department of the plant. It would be an indirect cost when the cost object is a product.

14-4   Exhibit 14-2 lists four criteria used to guide cost allocation decisions:
1.   Cause and effect.
2.   Benefits received.
3.   Fairness or equity.
4.   Ability to bear.
The cause-and-effect criterion and the benefits-received criterion are the dominant criteria when the purpose of the allocation is related to the economic decision purpose or the motivation purpose.

14-6   The total sales-mix variance arises from differences in the budgeted contribution margin of the actual and budgeted sales mix. The composite unit concept enables the effect of individual product changes to be summarized in a single intuitive number by using weights based on the mix of individual units in the actual and budgeted mix of products sold.

14-8   The sales-quantity variance can be decomposed into (a) a market-size variance (because the actual total market size in units is different from the budgeted market size in units), and (b) a market share variance (because the actual market share of a company is different from the budgeted market share of a company). Both variances use the budgeted average contribution margin per unit.

14-10   Customer profitability analysis highlights to managers how individual customers differentially contribute to total profitability. It helps managers to see whether customers who contribute sizably to total profitability are receiving a comparable level of attention from the organization.

14-12   No. A customer-profitability profile highlights differences in current period's profitability across customers. Dropping customers should be the last resort. An unprofitable customer in one period may be highly profitable in subsequent future periods. Moreover, costs assigned to individual customers need not be purely variable with respect to short-run elimination of sales to those customers. Thus, when customers are dropped, costs assigned to those customers may not disappear in the short run.

14-14   A process where the inputs are nonsubstitutable leaves workers no discretion as to the inputs (such as, types of materials or labor) to use. A process where the inputs are substitutable means there is discretion about the exact number and type of inputs to produce output.

14-16 (15-20 min.) **Cost allocation in hospitals, alternative allocation criteria.**

1.
   Direct costs   = $2.40

   Indirect costs   = $11.52 – $2.40 = $9.12

   Overhead rate   = $\dfrac{\$9.12}{\$2.40}$ = 380%

2.   The answers here are less than clear-cut in some cases.

Overhead Cost Item	Allocation Criteria
Processing of paperwork for purchase	Cause and effect
Supplies room management fee	Benefits received
Operating-room and patient-room handling costs	Cause and effect
Administrative hospital costs	Benefits received
University teaching-related costs	Ability to bear
Malpractice insurance costs	Ability to bear or benefits received
Cost of treating uninsured patients	Ability to bear
Profit component	None. This is not a cost.

3.   Assuming that Meltzer's insurance company is responsible for paying the $4,800 bill, Meltzer probably can only express outrage at the amount of the bill. The point of this question is to note that even if Meltzer objects strongly to one or more overhead items, it is his insurance company that likely has the greater incentive to challenge the bill. Individual patients have very little power in the medical arena. In contrast, insurance companies have considerable power and may decide that certain costs are not reimbursable—for example, the costs of treating uninsured patients.

14-18 (30 min.) Cost allocation to divisions.

1.

	Hotel	Restaurant	Casino	Rembrandt
Revenue	$16,425,000	$5,256,000	$12,340,000	$34,021,000
Direct costs	9,819,260	3,749,172	4,248,768	17,817,200
Segment margin	$ 6,605,740	$1,506,828	$ 8,091,232	16,203,800
Indirect costs				14,550,000
Income before taxes				$ 1,653,800
Segment margin %	40.22%	28.67%	65.57%	

2.

	Hotel	Restaurant	Casino	Rembrandt
Direct costs	$9,819,260	$3,749,172	$4,248,768	$17,817,200
Direct cost %	55.11%	21.04%	23.85%	100.00%
Square footage	80,000	16,000	64,000	160,000
Square footage %	50.00%	10.00%	40.00%	100.00%
# of Employees	200	50	250	500
# of Employees %	40.00%	10.00%	50.00%	100.00%

A: Cost allocation based on direct costs:

	Hotel	Restaurant	Casino	Rembrandt
Revenue	$16,425,000	$ 5,256,000	$12,340,000	$34,021,000
Direct costs	9,819,260	3,749,172	4,248,768	17,817,200
Segment margin	6,605,740	1,506,828	8,091,232	16,203,800
Allocated indirect costs	8,018,505	3,061,320	3,470,175	14,550,000
Segment pre-tax income	$(1,412,765)	$ (1,554,492)	$ 4,621,057	$ 1,653,800
Segment pre-tax income %	−8.60%	−29.58%	37.45%	

B: Cost allocation based on floor space:

	Hotel	Restaurant	Casino	Rembrandt
Allocated indirect costs	$7,275,000	$1,455,000	$5,820,000	$14,550,000
Segment pre-tax income	$ (669,260)	$ 51,828	$2,271,232	$ 1,653,800
Segment pre-tax income %	−4.07%	0.99%	18.41%	

C: Cost allocation based on # of employees

	Hotel	Restaurant	Casino	Rembrandt
Allocated indirect costs	$5,820,000	$1,455,000	$7,275,000	$14,550,000
Segment pre-tax income	$ 785,740	$ 51,828	$ 816,232	$ 1,653,800
Segment pre-tax income %	4.78%	0.99%	6.61%	

3. The segment pre-tax income percentages show the dramatic effect of choice of the cost allocation base on reported numbers:

Denominator	Hotel	Restaurant	Casino
Direct costs	−8.60%	−29.58%	37.45%
Floor space	−4.07	0.99	18.41
# of employees	4.78	0.99	6.61

The decision context should guide a. whether costs should be allocated, and b. the preferred cost allocation base. Decisions about, say, performance measurement may be made on a combination of financial and nonfinancial measures. It may well be that Rembrandt may prefer to exclude allocated costs from the financial measures to reduce areas of dispute.

Where cost allocation is required, the cause-and-effect and benefits-received criteria are recommended in Chapter 14. The $14,550,000 is a fixed overhead cost. This means that on a short-run basis, the cause-and-effect criterion is not appropriate but Rembrandt could attempt to identify the cost drivers for these costs in the long run when these costs are likely to be more variable. Rembrandt should look at how the $14,550,000 cost benefits the three divisions. This will help guide the choice of an allocation base in the short run.

4. The analysis in requirement 2 should not guide the decision on whether to shut down any of the divisions. The overhead costs are fixed costs in the short run. It is not clear how these costs would be affected in the long run if Rembrandt shut down one of the divisions. Also, each division is not independent of the other two. A decision to shut down, say, the restaurant likely would negatively affect the attendance at the casino and possibly the hotel. Rembrandt should examine the future revenue and future cost implications of different resource investments in the three divisions. This is a future-oriented exercise, whereas the analysis in requirement 2 is an analysis of past costs.

14-20 (20–30 min.) Customer profitability, service company.

1. (in thousands)

	Customer Revenues	Customer Costs	Customer Operating Income
Avery Group	$ 260	$182	$ 78
Duran Systems	180	184	(4)
Retail Systems	163	178	(15)
Wizard Partners	322	225	97
Santa Clara College	235	308	(73)
Grainger Services	80	74	6
Software Partners	174	100	74
Problem Solvers	76	108	(32)
Business Systems	137	110	27
Okie Enterprises	373	231	142

Solution Exhibits 14-20A and 14-20B present the summary results. The two most profitable customers provide 80% of total operating income.

2. The options Instant Service should consider include:

a. Increase the attention paid to Okie Enterprises and Wizard Partners. These are "key customers," and every effort has to be made to ensure they retain IS. IS may well want to suggest a minor price reduction to signal how important it is in their view to provide a cost-effective service to these customers.

b. Seek ways of reducing the costs or increasing the revenues of the problem accounts— Santa Clara College and Problem Solvers. For example, are the copying machines at Santa Clara outdated and in need of repair? If yes, an increased charge may be appropriate. Can IS provide better on-site guidelines to users about ways to reduce breakdowns?

c. As a last resort, IS may want to consider dropping particular accounts. For example, if Santa Clara College will not agree to a fee increase but has machines continually breaking down, IS may well decide that it is time not to bid on any more work for this customer.

3. Major problems in accurately estimating the operating costs of each customer are:

a. Basic underlying records may not be accurate. For example, some technicians include travel time, break time, etc., in their time records to create an appearance of high work effort.

b. Not all costs for individual repair people are easily assignable to individual customers. For example, how is the cost of a trip to pick up parts for three customers assigned among individual customers?

c. Many costs of IS are not related to specific customers. For example, advertising by IS is aimed at a general market rather than being targeted to a specific potential customer.

14-20 (Cont'd.)

SOLUTION EXHIBIT 14-20A
Panel A: Customers Ranked on Customer-Level Operating Income

	Customer Operating Income (1)	Customer Revenue (2)	Customer Operating Income Divided By Revenue (3) = (1) ÷ (2)	Cumulative Customer Operating Income (4)	Operating Income as a % of Total Operating Income (5) = (4) ÷ $300
Okie Ent.	$142	$ 373	38%	$142	47%
Wizard P.	97	322	30	239	80
Avery Group	78	260	30	317	106
Software P.	74	174	43	391	130
Business S.	27	137	20	418	139
Grainger S.	6	80	8	424	141
Duran S.	(4)	180	(2)	420	140
Retail S.	(15)	163	(9)	405	135
Problem S.	(32)	76	(42)	373	124
Santa Clara	(73)	235	(31)	300	100
	$300	$2,000			

SOLUTION EXHIBIT 14-20B
Bar Chart of Customer Operating Income

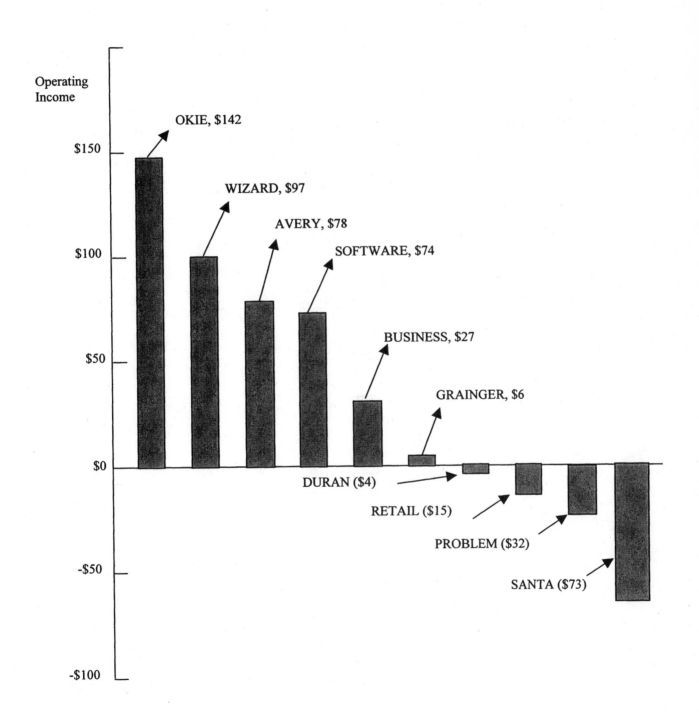

14-22   (30–40 min.) **Variance analysis, multiple products.**

1.

$$\text{Sales-volume variance} = \left(\begin{array}{c} \text{Actual sales} \\ \text{quantity in units} \end{array} - \begin{array}{c} \text{Budgeted sales} \\ \text{quantity in units} \end{array} \right) \times \begin{array}{c} \text{Budgeted contribution} \\ \text{margin per ticket} \end{array}$$

Lower-tier tickets	= (3,300 – 4,000) × $20	= $14,000 U
Upper-tier tickets	= (7,700 – 6,000) × $ 5	= $\underline{\quad 8,500}$ F
All tickets		$\underline{\underline{\$\ 5,500}}$ U

2.

$$\begin{array}{c} \text{Budgeted average} \\ \text{contribution margin per unit} \end{array} = \frac{(4,000 \times \$20) + (6,000 \times \$5)}{10,000}$$

$$= \frac{\$80,000 + \$30,000}{10,000} = \frac{\$110,000}{10,000}$$

$$= \$11 \text{ per unit (seat sold)}$$

Sales-mix percentages:

	Budgeted	Actual
Lower-tier	$\dfrac{4,000}{10,000} = 0.40$	$\dfrac{3,300}{11,000} = 0.30$
Upper-tier	$\dfrac{6,000}{10,000} = 0.60$	$\dfrac{7,700}{11,000} = 0.70$

14-22 (Cont'd.)

Solution Exhibit 14-22 presents the sales-volume, sales-quantity, and sales-mix variances for lower-tier tickets, upper-tier tickets, and in total for Detroit Penguins in 2004.

The sales-quantity variances can also be computed as:

$$\begin{matrix} \text{Sales-quantity} \\ \text{variance} \end{matrix} = \begin{pmatrix} \begin{matrix}\text{Actual units} \\ \text{of all tickets} \\ \text{sold}\end{matrix} - \begin{matrix}\text{Budgeted units} \\ \text{of all tickets} \\ \text{sold}\end{matrix} \end{pmatrix} \times \begin{matrix}\text{Budgeted} \\ \text{sales - mix} \\ \text{percentage}\end{matrix} \times \begin{matrix}\text{Budgeted} \\ \text{cont. margin} \\ \text{per ticket}\end{matrix}$$

The sales-quantity variances are:

Lower-tier tickets	= (11,000 – 10,000) × 0.40 × $20 =	$ 8,000 F
Upper-tier tickets	= (11,000 – 10,000) × 0.60 × $ 5 =	3,000 F
All tickets		$11,000 F

The sales-mix variance can also be computed as:

$$\begin{matrix} \text{Sales-mix} \\ \text{variance} \end{matrix} = \begin{matrix}\text{Actual units} \\ \text{of all tickets} \times \\ \text{sold}\end{matrix} \begin{pmatrix} \begin{matrix}\text{Actual sales -} \\ \text{mix percentage}\end{matrix} - \begin{matrix}\text{Budgeted sales -} \\ \text{mix percentage}\end{matrix} \end{pmatrix} \times \begin{matrix}\text{Budgeted} \\ \text{cont. margin} \\ \text{per ticket}\end{matrix}$$

The sales-mix variances are:

Lower-tier tickets	= 11,000 × (0.30 – 0.40) × $20 =	$22,000 U
Upper-tier tickets	= 11,000 × (0.70 – 0.60) × $ 5 =	5,500 F
All tickets		$16,500 U

3.   The Detroit Penguins increased average attendance by 10% per game. However, there was a sizable shift from lower-tier seats (budgeted contribution margin of $20 per seat) to the upper-tier seats (budgeted contribution margin of $5 per seat). The net result: the actual contribution margin was $5,500 below the budgeted contribution margin.

14-22 (Cont'd.)

SOLUTION EXHIBIT 14-22
Columnar Presentation of Sales-Volume, Sales-Quantity and Sales-Mix Variances for Detroit Penguins

	Flexible Budget: Actual Units of All Products Sold × Actual Sales Mix × Budgeted Contribution Margin per Unit (1)	Actual Units of All Products Sold × Budgeted Sales Mix × Budgeted Contribution Margin per Unit (2)	Static Budget: Budgeted Units of All Products Sold × Budgeted Sales Mix × Budgeted Contribution Margin per Unit (3)
Panel A: Lower-tier	$(11,000 \times 0.30^a) \times \$20$ $3,300 \times \$20$ $\$66,000$	$(11,000 \times 0.40^b) \times \$20$ $4,400 \times \$20$ $\$88,000$	$(10,000 \times 0.40^b) \times \$20$ $4,000 \times \$20$ $\$80,000$

$\uparrow$ ————— $22,000U$ ————— $\uparrow$ ————— $8,000 F$ ————— $\uparrow$
Sales-mix variance　　　　　　Sales-quantity variance
$\uparrow$ —————————— $14,000 U$ —————————— $\uparrow$
Sales-volume variance

Panel B: Upper-tier	$(11,000 \times 0.70^c) \times \$5$ $7,700 \times \$5$ $\$38,500$	$(11,000 \times 0.60^d) \times \$5$ $6,600 \times \$5$ $\$33,000$	$(10,000 \times 0.60^d) \times \$5$ $6,000 \times \$5$ $\$30,000$

$\uparrow$ ————— $5,500 F$ ————— $\uparrow$ ————— $3,000 F$ ————— $\uparrow$
Sales-mix variance　　　　　　Sales-quantity variance
$\uparrow$ —————————— $8,500 F$ —————————— $\uparrow$
Sales-volume variance

Panel C: All Tickets (Sum of Lower-tier and Upper-tier tickets)	$\$104,500^e$	$\$121,000^f$	$\$110,000^g$

$\uparrow$ ————— $16,500 U$ ————— $\uparrow$ ————— $11,000 F$ ————— $\uparrow$
Total sales-mix variance　　　　Total sales-quantity variance
$\uparrow$ —————————— $5,500 U$ —————————— $\uparrow$
Total sales-volume variance

F = favorable effect on operating income; U = unfavorable effect on operating income.

Actual Sales Mix:
^{a}Lower-tier= $3,300 \div 11,000$ = 30%
^{c}Upper-tier = $7,700 \div 11,000$ = 70%
$^e\$66,000 + 38,500 = \$104,500$

Budgeted Sales Mix:
^{b}Lower-tier = $4,000 \div 10,000$ = 40%
^{d}Upper-tier = $6,000 \div 10,000$ = 60%
$^f \$88,000 + \$33,000 = \$121,000$
$^g \$80,000 + \$30,000 = \$110,000$

14-22 (Cont'd.)

14-22 Excel Application

**Revenues, Sales Variances, and
Customer Profitability Analysis
Detroit Penguins**

Original Data

	Lower-Tier Tickets	Upper-Tier Tickets
Selling price	$35	$14
Downtown arena fee	10	6
Reservation network fee	5	3
Contribution margin per ticket	$20	$ 5

	Budgeted Seats Sold	Actual Seats Sold
Lower-Tier	4,000	3,300
Upper-Tier	6,000	7,700
Total	10,000	11,000

Problem 1
Sales Volume Variance calculations

Lower-tier tickets	$(14,000)	U
Upper-tier tickets	$ 8,500	F
All tickets	$ (5,500)	U

Problem 2

Sales - mix percentages

	Budgeted	Actual
Lower-tier	0.4	0.3
Upper-tier	0.6	0.7

Sales-quantity variance calculations

Lower-tier tickets	$ 8,000	F
Upper-tier tickets	$ 3,000	F
All tickets	$11,000	F

Sales-mix variance calculations

Lower-tier tickets	$(22,000)	U
Upper-tier tickets	$ 5,500	F
All tickets	$(16,500)	U

14-24 (60 min.) Variance analysis, multiple products.

1. Budget for 2003

	Selling Price (1)	Variable Cost per Unit (2)	Contrib. Margin per Unit (3) = (1) − (2)	Units Sold (4)	Sales Mix (5)	Contribution Margin (6) = (3) × (4)
Kola	$6.00	$4.00	$2.00	400,000	16%	$ 800,000
Limor	4.00	2.80	1.20	600,000	24	720,000
Orlem	7.00	4.50	2.50	1,500,000	60	3,750,000
Total				2,500,000	100%	$5,270,000

Actual for 2003

	Selling Price (1)	Variable Cost per Unit (2)	Contrib. Margin per Unit (3) = (1) − (2)	Units Sold (4)	Sales Mix (5)	Contribution Margin (6) = (3) × (4)
Kola	$6.20	$4.50	$1.70	480,000	16%	$ 816,000
Limor	4.25	2.75	1.50	900,000	30	1,350,000
Orlem	6.80	4.60	2.20	1,620,000	54	3,564,000
Total				3,000,000	100%	$5,730,000

Solution Exhibit 14-24 presents the sales-volume, sales-quantity, and sales-mix variances for each product and in total for 2003.

$$\text{Sales-volume variance} = \left[\begin{array}{c} \text{Actual sales} \\ \text{quantity} \\ \text{in units} \end{array} - \begin{array}{c} \text{Budgeted sales} \\ \text{quantity} \\ \text{in units} \end{array} \right] \times \begin{array}{c} \text{Budgeted} \\ \text{contrib. margin} \\ \text{per unit} \end{array}$$

Kola	= (480,000 − 400,000) × $2.00	=	$160,000 F
Limor	= (900,000 − 600,000) × $1.20	=	360,000 F
Orlem	= (1,620,000 − 1,500,000) × $2.50	=	300,000 F
Total			$820,000 F

$$\text{Sales-quantity variance} = \left[\begin{array}{c} \text{Actual units} \\ \text{of all products} \\ \text{sold} \end{array} - \begin{array}{c} \text{Budgeted units} \\ \text{of all products} \\ \text{sold} \end{array} \right] \times \begin{array}{c} \text{Budgeted} \\ \text{sales-mix} \\ \text{percentage} \end{array} \times \begin{array}{c} \text{Budgeted} \\ \text{contrib. margin} \\ \text{per unit} \end{array}$$

Kola	= (3,000,000 − 2,500,000) × 0.16 × $2.00	=	$ 160,000 F
Limor	= (3,000,000 − 2,500,000) × 0.24 × $1.20	=	144,000 F
Orlem	= (3,000,000 − 2,500,000) × 0.60 × $2.50	=	750,000 F
Total			$1,054,000 F

14-24 (Cont'd.)

Sales-mix variance		Actual units of all products sold	×	(Actual sales-mix percentage	−	Budgeted sales-mix percentage)	×	Budgeted contrib. margin per unit

Kola	= 3,000,000 × (0.16 – 0.16) × $2.00	=	$ 0
Limor	= 3,000,000 × (0.30– 0.24) × $1.20	=	216,000 F
Orlem	= 3,000,000 × (0.54 – 0.60) × $2.50	=	450,000 U
Total			$234,000 U

2.   The breakdown of the favorable sales-volume variance of $820,000 shows that the biggest contributor is the 500,000 unit increase in sales resulting in a favorable sales-quantity variance of $1,054,000. There is a partially offsetting unfavorable sales-mix variance of $234,000 in contribution margin.

SOLUTION EXHIBIT 14-24

Sales-Mix and Sales-Quantity Variance Analysis of Soda King for 2003

	Flexible Budget: Actual Units of All Products Sold × Actual Sales Mix × Budgeted Contribution Margin Per Unit	Actual Units of All Products Sold × Budgeted Sales Mix × Budgeted Contribution Margin Per Unit	Static Budget: Budgeted Units of All Products Sold × Budgeted Sales Mix × Budgeted Contribution Margin Per Unit
Kola	3,000,000 × 0.16 × $2 = $ 960,000	3,000,000 × 0.16 × $2 = $ 960,000	2,500,000 × 0.16 × $2 = $ 800,000
Limor	3,000,000 × 0.30 × $1.20 = 1,080,000	3,000,000 × 0.24 × $1.20 = 864,000	2,500,000 × 0.24 × $1.20 = 720,000
Orlem	3,000,000 × 0.54 × $2.50 = 4,050,000	3,000,000 × 0.60 × $2.50 = 4,500,000	2,500,000 × 0.60 × $2.50 = 3,750,000
	$6,090,000	$6,324,000	$5,270,000

$234,000 U	$1,054,000 F
Sales-mix variance	Sales-quantity variance

$820,000 F
Sales-volume variance

F = favorable effect on operating income; U= unfavorable effect on operating income

14-13

14-26 (40 min.) Allocation of central corporate costs to divisions.

1. The purposes for allocating central corporate costs to each division include:

a. **To provide information for economic decisions.** Allocations can signal to division managers that decisions to expand (contract) activities will likely require increases (decreases) in corporate costs that should be considered in the initial decision about expansion (contraction). When top management is allocating resources to divisions, analysis of relative division profitability should consider differential use of corporate services by divisions. Some allocation schemes can encourage the use of central services that would otherwise be underutilized. A common rationale related to this purpose is "to remind profit center managers that central corporate costs exist and that division earnings must be adequate to cover some share of those costs."

b. **Motivation.** Creates an incentive for division managers to control costs; for example, by reducing the number of employees at a division, a manager will save direct labor costs as well as central personnel and payroll costs allocated on the basis of number of employees. Allocation also creates incentives for division managers to monitor the effectiveness and efficiency with which central corporate costs are spent.

c. **Cost justification or reimbursement.** Some lines of business of Richfield Oil may be regulated with cost data used in determining "fair prices"; allocations of central corporate costs will result in higher prices being set by a regulator.

d. **Income measurement for external parties.** Richfield Oil may include allocations of central corporate costs in its external line-of-business reporting.

Instructors may wish to discuss the "Surveys of Company Practice" evidence from the United States, Canada, Australia, and the United Kingdom in Chapter 14 (p. 488).

2. Total costs in single pool = $3,000
Allocation base = $30,000 revenue
Allocation rate = $3,000 ÷ $30,000 = $0.10 per $1 of revenue
See Solution Exhibit 14-26 for additional answers.

14-26 (Cont'd.)

3.   See Solution Exhibit 14-26 for answer.

SOLUTION EXHIBIT 14-26
(in millions)

	Oil & Gas Upstream	Oil & Gas Downstream	Chemical Products	Copper Mining	Total
Revenues	$7,000	$16,000	$4,000	$3,000	$30,000
Operating costs	3,000	15,000	3,800	3,200	25,000
Allocated costs, $0.10 per $1 revenue	700	1,600	400	300	3,000
Division income	$3,300	$ (600)	$ (200)	$ (500)	$ 2,000

Allocation Base	Oil & Gas Upstream	Oil & Gas Downstream	Chemical Products	Copper Mining
1. Allocated on basis of identifiable assets	14/25	6/25	3/25	2/25
Total costs = $2,000	$1,120	$480	$240	$160
2. Allocated on basis of revenues	7/30	16/30	4/30	3/30
Total costs = $600	$140	$320	$ 80	$ 60
3. Allocated on basis of operating income (if positive)	40/52	10/52	2/52	--
Total costs = $208	$160	$ 40	$ 8	$ 0
4. Allocated on basis of number of employees	9/30	12/30	6/30	3/30
Total costs = $192	$ 57.6	$ 76.8	$ 38.4	$ 19.2

	Oil & Gas Upstream	Oil & Gas Downstream	Chemical Products	Copper Mining	Total
Revenues	$7,000	$16,000	$4,000	$3,000	$30,000
Operating costs	3,000	15,000	3,800	3,200	25,000
Cost Pool 1 Allocation	1,120	480	240	160	2,000
Cost Pool 2 Allocation	140	320	80	60	600
Cost Pool 3 Allocation	160	40	8	0	208
Cost Pool 4 Allocation	57.6	76.8	38.4	19.2	192
Division income	$2,522.4	$ 83.2	$ (166.4)	$ (439.2)	$ 2,000

4.   Strengths of Rhodes' proposal relative to existing single-cost pool method:

a.   Better able to capture cause-and-effect relationships. Interest on debt is more likely caused by the financing of assets than by revenues. Personnel and payroll costs are more likely caused by the number of employees than by revenues.

b.   Relatively simple. No extra information need be collected beyond that already available. (Some students will list the extra costs of Rhodes' proposal as a weakness. However, for a company with $30 billion in revenues, those extra costs are minimal.)

Weaknesses of Rhodes' proposal relative to existing single-cost pool method:

a.   May promote dysfunctional decision making. May encourage division managers to lease or rent assets rather than to purchase assets, even where it is economical for Richfield Oil to purchase them. This off-balance sheet financing will reduce the "identifiable assets" of the division and thus will reduce the interest on debt costs allocated to the division. (Richfield Oil could counteract this problem by incorporating leased and rented assets in the "identifiable assets" base.)

Note: Some students criticized Rhodes' proposal, even though agreeing that it is preferable to the existing single-cost pool method. These criticisms include:

a.   Proposal does not adequately capture cause-and-effect relationships for the legal and research and development cost pools. For these cost pools, specific identification of individual projects with an individual division can better capture cause-and-effect relationships.

b.   Proposal may give rise to disputes over the definition and valuation of "identifiable assets."

c.   Use of actual rather than budgeted amounts in the allocation bases creates interdependencies between divisions. Moreover, use of actual amounts means that division managers do not know cost allocation consequences of their decisions until the end of each reporting period.

d.   Separate allocation of fixed and variable costs would result in more refined cost allocations.

e.   Questionable that 100% of central corporate costs should be allocated. Many students argue that public affairs should not be allocated to any division, based on the notion that division managers may not control many of the individual expenditures in this cost pool.

14-28 (60 min.) **Customer-profitability analysis, customer cost hierarchy.**

1.

Item	April	Madison	Suitors	Design
Revenues at list prices				
$17,600^a \times \$200$; $12,400^b \times \$200$;				
$6,360^c \times \$200$; $6,250^d \times \$200$	\$3,520,000	\$2,480,000	\$1,272,000	\$1,250,000
Discount				
$17,600 \times \$60^e$; $12,400 \times \$40^f$;				
$6,360 \times \$30^g$; $6,250 \times \$20^h$	1,056,000	496,000	190,800	125,000
Revenues (at actual prices)	2,464,000	1,984,000	1,081,200	1,125,000
Cost of goods sold				
$17,600 \times \$110$; $12,400 \times \$110$;				
$6,360 \times \$110$; $6,250 \times \$110$	1,936,000	1,364,000	699,600	687,500
Gross Margin	528,000	620,000	381,600	437,500
Customer-level operating costs				
Order processing				
$44, 62, 212, 250 \times \$245$	10,780	15,190	51,940	61,250
Sales visits				
$8, 12, 22, 20 \times \$1,430$	11,440	17,160	31,460	28,600
Delivery – regular				
$41, 48, 166, 190 \times \$300$	12,300	14,400	49,800	57,000
Delivery – rushed				
$3, 14, 46, 60 \times \$850$	2,550	11,900	39,100	51,000
Total customer-level operating costs	37,070	58,650	172,300	197,850
Customer-level operating income	\$ 490,930	\$ 561,350	\$ 209,300	\$ 239,650

[a] $44 \times 400 = 17,600$
[b] $62 \times 200 = 12,400$
[c] $212 \times 30 = 6,360$
[d] $250 \times 25 = 6,250$
[e] $\$200 – \$140 = \$60$
[f] $\$200 – \$160 = \$40$
[g] $\$200 – \$170 = \$30$
[h] $\$200 – \$180 = \$20$

2. Key challenges facing Sims are:
   a. Reduce level of price discounting, especially by April
   b. Reduce level of customer-level costs, especially by Suitors and Design

The ABC cost system highlights areas where the Suitors and Design accounts are troublesome. They have:

   - A high number of orders,
   - A high number of customer visits, and
   - A high number of rushed deliveries.

Sims needs to consider whether this high level of activity can be reduced without reducing customer revenues.

3. Solution Exhibit 14-28 presents a customer cost hierarchy report for Zoot's Suits.

SOLUTION EXHIBIT 14-28
Income Statement of Zoot's Suits for 2003

			Customer Distribution Channels				
		Wholesale Customers			Retail Customers		
	Total (1)	Total (2)	April (3)	Madison (4)	Total (5)	Suitors (6)	Design (7)
Revenues (at actual prices)	$6,654,200	$4,448,000	$2,464,000	$1,984,000	$2,206,200	$1,081,200	$1,125,000
Customer-level optg. costs	5,152,970	3,395,720	1,973,070	1,422,650	1,757,250	871,900	885,350
Customer-level operating income	1,501,230	1,052,280	$ 490,930	$ 561,350	448,950	$ 209,300	$ 239,650
Distribution-channel costs	560,000	350,000			210,000		
Distribution-channel-level operating income	941,230	$ 702,280			$ 238,950		
Corporate-sustaining costs	250,000						
Operating income	$ 691,230						

14-18

14-30 (40 min.) **Customer loyalty clubs and profitability analysis.**

1.

Gold Program

Revenues	
2,430 × 20 × ($200 × 0.90)	$ 8,748,000
2,430 × 30 × ($200 × 0.80)	11,664,000
2,430 × 10 × ($200 × 0.70)	3,402,000
Total revenues	23,814,000
Variable Costs	
Hotel variable costs, 2,430 × 60 × $65	9,477,000
Wine Costs	
2,430 × 50 × $5	607,500
2,430 × 10 × $20	486,000
Restaurant costs	
2,430 × 20 × $10	486,000
2,430 × 30 × $15	1,093,500
2,430 × 10 × $20	486,000
Total variable costs	12,636,000
Contribution margin	$11,178,000

Silver Program
Revenues

8,340 × 20 × ($200 × 0.90)	$30,024,000
8,340 × 15 × ($200 × 0.80)	20,016,000
Total revenues	50,040,000
Variable Costs	
Hotel variable costs, 8,340 × 35 × $65	18,973,500
Wine costs, 8,340 × 35 × $5	1,459,500
Restaurant Costs	
8,340 × 20 × $10	1,668,000
8,340 × 15 × $15	1,876,500
Total variable costs	23,977,500
Contribution margin	$26,062,500

Bronze Program

Revenues, 80,300 × 10 × ($200 × 0.90)	$144,540,000
Variable costs	
Hotel variable costs, 80,300 × 10 × $65	52,195,000
Wine costs 80,300 × 10 × $5	4,015,000
Restaurant costs 80,300 × 10 × $10	8,030,000
Total variable costs	64,240,000
Contribution margin	$ 80,300,000

No Program

Revenues, 219,000 × 1 × $200	$43,800,000
Variable costs, 219,000 × 1 × $65	14,235,000
Contribution margin	$29,565,000

Loyalty Program	Total Revenues	Variable Costs	Contribution Margin	Contrib. Margin ÷ Total Revenues
Gold	$ 23,814,000	$ 12,636,000	$ 11,178,000	46.94%
Silver	50,040,000	23,977,500	26,062,500	52.08
Bronze	144,540,000	64,240,000	80,300,000	55.56
No program	43,800,000	14,235,000	29,565,000	67.50
Total	$262,194,000	$115,088,500	$147,105,500	

The no-program group of customers has the highest contribution margin per revenue dollar. However, it comprises only 16.71% ($43,800,000 ÷ $262,194,000) of total revenues. The gold program has the lowest contribution margin per revenue dollar. However, it is misleading to evaluate each program in isolation. A key aim of loyalty programs is to promote a high frequency of return business. The contribution margin to total revenue ratio of each program in isolation does not address this issue.

14-30 (Cont'd.)

2.

Revenues	$262,194,000
Variable costs	115,088,500
Contribution margin	147,105,500
Fixed costs	140,580,000
Operating income	$ 6,525,500

2. Number of room nights

Gold, 2,430 × 60	145,800
Silver, 8,340 × 35	291,900
Bronze, 80,300 × 10	803,000
No program, 219,000 × 1	219,000
	1,459,700

Average room rate per night: $\dfrac{\$262,194,000}{1,459,700} = \$179.62$

Average variable cost per night: $\dfrac{\$115,088,500}{1,459,700} = \$78.84$

3. Sherriton Hotels has fixed costs of $140,580,000. A key challenge is to attract a high number of repeat business customers. Loyalty programs aim to have customers return to Sherriton multiple times. Their aim is increasing the revenues beyond what they would be without the program. It is to be expected that the higher the level of nights stayed, the greater the inducements necessary to keep attracting the customer to return. However, given the low level of variable costs to room rates, there is considerable cushion available for Sherriton to offer high inducements for frequent stayers.

Sherriton could adopt a net present value analysis of customers who are in the different loyalty clubs. It would be informative for Sherriton to have information on how much of each customer's total lodging industry expenditures it captures. It may well want to give higher levels of inducements to frequent stayers if the current program attracts only, say, 30% of each of its frequent customer's total business in cities where it has lodging properties available.

14-32 (60 min.)   Variance analysis, sales-mix, and sales-quantity variances.

1. Actual Contribution Margins

Product	Actual Selling Price	Actual Variable Costs per Unit	Actual Contribution Margin per Unit	Actual Sales Volume in Units	Actual Contribution Dollars	Actual Contribution Percent
Palm Pro	$349	$178	$171	11,000	$ 1,881,000	16%
Palm CE	285	92	193	44,000	8,492,000	71%
PalmKid	102	73	29	55,000	1,595,000	13%
				110,000	$11,968,000	100%

The actual average contribution margin per unit is $108.80 ($11,968,000 ÷ 110,000 units).

Budgeted Contribution Margins

Product	Budgeted Selling Price	Budgeted Variable Costs per Unit	Budgeted Contribution Margin per Unit	Budgeted Sales Volume in Units	Budgeted Contribution Dollars	Budgeted Contribution Percent
Palm Pro	$379	$182	$197	12,500	$ 2,462,500	19%
Palm CE	269	98	171	37,500	6,412,500	49%
Palm Kid	149	65	84	50,000	4,200,000	32%
				100,000	$13,075,000	100%

The budgeted average contribution margin per unit is $130.75 ($13,075,000 ÷ 100,000 units).

2. Actual Sales Mix

Product	Actual Sales Volume in Units	Actual Sales Mix
Palm Pro	11,000	10.0% (11,000 ÷ 110,000)
Palm CE	44,000	40.0% (44,000 ÷ 110,000)
Palm Kid	55,000	50.0% (55,000 ÷ 110,000)
	110,000	100.0%

Budgeted Sales Mix

Product	Budgeted Sales Volume in Units	Budgeted Sales Mix
Palm Pro	12,500	12.5% (12,500 ÷ 100,000)
Palm CE	37,500	37.5% (37,500 ÷ 100,000)
Palm Kid	50,000	50.0% (50,000 ÷ 100,000)
	100,000	100.0%

14-32 (Cont'd.)

3. Sales-volume variance:

$$= \begin{pmatrix} \text{Actual sales} \\ \text{quantity} \\ \text{in units} \end{pmatrix} - \begin{pmatrix} \text{Budgeted sales} \\ \text{quantity} \\ \text{in units} \end{pmatrix} \times \begin{array}{c} \text{Budgeted} \\ \text{contrib. margin} \\ \text{per unit} \end{array}$$

PalmPro	(11,000	–	12,500)	×	$197	$ 295,500 U
PalmCE	(44,000	–	37,500)	×	$171	1,111,500 F
PalmKid	(55,000	–	50,000)	×	$ 84	420,000 F
Total sales-volume variance						$1,236,000 F

Sales-mix variance:

$$= \begin{array}{c} \text{Actual units} \\ \text{of all} \\ \text{products sold} \end{array} \times \begin{pmatrix} \text{Actual} \\ \text{sales mix} \\ \text{percentage} \end{pmatrix} - \begin{pmatrix} \text{Budgeted} \\ \text{sales mix} \\ \text{percentage} \end{pmatrix} \times \begin{array}{c} \text{Budgeted} \\ \text{contrib. margin} \\ \text{per unit} \end{array}$$

PalmPro	=	110,000	×	(0.10	–	0.125)	×	$197	$541,750 U
PalmCE	=	110,000	×	(0.40	–	0.375)	×	$171	470,250 F
PalmKid	=	110,000	×	(0.50	–	0.50)	×	$ 84	0 F
Total sales-mix variance									$ 71,500 U

Sales-quantity variance:

$$= \begin{pmatrix} \text{Actual units} \\ \text{of all} \\ \text{products sold} \end{pmatrix} - \begin{pmatrix} \text{Budgeted units} \\ \text{of all} \\ \text{products sold} \end{pmatrix} \times \begin{array}{c} \text{Budgeted} \\ \text{sales mix} \\ \text{percentage} \end{array} \times \begin{array}{c} \text{Budgeted} \\ \text{contrib. margin} \\ \text{per unit} \end{array}$$

PalmPro	(110,000	–	100,000)	×	0.125	×	$197	$ 246,250 F
PalmCE	(110,000	–	100,000)	×	0.375	×	$171	641,250 F
PalmKid	(110,000	–	100,000)	×	0.50	×	$ 84	420,000 F
Total sales-quantity variance								$1,307,500 F

14-32 (Cont'd.)

Solution Exhibit 14-32 presents the sales-volume variance, the sales-mix variance, and the sales-quantity variance for Palm Pro, Palm CE, and PalmKid and in total for Third Quarter 2004

SOLUTION EXHIBIT 14-32

Sales-Mix and Sales-Quantity Variance Analysis of Aussie Infonautics for Third Quarter 2004

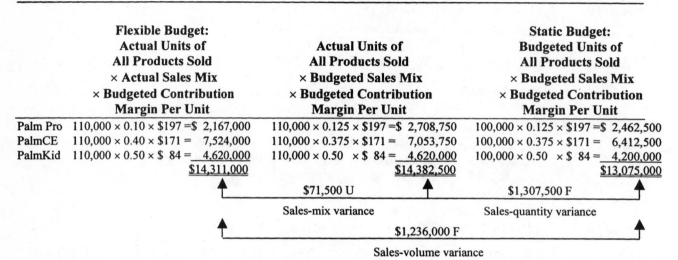

	Flexible Budget: Actual Units of All Products Sold × Actual Sales Mix × Budgeted Contribution Margin Per Unit	Actual Units of All Products Sold × Budgeted Sales Mix × Budgeted Contribution Margin Per Unit	Static Budget: Budgeted Units of All Products Sold × Budgeted Sales Mix × Budgeted Contribution Margin Per Unit
Palm Pro	110,000 × 0.10 × $197 =$ 2,167,000	110,000 × 0.125 × $197 =$ 2,708,750	100,000 × 0.125 × $197 =$ 2,462,500
PalmCE	110,000 × 0.40 × $171 = 7,524,000	110,000 × 0.375 × $171 = 7,053,750	100,000 × 0.375 × $171 = 6,412,500
PalmKid	110,000 × 0.50 × $ 84 = 4,620,000	110,000 × 0.50 × $ 84 = 4,620,000	100,000 × 0.50 × $ 84 = 4,200,000
	$14,311,000	$14,382,500	$13,075,000

$71,500 U → Sales-mix variance

$1,307,500 F → Sales-quantity variance

$1,236,000 F → Sales-volume variance

F = favorable effect on operating income; U= unfavorable effect on operating income

4.   The following factors help us understand the differences between actual and budgeted amounts.

- The difference in actual versus budgeted contribution margins was $1,107,000 unfavorable ($11,968,000 – $13,075,000). However, the contribution margin from the PalmCE exceeded budget by $2,079,500 while the contributions from the PalmPro and the PalmKid were lower than expected and offset this gain. This is attributable to lower unit sales in the case of PalmPro and lower contribution margins in the case of PalmKid.

- In percentage terms, the PalmCE accounted for 71% of actual contribution margin versus a planned 49% contribution margin. However, the PalmPro accounted for 16% versus planned 19% and the PalmKid accounted for only 13% versus a planned 32%.

- In unit terms (rather than in contribution terms), the PalmKid accounted for 50% of the sales mix as planned. However, the PalmPro accounted for only 10% versus a budgeted 12.5% and the PalmCE accounted for 40% versus a planned 37.5%.

- Variance analysis for the PalmPro shows an unfavorable sales-mix variance outweighing a favorable sales-quantity variance and producing an unfavorable sales-volume variance. The drop in sales-mix share was far larger than the gain from an overall greater quantity sold.

- The PalmCE gained both from an increase in share of the sales mix as well as from the increase in the overall number of units sold.

- The PalmKid maintained sales-mix share at 50%—as a result, the sales-mix variance is zero. However, PalmKid sales did gain from the overall increase in units sold.

- Overall, there was a favorable total sales-volume variance. However, the large drop in PalmKid's contribution margin per unit combined with a decrease in the actual number of PalmPro units sold as well as a drop in the actual contribution margin per unit below budget, led to the total contribution margin being much lower than budgeted.

Other factors could be discussed here—for example, it seems that the PalmKid did not achieve much success with a three digit price point—selling price was budgeted at $149 but dropped to $102. At the same time, variable costs increased. This could have been due to a marketing push that did not succeed.

14-34 (40 min.) Variance analysis, multiple products.

1, 2, and 3. Solution Exhibit 14-34 presents the sales-volume, sales-quantity, and sales-mix variances for each type of cookie and in total for Debbie's Delight Inc. in August 2003.

The sales-volume variances can also be computed as:

$$\text{Sales-volume variance} = \left(\begin{array}{c}\text{Actual sales} \\ \text{quantity in pounds}\end{array} - \begin{array}{c}\text{Budgeted sales} \\ \text{quantity in pounds}\end{array}\right) \times \begin{array}{c}\text{Budgeted contribution} \\ \text{margin per pound}\end{array}$$

The sales-volume variances are:

Chocolate chip	=	(57,600 – 45,000) × $2.00	=	$25,200 F
Oatmeal raisin	=	(18,000 – 25,000) × $2.30	=	16,100 U
Coconut	=	(9,600 – 10,000) × $2.60	=	1,040 U
White chocolate	=	(13,200 – 5,000) × $3.00	=	24,600 F
Macadamia nut	=	(21,600 – 15,000) × $3.10	=	20,460 F
All cookies				$53,120 F

The sales-quantity variance can also be computed as :

$$\text{Sales-quantity variance} = \left(\begin{array}{c}\text{Actual pounds} \\ \text{of all cookies} \\ \text{sold}\end{array} - \begin{array}{c}\text{Budgeted pounds} \\ \text{of all cookies} \\ \text{sold}\end{array}\right) \times \begin{array}{c}\text{Budgeted} \\ \text{sales-mix} \\ \text{percentage}\end{array} \times \begin{array}{c}\text{Budgeted} \\ \text{contribution} \\ \text{margin per pound}\end{array}$$

The sales-quantity variances are:

Chocolate chip	=	(120,000 – 100,000) × 0.45 × $2.00	=	$18,000 F
Oatmeal raisin	=	(120,000 – 100,000) × 0.25 × $2.30	=	11,500 F
Coconut	=	(120,000 – 100,000) × 0.10 × $2.60	=	5,200 F
White chocolate	=	(120,000 – 100,000) × 0.05 × $3.00	=	3,000 F
Macadamia nut	=	(120,000 – 100,000) × 0.15 × $3.10	=	9,300 F
All cookies				$47,000 F

14-34 (Cont'd.)

The sales-mix variance can also be computed as:

$$\begin{matrix} \text{Sales-mix} \\ \text{variance} \end{matrix} = \begin{pmatrix} \text{Actual sales-} \\ \text{mix percentage} \end{pmatrix} - \begin{pmatrix} \text{Budgeted sales-} \\ \text{mix percentage} \end{pmatrix} \times \begin{matrix} \text{Actual pounds} \\ \text{of all cookies} \\ \text{sold} \end{matrix} \times \begin{matrix} \text{Budgeted} \\ \text{contribution} \\ \text{margin per pound} \end{matrix}$$

The sales-mix variances are:

Chocolate chip	=	$(0.48 - 0.45) \times 120,000 \times \$2.00$	=	$ 7,200 F
Oatmeal raisin	=	$(0.15 - 0.25) \times 120,000 \times \$2.30$	=	27,600 U
Coconut	=	$(0.08 - 0.10) \times 120,000 \times \$2.60$	=	6,240 U
White chocolate	=	$(0.11 - 0.05) \times 120,000 \times \$3.00$	=	21,600 F
Macadamia nut	=	$(0.18 - 0.15) \times 120,000 \times \$3.10$	=	11,160 F
All cookies				$ 6,120 F

A summary of the variances is:

Sales-Volume Variance	
Chocolate chip	$25,200 F
Oatmeal raisin	16,100 U
Coconut	1,040 U
White chocolate	24,600 F
Macadamia nut	20,460 F
All cookies	$53,120 F

Sales-Mix Variance		Sales-Quantity Variance	
Chocolate chip	$ 7,200 F	Chocolate chip	$18,000 F
Oatmeal raisin	27,600 U	Oatmeal raisin	11,500 F
Coconut	6,240 U	Coconut	5,200 F
White chocolate	21,600 F	White chocolate	3,000 F
Macadamia nut	11,160 F	Macadamia nut	9,300 F
All cookies	$ 6,120 F	All cookies	$47,000 F

4.   Debbie's Delight shows a favorable sales-quantity variance because it sold more cookies in total than was budgeted. Together with the higher quantities, Debbie's also sold more of the high-contribution margin white chocolate and macadamia nut cookies relative to the budgeted mix—hence, Debbie's also showed a favorable total sales-mix variance.

14-34 (Cont'd.)

SOLUTION EXHIBIT 14-34

Columnar Presentation of Sales-Volume, Sales-Quantity, and Sales-Mix Variances for Debbie's Delight Inc.

	Flexible Budget: Actual Pounds of All Cookies Sold × Actual Sales Mix × Budgeted Contribution Margin per Pound (1)	Actual Pounds of All Cookies Sold × Budgeted Sales Mix × Budgeted Contribution Margin per Pound (2)	Static Budget: Budgeted Pounds of All Cookies Sold × Budgeted Sales Mix × Budgeted Contribution Margin per Pound (3)
Panel A: Chocolate Chip	$(120,000 \times 0.48^a) \times \$2$ $57,600 \times \$2$ $\$115,200$	$(120,000 \times 0.45^b) \times \$2$ $54,000 \times \$2$ $\$108,000$	$(100,000 \times 0.45^b) \times \$2$ $45,000 \times \$2$ $\$90,000$

$\$7,200$ F — Sales-mix variance $\qquad$ $\$18,000$ F — Sales-quantity variance

$\$25,200$ F — Sales-volume variance

Panel B: Oatmeal Raisin	$(120,000 \times 0.15^c) \times \$2.30$ $18,000 \times \$2.30$ $\$41,400$	$(120,000 \times 0.25^d) \times \$2.30$ $30,000 \times \$2.30$ $\$69,000$	$(100,000 \times 0.25^d) \times \$2.30$ $25,000 \times \$2.30$ $\$57,500$

$\$27,600$ U — Sales-mix variance $\qquad$ $\$11,500$ F — Sales-quantity variance

$\$16,100$ U — Sales-volume variance

Panel C: Coconut	$(120,000 \times 0.08^e) \times \$2.60$ $9,600 \times \$2.60$ $\$24,960$	$(120,000 \times 0.10^f) \times \$2.60$ $12,000 \times \$2.60$ $\$31,200$	$(100,000 \times 0.10^f) \times \$2.60$ $10,000 \times \$2.60$ $\$26,000$

$\$6,240$ U — Sales-mix variance $\qquad$ $\$5,200$ F — Sales-quantity variance

$\$1,040$ U — Sales-volume variance

F = favorable effect on operating income; U = unfavorable effect on operating income.

Actual Sales Mix:		Budgeted Sales Mix:	
[a]Chocolate Chip	$= 57,600 \div 120,000 = 48\%$	[b]Chocolate Chip	$= 45,000 \div 100,000 = 45\%$
[c]Oatmeal Raisin	$= 18,000 \div 120,000 = 15\%$	[d]Oatmeal Raisin	$= 25,000 \div 100,000 = 25\%$
[e]Coconut	$= 9,600 \div 120,000 = 8\%$	[f]Coconut	$= 10,000 \div 100,000 = 10\%$

14-34 (Cont'd.)

SOLUTION EXHIBIT 14-34 (Cont'd.)
Columnar Presentation of Sales-Volume, Sales-Quantity, and Sales-Mix Variances
for Debbie's Delight Inc.

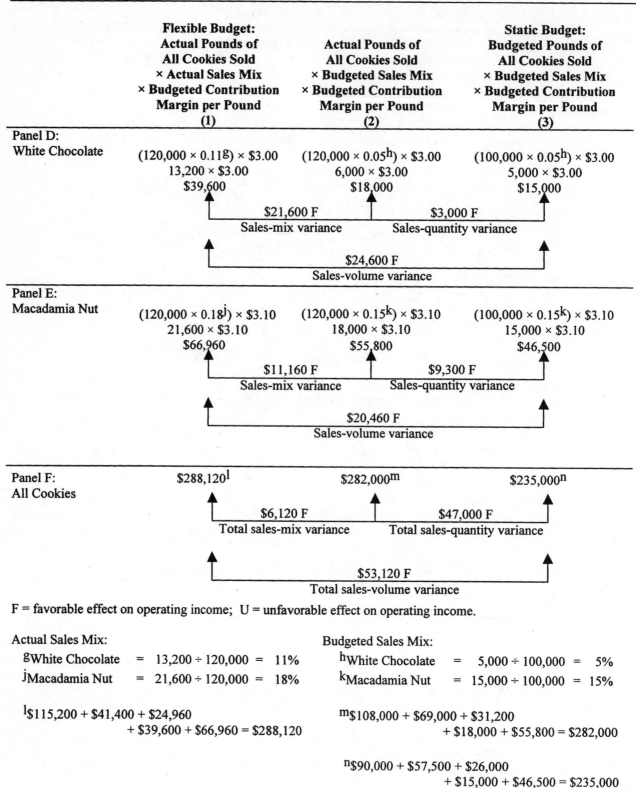

	Flexible Budget: Actual Pounds of All Cookies Sold × Actual Sales Mix × Budgeted Contribution Margin per Pound (1)	Actual Pounds of All Cookies Sold × Budgeted Sales Mix × Budgeted Contribution Margin per Pound (2)	Static Budget: Budgeted Pounds of All Cookies Sold × Budgeted Sales Mix × Budgeted Contribution Margin per Pound (3)
Panel D: White Chocolate	$(120{,}000 \times 0.11^g) \times \$3.00$ $13{,}200 \times \$3.00$ $\$39{,}600$	$(120{,}000 \times 0.05^h) \times \$3.00$ $6{,}000 \times \$3.00$ $\$18{,}000$	$(100{,}000 \times 0.05^h) \times \$3.00$ $5{,}000 \times \$3.00$ $\$15{,}000$

$\$21{,}600$ F — Sales-mix variance $\$3{,}000$ F — Sales-quantity variance

$\$24{,}600$ F — Sales-volume variance

Panel E: Macadamia Nut	$(120{,}000 \times 0.18^j) \times \$3.10$ $21{,}600 \times \$3.10$ $\$66{,}960$	$(120{,}000 \times 0.15^k) \times \$3.10$ $18{,}000 \times \$3.10$ $\$55{,}800$	$(100{,}000 \times 0.15^k) \times \$3.10$ $15{,}000 \times \$3.10$ $\$46{,}500$

$\$11{,}160$ F — Sales-mix variance $\$9{,}300$ F — Sales-quantity variance

$\$20{,}460$ F — Sales-volume variance

Panel F: All Cookies	$\$288{,}120^l$	$\$282{,}000^m$	$\$235{,}000^n$

$\$6{,}120$ F — Total sales-mix variance $\$47{,}000$ F — Total sales-quantity variance

$\$53{,}120$ F — Total sales-volume variance

F = favorable effect on operating income; U = unfavorable effect on operating income.

Actual Sales Mix:
[g] White Chocolate = $13{,}200 \div 120{,}000$ = 11%
[j] Macadamia Nut = $21{,}600 \div 120{,}000$ = 18%

[l] $\$115{,}200 + \$41{,}400 + \$24{,}960$
    $+ \$39{,}600 + \$66{,}960 = \$288{,}120$

Budgeted Sales Mix:
[h] White Chocolate = $5{,}000 \div 100{,}000$ = 5%
[k] Macadamia Nut = $15{,}000 \div 100{,}000$ = 15%

[m] $\$108{,}000 + \$69{,}000 + \$31{,}200$
     $+ \$18{,}000 + \$55{,}800 = \$282{,}000$

[n] $\$90{,}000 + \$57{,}500 + \$26{,}000$
    $+ \$15{,}000 + \$46{,}500 = \$235{,}000$

14-36 (20–25 min.)**Direct materials efficiency, mix and yield variances**
(Chapter Appendix).

1 & 2. Actual total quantity of all inputs used and actual input mix percentages for each input are as follows:

Chemical	Actual Quantity	Actual Mix Percentage		
Echol	24,080	$24,080 \div 86,000$	=	0.28
Protex	15,480	$15,480 \div 86,000$	=	0.18
Benz	36,120	$36,120 \div 86,000$	=	0.42
CT-40	10,320	$10,320 \div 86,000$	=	0.12
Total	86,000			1.00

Budgeted total quantity of all inputs allowed and budgeted input mix percentages for each input are as follows:

Chemical	Budgeted Quantity	Budgeted Mix Percentage		
Echol	25,200	$25,200 \div 84,000$	=	0.30
Protex	16,800	$16,800 \div 84,000$	=	0.20
Benz	33,600	$33,600 \div 84,000$	=	0.40
CT-40	8,400	$8,400 \div 84,000$	=	0.10
Total	84,000			1.00

Solution Exhibit 14-36 presents the total direct materials efficiency, yield, and mix variances for August 2003.

Total direct materials efficiency variance can also be computed as:

$$\text{Direct materials efficiency variance for each input} = \left(\text{Actual inputs} - \text{Budgeted inputs allowed for actual outputs achieved}\right) \times \text{Budgeted prices}$$

Echol	=	$(24,080 - 25,200) \times \$0.20$	=	\$224 F
Protex	=	$(15,480 - 16,800) \times \$0.45$	=	594 F
Benz	=	$(36,120 - 33,600) \times \$0.15$	=	378 U
CT40	=	$(10,320 - 8,400) \times \$0.30$	=	576 U
Total direct materials efficiency variance				$\underline{\$136}$ U

The total direct materials yield variance can also be computed as the sum of the direct materials yield variances for each input:

$$\text{Direct materials yield variance for each input} = \left(\begin{array}{c}\text{Actual total quantity of all direct materials inputs used}\end{array} - \begin{array}{c}\text{Budgeted total quantity of all direct materials inputs allowed for actual output achieved}\end{array}\right) \times \begin{array}{c}\text{Budgeted direct materials input mix percentage}\end{array} \times \begin{array}{c}\text{Budgeted price of direct materials inputs}\end{array}$$

Echol	=	$(86,000 - 84,000)$	$\times\ 0.30 \times \$0.20$ =	$2,000 \times 0.30 \times \$0.20$	=	\$120 U
Protex	=	$(86,000 - 84,000)$	$\times\ 0.20 \times \$0.45$ =	$2,000 \times 0.20 \times \$0.45$	=	180 U
Benz	=	$(86,000 - 84,000)$	$\times\ 0.40 \times \$0.15$ =	$2,000 \times 0.40 \times \$0.15$	=	120 U
CT40	=	$(86,000 - 84,000)$	$\times\ 0.10 \times \$0.30$ =	$2,000 \times 0.10 \times \$0.30$	=	60 U
Total direct materials yield variance						$\underline{\$480}$ U

14-36 (Cont'd.)

The total direct materials mix variance can also be computed as the sum of the direct materials mix variances for each input:

$$\begin{array}{c}\text{Direct}\\\text{materials}\\\text{mix variance}\\\text{for each input}\end{array} = \left(\begin{array}{c}\text{Actual}\\\text{direct materials}\\\text{input mix}\\\text{percentage}\end{array} - \begin{array}{c}\text{Budgeted}\\\text{direct materials}\\\text{input mix}\\\text{percentage}\end{array}\right) \times \begin{array}{c}\text{Actual total}\\\text{quantity of all}\\\text{direct materials}\\\text{inputs used}\end{array} \times \begin{array}{c}\text{Budgeted}\\\text{price of}\\\text{direct materials}\\\text{inputs}\end{array}$$

Echol	=	$(0.28 - 0.30) \times 86{,}000 \times \$0.20$	$= -0.02 \times 86{,}000 \times \$0.20$	=	\$344 F
Protex	=	$(0.18 - 0.20) \times 86{,}000 \times \$0.45$	$= -0.02 \times 86{,}000 \times \$0.45$	=	774 F
Benz	=	$(0.42 - 0.40) \times 86{,}000 \times \$0.15$	$= \;\;\;0.02 \times 86{,}000 \times \$0.15$	=	258 U
CT40	=	$(0.12 - 0.10) \times 86{,}000 \times \$0.30$	$= \;\;\;0.02 \times 86{,}000 \times \$0.30$	=	516 U
Total direct materials mix variance					\$344 F

3. Energy Products used a larger total quantity of direct materials inputs than budgeted, and so showed an unfavorable yield variance. The mix variance was favorable because the actual mix contained more of the cheapest input, Benz, and less of the most costly input, Protex, than the budgeted mix. The favorable mix variance offset some, but not all, of the unfavorable yield variance—the overall efficiency variance was unfavorable. Energy Products will find it profitable to shift to the cheaper mix only if the yield from this cheaper mix can be improved. Energy Products must also consider the effect on output quality of using the cheaper mix, and the potential consequences for future revenues.

SOLUTION EXHIBIT 14-36
Columnar Presentation of Direct Materials Efficiency, Yield and Mix Variances
for The Energy Products Company for August 2003

	Actual Total Quantity of All Inputs Used × Actual Input Mix × Budgeted Price (1)		Actual Total Quantity of All Inputs Used × Budgeted Input Mix × Budgeted Price (2)		Flexible Budget: Budgeted Total Quantity of All Inputs Allowed for Actual Output Achieved × Budgeted Input Mix × Budgeted Price (3)	
Echol	$86{,}000 \times 0.28 \times \$0.20 =$	\$ 4,816	$86{,}000 \times 0.30 \times \$0.20 =$	\$ 5,160	$84{,}000 \times 0.30 \times \$0.20 =$	\$ 5,040
Protex	$86{,}000 \times 0.18 \times \$0.45 =$	6,966	$86{,}000 \times 0.20 \times \$0.45 =$	7,740	$84{,}000 \times 0.20 \times \$0.45 =$	7,560
Benz	$86{,}000 \times 0.42 \times \$0.15 =$	5,418	$86{,}000 \times 0.40 \times \$0.15 =$	5,160	$84{,}000 \times 0.40 \times \$0.15 =$	5,040
CT40	$86{,}000 \times 0.12 \times \$0.30 =$	3,096	$86{,}000 \times 0.10 \times \$0.30 =$	2,580	$84{,}000 \times 0.10 \times \$0.30 =$	2,520
		\$20,296		\$20,640		\$20,160

	$344 F		$480 U	
	Total mix variance		Total yield variance	
		$136 U		
		Total efficiency variance		

F = favorable effect on operating income; U = unfavorable effect on operating income

14-38 (15–20 min.) **Customer profitability, responsibility for environmental clean-up, ethics.**

1. Customer-profitability analysis examines how individual customers differ in their profitability. The revenues and costs of each customer can be estimated with varying degrees of accuracy. Revenues of IF typically would be known at the time of sale. Many costs also would be known, e.g., the cost of materials used to manufacture the fluids sold to each customer. A major area of uncertainty is future costs associated with obligations arising from the sale. There are several issues here:

a. Uncertainty as to the existence and extent of legal liability. Each customer has primary responsibility to dispose of its own toxic waste. However, under some U.S. laws (such as the "Superfund" laws), suppliers to a company may be partially liable for disposal of toxic material. Papandopolis needs to determine the extent of IF's liability. It would be necessary to seek legal guidance on this issue.

b. Uncertainty as to when the liability will occur. The further in the future, the lower the amount of the liability (assuming discounting for the time-value of money occurs.)

c. Uncertainty as to the amount of the liability, given that the liability exists and the date of the liability can be identified. Papandopolis faces major difficulties here—see the answer to requirement 2.

Many companies argue that uncertainties related to (a), (b), and (c) make the inclusion of "hard-dollar estimates meaningless." However, at a minimum, a contingent liability should be recognized and included in the internal customer-profitability reports.

2. Papandopolis' controller may believe that if estimates of future possible legal exposure are sufficiently uncertain, then they should not be recorded. His concern about "smoking guns" may have a very genuine basis—that is, if litigation arises, third parties may misrepresent Papandopolis' concerns to the detriment of IF. Any written comments that she makes may surface 5 or 10 years later and be interpreted as "widespread knowledge" within IF that they have responsibility for large amounts of environmental clean-up.

Given this background, Papandopolis still has the responsibility to prepare a report in an objective and competent way. Moreover, she has visited 10 customer sites and has details as to their toxic-waste handling procedures. If Acme goes bankrupt and has no liability insurance, one of the "deep pockets" available to meet toxic waste handling costs is likely to be IF. At a minimum, she should report the likely bankruptcy and the existence of IF's contingent liability for toxic-waste clean-up in her report. Whether she quantifies this contingent liability is a more difficult question. Papandopolis has limited information available to make a meaningful quantification. She is not an employee of Acme Metal and has no information about Acme's liability insurance. Moreover, she does not know what other parties (such as other suppliers) are also jointly liable to pay Acme's clean-up costs.

The appropriate course appears to highlight the contingent liability but to not attempt to quantify it.

CHAPTER 15
ALLOCATION OF SUPPORT DEPARTMENT COSTS, COMMON COSTS, AND REVENUES

15-2 The dual-rate method provides information to division managers about cost behavior. Knowing how fixed costs and variable costs behave differently is useful in decision making.

15-4 Examples of bases used to allocate support department cost pools to operating departments include the number of employees, square feet of space, number of hours, and machine-hours.

15-6 Disagree. Allocating costs on "the basis of estimated long-run use by user department managers" means department managers can lower their cost allocations by deliberately underestimating their long-run use (assuming all other managers do not similarly underestimate their usage).

15-8 The reciprocal method is theoretically the most defensible method because it explicitly recognizes the mutual services provided among all departments, irrespective of whether those departments are operating or support departments.

15-10 All contracts with U.S. government agencies must comply with cost accounting standards issued by the Cost Accounting Standards Board (CASB).

15-12 Companies increasingly are selling packages of products or services for a single price. Revenue allocation is required when managers in charge of developing or marketing individual products in a bundle are evaluated using product-specific revenues.

15-14 Managers typically will argue that their individual product is the prime reason why consumers buy a bundle of products. Evidence on this argument could come from the sales of the products when sold as individual products. Other pieces of evidence include surveys of users of each product and surveys of people who purchase the bundle of products.

15-16 (20 min.) **Single-rate versus dual-rate allocation methods, support department.**

Bases available (kilowatt hours):

	Rockford	Peoria	Hammond	Kankakee	Total
Practical capacity	10,000	20,000	12,000	8,000	50,000
Expected monthly usage	8,000	9,000	7,000	6,000	30,000

1a.   Single-rate method based on practical capacity:

Total costs in pool	=	$6,000 + $9,000	= $15,000
Practical capacity	=	50,000 kilowatt hours	
Allocation rate	=	$15,000 ÷ 50,000	= $0.30 per hour of capacity

	Rockford	Peoria	Hammond	Kankakee	Total
Practical capacity in hours	10,000	20,000	12,000	8,000	50,000
Costs allocated at $0.30 per hour	$3,000	$6,000	$3,600	$2,400	$15,000

1b.   Single-rate method based on expected monthly usage:

Total costs in pool	= $6,000 + $9,000	= $15,000
Expected usage	= 30,000 kilowatt hours	
Allocation rate	= $15,000 ÷ 30,000	= $0.50 per hour of expected usage

	Rockford	Peoria	Hammond	Kankakee	Total
Expected monthly usage in hours	8,000	9,000	7,000	6,000	30,000
Costs allocated at $0.50 per hour	$4,000	$4,500	$3,500	$3,000	$15,000

2.   Variable-Cost Pool:

Total costs in pool	=	$6,000
Expected usage	=	30,000 kilowatt hours
Allocation rate	=	$0.20 per hour of expected usage

Fixed-Cost Pool:

Total costs in pool	=	$9,000
Practical capacity	=	50,000 kilowatt hours
Allocation rate	=	$0.18 per hour of capacity

	Rockford	Peoria	Hammond	Kankakee	Total
Variable-cost pool					
$0.20 × 8,000; 9,000; 7,000, 6,000	$1,600	$1,800	$1,400	$1,200	$ 6,000
Fixed-cost pool					
$0.18 × 10,000; 20,000; 12,000, 8,000	1,800	3,600	2,160	1,440	9,000
Total	$3,400	$5,400	$3,560	$2,640	$15,000

The dual-rate method permits a more refined allocation of the power department costs; it permits the use of different allocation bases for different cost pools. The fixed costs result from decisions most likely associated with the practical capacity level. The variable costs result from decisions most likely associated with monthly usage.

15-18 (20 min.) **Dual-rate cost-allocation method, budgeted versus actual costs, and practical capacity vs. actual quantities (continuation of 15-17).**

1. Charges with dual rate method.

Variable indirect cost rate	=	$1,500 per trip
Fixed indirect cost rate	=	$\dfrac{\$200{,}000 \text{ budgeted costs}}{250 \text{ trips at practical capacity}}$
	=	$800 per trip at practical capacity

Orange Juice Division
Variable indirect costs, $1,500 × 150	$225,000
Fixed indirect costs, $800 × 150	120,000
	$345,000

Grapefruit Juice Division
Variable indirect costs, $1,500 × 75	$112,500
Fixed indirect costs, $800 × 100	80,000
	$192,500

2. The dual rate changes how the fixed indirect cost component is treated. By using budgeted trips made, the Orange Juice Division is unaffected by changes from its own budgeted usage or that of other divisions.

15-20 (50 min.) **Support department cost allocation, reciprocal method (continuation of 15-19).**

1a.

	Support Departments		Operating Departments	
	A/H	IS	Govt.	Corp.
Costs	$600,000	$2,400,000		
Alloc. of A/H (0.25, 0.40, 0.35)	(861,538)	215,385	$ 344,615	$ 301,538
Alloc. of I.S. (0.10, 0.30, 0.60)	261,538	(2,615,385)	784,616	1,569,231
			$1,129,231	$1,870,769

Reciprocal Method Computation

$$A = \$600{,}000 + 0.10\ IS$$
$$IS = \$2{,}400{,}000 + 0.25A$$
$$IS = \$2{,}400{,}000 + 0.25\,(\$600{,}000 + 0.10\ IS)$$
$$= \$2{,}400{,}000 + \$150{,}000 + 0.025\ IS$$
$$0.975\,IS = \$2{,}550{,}000$$
$$IS = \$2{,}550{,}000 \div 0.975$$
$$= \$2{,}615{,}385$$
$$A = \$600{,}000 + 0.10\,(\$2{,}615{,}385)$$
$$= \$600{,}000 + \$261{,}538$$
$$= \$861{,}538$$

15-20 (Cont'd.)

1b.

	Support Departments		Operating Departments	
	A/H	IS	Govt.	Corp.
Costs	$600,000	$2,400,000		
1st Allocation of A/H				
(0.25, 0.40, 0.35)	(600,000)	150,000	$ 240,000	$ 210,000
		2,550,000		
1st Allocation of IS				
(0.10, 0.30, 0.60)	255,000	(2,550,000)	765,000	1,530,000
2nd Allocation of A/H				
(0.25, 0.40, 0.35)	(255,000)	63,750	102,000	89,250
2nd Allocation of IS				
(0.10, 0.30, 0.60)	6,375	(63,750)	19,125	38,250
3rd Allocation of A/H				
(0.25, 0.40, 0.35)	(6,375)	1,594	2,550	2,231
3rd Allocation of IS				
(0.10, 0.30, 0.60)	160	(1,594)	478	956
4th Allocation of A/H				
(0.25, 0.40, 0.35)	(160)	40	64	56
4th Allocation of IS				
(0.10, 0.30, 0.60)	4	(40)	12	24
5th Allocation of A/H				
(0.25, 0.40, 0.35)	(4)	1	2	1
5th Allocation of IS				
(0.10, 0.30, 0.60)	0	(1)	0	1
Total allocation	$ 0	$ 0	$1,129,231	$1,870,769

2.

		Govt. Consulting	Corp. Consulting
a.	Direct	$1,120,000	$1,880,000
b.	Step-Down (Ad/HR first)	1,090,000	1,910,000
c.	Step-Down (IS first)	1,168,000	1,832,080
d.	Reciprocal (linear equations)	1,129,231	1,870,769
e.	Reciprocal (repeated iterations)	1,129,231	1,870,769

The four methods differ in the level of support department cost allocation across support departments. The level of reciprocal service by support departments is material. Administrative/HR supplies 25% of its services to Information Systems. Information Systems supplies 10% of its services to Administrative/HR. The Information Department has a budget of $2,400,000 that is 400% higher than Administrative/HR.

The reciprocal method recognizes all the interactions and is thus the most accurate. It is especially clear from looking at the repeated iterations calculations.

15-20 Excel Application

Cost Allocation: Phoenix Consulting

Original Data
Department Costs

Administrative/Human Resources (A/H)	$600,000
Information Systems (I/S)	$2,400,000
Government Clients (GOVT)	$8,756,000
Corporate Clients (CORP)	$12,452,000

Support Relationships	**Used by:**			
Supplied by:	A/H	IS	GOVT	CORP
A/H	-	25%	40%	35%
IS	10%	-	30%	60%

Cost Allocation - Reciprical Method	A/H	IS	GOVT	CORP
Department costs before any interdepartmental cost allocations	$600,000	$2,400,000		
1st allocation of A/H costs	(600,000)	150,000	$ 240,000	$ 210,000
1st allocation of IS costs	255,000	(2,550,000)	765,000	1,530,000
2nd allocation of A/H costs	(255,000)	63,750	102,000	89,250
2nd allocation of IS costs	6,375	(63,750)	19,125	38,250
3rd allocation of A/H costs	(6,375)	1,594	2,550	2,231
3rd allocation of IS costs	160	(1,594)	478	956
4th allocation of A/H costs	(160)	40	64	56
4th allocation of IS costs	4	(40)	12	24
5th allocation of A/H costs	(4)	1	2	1
5th allocation of IS costs	0	(1)	0	1
Total costs of operating departments	$ -	$ -	$1,129,231	$1,870,769

15-22 (30 min.) **Reciprocal cost allocation** (continuation of 15-21).

1. The reciprocal allocation method explicitly includes the mutual services provided among all support departments. Interdepartmental relationships are fully incorporated into the support department cost allocations.

2.
$$AD = \$72,700 + .08333IS$$
$$IS = \$234,400 + .23077AD$$
$$AD = \$72,700 + [.08333(\$234,400 + .23077AD)]$$
$$= \$72,700 + [\$19,532.55 + 0.01923AD]$$
$$0.98077AD = \$92,232.55$$
$$AD = \$92,232.55 \div 0.98077$$
$$= \$94,041$$
$$IS = \$234,400 + (0.23077 \times \$94,041)$$
$$= \$256,102$$

	Support Depts		Operating Depts		
	Administ.	Info. Systems	Corporate	Consumer	Total
Costs Incurred	$72,700	$234,400	$ 998,270	$489,860	$1,795,230
Alloc. of Admin.					
(21/91, 42/91, 28/91)	(94,041)	21,702	43,404	28,935	
Alloc. of Info. Syst.					
(320/3,840, 1,920/3,840,					
1,600/3,840)	21,341	(256,102)	128,051	106,710	
	$ 0	$ 0	$1,169,725	$625,505	$1,795,230

15-6

15-22 (Cont'd.)

Solution Exhibit 15-22 presents the reciprocal method using repeated iterations.

SOLUTION EXHIBIT 15-22
Reciprocal Method of Allocating Support Department Costs for September 2004 at e-books Using Repeated Iterations

| | Support Departments | | Operating Departments | | |
	Administrative	Information Systems	Corporate Sales	Consumer Sales	Total
Budgeted manufacturing overhead costs before any interdepartmental cost allocation	$72,700	$234,400	$ 998,270	$489,860	$1,795,230
1st Allocation of Administrative (21/91, 42/91, 28/91)[a]	(72,700)	16,777 251,177	33,554	22,369	
1st Allocation of Information Systems (320/3,840, 1920/3840, 1,600/3,840)[b]	20,931	(251,777)	125,589	104,657	
2nd Allocation of Administrative (21/91, 42/91, 28/91)[a]	(20,931)	4,830	9,661	6,440	
2nd Allocation of Information Systems (320/3,840, 1,920/3,840, 1,600/3,840)[b]	402	(4,830)	2,415	2,013	
3rd Allocation of Administrative (21/91, 42/91, 28/91)[a]	(402)	93	185	124	
3rd Allocation of Information Systems (320/3,840, 1,920/3,840, 1,600/3,840)[b]	8	(93)	46	39	
4th Allocation of Administrative (21/91, 42/91, 28/91)[a]	(8)	2	4	2	
4th Allocation of Information Systems: (320/3,840, 1,920/3,840, 1,600/3,840)[b]	0	(2)	1	1	
Total budgeted manufacturing overhead of operating departments	$ 0	$ 0	$1,169,725	$625,505	$1,795,230

Total accounts allocated and reallocated (the numbers in parentheses in first two columns)
Administrative $72,700 + $20,931 + $402 + $8 = $94,041
Information Systems $251,177 + $4,830 + $93 + $2 = $256,102

[a]Base is (21 + 42 + 28) or 91 employees
[b]Base is (320 + 1,920 + 1,600) or 3,840 minutes

3. The reciprocal method is more accurate than the direct and step-down methods when there is reciprocal relationships among support departments.

A summary of the alternatives is:

	Corporate Sales	Consumer Sales
Direct method	$1,169,745	$625,485
Step-down method		
(Admin. first)	1,168,830	626,400
Reciprocal method	1,169,725	625,505

The reciprocal method is the preferred method, although for September 2004 the numbers do not appear materially different across the alternatives.

15-24 (20 min.) Allocation of common costs.

1.   Allocation of the $1,800 airfare: Alternative approaches include:

a.   The stand-alone cost allocation method. This method would allocate the air fare on the basis of each user's percentage of the total of the individual stand-alone costs:

$$\text{Baltimore employer} \qquad \frac{\$1,400}{(\$1,400 + \$1,100)} \quad \times \$1,800 = \quad \$1,008$$

$$\text{Chicago employer} \qquad \frac{\$1,100}{(\$1,400 + \$1,100)} \quad \times \$1,800 = \quad \underline{792}$$

$$\underline{\$1,800}$$

Advocates of this method often emphasize an equity or fairness rationale.

b.   The incremental cost allocation method. This requires the choice of a primary party and an incremental party.

If the Baltimore employer is the primary party, the allocation would be:

Baltimore employer	$1,400
Chicago employer	400
	$1,800

One rationale is Ernst was planning to make the Baltimore trip, and the Chicago stop was added subsequently. Some students have suggested allocating as much as possible to the Baltimore employer since Ernst was not joining them.

If the Chicago employer is the primary party, the allocation would be:

Chicago employer	$1,100
Baltimore employer	700
	$1,800

One rationale is that the Chicago employer is the successful recruiter and presumably receives more benefits from the recruiting expenditures.

15-24 (Cont'd.)

2.   Ernst should use the stand-alone allocation method because it treats both employers the same rather than one employer as the primary party and the other employer as the incremental party. Alternatively, Ernst could calculate the Shapley value that considers each employer in turn as the primary party: The Baltimore employer is allocated $1,400 as the primary party and $700 as the incremental party for an average of ($1,400 + $700) ÷ 2 = $1,050. The Chicago employer is allocated $1,100 as the primary party and $400 as the incremental party for an average of ($1,100 + 400) ÷ 2 = $750. The Shapley value approach would allocate $1,050 to the Baltimore employer and $750 to the Chicago employer.

3.   A simple approach is to split the $60 equally between the two employers. The limousine costs at the Sacramento end are not a function of distance traveled on the plane.

       An alternative approach is to add the $60 to the $1,800 and repeat requirement 1:

a.   Stand-alone cost allocation method:

Baltimore employer $\quad\dfrac{\$1,460}{(\$1,460 + \$1,160)} \quad \times\ \$1,860 = \$1,036$

Chicago employer $\quad\dfrac{\$1,160}{(\$1,460 + \$1,160)} \quad \times\ \$1,860 = \$\ 824$

b.   Incremental cost allocation method. With Baltimore employer as the primary party:

Baltimore employer	$1,460
Chicago employer	400
	$1,860

With Chicago employer as the primary party:

Chicago employer	$1,160
Baltimore employer	700
	$1,860

c.   Using Shapley value, Baltimore employer: (1,460 + $700) ÷ 2 = $1,080
                                      Chicago employer: ($400 + $1,160) ÷ 2 = $ 780

Note: Ask any students in the class how they handled this situation if they have faced it.

15-26 (10–15 min.) **Revenue allocation, bundled products, additional complexities (continuation of 15-25).**

Alternatives include:

a.   Use information about how each individual package is used to make the revenue allocations. Thus, if one party uses only lodging and food, the $700 is allocated among those two groups. This would be the most accurate approach, as it captures actual usage and non-usage of the facilities.

b.   Use the average nonusage information to compute an "adjusted unit selling price:"

Lodging: $640 × 1.00	$ 640
Food: $160 × 0.95	152
Recreation: $300 × 0.90	270
	$1,062

These adjusted revenues can be used in either the stand-alone or incremental methods. For example, the stand-alone allocations are:

Lodging: $\dfrac{\$640}{\$1,062} \times \$700$ = $422

Food: $\dfrac{\$152}{\$1,062} \times \$700$ = $100

Recreation: $\dfrac{\$270}{\$1,062} \times \$700$ = $178

$700

Using the incremental method with Recreation first, then lodging, and then Food:

Product	Revenue Allocated	Revenue Remaining to Be Allocated to Other Products
Recreation	$270	$700 − $270 = $430
Lodging	430	$430 − $430 = $ 0
Food	0	
	$700	

15-28 (15 min.) **Single-rate versus dual-rate cost-allocation methods**

1. Budgeted fixed rate = $\dfrac{\$1,000,000}{200,000}$ = \$ 5.00 per kilowatt-hour

    Budgeted variable rate = $\dfrac{\$2,000,000}{160,000}$ = \$12.50 per kilowatt-hour

    Single fixed and variable rate $\qquad$ = \$17.50 per kilowatt-hour

    Allocation to:

    Durham $\quad$ \$17.50 × 85,000 = \$1,487,500
    Charlotte \$17.50 × 40,000 = \$ 700,000
    Raleigh $\quad$ \$17.50 × 35,000 = \$ 612,500

2. Budgeted fixed rate $\quad$ = $\dfrac{\$1,000,000}{160,000}$ = \$ 6.25 per kilowatt-hour

    Budgeted variable rate = $\dfrac{\$2,000,000}{160,000}$ = \$12.50 per kilowatt-hour

    Single fixed and variable rate $\qquad$ = \$18.75 per kilowatt-hour

    Allocation to:

    Durham $\quad$ \$18.75 × 85,000 $\quad$ = \$1,593,750
    Charlotte \$18.75 × 40,000 $\quad$ = \$ 750,000
    Raleigh $\quad$ \$18.75 × 35,000 $\quad$ = \$ 656,250

3. Fixed Cost Rate: $\dfrac{\$1,000,000}{200,000}$ = \$5 per kilowatt-hour

    Variable Cost Rate: $\dfrac{\$2,000,000}{160,000}$ = \$12.50 per kilowatt-hour

    Allocation to Durham:

Fixed costs \$5 × 100,000	\$ 500,000
Variable costs \$12.50 × 85,000	1,062,500
Total	\$1,562,500

(15-28 cont.)
Allocation to Charlotte:

	Fixed costs $5 × 60,000	$ 300,000
	Variable costs $12.50 × 40,000	500,000
	Total	$ 800,000

Allocation to Raleigh:

	Fixed costs $5 × 40,000	$ 200,000
	Variable costs $12.50 × 35,000	437,500
	Total	$ 637,500

15-28 (Cont'd)

4. Fixed Cost Rate: $\dfrac{\$1,000,000}{160,000}$ = $6.25 per kilowatt-hour

Variable Cost Rate: $\dfrac{\$2,000,000}{160,000}$ = $12.50 per kilowatt-hour

Allocation to Durham:
Fixed costs $6.25 × 80,000	$ 500,000
Variable costs $12.50 × 85,000	1,062,500
Total	$1,562,500

Allocation to Charlotte:
Fixed costs $6.25 × 50,000	$ 312,500
Variable costs $12.50 × 40,000	500,000
Total	$ 812,500

Allocation to Raleigh:
Fixed costs $6.25 × 30,000	$ 187,500
Variable costs $12.50 × 35,000	437,500
Total	$ 625,000

15-30 (30 min.) Cost allocation, actual versus budgeted usage (CMA, revised).

1. Problems with the monthly allocation report include:

a. The single-rate method used does not distinguish between fixed vs. variable costs.
b. Actual costs and actual quantities are used. This results in managers not knowing cost rates until year-end.
c. Monthly time periods are used to determine cost rates. The use of a monthly time period can result in highly variable cost rates depending on seasonality, days in a month, demand surges and so on.

2. Budgeted variable cost (based on normal usage):

$$\frac{\$7,500,000}{100,000,000} = \$0.075 \text{ per kwh}$$

15-30 (Cont'd.)

Monthly Allocation Report
November 2003

Allocations of Variable Costs (based on budgeted rate × actual usage)*

To Department A: 60,000,000 × $0.075 $4,500,000
To Department B: 20,000,000 × $0.075   1,500,000
     $6,000,000

*There will be $1,500,000 of unallocated variable costs for November 2003.

Allocation of fixed costs (Based on budgeted usage × budgeted amount)

To Department A: 60% × $30,000,000 $18,000,000
To Department B: 40% × $30,000,000   12,000,000
Total $30,000,000

Or alternatively,

$$\text{Budgeted fixed cost rate} = \frac{\text{Budgeted fixed costs}}{\text{Budgeted kwh}} = \frac{\$30,000,000}{60,000,000 + 40,000,000}$$

$$= \$0.30 \text{ per kwh}$$

Allocation of fixed costs (based on budgeted usage)
To Department A: $0.30 × 60,000,000 kwh = $18,000,000
To Department B: $0.30 × 40,000,000 kwh = 12,000,000
Total $30,000,000

Department A allocation of costs

Variable costs	$ 4,500,000
Fixed costs	18,000,000
Total	$22,500,000

Department B allocation of costs

Variable costs	$ 1,500,000
Fixed costs	12,000,000
Total	$13,500,000

3. Under Lamb's allocation report, the production manager has both risk-exposure and uncertainty concerns:

Risk-exposure—Changes in the demand for energy by Department A affect the costs Lamb will report for Department B. Increases in demand by A will reduce B's cost per kwh and vice versa. Department B's production manager may seek to curtail production in periods when Departments A's production declines. This could create an ever-diminishing cycle of production. Alternatively, Department B may subcontract outside to avoid a higher energy rate, even if it is not in Bulldog's best interest to subcontract.

Uncertainty—When actual costs are used, managers cannot plan costs with certainty. Managers typically have less ability to bear uncertainty than do companies. The result is that managers may reject alternatives that are good risks from Bulldog's perspective but not attractive risks for themselves.

15-32 (40-60 min.) **Support department cost allocations; single-department cost pools; direct, step-down, and reciprocal methods.**

All the following computations are in dollars.
1.

Direct method:		**To X**		**To Y**	
A	$250/400 \times \$100,000 =$	\$62,500	$150/400 \times \$100,000$	$=$	\$37,500
B	$100/500 \times \$40,000 =$	8,000	$400/500 \times \$40,000$	$=$	32,000
Total		$\underline{\$70,500}$			$\underline{\$69,500}$

Step-down method, allocating A first:

	A	**B**	**X**	**Y**
Costs to be allocated	$100,000	$40,000	—	—
Allocate A: (100; 250; 150 ÷ 500)	(100,000)	20,000	$50,000	$30,000
Allocate B: (100; 400 ÷ 500)	—	(60,000)	12,000	48,000
Total	$\underline{\$\quad 0}$	$\underline{\$\quad 0}$	$\underline{\$62,000}$	$\underline{\$78,000}$

Step-down method, allocating B first:

	A	**B**	**X**	**Y**
Costs to be allocated	$100,000	$ 40,000	—	—
Allocate B: (500; 100; 400 ÷ 1,000)	20,000	(40,000)	$ 4,000	$16,000
Allocate A: (250/400, 150/400)	(120,000)	—	75,000	45,000
Total	$\underline{\$\quad 0}$	$\underline{\$\quad 0}$	$\underline{\$79,000}$	$\underline{\$61,000}$

Note that these methods produce significantly different results, so the choice of method may frequently make a difference in the budgeted department overhead rates.

15-32 (Cont'd.)

Reciprocal method:

Stage 1: Let   A = total costs of materials-handling department
             B = total costs of power-generating department
      (1)   A = $100,000 + 0.5B
      (2)   B = $ 40,000 + 0.2A

Stage 2: Substituting in (1):   A = $100,000 + 0.5($40,000 + 0.2A)
                             A = $100,000 + $20,000   + 0.1A
                       0.9A = $120,000
                             A = $133,333

        Substituting in (2):   B = $40,000 + 0.2($133,333)
                             B = $66,666

Stage 3:

	A	B	X	Y
Original amounts	100,000	40,000	—	—
Allocation of A	(133,333)	26,666(20%)	66,667(50%)	40,000(30%)
Allocation of B	33,333(50%)	(66,666)	6,667(10%)	26,666(40%)
Totals accounted for	—	—	73,334	66,666

15-32 (Cont'd.)

SOLUTION EXHIBIT 15-32
Reciprocal Method of Allocating Support Department Costs for Manes Company Using Repeated Iterations.

	Support Departments		Operating Departments	
	A	B	X	Y
Budgeted manufacturing overhead costs before any interdepartmental cost allocations	$100,000	$40,000		
1st Allocation of Dept. A: (2/10, 5/10, 3/10)ᵃ	(100,000)	20,000 ――――― 60,000	$50,000	$30,000
1st Allocation of Dept. B (5/10, 1/10, 4/10)ᵇ	30,000	(60,000)	6,000	24,000
2nd Allocation of Dept. A (2/10, 5/10, 3/10)ᵃ	(30,000)	6,000	15,000	9,000
2nd Allocation of Dept B: (5/10, 1/10, 4/10)ᵇ	3,000	(6,000)	600	2,400
3rd Allocation of Dept A: (2/10, 5/10, 3/10)ᵃ	(3,000)	600	1,500	900
3rd Allocation of Dept. B: (5/10, 1/10, 4/10)ᵇ	300	(600)	60	240
4th Allocation of Dept. A (2/10, 5/10, 3/10)ᵃ	(300)	60	150	90
4th Allocation of Dept. B (5/10, 1/10, 4/10)ᵇ	30	(60)	6	24
5th Allocation of Dept A (2/10, 5/10, 3/10)	(30)	6	15	9
5th Allocation of Dept B (5/10, 1/10, 4/10)	3	(6)	1	2
6th Allocation of Dept A (2/10, 5/10, 3/10)	(3)	0	2	1
Total budgeted manufacturing overhead of operating departments	$ 0	$ 0	$73,334	$66,666

Total accounts allocated and reallocated (the numbers in parentheses in first two columns)
Plant Maintenance: $100,000 + $30,000 + $3,000 + $300 + $30 + $3 = $133,333
Information Systems: $60,000 + $6,000 + $600 + $60 + $6 = $66,666

ᵃBase is (100 + 250 +150) or 500 labor-hours; $100 \div 500 = 2/10$, $250 \div 500 = 5/10$, $150 \div 500 = 3/10$.
ᵇBase is (500 + 100 + 400) or 1,000 kwhours ; $500 \div 1,000 = 5/10$, $100 \div 1,000 = 1/10$, $400 \div 1,000 = 4/10$.

Comparison of methods:

Method of Allocation	X	Y
Direct method	$70,500	$69,500
Step-down: A first	62,000	78,000
Step-down: B first	79,000	61,000
Reciprocal method	73,334	66,666

Note that *in this case* the direct method produces answers that are the closest to the "correct" answers (that is, those from the reciprocal method), step-down allocating B first is next, and step-down allocating A first is least accurate.

15-32 (Cont'd.)

2. At first glance, it appears that the cost of power is $40 per unit plus the material handling costs. If so, Manes would be better off by purchasing from the power company. However, the decision should be influenced by the effects of the interdependencies and the fixed costs. Note that the power needs would be less (students miss this) if they were purchased from the outside:

	Outside Power Units Needed
X	100
Y	400
A (500 units minus 20% of 500 units, because there is no need to service the nonexistent power department)	400
Total units	900

Total costs, 900 × $40 = $36,000

In contrast, the total costs that would be saved by not producing the power inside would depend on the effects of the decision on various costs:

	Avoidable Costs of 1000 Units of Power Produced Inside
Variable indirect labor and indirect material costs	$10,000
Supervision in power department	10,000
Materials handling, 20% of $70,000*	14,000
Probable minimum cost savings	$34,000
Possible additional savings:	
a. Can any supervision in materials handling be saved because of overseeing less volume? Minimum savings is probably zero; the maximum is probably 20% of $10,000 or $2,000.	?
b. Is any depreciation a truly variable, wear-and-tear type of cost?	?
Total savings by not producing 1000 units of power	$34,000 + ?

* Materials handling costs are higher because the power department uses 20% of materials handling. Therefore, materials-handling costs will decrease by 20%.

In the short run (at least until a capital investment in equipment is necessary), the data suggest continuing to produce internally because the costs eliminated would probably be less than the comparable purchase costs.

15-34 (50-60 min.) **Revenue allocation, bundled products.**

1a.   Stand-alone revenues in 2003:

Fraîche ($100 × 20,000)	$2,000,000
Désarmer ($80 × 37,500)	3,000,000
Innocence ($250 × 20,000)	5,000,000

The weights for Fraîche + Désarmer suite:

$$\text{Fraîche:} \quad \frac{\$2\text{ million}}{\$2\text{ million} + \$3\text{ million}} \times \$150 = \$60$$

$$\text{Désarmer:} \quad \frac{\$3\text{ million}}{\$2\text{ million} + \$3\text{ million}} \times \$150 = \$90$$

The weights for Fraîche + Innocence suite:

$$\text{Fraîche:} \quad \frac{\$2\text{ million}}{\$2\text{ million} + \$5\text{ million}} \times \$280 = \$80$$

$$\text{Innocence:} \quad \frac{\$5\text{ million}}{\$2\text{ million} + \$5\text{ million}} \times \$280 = \$200$$

b.   Fraîche + Désarmer suite:

Product	Revenue Allocated	Revenue Remaining to be Allocated
Désarmer	$ 80	$70 ($150 − $80)
Fraîche	70	0
Total revenue allocated	$150	

Fraîche + Innocence suite:

Product	Revenue Allocated	Revenue Remaining to be Allocated
Innocence	$250	$30 ($280 − $250)
Fraîche	30	0
Total revenue allocated	$280	

15-34 (Cont'd.)

2. Each product will be considered as a primary product and first incremental product. An average revenue is the final revenue allocation to the product. This approach is illustrated below.

Fraîche + Désarmer suite:

<u>Fraîche</u>

Allocation as the primary product	$100
Allocation as the incremental product ($150 – $80)	70
Total	$170
Allocation ($170 ÷ 2)	$ 85

<u>Désarmer</u>

Allocation as the primary product	$ 80
Allocation as the incremental product ($150 – $100)	50
Total	$130
Allocation ($130 ÷ 2)	$ 65

According to this approach, Fraîche's revenue allocation is $85 and Désarmer's revenue allocation is $65 out of the total suite revenue of $150.

Fraîche + Innocence suite:

<u>Fraîche</u>

Allocation as the primary product	$100
Allocation as the incremental product ($280 – $250)	30
Total	$130
Allocation ($130 ÷ 2)	$ 65

<u>Innocence</u>

Allocation as the primary product	$250
Allocation as the incremental product ($280 – $100)	180
Total	$430
Allocation ($430 ÷ 2)	$215

Fraîche is allocated $65 revenue and Innocence is allocated $215 revenue out of the total suite revenue of $280.

An alternative approach is to take into account both the price and the units sold, that is, total revenues from each product when calculating the weights.

On a stand-alone basis, the price of Fraîche plus Désarmer is $100 + $80 = $180.

On a stand-alone basis the revenues are

Fraîche	$2,000,000
Désarmer	3,000,000
Total	$5,000,000

15-34 (Cont'd.)

So Fraîche accounts for 40% ($2,000,000 ÷ $5,000,000) and Désarmer 60% ($3,000,000 ÷ 5,000,000) of total revenues from Fraîche and Désarmer.

Applying these percentages to the total stand-alone price of $180, we get revenue-weighted prices of $180 × 40% = $72 for Fraîche and $180 × 60% = $108 for Désarmer.

Using these revenue-weighted prices and considering each product as the primary product and then the incremental product:

Fraîche and Désarmer suite:

<u>Fraîche</u>

Allocation as the primary product	$ 72
Allocation as the incremental product ($150 – $108)	42
Total	$114
Allocation ($114 ÷ 2)	$ 57

<u>Désarmer</u>

Allocation as the primary product	$108
Allocation as the incremental product ($150 – $72)	78
Total	$186
Allocation ($186 ÷ 2)	93

On a stand-alone basis, the price of Fraîche + Innocence is $100 + $250 = $350.
On a stand-alone basis, the revenues are

Fraîche	$2,000,000
Innocence	5,000,000
Total	$7,000,000

So Fraîche accounts for 2/7 ($2,000,000 ÷ $7,000,000) and Innocence 5/7 ($5,000,000 ÷ $7,000,000) of total revenues from Fraîche and Innocence.

Applying these percentages to the total stand-alone price of $350, we get revenue-weighted prices of $350 × 2/7 = $100 for Fraîche and $350 × 5/7 = $250 for Innocence.

Using these revenue-weighted prices and considering each product as the primary product and then the incremental product:

Fraîche and Innocence suite:

<u>Fraîche</u>

Allocation as the primary product	$100
Allocation as the incremental product ($280 – $250)	30
Total	$130
Allocation ($130 ÷ 2)	$ 65

<u>Innocence</u>

Allocation as the primary product	$250
Allocation as the incremental product ($280 – $100)	$180
Total	$430
Allocation ($430 ÷ 2)	$215

15-34 (Cont'd.)

A summary of the price allocations for the bundled products under different methods follows

	Stand-alone Revenue Allocation (1)	Incremental With Fraîche Primary (2)	Incremental With Désarmer/ Innocence Primary (3)	Shapley Value Based on Price (4)	Shapely Value Based on Revenue- Weighted Price (5)
Fraîche	$ 60	$100	$ 70	$ 85	$ 57
Désarmer	90	50	80	65	93
Total	$150	$150	$150	$150	$150
Fraîche	$ 80	$100	$ 30	$ 65	$ 65
Innocence	200	180	250	215	215
Total	$280	$280	$280	$280	$280

Note that the Shapley value calculations based on price and revenue-weighted prices are the same for Fraîche and Innocence because the same number of units of each of these products is sold (20,000 units). In general, the Shapely value calculations based on revenue-weighted prices gives the most fair allocation of prices to each product in the bundle because it considers not only the prices of each product sold but also the units. Thus, if one of the products in the bundle sells very few units, it gets very few revenues allocated to it even if it sells for a high price. The table above also indicates that the stand-alone revenue allocation method closely approximates the Shapley value calculations based on revenue-weighted prices. Note that columns 2, 3, and 4 in the above table all allocate more revenues with Fraîche-Désarmer bundle to Fraîche because Fraîche sells for a higher price ($100 versus $80). But the allocations in these columns ignore the important fact that Fraîche sells far fewer units than Désarmer (20,000 versus 37,500).

15-36 (60-80 min.) Allocating costs of support departments; dual rates; direct, step-down, and reciprocal methods.

1.   Solution Exhibit 15-36 presents the costs allocated to each assembly department under the four service department cost allocation methods.

The linear equations underlying the complete reciprocated costs reported in Solution Exhibit 15-36 (in 000s) are:

Fixed-Cost Pool:

$$ES = \$2,700 + 0.20IS$$
$$IS = \$8,000 + 0.10ES$$

$$ES = \$2,700 + 0.20 (\$8,000 + 0.10ES)$$
$$ES = \$4,300 + 0.02ES$$
$$0.98ES = \$4,300$$
$$ES = \$4,300 \div 0.98 = \$4,387.76$$

$$IS = \$8,000 + 0.10 (\$4,387.76)$$

$$= \quad \$8,438.78$$

15-36 (Cont'd.)

Variable-Cost Pool:

ES	=	$\$8,500 + 0.25IS$
IS	=	$\$3,750 + 0.15ES$
ES	=	$\$8,500 + 0.25 (\$3,750 + 0.15ES)$
ES	=	$\$9,437.5 + 0.0375ES$
0.9625ES	=	$\$9,437.5$
ES	=	$\$9,437.5 \div 0.9625 = \$9,805.19$
IS	=	$\$3,750 + 0.15 (\$9,805.19)$
	=	$\$3,750 + \$1,470.78 = \$5,220.78$

The repeated iterations underlying the complete reciprocated costs reported in Fixed-Cost Pool:

	Support Departments		**Operating Departments**	
			Home Security	**Business Security**
	ES	**IS**	**Systems**	**Systems**
Costs	$2,700.00	$8,000.00		
1st Allocation of ES				
(.1, .4, .5)	(2,700.00)	270.00	$1,080.00	$1,350.00
		8,270.00		
1st Allocation of IS				
(.2, .3, .5)	1,654.00	(8,270.00)	2,481.00	4,135.00
2nd Allocation of ES				
(.1, .4, .5)	(1,654.00)	165.40	661.60	827.00
2nd Allocation of IS				
(.2, .3, .5)	33.08	(165.40)	49.62	82.70
3rd Allocation of ES				
(.1, .4, .5)	(33.08)	3.31	13.23	16.54
3rd Allocation of IS				
(.2, .3, .5)	0.66	(3.31)	0.99	1.66
4th Allocation of ES				
(.1, .4, .5)	(0.66)	0.07	0.26	0.33
4th Allocation of IS				
(.2, .3, .5)	0.01	(0.07)	0.02	0.04
5th Allocation of ES				
(.1, .4, .5)	(0.01)	0	0.01	0
Fixed-costs allocation	$ 0	$ 0	$4,286.73	$6,413.27

15-36 (Cont'd.)

The reported iterations underlying the complete reciprocated costs reported in Variable-Cost Pool:

| | Support Departments | | Operating Departments | |
	ES	IS	Home Security Systems	Business Security Systems
Costs	$8,500.00	$3,750.00		
1st Allocation of ES				
(.15, .30, .55)	(8,500.00)	1, 275.00	$2,550.00	$4,675.00
		5,025.00		
1st Allocation of IS				
(.25, .15, .60)	1,256.25	(5,025.00)	753.75	3,015.00
2nd Allocation of ES				
(.15, .30, .55)	(1,256.25)	188.44	376.87	690.94
2nd Allocation of IS				
(.25, .15, .60)	47.11	(188.44)	28.27	113.06
3rd Allocation of ES				
(.15, .30, .55)	(47.11)	7.07	14.13	25.91
3rd Allocation of IS				
(.25, .15, .60)	1.77	(7.07)	1.06	4.24
4th Allocation of ES				
(.15, .30, .55)	(1.77)	0.27	0.53	0.97
4th Allocation of IS				
(.25, .15, .60)	0.07	(0.27)	0.04	0.16
5th Allocation of ES				
(.15, .30, .55)	(0.07)	0	0.03	0.04
Variable-cost allocation	$ 0	$ 0	$3,724.68	$8,525.32

15-36 (Cont'd.)

SOLUTION EXHIBIT 15-36
(in thousands)

	Engineering Support	Information Systems Support	Home Security Systems	Business Security Systems
a. Direct Method				
Fixed- Cost Pool	$ 2,700	$ 8,000		
Eng. Support (4/9, 5/9)	(2,700)		$1,200.00	$1,500.00
Info. Support (3/8, 5/8)		(8,000)	3,000.00	5,000.00
			$4,200.00	$6,500.00
Variable-Cost Pool:	$ 8,500	$ 3,750		
Eng. Support (30/85, 55/85)	(8,500)		$3,000.00	$5,500.00
Info. Support (15/75,60/75)		(3,750)	750.00	3,000.00
			$3,750.00	$8,500.00
b. Step-down (Information First)				
Fixed-Cost Pool:	$ 2,700	$ 8,000		
Info. Support (.2, .3, .5)	1,600	(8,000)	$2,400.00	$4,000.00
Eng. Support (4/9, 5/9)	(4,300)	—	1,911.11	2,388.89
			$4,311.11	$6,388.89
Variable-Cost Pool:	$ 8,500	$ 3,750		
Info. Support (.25, .15, .60)	937.5	(3,750)	$ 562.50	$2,250.00
Eng. Support (30/85, 55/85)	(9,437.5)	—	3,330.88	6,106.62
			$3,893.38	$8,356.62
c. Step-down (Engineering First):				
Fixed-Cost Pool:	$ 2,700	$ 8,000		
Eng. Support (.1, .4, .5)	(2,700)	270	$1,080.00	$1,350.00
Info. Support (3/8, 5/8)		(8,270)	3,101.25	5,168.75
			$4,181.25	$6,518.75
Variable-Cost Pool:	$ 8,500	$ 3,750		
Eng. Support (.15, .30, .55)	(8,500)	1,275	$2,550.00	$4,675.00
Info. Support (.2, .8)		(5,025)	1,005.00	4,020.00
			$3,555.00	$8,695.00
d. Reciprocal Method				
Fixed-Cost Pool:	$ 2,700	$ 8,000.00		
Eng. Support (.1, .4, .5)	(4,387.76)	438.78	$1,755.10	$2,193.88
Info. Support (.2, .3, .5)	1,687.76	(8,438.78)	2,531.63	4,219.39
			$4,286.73	$6,413.27
Variable-Cost Pool:	$ 8,500.00	$ 3,750.00		
Eng. Support (.15, .30, .55)	(9,805.19)	1,470.78	$2,941.56	$5,392.85
Info. Support (.25, .15, .60)	1,305.19	(5,220.78)	783.12	3,132.47
			$3,724.68	$8,525.32

15-36 (Cont'd.)

A summary of the costs allocated under each method from Solution Exhibit 15-36 is:

(In Thousands)		Home Security Systems	Business Security Systems
a.	Direct Method:		
	Fixed-cost pool	$4,200.00	$ 6,500.00
	Variable-cost pool	3,750.00	8,500.00
		$7,950.00	$15,000.00
b.	Step-down (Information First):		
	Fixed-cost pool	$4,311.11	$ 6,388.89
	Variable-cost pool	3,893.38	8,356.62
		$8,204.49	$14,745.51
c.	Step-down (Engineering First):		
	Fixed-cost pool	$4,181.25	$ 6,518.75
	Variable-cost pool	3,555.00	8,695.00
		$7,736.25	$15,213.75
d. & e.	Reciprocal Method:		
	Fixed-cost pool	$4,286.73	$ 6,413.27
	Variable-cost pool	3,724.68	8,525.32
		$8,011.41	$14,938.59

2. Support department costs allocated per unit:

		Home Security Systems Alloc. Costs ÷ $7,950 units	Business Security Systems Alloc. Costs ÷ $3,750 units
a.	Direct method	$1,000	$4,000
b.	Step-down (Information first)	1,032	3,932
c.	Step-down (Engineering first)	973	4,057
d. & e.	Reciprocal method	1,008	3,984

3. Factors that might explain why the reciprocal method is not more widely used in practice include:

a. Managers find the reciprocal method difficult to understand, especially where there are many support departments.

b. The final cost allocations yielded by using the reciprocal method differ little in some cases from those yielded by using the direct or step-down methods. As illustrated in requirement 2, the differences among the four methods in this problem appear small.

c. It is costly to maintain records of the use of the support departments by other support departments.

4. The manager of the Home Security Department would prefer the step-down method with the sequence starting with Engineering Support. This alternative results in the lowest amount ofsupport departments' costs allocated to Home Security Systems.

CHAPTER 16
COST ALLOCATION: JOINT PRODUCTS AND BYPRODUCTS

16-2 A *joint cost* is a cost of a production process that yields multiple products simultaneously. A s*eparable cost* is a cost incurred beyond the splitoff point that is assignable to each of the specific products identified at the splitoff point.

16-4 A *product* is any output that has a positive sales value (or an output that enables an organization to avoid incurring costs). In some joint-cost settings, outputs can occur that do not have a positive sales value. The offshore processing of hydrocarbons yields water that is recycled back into the ocean as well as yielding oil and gas. The processing of mineral ore to yield gold and silver also yields dirt as an output, which is recycled back into the ground.

16-6 The joint production process yields individual products that are either sold this period or held as inventory to be sold in subsequent periods. Hence, the joint costs need to be allocated between total production rather than just those sold this period.

16-8 Both methods use market selling-price data in allocating joint costs, but they differ in which sales-price data they use. The *sales value at splitoff method* allocates joint costs to joint products on the basis of the relative total sales value at the splitoff point of the total production of these products during the accounting period. The *net realizable value method* allocates joint costs to joint products on the basis of the relative net realizable value (the final sales value minus the separable costs of production and marketing) of the total production of the joint products during the accounting period.

16-10 The NRV method can be simplified by assuming (a) a standard set of post-splitoff point processing steps, and (b) a standard set of selling prices. The use of (a) and (b) achieves the same benefits that the use of standard costs does in costing systems.

16-12 No. Any method used to allocate joint costs to individual products that is applicable to the problem of joint product-cost allocation should not be used for management decisions regarding whether a product should be sold or processed further. When a product is an inherent result of a joint process, the decision to process further should not be influenced by either the size of the total joint costs or by the portion of the joint costs assigned to particular products. Joint costs are irrelevant for these decisions. The only relevant items for these decisions are the incremental revenue and the incremental costs beyond the splitoff point.

16-14 Two methods to account for byproducts are:
a. Production method - recognizes byproducts in the financial statements at the time production is completed.
b. Sales method - delays recognition of byproducts until the time of sale.

16-16 (20-30 min.) Joint-cost allocation, insurance settlement.

1. (a) Sales value at splitoff-point method.

	Pounds of Product	Wholesale Selling Price per Pound	Sales Value at Splitoff	Weighting: Sales Value at Splitoff	Joint Costs Allocated	Allocated Costs per Pound
Breasts	100	$1.10	$110	0.675	$ 67.50	0.6750
Wings	20	0.40	8	0.049	4.90	0.2450
Thighs	40	0.70	28	0.172	17.20	0.4300
Bones	80	0.20	16	0.098	9.80	0.1225
Feathers	10	0.10	1	0.006	0.60	0.0600
	250		$163	1.000	$100.00	

Costs of Destroyed Product

Breasts: $0.6750 per pound × 20 pounds = $13.50

Wings: $0.2450 per pound × 10 pounds = 2.45

$15.95

b. Physical measures method

	Pounds of Product	Weighting: Physical Measures	Joint Costs Allocated	Allocated Costs per Pound
Breasts	100	0.400	$ 40.00	$0.400
Wings	20	0.080	8.00	0.400
Thighs	40	0.160	16.00	0.400
Bones	80	0.320	32.00	0.400
Feathers	10	0.040	4.00	0.400
	250	1.000	$100.00	

Costs of Destroyed Product

Breast: $0.40 per pound × 20 pounds = $ 8

Wings: $0.40 per pound × 10 pounds = 4

$12

Note: Although not required, it is useful to highlight the individual product profitability figures:

Product	Sales Value	Sales Value at Splitoff Method		Physical Measures Method	
		Joint Costs Allocated	Gross Income	Joint Costs Allocated	Gross Income
Breasts	$110	$67.50	$42.50	$40.00	$70.00
Wings	8	4.90	3.10	8.00	0.00
Thighs	28	17.20	10.80	16.00	12.00
Bones	16	9.80	6.20	32.00	(16.00)
Feathers	1	0.60	0.40	4.00	(3.00)

16–16 (Cont'd.)

2.   The sales-value at splitoff method captures the benefits-received criterion of cost allocation and is the preferred method. The costs of processing a chicken are allocated to products in proportion to the ability to contribute revenue. Chicken Little's decision to process chicken is heavily influenced by the revenues from breasts and thighs. The bones provide relatively few benefits to Chicken Little despite their high physical volume.

The physical measures method shows profits on breasts and thighs and losses on bones and feathers. Given that Chicken Little has to jointly process all the chicken products, it is non-intuitive to single out individual products that are being processed simultaneously as making losses while the overall operations make a profit. Chicken Little is processing chicken mainly for breasts and thighs and not for wings, bones, and feathers, while the physical measure method allocates a disproportionate amount of costs to wings, bones and feathers.

16-18 (10 min.) Net realizable value method.

A diagram of the situation is in Solution Exhibit 16-18 (all numbers are in thousands).

	Cooking Oil	Soap Oil	Total
Final sales value of total production, CO, 1,000 × $50; SO, 500 × $25	$50,000	$12,500	$62,500
Deduct separable costs to complete and sell	30,000	7,500	37,500
Net realizable value at splitoff point	$20,000	$ 5,000	$25,000
Weighting	$\dfrac{\$20,000}{\$25,000} = 0.8$	$\dfrac{\$5,000}{\$25,000} = 0.2$	
Joint costs allocated, CO, 0.8 × $24,000; SO, 0.2 × $24,000	$19,200	$ 4,800	$24,000

16–18 (Cont'd.)

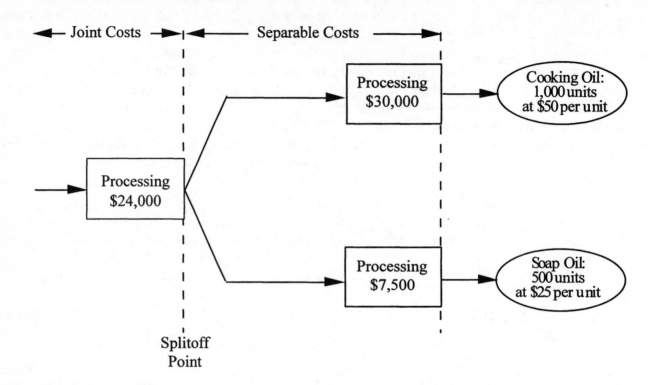

16-18 Excel Application

Cost Allocation: Joint Products and Byproducts
Illawara, Inc.

Original Data

Joint Costs ($1,000's)	$24,000

	Cooking Oil	Soap Oil
Separable Costs ($1,000's)	$30,000	$7,500
Selling Price (per drum)	50	25
Sales Volume (1,000's of drums)	1,000	500

Joint Cost Allocation (all numbers in thousands)

	Cooking Oil	Soap Oil	Total
1. Final sales value of production	$50,000	$12,500	$62,500
(Cooking oil, 1,000,000 drums x $50; Soap oil, 500,000 drums x $25)			
2. Deduct separable costs to complete and sell	30,000	7,500	37,500
3. Net realizable value at splitoff point	$20,000	$5,000	25,000
4. Weighting (Cooking oil, $20,000/$25,000; Soap oil, $5,000/$25,000)	0.8	0.2	
5. Joint costs allocated	$19,200	$4,800	$24,000
(Cooking oil, 0.8 x $24,000; Soap oil, 0.2 x $24,000)			

16-20 (40 min.) Alternative methods of joint-cost allocation, ending inventories.

Total production for the year was:

	Sold	Ending Inventories	Total Production
X	120	180	300
Y	340	60	400
Z	475	25	500

A diagram of the situation is in Solution Exhibit 16-20.

1.   a. Net realizable value (NRV) method:

	X	Y	Z	Total
Final sales value of total production, X, 300 × $1,500; Y, 400 × $1,000; Z, 500 × $700	$450,000	$400,000	$350,000	$1,200,000
Deduct separable costs	—	—	200,000	200,000
Net realizable value at splitoff point	$450,000	$400,000	$150,000	$1,000,000

Weighting:

$$\frac{\$450}{\$1,000}=0.45 \qquad \frac{\$400}{\$1,000}=0.40 \qquad \frac{\$150}{\$1,000}=0.15$$

	X	Y	Z	Total
Joint costs allocated, 0.45, 0.40 , 0.15 × $400,000	$180,000	$160,000	$60,000	$400,000

Ending Inventory Percentages:

	X	Y	Z
Ending inventory	180	60	25
Total production	300	400	500
Ending inventory percentage	60%	15%	5%

Income Statement

	X	Y	Z	Total
Revenues, X, 120 × $1,500; Y, 340 × $1,000; Z, 475 × $700	$180,000	$340,000	$332,500	$852,500
Cost of goods sold:				
Joint costs allocated	180,000	160,000	60,000	400,000
Separable costs	—	—	200,000	200,000
Cost of goods available for sale	180,000	160,000	260,000	600,000
Deduct ending inventory, X, 60%; Y, 15%; Z, 5%	108,000	24,000	13,000	145,000
Cost of goods sold	72,000	136,000	247,000	455,000
Gross margin	$108,000	$204,000	$85,500	$397,500
Gross-margin percentage	60%	60%	25.71%	

16-20 (Cont'd.)

b. Constant gross-margin percentage NRV method:

Step 1:

Final sales value of prodn., $(300 \times \$1,500) + (400 \times \$1,000) + (500 \times \$700)$	$1,200,000
Deduct joint and separable costs, $400,000 + $200,000	600,000
Gross margin	$ 600,000
Gross-margin percentage, $600,000 ÷ $1,200,000	50%

	X	Y	Z	Total
Final sales value of total production,				
X, 300 × $1,500; Y, 400 × $1,000;				
Z, 500 × $700	$450,000	$400,000	$350,000	$1,200,000
Step 2: Deduct gross margin, using overall gross-margin percentage of sales, 50%	225,000	200,000	175,000	600,000
Step 3: Deduct separable costs			200,000	200,000
Joint costs allocated	$225,000	$200,000	$(25,000)	$ 400,000

The negative joint-cost allocation to Product Z illustrates one "unusual" feature of the constant gross-margin percentage NRV method. Some products may receive negative cost allocations in order that all individual products have the same gross-margin percentage.

Income Statement

	X	Y	Z	Total
Revenues X, 120 × $1,500; Y, 340 × $1,000; Z, 475 × $700	$180,000	$340,000	$332,500	$852,500
Cost of goods sold:				
Joint costs allocated	225,000	200,000	(25,000)	400,000
Separable costs	-	-	200,000	200,000
Cost of goods available for sale	225,000	200,000	175,000	600,000
Deduct ending inventory,				
X, 60%; Y, 15%; Z, 5%	135,000	30,000	8,750	173,750
Cost of goods sold	90,000	170,000	166,250	426,250
Gross margin	$ 90,000	$170,000	$166,250	$426,250
Gross-margin percentage	50%	50%	50%	50%

16-6

16-20 (Cont'd.)

Summary

	X	Y	Z	Total
a. Estimated NRV method:				
Inventories on balance sheet	$108,000	$ 24,000	$ 13,000	$145,000
Cost of goods sold on income statement	72,000	136,000	247,000	455,000
				$600,000
b. Constant gross-margin percentage NRV method				
Inventories on balance sheet	$135,000	$ 30,000	$ 8,750	$173,750
Cost of goods sold on income statement	90,000	170,000	166,250	426,250
				$600,000

2.   Gross-margin percentages:

	X	Y	Z
Estimated NRV method	60%	60%	25.71%
Constant gross-margin percentage NRV	50%	50%	50.00%

SOLUTION EXHIBIT 16-20

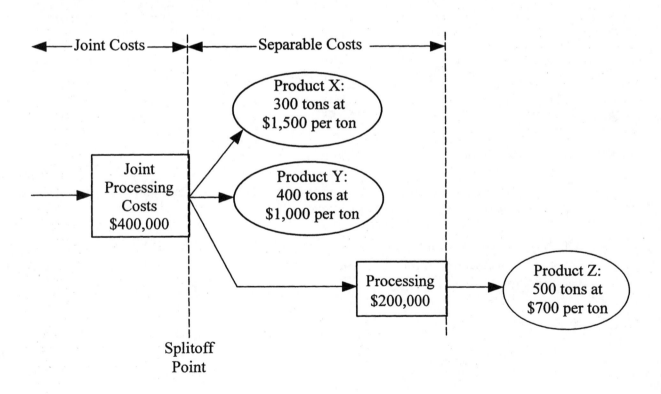

16-22 (20 min.) **Joint-cost allocation, physical-measures method.**
(continuation of 16-21).

1.

		Crude Oil	NGL	Total
1.	Final sales value of total production	$2,700	$750	$ 3,450
2.	Deduct separable costs	175	105	280
3.	NRV at splitoff	$2,525	$645	$3,170
4.	Weighting (2,525; 645÷3,170)	0.7965	0.2035	
5.	Joint costs allocated (Weights × $1,800)	$1,433.70	$366.30	$1,800

	Crude Oil	NGL	Total
Revenues	$2,700.00	$750.00	$3,450
Cost of good sold			
Joint costs	1,433.70	366.30	1,800
Separable costs	175.00	105.00	280
Total cost of goods sold	1,608.70	471.30	2,080
Gross margin	$1,091.30	$278.70	$1,370

2.   The State's proposed method results in large profits on crude oil and large losses on gas:

	Crude Oil	NGL	Gas	Total
Revenues	$2,700	$750	$ 0	$3,450
Cost of goods sold				
Joint costs	270	90	1,440	1,800
Separable costs	175	105	0	280
Total cost of goods sold	445	195	1,440	2,080
Gross margin	$2,255	$555	$(1,440)	$1,370

The main points to note are:

a.   Gas is not a salable product. It is simply a recycled output that adds no revenues. Indeed, costs are incurred to recycle the gas.

b.   The physical measure method has all the problems alluded to in the literature—e.g., it ignores the revenue earning potential of products, and it may not have a consistent denominator.

16-24 (30 min.) **Accounting for a main product and a byproduct.**

	Method A, Recognized at Production	Method B, Recognized at Sale
1. Revenues		
Main product	$160,000[a]	$160,000
Byproduct	---	2,800[d]
Total revenues	160,000	162,800
Cost of goods sold		
Total manufacturing costs	120,000	120,000
Deduct byproduct revenue	4,000[b]	0
Net manufacturing costs	116,000	120,000
Deduct main product inventory	23,200[c]	24,000[e]
Cost of goods sold	92,800	96,000
Gross margin	$ 67,200	$ 66,800

a. $8,000 \times \$20.00$

b. $2,000 \times \$2.00$

c. $\left(\dfrac{2,000}{10,000} \times \$116,000\right) = \$23,200$

d. $1,400 \times \$2.00$

e. $\left(\dfrac{2,000}{10,000} \times \$120,000\right) = \$24,000$

	Method A, Recognized at Production	Method B, Recognized at Sale
2. Rainbow Dew	$23,200	$24,000
Resi-Dew	1,200[a]	0

a. Ending inventory shown at unrealized selling price.

BI + Production – Sales = EI

0 + 2,000 – 1,400 = 600 gallons

Ending inventory = 600 gallons × $2 per gallon = $1,200

16-26 (40 min.) **Alternative methods of joint-cost allocation, product-mix decision.**

1. Joint costs = $300,000
a. **Sales value at splitoff method**

		Select	White	Knotty	Total
1.	Sales value of total prodn. at splitoff (30,000 × $8, 50,000 × $4, 20,000 × $3)	$240,000	$200,000	$60,000	$500,000
2.	Weighting (240/500, 200/500, 60/500)	0.48	0.40	0.12	
3.	Joint costs allocated (0.48, 0.40, 0.12 × $300,000)	$144,000	$120,000	$36,000	$300,000
4.	Total cost computation				
	Joint costs	$144,000	$120,000	$36,000	$300,000
	Separable processing costs	60,000	90,000	15,000	165,000
	Total costs	$204,000	$210,000	$51,000	$465,000
	Total board feet	25,000	40,000	15,000	
	Total cost per board foot	$8.16	$5.25	$3.40	

b. **Physical-measures method**

		Select	White	Knotty	Total
1.	Physical measure of production (board feet)	30,000	50,000	20,000	100,000
2.	Weighting (30/100, 50/100, 20/100)	0.30	0.50	0.20	
3.	Joint costs allocated (0.30, 0.50, 0.20 × $300,000)	$ 90,000	$150,000	$60,000	$300,000
4.	Total cost computation				
	Joint costs	$ 90,000	$150,000	$60,000	$300,000
	Separable processing	60,000	90,000	15,000	165,000
	Total costs	$150,000	$240,000	$75,000	$465,000
	Total board feet	25,000	40,000	15,000	
	Total cost per board foot	$6.00	$6.00	$5.00	

c. Net realizable value method

	Select	White	Knotty	Total
1. Final sales value of total production				
(25,000 × $16, 40,000 × $9, 15,000 × $7)	$400,000	$360,000	$105,000	$865,000
2. Deduct separable costs	60,000	90,000	15,000	165,000
3. NRV at splitoff	$340,000	$270,000	$90,000	$700,000
4. Weighting (340/700, 270/700, 90/700)	0.4857	0.3857	0.1286	
5. Joint costs allocated				
(0.4857, 0.3857, 0.1286 × $300,000)	$145,710	$115,710	$38,580	$300,000
Total cost computation				
Joint costs	$145,710	$115,710	$38,580	$300,000
Separable processing	60,000	90,000	15,000	165,000
Total costs	$205,710	$205,710	$53,580	$465,000
Total units	25,000	40,000	15,000	
Unit cost	$8.23	$5.14	$3.57	

2.	Select	White	Knotty	Total
a. Sales value at splitoff				
($8.16 × 1,000, $5.25 × 2,000, $3.40 × 500)	$8,160	$10,500	$1,700	$20,360
b. Physical measures				
($6.00 × 1,000, $6.00 × 2,000, $5.00 × 500)	6,000	12,000	2,500	20,500
c. Estimated NRV				
($8.23 × 1,000, $5.14 × 2,000, $3.57 × 500)	8,230	10,280	1,785	20,295

3. **Raw to Select Oak**

Incremental revenues: $400,000 – $240,000	$160,000
Deduct incremental processing costs	60,000
Increase in operating income	$100,000

Raw to White Oak

Incremental revenues: $360,000 – $200,000	$160,000
Deduct incremental processing costs	90,000
Increase in operating income	$ 70,000

Raw to Knotty Oak

Incremental revenues: $105,000 – $60,000	$ 45,000
Deduct incremental processing costs	15,000
Increase in operating income	$ 30,000

Pacific Lumber is maximizing its total August 2004 operating income by fully processing each raw oak product into its finished product form.

16-28 (40-60 min.) **Comparison of alternative joint-cost allocation methods, further-process decision, chocolate products.**

1a. Sales value at splitoff method:

	Chocolate-Powder Liquor Base	Milk-Chocolate Liquor Base	Total
Sales value of prodn. at splitoff, 200[a] × $21; 300[b] × $26	$4,200	$7,800	$12,000
Weighting	$\dfrac{\$4,200}{\$12,000} = 0.35$	$\dfrac{\$7,800}{\$12,000} = 0.65$	
Joint costs allocated, 0.35 × $10,000; 0.65 × $10,000	$3,500	$6,500	$10,000

[a](2,000/200) × 20   [b](3,400/340) × 30

1b. Physical-measure method:

	Chocolate-Powder Liquor Base	Milk-Chocolate Liquor Base	Total
200 (10 × 20) gallons; 300 (10 × 30) gallons	200 gallons	300 gallons	500 gallons
Weighting	$\dfrac{200}{500} = 0.40$	$\dfrac{300}{500} = 0.60$	
Joint costs allocated, 0.40 × $10,000; 0.60 × $10,000	$4,000	$6,000	$10,000

1c. Net realizable value method:

	Chocolate-Powder Liquor Base	Milk-Chocolate Liquor Base	Total
Final sales value of total production, 2,000 × $4; 3,400 × $5	$8,000	$17,000	$25,000
Deduct separable costs to complete and sell	4,250	8,750	13,000
Net realizable value at splitoff point	$3,750	$ 8,250	$12,000
Weighting	$\dfrac{\$3,750}{\$12,000} = 0.3125$	$\dfrac{\$8,250}{\$12,000} = 0.6875$	
Joint costs allocated, 0.3125 × $10,000; 0.6875 × $10,000	$3,125	$ 6,875	$10,000

16-28 (Cont'd.)

1d.   Constant gross-margin percentage NRV method:

Step 1:

Final sales value of total production,	
$\quad$ (2,000 × \$4) + (3,400 × \$5)	\$25,000
Deduct joint and separable costs,	
$\quad$ (\$10,000 + \$4,250 + \$8,750)	23,000
Gross margin	\$ 2,000
Gross-margin percentage (\$2,000 ÷ \$25,000)	8%

Step 2:

	Chocolate-Powder Liquor Base	Milk-Chocolate Liquor Base	Total
Final sales value of total production (2000 × \$4); (3,400 × \$5)	\$8,000	\$17,000	\$25,000
Deduct gross margin, using overall gross-margin percentage of sales (8%)	640	1,360	2,000
Cost of goods available for sale	7,360	15,640	23,000

Step 3:

	Chocolate-Powder Liquor Base	Milk-Chocolate Liquor Base	Total
Deduct separable costs to complete and sell	4,250	8,750	13,000
Joint costs allocated	\$3,110	\$ 6,890	\$10,000

16-28(Cont'd.)

2.

		Chocolate-Powder Liquor Base	Milk-Chocolate Liquor Base	Total
a.	Revenues	$8,000	$17,000	$25,000
	Joint costs	3,500	6,500	10,000
	Separable costs	4,250	8,750	13,000
	Total costs	7,750	15,250	23,000
	Gross margin	$ 250	$ 1,750	$ 2,000
	Gross-margin percentage	3.125%	10.294%	8%
b.	Revenues	$8,000	$17,000	$25,000
	Joint costs	4,000	6,000	10,000
	Separable costs	4,250	8,750	13,000
	Total costs	8,250	14,750	23,000
	Gross margin	$ (250)	$ 2,250	$ 2,000
	Gross-margin percentage	(3.125)%	13.235%	8%
c.	Revenues	$8,000	$17,000	$25,000
	Joint costs	3,125	6,875	10,000
	Separable costs	4,250	8,750	13,000
	Total costs	7,375	15,625	23,000
	Gross margin	$ 625	$ 1,375	$ 2,000
	Gross-margin percentage	7.812%	8.088%	8%
d.	Revenues	$8,000	$17,000	$25,000
	Joint costs	3,110	6,890	10,000
	Separable costs	4,250	8,750	13,000
	Total costs	7,360	15,640	23,000
	Gross margin	$ 640	$ 1,360	$ 2,000
	Gross-margin percentage	8%	8%	8%

3. Further processing of chocolate-powder liquor base into chocolate powder:

Incremental revenue, $8,000 – $4,200	$ 3,800
Incremental costs	4,250
Incremental operating income from further processing	$ (450)

Further processing of milk-chocolate liquor base into milk chocolate:

Incremental revenue, $17,000 – $7,800	$ 9,200
Incremental costs	8,750
Incremental operating income from further processing	$ 450

Roundtree Chocolates could increase operating income by $450 (to $2,450) if chocolate-powder liquor base is sold at the splitoff point and if milk-chocolate liquor base is further processed into milk chocolate.

16-30 (25 min.) **Joint-cost allocation, relevant costs** (R. Capettini, adapted).

1.   The "four-day progressive product trimming" ignores the fundamental point that the $300 cost to buy the pig is a joint cost. A pig is purchased as a whole. The butcher's challenge is to maximize the total revenues minus incremental costs (assumed zero) from the sale of all products.

At each stage, the decision made ignores the general rule that product emphasis decisions should consider relevant revenues and relevant costs. Allocated joint costs are not relevant. For example, the Day 1 decision to drop bacon ignores the fact that the $300 joint cost has been paid to acquire the whole pig. The $144 of revenues are relevant inflows. This same position also holds for the Day 2 to Day 4 decisions.

2.   The revenue amounts are the figures to use in the sales value at splitoff method:

Product	Revenue	Weighting	Joint Costs Allocated
Pork chops	$120	0.2899	$ 86.97
Ham	150	0.3623	108.69
Bacon	144	0.3478	104.34
	$414	1.0000	$300.00

3.   No. The decision to sell or not sell individual products should consider relevant revenues and relevant costs. In the butcher's context, the relevant costs would be the additional time and other incidentals to take each pig part and make it a salable product. The relevant revenues would be the difference between the selling price at the consumer level for the pig parts and what the butcher may receive for the whole pig.

16-32 (30 min.) **NRV method, byproducts** (CMA, adapted).

1.   a.   For the month of November 2003, Princess Corporation's output was:
- apple slices   89,100
- applesauce   81,000
- apple juice   67,500
- animal feed   27,000

These amounts were calculated as follows:

Product	Input	Proportion	Total Pounds	Pounds Lost	Net Pounds
Slices	270,000 lbs.	0.33	89,100	–	89,100
Sauce	270,000	0.30	81,000	–	81,000
Juice	270,000	0.27	72,900	5,400	67,500[a]
Feed	270,000	0.10	27,000	–	27,000
		1.00	270,000	5,400	264,600

[a]Net pounds: = $72,900 - (0.08 \times \text{net pounds})$
1.08 net pounds   =   72,900
Net pounds   =   67,500

b. The net realizable value for each of the three main products is calculated below:

Product	Net Pounds	Price	Revenue	Separable Costs	Net Realizable Value
Slices	89,100	$0.80	$ 71,280	$11,280	$ 60,000
Sauce	81,000	0.55	44,550	8,550	36,000
Juice	67,500	0.40	27,000	3,000	24,000
			$142,830	$22,830	$120,000

c. and d.

The net realizable value of the byproduct is deducted from the production costs prior to allocation to the joint products, as presented below:

Allocation of Cutting Department Costs
to Joint Products and Byproducts

Net realizable value
(NRV) of byproduct
= Byproduct revenue – Separable costs
= $0.10 (27,000 lbs) – $700
= $2,700 – $700
= $2,000

Costs to be allocated
= Joint costs – NRV of byproduct
= $60,000 – $2,000
= $58,000

Product	Revenue	Separable Costs	Joint Costs[a]	Gross Margin
Slices	$ 71,280	$11,280	$29,000	$31,000
Sauce	44,550	8,550	17,400	18,600
Juice	27,000	3,000	11,600	12,400
	$142,830	$22,830	$58,000	$62,000

[a] Allocated using NRV of the three joint products from requirement 1b:

Slices   ($60,000 ÷ $120,000) × $58,000 = $29,000
Sauce   ($36,000 ÷ $120,000) × $58,000 = 17,400
Juice   ($24,000 ÷ $120,000) × $58,000 = 11,600

2. The gross-margin dollar information by main product is determined by the arbitrary allocation of joint production costs. As a result, these cost figures and the resulting gross-margin information are of little significance for planning and control purposes. The allocation is made only for purposes of inventory costing and income determination.

16-34 (20 min.) Byproduct, disposal costs, ethics.

1. The comparative analysis prepared by the cost accountant is flawed. In the process further alternative, he has erroneously included the $250,000 allocated joint costs. Allocated joint costs are irrelevant because they are not incremental costs of the alternative being considered. If the joint costs allocated are taken out, it becomes clear that financially it would be to the advantage of the company to process further the product as it would increase the operating income by $150,000 [$500,000 − ($300,000 + $50,000)]. Furthermore, the dumping alternative does not consider potential future costs that may arise from environmental liabilities.

2. It appears that there would be no legal ramifications if the company decided to dump the hazardous product into the Gulf. The country either may have no laws against such dumping, or even if they exist, they are not enforced in accordance with the government policy. A more important consideration, however, is the ethical implications. To knowingly dump a hazardous material into the Gulf would certainly result in water pollution. This is an unacceptable action from a societal standpoint. *It is important to remember that an act that does not violate any laws is not necessarily an ethical act.* Ethical considerations go beyond legal considerations. In different parts of the world, legal systems are imperfect and not comprehensive. It is the responsibility of top management to take a broader, societal view when making decisions. In other words, a business should take its social responsibility seriously, by making it an integral part of the decision-making process. In the long run it is in the best interest of all stakeholders as well as the business itself.

17-2 Process costing systems separate costs into cost categories according to the timing of when costs are introduced into the process. Often, only two cost classifications, direct materials and conversion costs, are necessary. Direct materials are frequently added at one point in time, often the start or the end of the process, and all conversion costs are added at about the same time, but in a pattern different from direct materials costs.

17-4 The accuracy of the estimates of completion depend on the care and skill of the estimator and the nature of the process. Aircraft blades may differ substantially in the finishing necessary to obtain a final product. The amount of work necessary to finish a product may not always be easy to ascertain in advance.

17-6 Three inventory methods associated with process costing are:
- Weighted average.
- First-in, first-out.
- Standard costing.

17-8 FIFO computations are distinctive because they assign the cost of the previous accounting period's equivalent units in beginning work-in-process inventory to the first units completed and transferred out of the process and assigns the cost of equivalent units worked on during the current period first to complete beginning inventory, next to start and complete new units, and finally to units in ending work-in-process inventory. In contrast, the weighted-average method costs units completed and transferred out and in ending work in process at the same average cost.

17-10 A major advantage of FIFO is that managers can judge the performance in the current period independently from the performance in the preceding period.

17-12 Standard-cost procedures are particularly appropriate to process-costing systems where there are various combinations of materials and operations used to make a wide variety of similar products as in the textiles, paints, and ceramics industries. Standard-cost procedures also avoid the intricacies involved in detailed tracking with weighted-average or FIFO methods when there are frequent price variations over time.

17-14 No. Transferred-in costs or previous department costs are costs incurred in a previous department that have been charged to a subsequent department. These costs may be costs incurred in that previous department during this accounting period or a preceding accounting period.

17-16 (25 min.) **Equivalent units, zero beginning inventory.**

1. Direct materials cost per unit ($720,000 ÷ 10,000)	$ 72
Conversion cost per unit ($760,000 ÷ 10,000)	76
Assembly Department cost per unit	$148

17-16 (Cont'd.)

2a. Solution Exhibit 17-16A calculates the equivalent units of direct materials and conversion costs in the Assembly Department of International Electronics in February 2004.

Solution Exhibit 17-16B computes equivalent units costs.

2b.
Direct materials cost per unit	$ 72
Conversion cost per unit	80
Assembly Department cost per unit	$152

3. The difference in the Assembly Department cost per unit calculated in requirements 1 and 2 arises because the costs incurred in January and February are the same but fewer equivalent units of work are done in February relative to January. In January, all 10,000 units introduced are fully completed resulting in 10,000 equivalent units of work done with respect to direct materials and conversion costs. In February, of the 10,000 units introduced, 10,000 equivalent units of work is done with respect to direct materials but only 9,500 equivalent units of work is done with respect to conversion costs. The Assembly Department cost per unit is, therefore, higher.

SOLUTION EXHIBIT 17-16A

Steps 1 and 2: Summarize Output in Physical Units and Compute Equivalent Units
Assembly Department of International Electronics for February 2004

		(Step 2)	
	(Step 1)	Equivalent Units	
Flow of Production	Physical Units	Direct Materials	Conversion Costs
Work in process, beginning	0		
Started during current period	10,000		
To account for	10,000		
Completed and transferred out during current period	9,000	9,000	9,000
Work in process, ending*	1,000		
1,000 × 100%; 1,000 × 50%		1,000	500
Accounted for	10,000		
Work done in current period only		10,000	9,500

*Degree of completion in this department: direct materials, 100%; conversion costs, 50%.

SOLUTION EXHIBIT 17-16B

Compute Equivalent Unit Costs,
Assembly Department of International Electronics for February 2004

	Total Production Costs	Direct Materials	Conversion Costs
(Step 3) Costs added during February	$1,480,000	$720,000	$760,000
Divide by equivalent units of work done in current period (Solution Exhibit 17-16A)		÷ 10,000	÷ 9,500
Cost per equivalent unit		$ 72	$ 80

17-18 (25 min.) **Zero beginning inventory, materials introduced in middle of process.**

1.   Solution Exhibit 17-18A shows equivalent units of work done in the current period of Chemical P, 50,000; Chemical Q, 35,000; Conversion costs, 45,000.

2.   Solution Exhibit 17-18B calculates cost per equivalent unit of work done in the current period for Chemical P, Chemical Q, and Conversion costs, summarizes the total Mixing Department costs for July 2004, and assigns these costs to units completed (and transferred out) and to units in ending work in process.

SOLUTION EXHIBIT 17-18A
Steps 1 and 2: Summarize Output in Physical Units and Compute Equivalent Units
Mixing Department of Vaasa Chemicals for July 2004

| | (Step 1) | (Step 2) Equivalent Units | | |
| | Physical | | | Conversion |
Flow of Production	Units	Chemical P	Chemical Q	Costs
Work in process, beginning	0			
Started during current period	50,000			
To account for	50,000			
Completed and transferred out during current period	35,000	35,000	35,000	35,000
Work in process, ending*	15,000			
15,000 × 100%; 15,000 × 0%;				
15,000 × 66 2/3%	_____	15,000	0	10,000
Accounted for	50,000			
Work done in current period only		50,000	35,000	45,000

*Degree of completion in this department: Chemical P, 100%; Chemical Q, 0%; conversion costs, 66 2/3%.

17-18 (Cont'd.)

SOLUTION EXHIBIT 17-18B
Steps 3, 4, and 5: Compute Equivalent Unit Costs, Summarize Total Costs to Account For, and Assign Costs to Units Completed and to Units in Ending Work in Process, Mixing Department of Vaasa Chemicals for July 2004

	Total Production Costs	Chemical P	Chemical Q	Conversion Costs
(Step 3) Costs added during July	$455,000	$250,000	$70,000	$135,000
Divide by equivalent units of work done in current period (Solution Exhibit 17-18A)		÷ 50,000	÷35,000	÷ 45,000
Cost per equivalent unit		$ 5	$ 2	$ 3
(Step 4) Total costs to account for	$455,000			
(Step 5) Assignment of costs:				
Completed and transferred out (35,000 units)	$350,000	(35,000*× $5) +	(35,000*×$2) +	(35,000*×$3)
Work in process ending (15,000 units)				
Chemical P	75,000	15,000† × $5		
Chemical Q	0		0† × $2	
Conversion costs	30,000			10,000†×$3
Total work in process	105,000			
Total costs accounted for	$455,000			

*Equivalent units completed and transferred out from Solution Exhibit 17-18A, Step 2.
†Equivalent units in work in process, ending from Solution Exhibit 17-18A, Step 2.

17-20 (20 min.) **Weighted-average method, assigning costs (continuation of 17-19).**

Solution Exhibit 17-20 calculates cost per equivalent unit of work done to date in the Assembly Department of Aerospatiale, summarizes total costs to account for, and assigns costs to units completed and to units in ending work-in-process inventory.

SOLUTION EXHIBIT 17-20
Steps 3, 4, and 5: Compute Equivalent Unit Costs, Summarize Total Costs to Account For, and Assign Costs to Units Completed and to Units in Ending Work in Process
Weighted-Average Method of Process Costing, Satellite Assembly Department of Aerospatiale for May 2004

		Total Production Costs	Direct Materials	Conversion Costs
(Step 3)	Work in process, beginning (given)	$ 5,844,000	$ 4,933,600	$ 910,400
	Costs added in current period (given)	46,120,000	32,200,000	13,920,000
	Costs incurred to date		$37,133,600	$14,830,400
	Divide by equivalent units of work done to date (Solution Exhibit 17-19)		÷ 53.2	÷ 49.6
	Cost per equivalent unit of work done to date		$ 698,000	$ 299,000
(Step 4)	Total costs to account for	$51,964,000		
(Step 5)	Assignment of costs:			
	Completed and transferred out (46 units)	$45,862,000	(46*× $698,000) + (46* × $299,000)	
	Work in process, ending (12 units)			
	Direct materials	5,025,600	7.2†× $698,000	
	Conversion costs	1,076,400		3.6† × $299,000
	Total work in process	6,102,000		
	Total costs accounted for	$51,964,000		

*Equivalent units completed and transferred out from Solution Exhibit 17-19, Step 2.
†Equivalent units in work in process, ending from Solution Exhibit 17-19, Step 2.

17-22 (20 min.) FIFO method, assigning costs (continuation of 17-21).

Solution Exhibit 17-22 calculates cost per equivalent unit of work done in May 2004 in the Assembly Department of Aerospatiale, summarizes total costs to account for, and assigns costs to units completed and to units in ending work-in-process inventory.

SOLUTION EXHIBIT 17-22
Steps 3, 4, and 5: Compute Equivalent Unit Costs, Summarize Total Costs to Account For, and Assign Costs to Units Completed and to Units in Ending Work in Process
FIFO Method of Process Costing, Satellite Assembly Division of Aerospatiale for May 2004

	Total Production Costs	Direct Materials	Conversion Costs
Work in process, beginning ($4,933,600 + $910,400)	$ 5,844,000	(costs of work done before current period)	
(Step 3) Costs added in current period (given)	46,120,000	$32,200,000	$ 13,920,000
Divide by equivalent units of work done in current period (Solution Exhibit 17-21)		$\div$ 46	$\div$ 46.4
Cost per equivalent unit of work done in current period		$ 700,000	$ 300,000
(Step 4) Total costs to account for	$51,964,000		
(Step 5) Assignment of costs:			
Completed and transferred out (46 units):			
Work in process, beginning (8 units)	$ 5,844,000		
Direct materials added in current period	560,000	0.8* × $700,000	
Conversion costs added in current period	1,440,000		4.8* × $300,000
Total from beginning inventory	7,844,000		
Started and completed (38 units)	38,000,000	(38[†] × $700,000) + (38[†] × $300,000)	
Total costs of units completed & transf. out	45,844,000		
Work in process, ending (12 units)			
Direct materials	5,040,000	7.2[#] × $700,000	
Conversion costs	1,080,000		3.6[#] × $300,000
Total work in process, ending	6,120,000		
Total costs accounted for	$51,964,000		

*Equivalent units used to complete beginning work in process from Solution Exhibit 17-21, Step 2.
[†]Equivalent units started and completed from Solution Exhibit 17-21, Step 2.
[#]Equivalent units in work in process, ending from Solution Exhibit 17-21, Step 2.

17-24 (25 min.) Weighted-average method, assigning costs.

1. & 2.   Solution Exhibit 17-24 calculates the cost per equivalent unit of work done to date for direct materials and conversion costs, summarizes total costs to account for, and assigns these costs to units completed and transferred out and to units in ending work-in-process inventory.

SOLUTION EXHIBIT 17-24

Steps 3, 4, and 5: Compute Equivalent Unit Costs, Summarize Total Costs to Account For, and Assign Costs to Units Completed and to Units in Ending Work in Process
Weighted-Average Method of Process Costing, Chatham Company for July 2004

		Total Production Costs	Direct Materials	Conversion Costs
(Step 3)	Work in process, beginning (given)	$130,000	$ 60,000	$ 70,000
	Costs added in current period (given)	651,000	280,000	371,000
	Costs incurred to date		$340,000	$441,000
	Divide by equivalent units of work done to date (given)		÷ 50,000	÷ 42,000
	Cost per equivalent unit of work done to date		$ 6.80	$ 10.50
(Step 4)	Total costs to account for	$781,000		
(Step 5)	Assignment of costs:			
	Completed and transferred out (34,000 units)	$588,200	(34,000* × $6.80) +	(34,000* × $10.50)
	Work in process, ending (16,000 units)			
	Direct materials	108,800	16,000[†] × $6.80	
	Conversion costs	84,000		8,000[†] × $10.50
	Total work in process	192,800		
	Total costs accounted for	$781,000		

*Equivalent units completed and transferred out (given).
[†]Equivalent units in work in process, ending (given).

17-26 (30 min.) **Standard-costing method, assigning costs** (Refer to the information in Exercise 17-24).

1. The calculations of equivalent units for direct materials and conversion costs are identical to the calculations of equivalent units under the FIFO method. Solution Exhibit 17-26A shows the equivalent unit calculations for standard costing given by the equivalent units of work done in July 2004. Solution Exhibit 17-26B uses the standard costs (direct materials, $6.50; conversion costs, $10.30) to summarize total costs to account for, and to assign these costs to units completed and transferred out and to units in ending work-in-process inventory.

2. Solution Exhibit 17-26 shows the direct materials and conversion costs variances for

Direct materials	$20,000 U
Conversion costs	$10,500 U

SOLUTION EXHIBIT 17-26A
Steps 1 and 2: Summarize Output in Physical Units and Compute Equivalent Units
FIFO Method of Process Costing, Chatham Company for July 2004

	(Step 1)	(Step 2) Equivalent Units	
Flow of Production	Physical Units	Direct Materials	Conversion Costs
Work in process, beginning (given)	10,000	(work done before current period)	
Started during current period (given)	40,000		
To account for	50,000		
Completed and transferred out during current period:			
From beginning work in process[§]	10,000		
10,000 × (100% − 100%); 10,000 × (100% − 70%)		0	3,000
Started and completed	24,000[†]		
24,000 × 100%, 24,000 × 100%		24,000	24,000
Work in process, ending* (given)	16,000		
16,000 × 100%; 16,000 × 50%		16,000	8,000
Accounted for	50,000		
Work done in current period only		40,000	35,000

[§]Degree of completion in this department: direct materials, 100%; conversion costs, 70%.

[†]34,000 physical units completed and transferred out minus 10,000 physical units completed and transferred out from beginning work-in-process inventory.

*Degree of completion in this department: direct materials, 100%; conversion costs, 50%.

SOLUTION EXHIBIT 17-26B

Steps 3, 4, and 5: Compute Equivalent Unit Costs, Summarize Total Costs to Account For, and Assign Costs to Units Completed and to Units in Ending Work in Process
Use of Standard Costs in Process Costing, Chatham Company for July 2004.

	Total Production Costs	Direct Materials	Conversion Costs
(Step 3) Standard cost per equivalent unit (given)		$ 6.50	$ 10.30
Work in process, beginning (given)			
Direct materials, 10,000 × $6.50; Conversion costs, 7,000 × $10.30	$137,100		
Costs added in current period at standard costs			
Direct materials, 40,000 × $6.50;			
Conversion costs, 35,000 × $10.30	620,500	$260,000	$360,500
(Step 4) Costs to account for	$757,600		
(Step 5) Assignment of costs at standard costs:			
Completed and transferred out (34,000 units):			
Work in process, beginning (10,000 units)	$137,100		
Direct materials added in current period	0	0* × $6.50	
Conversion costs added in current period	30,900		3,000* × $10.30
Total from beginning inventory	168,000		
Started and completed (24,000 units)	403,200	(24,000† × $6.50) +	(24,000† × $10.30)
Total costs of units transferred out	571,200		
Work in process, ending (16,000 units)			
Direct materials	104,000	16,000# × $6.50	
Conversion costs	82,400		8,000# × $10.30
Total work in process, ending	186,400		
Total costs accounted for	$757,600		
Summary of variances for current performance:			
Costs added in current period at standard prices (see above)		$260,000	$360,500
Actual costs incurred (given)		280,000	371,000
Variance		$ 20,000 U	$ 10,500 U

*Equivalent units to complete beginning work in process from Solution Exhibit 17-25A, Step 2.
†Equivalent units started and completed from Solution Exhibit 17-25A, Step 2.
#Equivalent units in work in process, ending from Solution Exhibit 17-25A, Step 2.

17-28 (35–40 min.) **Transferred-in costs, FIFO method.**

1. & 2.   Solution Exhibit 17-28A calculates the equivalent units of work done in the current period (for transferred-in costs, direct-materials, and conversion costs) to complete beginning work-in-process inventory, to start and complete new units, and to produce ending work in process. Solution Exhibit 17-28B calculates the cost per equivalent unit of work done in the current period for transferred-in costs, direct materials, and conversion costs, summarizes total costs to account for, and assigns these costs to units completed and transferred out and to units in ending work-in-process inventory.

SOLUTION EXHIBIT 17-28A
Steps 1 and 2: Summarize Output in Physical Units and Compute Equivalent Units
FIFO Method of Process Costing
Cooking Department of Hideo Chemicals for June 2004

| | (Step 1) | (Step 2) Equivalent Units | | |
Flow of Production	Physical Units	Transferred-in Costs	Direct Materials	Conversion Costs
Work in process, beginning (given)	40	(work done before current period)		
Transferred in during current period (given)	80			
To account for	120			
Completed and transferred out during current period:				
From beginning work in process[§]	40			
40 × (100% – 100%); 40 × (100% – 0%); 40 × (100% – 75%)		0	40	10
Started and completed	50[†]			
50 × 100%; 50 × 100%; 50 × 100%		50	50	50
Work in process, ending* (given)	30			
30 × 100%; 30 × 0%; 30 × 50%		30	0	15
Accounted for	120			
Work done in current period only		80	90	75

[§]Degree of completion in this department: Transferred-in costs, 100%; direct materials, 0%; conversion costs, 75%.
[†]90 physical units completed and transferred out minus 40 physical units completed and transferred out from beginning work-in-process inventory.
*Degree of completion in this department: transferred-in costs, 100%; direct materials, 0%; conversion costs, 50%.

17-28 (Cont'd.)

SOLUTION EXHIBIT 17-28B
Steps 3, 4, and 5: Compute Equivalent Unit Costs, Summarize Total Costs to Account For, and Assign Costs to Units Completed and to Units in Ending Work in Process
FIFO Method of Process Costing
Cooking Department of Hideo Chemicals for June 2004

	Total Production Costs	Transferred -in Costs	Direct Materials	Conversion Costs
Work in process, beginning ($39,200 + $0 + $18,000)	$ 57,200	(Costs of work done before current period)		
(Step 3) Costs added in current period (given)	171,325	$85,600	$36,000	$49,725
Divide by equivalent units of work done in current period (Solution Exhibit 17-28A)		÷ 80	÷ 90	÷ 75
Cost per equiv. unit of work done in current period		$ 1,070	$ 400	$ 663
(Step 4) Total costs to account for	$228,525			
(Step 5) Assignment of costs:				
Completed and transferred out (90 units):				
Work in process, beginning (40 units)	$ 57,200			
Transferred-in costs added in current period	0	0*×$1,070		
Direct materials added in current period	16,000		40*×$400	
Conversion costs added in current period	6,630			10*×$663
Total from beginning inventory	79,830			
Started and completed (50 units)	106,650	(50†× $1,070) + (50†× $400)+ (50†×$663)		
Total costs of units completed & tfd. out	186,480			
Work in process, ending (30 units)				
Transferred-in costs	32,100	30#×$1,070		
Direct materials	0		0#×$400	
Conversion costs	9,945			15#×$663
Total work in process, ending	42,045			
Total costs accounted for	$228,525			

*Equivalent units used to complete beginning work in process from Solution Exhibit 17-28A, Step 2.
†Equivalent units started and completed from Solution Exhibit 17-28A, Step 2.
#Equivalent units in work in process, ending from Solution Exhibit 17-28A, Step 2.

17-30 (25 min.) Weighted-average method.

1.   Solution Exhibit 17-30A shows equivalent units of work done to date
        Direct materials   100 equivalent units
        Conversion costs   97 equivalent units

2. & 3. Solution Exhibit 17-30B calculates cost per equivalent unit of work done to date, summarizes the total Assembly Department costs for October 2004, and assigns these costs to units completed (and transferred out) and to units in ending work in process using the weighted-average method.

17-30 (Cont'd.)

SOLUTION EXHIBIT 17-30A
Steps 1 and 2: Summarize Output in Physical Units and Compute Equivalent Units
Weighted-Average Method of Process Costing, Assembly Department of Global Defense Inc. for
October 2004

Flow of Production	(Step 1) Physical Units (given)	(Step 2) Equivalent Units	
		Direct Materials	Conversion Costs
Work in process, beginning	20		
Started during current period	80		
To account for	100		
Completed and transferred out during current period	90	90	90
Work in process, ending*	10		
10 × 100%; 10 × 70%		10	7
Accounted for	100		
Work done to date		100	97

*Degree of completion in this department: direct materials, 100%; conversion costs, 70%.

SOLUTION EXHIBIT 17-30B
Steps 3, 4, and 5: Compute Equivalent Unit Costs, Summarize Total Costs to Account For, and
Assign Costs to Units Completed and to Units in Ending Work in Process
Weighted-Average Method of Process Costing, Assembly Department of Global Defense Inc.
for October 2004

		Total Production Costs	Direct Materials	Conversion Costs
(Step 3)	Work in process, beginning (given)	$ 580,000	$ 460,000	$ 120,000
	Costs added in current period (given)	2,935,000	2,000,000	935,000
	Costs incurred to date		$2,460,000	$1,055,000
	Divide by equivalent units of work done to date (Solution Exhibit 17-30A)		÷ 100	÷ 97
	Cost per equivalent unit of work done to date		$ 24,600	$10,876.29
(Step 4)	Total costs to account for	$3,515,000		
(Step 5)	Assignment of costs:			
	Completed and transferred out (90 units)	$3,192,866	(90* × $24,600) + (90* × $10,876.29)	
	Work in process, ending (10 units)			
	Direct materials	246,000	10[†] × $24,600	
	Conversion costs	76,134		7[†] × $10,876.29
	Total work in process, ending	322,134		
	Total costs accounted for	$3,515,000		

*Equivalent units completed and transferred out from Solution Exhibit 17-30A, Step 2.
[†]Equivalent units in work in process, ending from Solution Exhibit 17-30A, Step 2.

17-30 (Cont'd.)

17-30 Excel Application

Process Costing
Global Defense, Inc.
Original Data

	Physical Units (Missiles)	Direct Materials	Conversion Costs
Work in process, October 1	20	$460,000	$120,000
Started during October 2004	80		
Completed during October 2004	90		
Work in process, October 31	10		
Costs added during October 2004		$2,000,000	$935,000

Problem 1

Flow of Production	Physical Units	Direct Materials	Conversion Costs
Work in process, beginning	20		
Started during current period	80		
To account for	100		
Good units completed and transferred out during current period	90	90	90
Work in process, ending	10		
10 x 100%; 10 x 70%		10	7
Accounted for	100		
Work done to date		100	97

Problem 2

	Total Production Costs	Direct Materials	Conversion Costs
Work in process, beginning	$ 580,000	$ 460,000	$ 120,000
Costs added in current period	2,935,000	2,000,000	935,000
Costs incurred to date		$2,460,000	$1,055,000
Equivalent units of work done to date		100	97
Cost per equivalent unit of work done to date		$ 4,600	$10,876.29

Problem 3

	Total Production Costs	Direct Materials	Conversion Costs
Total costs to account for	$3,515,000		
Assignment of costs:			
Completed and transferred out	$3,192,866	2,214,000	978,866
Work in process, ending			
Direct materials	246,000		
Conversion costs	76,134		
Total work in process ending	322,134		
Total costs accounted for	$3,515,000		

17-32 (20 min.) **FIFO method (continuation of 17-30 and 17-31).**

1.   The equivalent units of work done in the current period in the Assembly Department in October 2004 for direct materials and conversion costs are shown in Solution Exhibit 17-32A.

2.   The cost per equivalent unit of work done in the current period in the Assembly Department in October 2004 for direct materials and conversion costs is calculated in Solution Exhibit 17-32B.

3.   Solution Exhibit 17-32B summarizes the total Assembly Department costs for October 2004, and assigns these costs to units completed (and transferred out) and units in ending work in process under the FIFO method.
       The cost per equivalent unit of beginning inventory and of work done in the current period differ:

	Beginning Inventory	Work Done in Current Period
Direct materials	$23,000 ($460,000 ÷ 20 equiv. units)	$25,000
Conversion costs	$10,000 ($120,000 ÷ 12 equiv. units)	$11,000

	Direct Materials	Conversion Costs
Cost per equivalent unit (weighted-average)	$24,600*	$10,876.29*
Cost per equivalent unit (FIFO)	$25,000**	$11,000**

*from Solution Exhibit 17-30B
**from Solution Exhibit 17-32B

The cost per equivalent unit differs between the two methods because each method uses different costs to calculate the numerator of the calculation. FIFO uses only the costs added during the period whereas weighted-average uses the costs from the beginning work-in-process as well as costs added during the period. Both methods also use different equivalent units in the denominator.
       The following table summarizes the costs assigned to units completed and those still in process under the weighted-average and FIFO process-costing methods for our example.

	Weighted Average (Solution Exhibit 17-30B)	FIFO (Solution Exhibit 17-32B)	Difference
Cost of units completed and transferred out	$3,192,866	$3,188,000	−$4,866
Work in process, ending	322,134	327,000	+$4,866
Total costs accounted for	$3,515,000	$3,515,000	

The FIFO ending inventory is higher than the weighted-average ending inventory by $4,866. This is because FIFO assumes that all the lower-cost prior-period units in work in process are the first to be completed and transferred out while ending work in process consists of only the higher-cost current-period units.   The weighted-average method, however, smoothes out cost per equivalent unit by assuming that more of the higher-cost units are completed and transferred out, while some of the lower-cost units in beginning work in process are placed in ending work in process.   Hence, in this case, the weighted-average method results in a higher cost of units completed and transferred out and a lower ending work-in-process inventory relative to FIFO.

SOLUTION EXHIBIT 17-32A
Steps 1 and 2: Summarize Output in Physical Units and Compute Equivalent Units
FIFO Method of Process Costing, Assembly Department of Global Defense Inc. for October 2004

Flow of Production	(Step 1) Physical Units	(Step 2) Equivalent Units Direct Materials	Conversion Costs
Work in process, beginning (given)	20	(work done before current	
Started during current period (given)	80	period)	
To account for	100		
Completed and transferred out during current period:			
From beginning work in process[§]	20		
20 × (100% − 100%); 20 × (100% − 60%)		0	8
Started and completed	70[†]		
70 ×100%, 70 × 100%		70	70
Work in process, ending* (given)	10		
10 × 100%; 10 × 70%		10	7
Accounted for	100		
Work done in current period only		80	85

[§]Degree of completion in this department: direct materials, 100%; conversion costs, 60%.

[†]90 physical units completed and transferred out minus 20 physical units completed and transferred out from beginning work-in-process inventory.

*Degree of completion in this department: direct materials, 100%; conversion costs, 70%.

17-32 (Cont'd.)

SOLUTION EXHIBIT 17-32B

Steps 3, 4, and 5: Compute Equivalent Unit Costs, Summarize Total Costs to Account For, and Assign Costs to Units Completed and to Units in Ending Work in Process
FIFO Method of Process Costing, Assembly Department of Global Defense Inc. for October 2004

	Total Production Costs	Direct Materials	Conversion Costs
Work in process, beginning ($460,000 + $120,000)	$ 580,000	(costs of work done before current period)	
(Step 3) Costs added in current period (given)	2,935,000	$2,000,000	$935,000
Divide by equivalent units of work done in current period (Solution Exhibit 17-32A)		÷ 80	÷ 85
Cost per equivalent unit of work done in current period		$ 25,000	$ 11,000
(Step 4) Total costs to account for	$3,515,000		
(Step 5) Assignment of costs:			
Completed and transferred out (90 units):			
Work in process, beginning (20 units)	$ 580,000		
Direct materials added in current period	0	0* × $25,000	
Conversion costs added in current period	88,000		8* × $11,000
Total from beginning inventory	668,000		
Started and completed (70 units)	2,520,000	(70† × $25,000) + (70† × $11,000)	
Total costs of units completed & transf. out	3,188,000		
Work in process, ending (10 units)			
Direct materials	250,000	10# × $25,000	
Conversion costs	77,000		7# × $11,000
Total work in process, ending	327,000		
Total costs accounted for	$3,515,000		

*Equivalent units used to complete beginning work in process from Solution Exhibit 17-32A, Step 2.
†Equivelant units started and completed from Solution Exhibit 17-32A, Step 2.
#Equivalent units in work in process, ending from Solution Exhibit 17-32A, Step 2.

17-34 (30 min.) Transferred-in costs, FIFO method (continuation of 17-33).

1.   As explained in Problem 17-33, requirement 1, transferred-in costs are 100% complete and direct materials are 0% complete in both beginning and ending work-in-process inventory.

2.   The equivalent units of work done in October 2004 in the Testing Department for transferred-in costs, direct materials, and conversion costs are calculated in Solution Exhibit 17-34A.

3.   Solution Exhibit 17-34B calculates the cost per equivalent unit of work done in October 2004 in the Testing Department for transferred-in costs, direct materials, and conversion costs, summarizes total Testing Department costs for October 2004, and assigns these costs to units completed and transferred out and to units in ending work in process using the FIFO method.

17-34 (Cont'd.)

4. Journal entries:

   a. Work in Process—Testing Department   3,188,000
         Work in Process—Assembly Department   3,188,000
      Cost of goods completed and transferred out
         during October from the Assembly Dept. to
         the Testing Dept.

   b. Finished Goods   9,281,527
         Work in Process—Testing Department   9,281,527
      Cost of goods completed and transferred out
         during October from the Testing Department
         to Finished Goods inventory.

SOLUTION EXHIBIT 17-34A

Steps 1 and 2: Summarize Output in Physical Units and Compute Equivalent Units
FIFO Method of Process Costing
Testing Department of Global Defense Inc. for October 2004

| | (Step 1) | (Step 2) Equivalent Units | | |
Flow of Production	Physical Units	Transferred-in Costs	Direct Materials	Conversion Costs
Work in process, beginning (given)	30	(work done before current period)		
Transferred-in during current period (given)	90			
To account for	120			
Completed and transferred out during current period:				
From beginning work in process[§]	30			
$30 \times (100\% - 100\%)$; $30 \times (100\% - 0\%)$;				
$30 \times (100\% - 70\%)$		0	30	9
Started and completed	75[†]			
$75 \times 100\%$; $75 \times 100\%$; $75 \times 100\%$		75	75	75
Work in process, ending* (given)	15			
$15 \times 100\%$; $15 \times 0\%$; $15 \times 60\%$		15	0	9
Accounted for	120			
Work done in current period only		90	105	93

[§] Degree of completion in this department: Transferred-in costs, 100%; direct materials, 0%; conversion costs, 70%.

[†]105 physical units completed and transferred out minus 30 physical units completed and transferred out from beginning work-in-process inventory.

*Degree of completion in this department: transferred-in costs, 100%; direct materials, 0%; conversion costs, 60%.

17-34 (Cont'd.)

SOLUTION EXHIBIT 17-34B
Steps 3, 4, and 5: Compute Equivalent Unit Costs, Summarize Total Costs to Account For, and Assign Costs to Units Completed and to Units in Ending Work in Process
FIFO Method of Process Costing
Testing Department of Global Defense Inc. for October 2004

		Total Production Costs	Transferred -in Costs	Direct Materials	Conversion Costs
	Work in process, beginning ($331,800 + $0 + $980,060))	$1,311,860	(Costs of work done before current period)		
(Step 3)	Costs added in current period (given)	8,654,000	$3,188,000	$3,885,000	$1,581,000
	Divide by equivalent units of work done in current period (Solution Exhibit 17-34A)		÷ 90	÷ 105	÷ 93
	Cost per equiv. unit of work done in current period		$ 35,422.22	$ 37,000	$ 17,000
(Step 4)	Total costs to account for	$9,965,860			
(Step 5)	Assignment of costs:				
	Completed and transferred out (105 units):				
	Work in process, beginning (30 units)	$1,311,860			
	Tfd-in costs added in current period	0	0*× $35,422.22		
	Direct materials added in current period	1,110,000		30*×$37,000	
	Conversion costs added in current period	153,000			9*×$17,000
	Total from beginning inventory	2,574,860			
	Started and completed (75 units)	6,706,667	(75†×$35,422.22)+(75†×$37,000)+(75†×$17,000)		
	Total costs of units completed & tfd. out	9,281,527			
	Work in process, ending (15 units)				
	Transferred-in costs	531,333	15#× $35,422.22		
	Direct materials	0		0#×$37,000	
	Conversion costs	153,000			9#×$17,000
	Total work in process, ending	684,333			
	Total costs accounted for	$9,965,860			

*Equivalent units used to complete beginning work in process from Solution Exhibit 17-34A, Step 2.
†Equivalent units started and completed from Solution Exhibit 17-34A, Step 2.
#Equivalent units in work in process, ending from Solution Exhibit 17-34A, Step 2.

17-36 (5–10 min.) **Journal entries (continuation of 17-35).**

1. Work in Process—Forming Department   70,000
       Accounts Payable   70,000
     To record direct materials purchased and
       used in production during April

2. Work in Process—Forming Department   42,500
       Various Accounts   42,500
     To record Forming Department conversion
       costs for April

3. Work in Process—Finishing Department   104,000
       Work in Process—Forming Department   104,000
     To record cost of goods completed and transferred
       out in April from the Forming Department
       to the Finishing Department

Work in Process—Forming Department			
Beginning inventory, April 1	9,625	3. Transferred out to	
1. Direct materials	70,000	Work in Process—Finishing	104,000
2. Conversion costs	42,500		
Ending inventory, April 30	18,125		

17-38 (30 min.) **Transferred-in costs, weighted average**
                (related to 17-35 through 17-37).

1.   Solution Exhibit 17-38A computes the equivalent units of work done to date in the Finishing Department for transferred-in costs, direct materials, and conversion costs.

       Solution Exhibit 17-38B calculates the cost per equivalent unit of work done to date in the Finishing Department for transferred-in costs, direct materials, and conversion costs, summarizes total Finishing Department costs for April 2004, and assigns these costs to units completed and transferred out and to units in ending work in process using the weighted-average method.

2.   Journal entries:
     a.   Work in Process—Finishing Department   104,000
            Work in Process—Forming Department   104,000
         Cost of goods completed and transferred out
            during April from the Forming Department
            to the Finishing Department

     b.   Finished Goods   168,552
            Work in Process—Finishing Department   168,552
         Cost of goods completed and transferred out
            during April from the Finishing Department
            to Finished Goods inventory

17-38 (Cont'd.)

SOLUTION EXHIBIT 17-38A
Steps 1 and 2: Summarize Output in Physical Units and Compute Equivalent Units
Weighted-Average Method of Process Costing
Finishing Department of Star Toys for April 2004

	(Step 1) Physical Units (given)	(Step 2) Equivalent Units		
Flow of Production		**Transferred-in Costs**	**Direct Materials**	**Conversion Costs**
Work in process, beginning	500			
Transferred in during current period	2,000			
To account for	2,500			
Completed and transferred out during current period	2,100	2,100	2,100	2,100
Work in process, ending*	400			
400 × 100%; 400 × 0%; 400 × 30%		400	0	120
Accounted for	2,500			
Work done to date		2,500	2,100	2,220

*Degree of completion in this department: transferred-in costs, 100%; direct materials, 0%; conversion costs, 30%.

SOLUTION EXHIBIT 17-38B
Steps 3, 4, and 5: Compute Equivalent Unit Costs, Summarize Total Costs to Account For, and Assign Costs to Units Completed and to Units in Ending Work in Process
Weighted-Average Method of Process Costing
Finishing Department of Star Toys for April 2004

	Total Production Costs	**Transferred-in Costs**	**Direct Materials**	**Conversion Costs**
(Step 3) Work in process, beginning (given)	$ 25,000	$ 17,750	$ 0	$ 7,250
Costs added in current period (given)	165,500	104,000	23,100	38,400
Costs incurred to date		$121,750	$23,100	$45,650
Divide by equivalent units of work done to date (Solution Exhibit 17-38A)		÷ 2,500	÷ 2,100	÷ 2,220
Equivalent unit costs of work done to date		$ 48.70	$ 11	$20.563
(Step 4) Total costs to account for	$190,500			
(Step 5) Assignment of costs:				
Completed and transferred out (2,100 units)	$168,552	(2,100*×$48.70) + (2,100* × $11) + (2,100*× $20.563)		
Work in process, ending (400 units)				
Transferred-in costs	19,480	400†×$48.70		
Direct materials	0		0† × $11	
Conversion costs	2,468			120† × $20.563
Total work in process, ending	21,948			
Total costs accounted for	$190,500			

*Equivalent units completed and transferred out from Solution Exhibit 17-38A, Step 2.
†Equivalent units in work in process, ending from Solution Exhibit 17-38A, Step 2.

17-40 (45 min.) Transferred-in costs, weighted-average and FIFO methods.

1. Solution Exhibit 17-40A computes the equivalent units of work done to date in the Drying and Packaging Department for transferred-in costs, direct materials, and conversion costs. Solution Exhibit 17-40B calculates the cost per equivalent unit of work done to date in the Drying and Packaging Department for transferred-in costs, direct materials, and conversion costs, summarizes total Drying and Packaging Department costs for week 37, and assigns these costs to units completed and transferred out and to units in ending work in process using the weighted-average method.

2. Solution Exhibit 17-40C computes the equivalent units of work done in week 37 in the Drying and Packaging Department for transferred-in costs, direct materials, and conversion costs. Solution Exhibit 17-40D calculates the cost per equivalent unit of work done in week 37 in the Drying and Packaging Department for transferred-in costs, direct materials, and conversion costs, summarizes total Drying and Packaging Department costs for week 37, and assigns these costs to units completed and transferred out and to units in ending work in process using the FIFO method.

SOLUTION EXHIBIT 17-40A
Steps 1 and 2: Summarize Output in Physical Units and Compute Equivalent Units
Weighted-Average Method of Process Costing
Drying and Packaging Department of Frito-Lay Inc. for Week 37

	(Step 1) Physical Units (given)	(Step 2) Equivalent Units		
Flow of Production		Transferred-in Costs	Direct Materials	Conversion Costs
Work in process, beginning	1,250			
Transferred in during current period	5,000			
To account for	6,250			
Completed and transferred out during current period	5,250	5,250	5,250	5,250
Work in process, ending*	1,000			
1,000 × 100%; 1,000 × 0%; 1,000 × 40%		1,000	0	400
Accounted for	6,250			
Work done to date		6,250	5,250	5,650

*Degree of completion in this department: transferred-in costs, 100%; direct materials, 0%; conversion costs, 40%.

17-40 (Cont'd.)

SOLUTION EXHIBIT 17-40B

Steps 3, 4, and 5: Compute Equivalent Unit Costs, Summarize Total Costs to Account For, and Assign Costs to Units Completed and to Units in Ending Work in Process

Weighted-Average Method of Process Costing

Drying and Packaging Department of Frito-Lay Inc. for Week 37

	Total Production Costs	Transferred-in Costs	Direct Materials	Conversion Costs
(Step 3) Work in process, beginning (given)	$ 38,060	$ 29,000	$ 0	$ 9,060
Costs added in current period (given)	159,600	96,000	25,200	38,400
Costs incurred to date		$125,000	$25,200	$47,460
Divide by equivalent units of work done to date (Solution Exhibit 17-40A)		÷ 6,250	÷ 5,250	÷ 5,650
Equivalent unit costs of work done to date		$ 20	$ 4.80	$ 8.40
(Step 4) Total costs to account for	$197,660			
(Step 5) Assignment of costs:				
Completed and transferred out (5,250 units)	$174,300	5,250*× $20 + 5,250*× $4.80 + 5,250*× $8.40		
Work in process, ending (1,000 units)				
Transferred-in costs	20,000	1,000†× $20		
Direct materials	0		0† × $4.80	
Conversion costs	3,360			400† × $8.40
Total work in process, ending	23,360			
Total costs accounted for	$197,660			

*Equivalent units completed and transferred out from Solution Exhibit 17-40A, Step 2.

†Equivalent units in work in process, ending from Solution Exhibit 17-40A, Step 2.

17-40 (Cont'd.)

SOLUTION EXHIBIT 17-40C
Steps 1 and 2: Summarize Output in Physical Units and Compute Equivalent Units
FIFO Method of Process Costing
Drying and Packaging Department of Frito-Lay Inc. for Week 37

	(Step 1)	(Step 2) Equivalent Units		
Flow of Production	**Physical Units**	**Transferred-in Costs**	**Direct Materials**	**Conversion Costs**
Work in process, beginning (given)	1,250	(work done before current period)		
Transferred-in during current period (given)	5,000			
To account for	6,250			
Completed and transferred out during current period:				
From beginning work in process[§]	1,250			
1,250 × (100% − 100%); 1,250 × (100% − 0%);				
1,250 × (100% − 80%)		0	1,250	250
Started and completed	4,000[†]			
4,000 × 100%; 4,000 × 100%; 4,000 × 100%		4,000	4,000	4,000
Work in process, ending* (given)	1,000			
1,000 × 100%; 1,000 × 0%; 1,000 × 40%		1,000	0	400
Accounted for	6,250			
Work done in current period only		5,000	5,250	4,650

[§]Degree of completion in this department: Transferred-in costs, 100%; direct materials, 0%; conversion costs, 80%.
[†]5,250 physical units completed and transferred out minus 1,250 physical units completed and transferred out from beginning work-in-process inventory.
*Degree of completion in this department: transferred-in costs, 100%; direct materials, 0%; conversion costs, 40%.

SOLUTION EXHIBIT 17-40D
Steps 3, 4, and 5: Compute Equivalent Unit Costs, Summarize Total Costs to Account For, and Assign Costs to Units Completed and to Units in Ending Work in Process
FIFO Method of Process Costing
Drying and Packaging Department of Frito-Lay Inc. for Week 37

		Total Production Costs	Transferred -in Costs	Direct Materials	Conversion Costs
	Work in process, beginning ($9,060 + $0 + $28,920)	$ 37,980	(Costs of work done before current period)		
(Step 3)	Costs added in current period (given)	157,600	$94,000	$25,200	$38,400
	Divide by equivalent units of work done in current period (Solution Exhibit 17-40C)		÷ 5,000	÷ 5,250	÷ 4,650
	Cost per equiv. unit of work done in current period		$ 18.80	$ 4.80	$ 8.258
(Step 4)	Total costs to account for	$195,580			
(Step 5)	Assignment of costs:				
	Completed and transferred out (5,250 units):				
	Work in process, beginning (1,250 units)	$ 37,980			
	Transferred-in costs added in current period	0	0*× $18.80		
	Direct materials added in current period	6,000		1,250*× $4.80	
	Conversion costs added in current period	2,065			250*× $8.258
	Total from beginning inventory	46,045			
	Started and completed (4,000 units)	127,432	(4,000†× $18.80)+(4,000†× $4.80) +(4,000†×$8.258)		
	Total costs of units completed & tfd. out	173,477			
	Work in process, ending (1,000 units)				
	Transferred-in costs	18,800	1,000#×$18.80		
	Direct materials	0		0#×$4.80	
	Conversion costs	3,303			400#×$8.258
	Total work in process, ending	22,103			
	Total costs accounted for	$195,580			

*Equivalent units used to complete beginning work in process from Solution Exhibit 17-40C, Step 2.
†Equivalent units started and completed from Solution Exhibit 17-40C, Step 2.
#Equivalent units in work in process, ending from Solution Exhibit 17-40C, Step 2.

17-42 (25-30 min.) Operation costing, equivalent units.

1. Materials and conversion costs of each operation, the total units produced, and the material and conversion cost per unit for the month of May are as follows:

	Extrusion	Form	Trim	Finish
1. Units produced	11,000	11,000	5,000	2,000
2. Materials costs	$132,000	$ 44,000	$15,000	$12,000
3. Materials cost per unit (2 ÷1)	12.00	4.00	3.00	6.00
4. Conversion costs	269,500	132,000	69,000	42,000
5. Conversion cost per unit (4 ÷ 1)	24.50	12.00	13.80	21.00

The unit cost and total costs in May for each product are as follows:

Cost Elements	Standard Model	Deluxe Model	Executive Model
Extrusion materials	$ 12.00	$ 12.00	$ 12.00
Form materials	4.00	4.00	4.00
Trim materials	–	3.00	3.00
Finish materials	–	–	6.00
Extrusion conversion	24.50	24.50	24.50
Form conversion	12.00	12.00	12.00
Trim conversion	–	13.80	13.80
Finish conversion	–	–	21.00
Total unit cost	$ 52.50	$ 69.30	$ 96.30
Multiply by units produced	× 6,000	× 3,000	× 2,000
Total product costs	$315,000	$207,900	$192,600

2.

	Unit Cost	Equivalent Units	Total Costs
Deluxe model work-in process costs at the trim operation			
Extrusion material (100% complete when transferred in)	$12.00	1,000	$12,000
Extrusion conversion (100% complete when transferred in)	24.50	1,000	24,500
Form material (100% complete when transferred in)	4.00	1,000	4,000
Form conversion (100% complete when transferred in)	12.00	1,000	12,000
Trim material (100% complete)	3.00	1,000	3,000
Trim conversion (60% complete)	13.80	600*	8,280
Work-in-process costs			$63,780

*1,000 units × 60% complete

17-44 (45 min.) Transferred-in costs, equivalent unit costs, working backward.

1. The equivalent units of work done in the current period for each cost category are computed in Solution Exhibit 17-44B using data on costs added in current period and cost per equivalent unit of work done in current period.

	Transferred-In Costs	Direct Materials	Conversion Costs
Costs added in current period	$58,500	$57,000	$57,200
Divided by cost per equivalent unit of work done in current period	÷ $6.50	÷ $3	÷ $5.20
Equivalent units of work done in current period	9,000	19,000	11,000

2. $$\text{Physical units completed and transferred out} = \text{Physical units in beginning work in process} + \text{Physical units added} - \text{Physical units in ending work in process}$$

$$= 15,000 + 9,000 - 5,000 = 19,000$$

Solution Exhibit 17-44A shows the equivalent units of work done in June to complete beginning work in process and the equivalent units of work done in June to start and complete 4,000 units. Note that direct materials in beginning work in process is 0% complete because it is added only when the process is 80% complete and the beginning WIP is only 60% complete. We had calculated the total equivalent units of work done in the current period in requirement 1: transferred-in costs, 9,000; direct materials, 19,000; and conversion costs, 11,000. The missing number is the equivalent units of each cost category in ending work in process (see Solution Exhibit 17-44A).

Transferred-in costs	5,000
Direct materials	0
Conversion costs	1,000

3. Percentage of completion for each cost category in ending work in process can be calculated by dividing equivalent units in ending work in process for each cost category by physical units of work in process (5,000 units).

Transferred-in costs	5,000 ÷ 5,000 = 100%
Direct materials	0 ÷ 5,000 = 0%
Conversion costs	1,000 ÷ 5,000 = 20%

4. Solution Exhibit 17-44B summarizes the total costs to account for, and assigns these costs to units completed and transferred out and to units in ending work in process.

17-44 (Cont'd.)

SOLUTION EXHIBIT 17-44A
Steps 1 and 2: Summarize Output in Physical Units and Compute Equivalent Units
FIFO Method of Process Costing
Thermo-assembly Department of Lennox Plastics for June 2004

Flow of Production	(Step 1) Physical Units	(Step 2) Equivalent Units		
		Transferred-in Costs	Direct Materials	Conversion Costs
Work in process, beginning (given)	15,000	(work done before current period)		
Transferred-in during current period (given)	9,000			
To account for	24,000			
Completed and transferred out during current period:				
From beginning work in process§	15,000			
15,000 × (100% – 100%); 15,000 × (100% – 0%); 15,000 × (100% – 60%)		0	15,000	6,000
Started and completed	4,000†			
4,000 × 100%; 4,000 × 100%; 4,000 × 100%		4,000	4,000	4,000
Work in process, ending* (given)	5,000			
5,000 × 100%; 5,000 × 0%; 5,000 × 20%		5,000	0	1,000
Accounted for	24,000			
Work done in current period only (from Solution Exhibit 17-44B)		9,000	19,000	11,000

§Degree of completion in this department: Transferred-in costs, 100%; direct materials, 0%; conversion costs, 60%.

†19,000 physical units completed and transferred out minus 15,000 physical units completed and transferred out from beginning work-in-process inventory.

*Degree of completion in this department: transferred-in costs, 100%; direct materials, 0%; conversion costs, 20%.

17-44 (Cont'd.)

SOLUTION EXHIBIT 17-44B
Steps 3, 4, and 5: Compute Equivalent Unit Costs, Summarize Total Costs to Account For, and Assign Costs to Units Completed and to Units in Ending Work in Process
FIFO Method of Process Costing
Thermo-assembly Department of Lennox Plastics for June 2004

		Total Production Costs	Transferred-in Costs	Direct Materials	Conversion Costs
	Work in process, beginning ($90,000 + $0 + $45,000)	$135,000	(Costs of work done before current period)		
(Step 3)	Costs added in current period (given)	172,700	$58,500	$57,000	$57,200
	Divide by equivalent units of work done in current period		÷ 9,000	÷19,000	÷11,000
	Cost per equiv. unit of work done in current period		$ 6.50	$ 3	$ 5.20
(Step 4)	Total costs to account for	$307,700			
(Step 5)	Assignment of costs:				
	Completed and transferred out (19,000 units):				
	Work in process, beginning (15,000 units)	$135,000			
	Transferred-in costs added in current period	0	0* × $6.50		
	Direct materials added in current period	45,000		15,000* × $3	
	Conversion costs added in current period	31,200			6,000* × $5.20
	Total from beginning inventory	211,200			
	Started and completed (4,000 units)	58,800	(4,000† × $6.50) + (4,000† × $3) + (4,000† × $5.20)		
	Total costs of units completed & tfd. out	270,000			
	Work in process, ending (5,000 units)				
	Transferred-in costs	32,500	5,000# × $6.50		
	Direct materials	0		0# × $3	
	Conversion costs	5,200			1,000# × $5.20
	Total work in process, ending	37,700			
	Total costs accounted for	$307,700			

*Equivalent units used to complete beginning work in process from Solution Exhibit 17-44A, Step 2.
†Equivalent units started and completed from Solution Exhibit 17-44A, Step 2.
#Equivalent units in work in process, ending from Solution Exhibit 17-44A, Step 2.

CHAPTER 18
SPOILAGE, REWORK, AND SCRAP

18-2 Spoilage—units of production that do not meet the standards required by customers for good units and that are discarded or sold for reduced prices.

Rework—units of production that do not meet the standards required by customers for finished units that are subsequently repaired and sold as acceptable finished units.

Scrap—material left over when making a product. It has low sales value compared with the sales value of the product.

18-4 Abnormal spoilage is spoilage that is not expected to arise under efficient operating conditions. Costs of abnormal spoilage are "lost costs," measures of inefficiency that should be written off directly as losses for the accounting period.

18-6 Normal spoilage typically is expressed as a percentage of good units passing the inspection point. Given actual spoiled units, we infer abnormal spoilage as follows:

Abnormal spoilage = Actual spoilage – Normal spoilage

18-8 Yes. Normal spoilage rates should be computed from the good output or from the *normal* input, not the *total* input. Normal spoilage is a given percentage of a certain output base. This base should never include abnormal spoilage, which is included in total input. Abnormal spoilage does not vary in direct proportion to units produced, and to include it would cause the normal spoilage count to fluctuate irregularly and not vary in direct proportion to the output base.

18-10 No. If abnormal spoilage is detected at a different point in the production cycle than normal spoilage, then unit costs would differ. If, however normal and abnormal spoilage are detected at the same point in the production cycle, their unit costs would be the same.

18-12 No. Unless there are special reasons for charging normal rework to jobs that contained the bad units, the costs of extra materials, labor, and so on are usually charged to manufacturing overhead and allocated to all jobs.

18-14 A company is justified in inventorying scrap when its estimated net realizable value is significant and the time between storing it and selling or reusing it is quite long.

18-16 (5-10 min.) **Normal and abnormal spoilage in units.**

1.	Total spoiled units	12,000
	Normal spoilage in units, 5% × 132,000	6,600
	Abnormal spoilage in units	5,400
2.	Abnormal spoilage, 5,400 × $10	$ 54,000
	Normal spoilage, 6,600 × $10	66,000
	Potential savings, 12,000 × $10	$120,000

18-16 (Cont'd.)

Regardless of the targeted normal spoilage, abnormal spoilage is non-recurring and avoidable. The targeted normal spoilage rate is subject to change. Many companies have reduced their spoilage to almost zero, which would realize all potential savings. Of course, zero spoilage usually means higher-quality products, more customer satisfaction, more employee satisfaction, and various effects on nonmanufacturing (for example, purchasing) costs of direct materials.

18-18 (20–25 min.) Weighted-average method, assigning costs (continuation of 18-17).

Solution Exhibit 18-18 calculates the costs per equivalent unit for direct materials and conversion costs, summarizes total costs to account for, and assigns these costs to units completed and transferred out (including normal spoilage), to abnormal spoilage, and to units in ending work in process.

SOLUTION EXHIBIT 18-18
Compute Equivalent Unit Costs, Summarize Total Costs to Account For, and Assign Costs to Units Completed, to Spoilage Units, and to Units in Ending Work in Process
Weighted-Average Method of Process Costing
Gray Manufacturing Company, November 2003

		Total Production Costs	Direct Materials	Conversion Costs
(Step 3)	Work in process, beginning (given)	$ 2,533	$ 1,423	$ 1,110
	Costs added in current period (given)	39,930	12,180	27,750
	Costs incurred to date		13,603	28,860
	Divided by equivalent units of work done to date		÷11,150	÷ 9,750
	Equivalent unit costs of work done to date		$ 1.22	$ 2.96
(Step 4)	Total costs to account for	$42,463		
(Step 5)	Assignment of costs			
	Good units completed and transferred out (9,000 units)			
	Costs before adding normal spoilage	$37,620	$(9,000^\# \times \$1.22) + (9,000^\# \times \$2.96)$	
	Normal spoilage (100 units)	418	$(100^\# \times \$1.22) + (100^\# \times \$2.96)$	
(A)	Total cost of good units completed & transf. out	38,038		
(B)	Abnormal spoilage (50 units)	209	$(50^\# \times \$1.22) + (50^\# \times \$2.96)$	
	Work in process, ending (2,000 units)			
	Direct materials	2,440	$2,000^\# \times \$1.22$	
	Conversion costs	1,776		$600^\# \times \$2.96$
(C)	Total work in process, ending	4,216		
(A)+(B)+(C)	Total costs accounted for	$42,463		

$^\#$Equivalent units of direct materials and conversion costs calculated in Step 2 in Solution Exhibit 18-17.

18-20 (20–25 min.) **FIFO method, assigning costs (continuation of 18-19).**

Solution Exhibit 18-20 calculates the costs per equivalent unit for direct materials and conversion costs, summarizes total costs to account for, and assigns these costs to units completed and transferred out (including normal spoilage), to abnormal spoilage, and to units in ending work in process.

SOLUTION EXHIBIT 18-20
Compute Equivalent Unit Costs, Summarize Total Costs to Account For, and Assign Costs to Units Completed, to Spoilage Units, and to Units in Ending Work in Process
FIFO Method of Process Costing
Gray Manufacturing Company, November 2003

		Total Production Costs	Direct Materials	Conversion Costs
(Step 3)	Work in process, beginning (given: $1,423 + $1,110)	$ 2,533		
	Costs added in current period (given)	39,930	$12,180	$27,750
	Divided by equivalent units of work done in current period		÷10,150	÷ 9,250
	Equivalent unit costs of work done in current period		$ 1.20	$ 3
(Step 4)	Total costs to account for	$42,463		
(Step 5)	Assignment of costs:			
	Good units completed and transferred out (9,000 units)			
	Work in process, beginning (1,000 units)	$ 2,533		
	Direct materials added in current period	0	$0^§ \times 1.20	
	Conversion costs added in current period	1,500		$500^§ \times 3
	Total from beginning inventory before normal spoilage	4,033		
	Started and completed before normal spoilage (8,000 units)	33,600	$(8,000^§ \times $1.20) + (8,000^§ \times $3)$	
	Normal spoilage (100 units)	420	$(100^§ \times $1.20) + (100^§ \times $3)$	
(A)	Total cost of good units transferred out	38,053		
(B)	Abnormal spoilage (50 units)	210	$(50^§ \times $1.20) + (50^§ \times $3)$	
	Work in process, ending (2,000 units)			
	Direct materials	2,400	$2,000^§ \times 1.20	
	Conversion costs	1,800		$600^§ \times 3
(C)	Total work in process, ending	4,200		
(A)+(B)+(C)	Total costs accounted for	$42,463		

§Equivalent units of direct materials and conversion costs calculated in Step 2 in Solution Exhibit 18-19.

18-22 (30 min.)   **FIFO method, spoilage** (Refer to the information in 18-21).

1.   Solution Exhibit 18-22, Panel A, calculates the equivalent units of work done in the current period for each cost category in March 2004.

2. & 3. Solution Exhibit 18-22, Panel B, calculates the cost per equivalent unit for each cost category, summarizes total costs to account for, and assigns these costs to units completed (including normal spoilage), to abnormal spoilage, and to units in ending work in process using the FIFO method.

SOLUTION EXHIBIT 18-22
First-in, First-out (FIFO) Method of Process Costing with Spoilage
Wang Manufacturing Company, March 2004

PANEL A: Steps 1 and 2—Summarize Output in Physical Units and Compute Equiv. Units

| | (Step 1) | Step (2) Equivalent Units | |
Flow of Production	Physical Units	Direct Materials	Conversion Costs
Work in process, beginning (given)	30,000		
Started during current period (given)	50,000		
To account for	80,000		
Good units completed and transferred out during current period:			
From beginning work in process‖ 30,000 × (100% − 100%); 30,000 × (100% − 60%)	30,000	0	12,000
Started and completed 10,000 × 100%; 10,000 × 100%	10,000#	10,000	10,000
Normal spoilage* 6,000 × 100%; 6,000 × 100%	6,000	6,000	6,000
Abnormal spoilage† 2,000 × 100%; 2,000 × 100%	2,000	2,000	2,000
Work in process ending ‡ 32,000 × 100%; 32,000 × 75%	32,000	32,000	24,000
Accounted for	80,000		
Work done in current period only		50,000	54,000

‖ Degree of completion in this department: direct materials, 100%; conversion costs, 60%.
40,000 physical units completed and transferred out minus 30,000 physical units completed and transferred out from beginning work in process inventory.
*Degree of completion of normal spoilage in this department: direct materials, 100%; conversion costs, 100%.
† Degree of completion of abnormal spoilage in this department: direct materials, 100%; conversion costs, 100%.
‡ Degree of completion in this department: direct materials, 100%; conversion costs, 75%.

18-22 (Cont'd.)

PANEL B: Steps 3, 4, and 5—Compute Equivalent Unit Costs, Summarize Total Costs to Account For, and Assign Costs to Units Completed, to Spoilage Units, and to Units in Ending Work in Process

	Total Production Costs	Direct Materials	Conversion Costs
(Step 3) Work in process, beginning (given) ($240,000 + $180,000)	$ 420,000		
Costs added in current period (given)	1,003,200	$420,000	$583,200
Divide by equivalent units of work done in current period		÷ 50,000	÷ 54,000
Equivalent unit costs of work done in current period		$8.40	$10.80
(Step 4) Total costs to account for	$1,423,200		
(Step 5) Assignment of costs			
Goods units completed and transferred out (40,000 units)			
Work in process, beginning (30,000 units)	$ 420,000		
Direct materials added in current period	0	$0^{\S} \times \$8.40$	
Conversion costs added in current period	129,600		$12,000^{\S} \times \$10.80$
Total from beginning inventory before normal spoilage	549,600		
Started and completed before normal spoilage (10,000 units)	192,000	$(10,000^{\S} \times \$8.40)$ +	$(10,000^{\S} \times \$10.80)$
Normal spoilage (6,000 units)	115,200	$(6,000^{\S} \times \$8.40)$ +	$(6,000^{\S} \times \$10.80)$
(A) Total cost of good units transferred out	856,800		
(B) Abnormal spoilage (2,000 units)	38,400	$(2,000^{\S} \times \$8.40)$ +	$(2,000^{\S} \times \$10.80)$
Work in process, ending (32,000 units)			
Direct materials	268,800	$32,000^{\S} \times \$8.40$	
Conversion costs	259,200		$24,000^{\S} \times \$10.80$
(C) Total work in process, ending	528,000		
(A)+(B)+(C) Total costs accounted for	$1,423,200		

§ Equivalent units of direct materials and conversion costs calculated in Step 2 in Panel A.

18-24 (25 min.) **Weighted-average method, spoilage.**

1. Solution Exhibit 18-24, Panel A, calculates the equivalent units of work done to date for each cost category in September 2003.

2. & 3. Solution Exhibit 18-24, Panel B, calculates the costs per equivalent unit for each cost category, summarizes total costs to account for, and assigns these costs to units completed (including normal spoilage), to abnormal spoilage, and to units in ending work in process using the weighted-average method.

SOLUTION EXHIBIT 18-24
Weighted-Average Method of Process Costing with Spoilage
Superchip, September 2003

PANEL A: Steps 1 and 2—Summarize Output in Physical Units and Compute Equivalent Units

Flow of Production	(Step 1) Physical Units (given)	(Step 2) Equivalent Units	
		Direct Materials	Conversion Costs
Work in process, beginning	400		
Started during current period	1,700		
To account for	2,100		
Good units completed and transferred out during current period:	1,400	1,400	1,400
Normal spoilage*	210		
210 × 100%; 210 × 100%		210	210
Abnormal spoilage[†]	190		
190 × 100%; 190 ×100%		190	190
Work in process, ending[‡]	300		
300 × 100%; 300 × 40%		300	120
Accounted for	2,100		
Work done to date		2,100	1,920

*Normal spoilage is 15% of good units transferred out: 15% × 1,400 = 210 units. Degree of completion of normal spoilage in this department: direct materials, 100%; conversion costs, 100%.

[†]Abnormal spoilage = Actual spoilage – Normal spoilage = 400 – 210 = 190 units. Degree of completion of abnormal spoilage in this department: direct materials, 100%; conversion costs, 100%.

[‡]Degree of completion in this department: direct materials, 100%; conversion costs, 40%.

18-24 (Cont'd.)

PANEL B: Steps 3, 4, and 5—Compute Equivalent Unit Costs, Summarize Total Costs to Account For, and Assign Costs to Units Completed, to Spoilage Units, and to Units in Ending Work in Process

		Total Production Costs	Direct Materials	Conversion Costs
(Step 3)	Work in process, beginning (given)	$ 74,200	$ 64,000	$ 10,200
	Costs added in current period (given)	531,600	378,000	153,600
	Costs incurred to date		442,000	163,800
	Divided by equivalent units of work done to date		÷ 2,100	÷ 1,920
	Equivalent unit costs of work done to date		$210.476	$85.3125
(Step 4)	Total costs to account for	$605,800		
(Step 5)	Assignment of costs			
	Good units completed and transferred out (1,400 units)			
	Costs before adding normal spoilage	$414,104	$(1,400^{\#} \times \$210.476) + (1,400^{\#} \times \$85.3125)$	
	Normal spoilage (210 units)	62,116	$(210^{\#} \times \$210.476) + (210^{\#} \times \$85.3125)$	
(A)	Total cost of good units completed & transf. out	476,220		
(B)	Abnormal spoilage (190 units)	56,199	$(190^{\#} \times \$210.476) + (190^{\#} \times \$85.3125)$	
	Work in process, ending (300 units)			
	Direct materials	63,143	$300^{\#} \times \$210.476$	
	Conversion costs	10,238		$120^{\#} \times \$85.3125$
(C)	Total work in process, ending	73,381		
(A)+(B)+(C)	Total costs accounted for	$605,800		

$^{\#}$ Equivalent units of direct materials and conversion costs calculated in Step 2 in Panel A.

18-26 (30 min.) **Standard costing method, spoilage** (Refer to the information in Exercise 18-24).

1. Solution Exhibit 18-26A, shows the computation of the equivalent units of work done in September 2003 for direct materials (1,700 units) and conversion costs (1,800 units).

2. The direct materials cost per equivalent unit of beginning work in process and of work done in September 2003 is the standard cost of $205 given in the problem.

    The conversion cost per equivalent unit of beginning work in process and of work done in September 2003 is the standard cost of $80 given in the problem.

3. Solution Exhibit 18-26B summarizes the total costs to account for, and assigns these costs to units completed (including normal spoilage), to abnormal spoilage, and to units in ending work in process using the standard costing method.

SOLUTION EXHIBIT 18-26A
First-in, First-out (FIFO) Method of Process Costing with Spoilage
Superchip, September 2003

Steps 1 and 2—Summarize Output in Physical Units and Compute Equivalent Units

Flow of Production	(Step 1) Physical Units	(Step 2) Equivalent Units	
		Direct Materials	Conversion Costs
Work in process, beginning (given)	400		
Started during current period (given)	1,700		
To account for	2,100		
Good units completed and transferred out during current period:			
From beginning work in process[‖]	400		
400 × (100% −100%); 400 × (100% − 30%)		0	280
Started and completed	1,000[#]		
1,000 × 100%; 1,000 × 100%		1,000	1,000
Normal spoilage*	210		
210 × 100%; 210 × 100%		210	210
Abnormal spoilage[†]	190		
190 × 100%; 190 × 100%		190	190
Work in process, ending[‡]	300		
300 × 100%; 300 × 40%		300	120
Accounted for	2,100		
Work done in current period only		1,700	1,800

[‖]Degree of completion in this department: direct materials, 100%; conversion costs, 30%.

[#]1,400 physical units completed and transferred out minus 400 physical units completed and transferred out from beginning work in process inventory.

*Normal spoilage is 15% of good units transferred out: 15% × 1,400 = 210 units. Degree of completion of normal spoilage in this department: direct materials, 100%; conversion costs, 100%.

[†]Abnormal spoilage = Actual spoilage − Normal spoilage = 400 − 210 = 190 units. Degree of completion of abnormal spoilage in this department: direct materials, 100%; conversion costs, 100%.

[‡]Degree of completion in this department: direct materials, 100%; conversion costs, 40%.

18-26 (Cont'd.)

SOLUTION EXHIBIT 18-26B
Standard Costing Method of Process Costing with Spoilage
Superchip, September 2003

Steps 3, 4, and 5—Compute Equivalent Unit Costs, Summarize Total Costs to Account For, and Assign Costs to Units Completed, to Spoilage Units, and to Units in Ending Work in Process

		Total Production Costs	Direct Materials	Conversion Costs
(Step 3)	Standard costs per equivalent unit (given)	$285	$205	$80
	Work in process, beginning*	$91,600		
	Costs added in current period at standard prices			
	Direct materials, 1,700 × $205; conversion costs, 1,800 × $80	492,500	$348,500	$144,000
(Step 4)	Costs to account for	$584,100		
(Step 5)	Assignment of costs at standard costs:			
	Good units completed and transferred out (1,400 units)			
	Work in process, beginning (400 units)	$91,600		
	Direct materials added in current period	0	$0^{\S} \times \$205$	
	Conversion costs added in current period	22,400		$280^{\S} \times \$80$
	Total from beginning inventory before normal spoilage	114,000		
	Started and completed before normal spoilage (1,000 units)	285,000	$(1,000^{\S} \times \$205)$ +	$(1,000^{\S} \times \$80)$
	Normal spoilage (210 units)	59,850	$(210^{\S} \times \$205)$ +	$(210^{\S} \times \$80)$
(A)	Total cost of good units transferred out	458,850		
(B)	Abnormal spoilage (190 units)	54,150	$(190^{\S} \times \$205)$ +	$(190^{\S} \times \$80)$
	Work in process, ending (300 units)			
	Direct materials	61,500	$300^{\S} \times \$205$	
	Conversion costs	9,600		$120^{\S} \times \$80$
(C)	Total work in process, ending	71,100		
(A)+(B)+(C)	Total costs accounted for	$584,100		

*Work in process, beginning has 400 equivalent units (400 physical units × 100%) of direct materials and 120 equivalent units (400 physical units × 30%) of conversion costs. Hence work in process, beginning inventory at standard costs equals ($205 × 400) + ($80 × 120) = $82,000 + $9,600 = $91,600.

§Equivalent units of direct materials and conversion costs calculated in Step 2 in Solution Exhibit 18-25, Panel A.

18-28 (15 min.) **Reworked units, costs of rework.**

1. The two alternative approaches to account for the materials costs of reworked units are:
   a. To charge the costs of rework to the current period as a separate expense item as abnormal rework. This approach would highlight to White Goods the costs of the supplier problem.
   b. To charge the costs of the rework to manufacturing overhead as normal rework.

2. The $50 tumbler cost is the cost of the actual tumblers included in the washing machines. The $44 tumbler units from the new supplier were eventually never used in any washing machine and that supplier is now bankrupt. The units must now be disposed of at zero disposal value.

3. The total costs of rework due to the defective tumbler units include:
   a. The labor and other conversion costs spent on substituting the new tumbler units.
   b. The costs of any extra negotiations to obtain the replacement tumbler units.
   c. Any higher price the existing supplier may have charged to do a rush order for the replacement tumbler units.
   d. Ordering costs for the replacement tumbler units.

18-30 (30 min.) **Weighted-average method, spoilage.**

Solution Exhibit 18-30 calculates the equivalent units of work done to date for each cost category, presents computations of the costs per equivalent unit for each cost category, summarizes total costs to account for, and assigns these costs to units completed (including normal spoilage), to abnormal spoilage, and to units in ending work in process using the weighted-average method.

SOLUTION EXHIBIT 18-30
Weighted-Average Method of Process Costing with Spoilage
Cleaning Department of the Alston Company for May

PANEL A: Steps 1 and 2—Summarize Output in Physical Units and Compute Equivalent Units

Flow of Production	(Step 1) Physical Units (given)	(Step 2) Equivalent Units	
		Direct Materials	Conversion Costs
Work in process, beginning	1,000		
Started during current period	9,000		
To account for	10,000		
Good units completed and transferred out during current period:	7,400	7,400	7,400
Normal spoilage*	740		
740 × 100%; 740 × 100%		740	740
Abnormal spoilage†	260		
260 × 100%; 260 ×100%		260	260
Work in process, ending‡	1,600		
1,600 × 100%; 1,600 × 25%		1,600	400
Accounted for	10,000		
Work done to date		10,000	8,800

*Normal spoilage is 10% of good units transferred out: 10% × 7,400 = 740 units. Degree of completion of normal spoilage in this department: direct materials, 100%; conversion costs, 100%.

†Abnormal spoilage = 260 units. Degree of completion of abnormal spoilage in this department: direct materials, 100%; conversion costs, 100%.

‡Degree of completion in this department: direct materials, 100%; conversion costs, 25%.

PANEL B: Steps 3, 4, and 5—Compute Equivalent Unit Costs, Summarize Total Costs to Account For, and Assign Costs to Units Completed, to Spoilage Units, and to Units in Ending Work in Process

		Total Production Costs	Direct Materials	Conversion Costs
(Step 3)	Work in process, beginning (given)	$ 1,800	$ 1,000	$ 800
	Costs added in current period (given)	17,000	9,000	8,000
	Costs incurred to date		10,000	8,800
	Divided by equivalent units of work done to date		÷10,000	÷ 8,800
	Equivalent unit costs of work done to date		$ 1	$ 1
(Step 4)	Total costs to account for	$18,800		
(Step 5)	Assignment of costs			
	Good units completed and transferred out (7,400 units)			
	Costs before adding normal spoilage	$14,800	$7,400^{\#} \times \$1 +$	$7,400^{\#} \times \$1$
	Normal spoilage (740 units)	1,480	$740^{\#} \times \$1 +$	$740^{\#} \times \$1$
(A)	Total cost of good units completed & transferred out	16,280		
(B)	Abnormal spoilage (260 units)	520	$260^{\#} \times \$1 +$	$260^{\#} \times \$1$
	Work in process, ending (1,600 units)			
	Direct materials	1,600	$1,600^{\#} \times \$1$	
	Conversion costs	400		$400^{\#} \times \$1$
(C)	Total work in process, ending	2,000		
(A)+(B)+(C)	Total costs accounted for	$18,800		

[#]Equivalent units of direct materials and conversion costs calculated in Step 2 in Panel A above.

18-32 (35 min.) Weighted-average method, Milling Department (continuation of 18-30).

For the Milling Department, Solution Exhibit 18-32 calculates the equivalent units of work done to date for each cost category, presents computations of the costs per equivalent unit for each cost category, summarizes total costs to account for, and assigns these costs to units completed (including normal spoilage), to abnormal spoilage, and to units in ending work in process using the weighted-average method.

SOLUTION EXHIBIT 18-32
Weighted-Average Method of Process Costing with Spoilage
Milling Department of the Alston Company for May

PANEL A: Steps 1 and 2—Summarize Output in Physical Units and Compute Equivalent Units

Flow of Production	(Step 1) Physical Units (given)	(Step 2) Equivalent Units		
		Transferred-in Costs	Direct Materials	Conversion Costs
Work in process, beginning	3,000			
Started during current period	7,400			
To account for	10,400			
Good units completed and transferred out during current period:	6,000	6,000	6,000	6,000
Normal spoilage*	300			
300 × 100%; 300 × 100%; 300 × 100%		300	300	300
Abnormal spoilage[†]	100			
100 × 100%; 100 ×100%, 100 × 100%		100	100	100
Work in process, ending[‡]	4,000			
4,000 × 100%; 4,000 × 0%; 4,000 × 25%		4,000	0	1,000
Accounted for	10,400			
Work done to date		10,400	6,400	7,400

*Normal spoilage is 5% of good units transferred out: 5% × 6,000 = 300 units. Degree of completion of normal spoilage in this department: transferred-in costs, 100%; direct materials, 100%; conversion costs, 100%.

[†]Abnormal spoilage = 100 units. Degree of completion of abnormal spoilage in this department: transferred-in costs, 100%; direct materials, 100%; conversion costs, 100%.

[‡]Degree of completion in this department: transferred-in costs, 100%; direct materials, 0%; conversion costs, 25%.

PANEL B: Steps 3, 4, and 5—Compute Equivalent Unit Costs, Summarize Total Costs to Account For, and Assign Costs to Units Completed, to Spoilage Units, and to Units in Ending Work in Process

		Total Production Costs	Transferred-in costs	Direct Materials	Conversion Costs
(Step 3)	Work in process, beginning (given)	$ 8,900	$ 6,450	$ 0	$2,450
	Costs added in current period (given)	21,870	16,280*	640	4,950
	Costs incurred to date		22,730	640	7,400
	Divided by equivalent units of work done to date		÷10,400	÷ 6,400	÷7,400
	Equivalent unit costs of work done to date		$2.1856	$ 0.10	$ 1
(Step 4)	Total costs to account for	$30,770			
(Step 5)	Assignment of costs				
	Good units completed and transferred out (6,000 units)				
	Costs before adding normal spoilage	$19,713	6,000[#] × ($2.1856 + $0.10 + $1)		
	Normal spoilage (300 units)	986	300[#] × ($2.1856 + $0.10 + $1)		
(A)	Total cost of good units completed & transferred out	20,699			
(B)	Abnormal spoilage (100 units)	329	100[#] × ($2.1856 + $0.10 + $1)		
	Work in process, ending (4,000 units)				
	Transferred-in costs	8,742	4,000[#] × $2.1856		
	Direct materials	0		0[#] × $0.10	
	Conversion costs	1,000			1,000[#] × $1
(C)	Total work in process, ending	9,742			
(A)+(B)+(C)	Total costs accounted for	$30,770			

[#]Equivalent units of direct materials and conversion costs calculated in Step 2 in Panel A above.
*Total costs of good units completed and transferred out in Step 5 Panel B of Solution Exhibit 18-30.

18-34 (20–25 min.) **Job-costing spoilage and scrap** (F. Mayne).

1. a. Materials Control   600

       Manufacturing Department Overhead Control   800

          Work-in-Process Control   1,400

          (650 + 500 + 250 = 1,400)

     b. Accounts Receivable   1,250

          Work-in-Process Control   1,250

2. a. The clause does not specify whether the 1% calculation is to be based on the input cost ($26,951 + $15,076 + $7,538) or the cost of the good output before the "1% normal spoilage" is added.

     b. *If the inputs are used to determine the 1%:*

$$\$26,951 + \$15,076 + \$7,538 = \$49,565$$

1% of $49,565 = $495.65 or $496, rounded. Then, the entry to leave the $496 "normal spoilage" cost on the job, remove the salvageable material, and charge manufacturing overhead would be:

Materials Control   600

Manufacturing Department Overhead Control   304

      Work-in-Process Control   904

($800 spoilage minus $496 = $304 spoilage

cost that is taken out of the job;

$600 salvage value plus $304 = $904; or

$1,400 minus $496 = $904)

     If the outputs are used to determine the 1%:

$$\begin{array}{rr} \$26,951 - \$650 = & \$26,301 \\ 15,076 - 500 = & 14,576 \\ \underline{7,538} - 250 = & \underline{7,288} \\ \underline{\$49,565} & \underline{\$48,165} \end{array}$$

Then, $48,165 \times 1\% = \$481.65$ or $482, rounded. The journal entry would be:

Materials Control   600

Manufacturing Department Overhead Control   318

      Work-in-Process Control   918

18-36 (30 min.) Job costing, scrap.

1. Materials Control 7,000
    Materials–Related Manufacturing Overhead Control 7,000
(To record scrap common to all jobs at the time it is
returned to the storeroom)

2. Cash or Accounts Receivable 7,000
    Materials Control 7,000
(To record sale of scrap from the storeroom)

3. A summary of the manufacturing costs for HM3 and JB4 before considering the value of scrap are as follows:

	HM3		JB4		Total Costs
	Cost per Unit (1)	Total Costs (2) = (1) × 20,000	Cost per Unit (3)	Total Costs (4) = (3) × 10,000	(5) = (2)+(4)
Direct materials	$10	$200,000	$15	$150,000	$350,000
Direct manufacturing labor	3	60,000	4	40,000	100,000
Materials-related manufacturing overhead (20% of direct materials)	2	40,000	3	30,000	70,000
Other manufacturing overhead (200% of direct manufacturing labor)	6	120,000	8	80,000	200,000
Total	$21	$420,000	$30	$300,000	$720,000

The value of scrap of $7,000 generated during March will reduce materials-related manufacturing overhead costs by $7,000 from $70,000 to $63,000. Materials-related manufacturing overhead will then be allocated at 18% of direct materials costs ($63,000 ÷ $350,000 = 0.18)

The revised manufacturing cost per unit would then be:

	HM3		JB4		Total Costs
	Cost per Unit (1)	Total Costs (2) = (1) × 20,000	Cost per Unit (3)	Total Costs (4) = (3) × 10,000	(5) = (2)+(4)
Direct materials	$10.00	$200,000	$15.00	$150,000	$350,000
Direct manufacturing labor	3.00	60,000	4.00	40,000	100,000
Materials-related manufacturing overhead (18% of direct materials)	1.80	36,000	2.70	27,000	63,000
Other manufacturing overhead 200% of direct manufacturing labor)	6.00	120,000	8.00	80,000	200,000
Total	$20.80	$416,000	$29.70	$297,000	$713,000

18-38 (25–35 min.) **Weighted-average method, inspection at 80% completion** (A. Atkinson) (Chapter Appendix).

The computation and allocation of spoilage is the most difficult part of this problem. The units in the ending inventory have passed inspection. Therefore, of the 80,000 units to account for (10,000 beginning + 70,000 started), 10,000 must have been spoiled in June [80,000 − (50,000 completed + 20,000 ending inventory)]. Normal spoilage is 7,000 [0.10 × (50,000 + 20,000)]. The 3,000 remainder is abnormal spoilage (10,000 − 7,000).

Solution Exhibit 18-38, Panel A, calculates the equivalent units of work done for each cost category. We comment on several points in this calculation:

- Ending work in process includes an element of normal spoilage since all the ending WIP have passed the point of inspection—inspection occurs when production is 80% complete, while the units in ending WIP are 95% complete.
- Spoilage includes no direct materials units because spoiled units are detected and removed from the finishing activity when inspection occurs at the time production is 80% complete. Direct materials are added only later when production is 90% complete.
- Direct materials units are included for ending work in process, which is 95% complete, but not for beginning work in process, which is 25% complete. The reason is that direct materials are added when production is 90% complete. The ending work in process, therefore, contains direct materials units; the beginning work in process does not.

Solution Exhibit 18-38, Panel B, computes the costs per equivalent unit for each cost category, summarizes total costs to account for, and assigns these costs to units completed (including normal spoilage), to abnormal spoilage, and to units in ending work in process using the weighted-average method. The cost of ending work in process includes the assignment of normal spoilage costs since these units have passed the point of inspection. The costs assigned to each cost category are as follows:

Cost of good units completed and transferred out (including normal spoilage costs on good units)	$1,877,350
Abnormal spoilage	67,710
Cost of ending work in process (including normal spoilage costs on ending work in process)	734,140
Total costs assigned and accounted for	$2,679,200

SOLUTION EXHIBIT 18-38
Weighted-Average Method of Process Costing with Spoilage
Finishing Department of the Ottawa Manufacturing Company for June

PANEL A: Steps 1 and 2—Summarize Output in Physical Units and Compute Equivalent Units

Flow of Production	(Step 1) Physical Units (given)	(Step 2) Equivalent Units		
		Transferred-in Costs	Direct Materials	Conversion Costs
Work in process, beginning	10,000			
Started during current period	70,000			
To account for	80,000			
Good units completed and transferred out during current period:	50,000	50,000	50,000	50,000
Normal spoilage on good units*	5,000			
5,000 × 100%; 5,000 × 0%; 5,000 × 80%		5,000	0	4,000
Work in process, ending‡	20,000			
20,000 × 100%; 20,000 × 100%; 20,000 × 95%		20,000	20,000	19,000
Normal spoilage on ending WIP**	2,000			
2,000 × 100%; 2,000 × 0%; 2,000 × 80%		2,000	0	1,600
Abnormal spoilage†	3,000			
3,000 × 100%; 3,000 × 0%; 3,000 × 80%		3,000	0	2,400
Accounted for	80,000			
Work done to date		80,000	70,000	77,000

*Normal spoilage is 10% of good units that pass inspection: 10% × 50,000 = 5,000 units. Degree of completion of normal spoilage in this department: transferred-in costs, 100%; direct materials, 0%; conversion costs, 80%.

‡Degree of completion in this department: transferred-in costs, 100%; direct materials, 100%; conversion costs, 95%.

**Normal spoilage is 10% of the good units in ending WIP that have passed the inspection point, 10% × 20,000 = 2,000 units. Degree of completion of normal spoilage in this department: transferred-in costs, 100%; direct materials, 0%; conversion costs, 80%.

†Abnormal spoilage = Actual spoilage − Normal spoilage = 10,000 − 7,000 = 3,000 units. Degree of completion of abnormal spoilage in this department: transferred-in costs, 100%; direct materials, 0%; conversion costs, 80%.

PANEL B: Steps 3, 4, and 5—Compute Equivalent Unit Costs, Summarize Total Costs to Account For, and Assign Costs to Units Completed, to Spoilage Units, and to Units in Ending Work in Process

		Total Production Costs	Transferred-in Costs	Direct Materials	Conversion Costs
(Step 3)	Work in process, beginning (given)	$ 124,900	$ 82,900	$ –	$ 42,000
	Costs added in current period (given)	2,554,300	647,500	655,200	1,251,600
	Costs incurred to date		730,400	655,200	1,293,600
	Divided by equivalent units of work done to date		÷ 80,000	÷ 70,000	÷ 77,000
	Equivalent unit costs of work done to date		$ 9.13	$ 9.36	$ 16.80
(Step 4)	Total costs to account for	$2,679,200			
(Step 5)	Assignment of costs				
	Good units completed and transferred out (50,000 units)				
	Costs before adding normal spoilage	$1,764,500	50,000# × ($9.13 + $9.36 + $16.80)		
	Normal spoilage (5,000 units)	112,850	(5,000# × $9.13) + (0# × $9.36) + (4,000# × $16.80)		
(A)	Total cost of good units completed & transferred out	1,877,350			
(B)	Abnormal spoilage (3,000 units)	67,710	(3,000# × $9.13) + (0# × $9.36) + (2,400# × $16.80)		
	Work in process, ending (20,000 units)				
	WIP ending, before normal spoilage	689,000	(20,000# × $9.13) + (20,000# × $9.36)+(19,000# × $16.80)		
	Normal spoilage on ending WIP	45,140	(2,000# × $9.13) + (0# × $9.36) + (1,600# × $16.80)		
(C)	Total costs of ending WIP	734,140			
(A)+(B)+(C)	Total costs accounted for	$2,679,200			

#Equivalent units of transferred-in costs, direct materials, and conversion costs calculated in Step 2 in Panel A.

18-40 (35 min.) FIFO method, spoilage, working backward.

1. Equivalent units of work done in the current period can be calculated using Step 2 as follows:

	Direct Materials	Conversion Costs
Costs added in January	$1,480,000	$942,000
Divided by cost per equivalent unit of work done in January	÷ $20	÷ $12
Equivalent units of work done in January	74,000	78,500

2. Solution Exhibit 18-40, Panel A, shows the equivalent units of work done (a) to complete beginning work-in-process inventory, (b) to start and complete new units, (c) for normal spoilage, and (d) for abnormal spoilage. The sum of these equivalent units is then subtracted from the total equivalent units of work done in January (direct materials, 74,000, and conversion costs, 78,500) to determine the equivalent units in ending work in process (direct materials, 15,000, and conversion costs, 12,000).

18-40 (Cont'd.)

3.   The physical units of ending work in process can be calculated by taking total physical units to account for, 84,000 (beginning work in process, 10,000 plus units started 74,000) and subtracting good units completed and transferred out, 61,000; normal spoilage, 6,710; and abnormal spoilage, 1,290, to obtain 15,000 physical units in ending work in process.

The percentage of completion of ending work in process for each cost category can then be calculated as follows:

	Direct Materials	Conversion Costs
Equivalent units of ending work in process (requirement 2)	15,000	12,000
Divided by physical units of ending work in process	÷15,000	÷15,000
Percentage of completion of ending work in process	100%	80%

4.   Solution Exhibit 18-40, Panel B summarizes total costs to account for, and assigns these costs to units completed and transferred out (including normal spoilage), to abnormal spoilage, and to units in ending work in process.

SOLUTION EXHIBIT 18-40
First-in, First-out (FIFO) Method of Process Costing with Spoilage
Cooking Department of Spicer Inc. for January

PANEL A: Steps 1 and 2—Summarize Output in Physical Units and Compute Equivalent Units

	(Step 1)	(Step 2) Equivalent Units	
Flow of Production	Physical Units	Direct Materials	Conversion Costs
Work in process, beginning (given)	10,000		
Started during current period (given)	74,000		
To account for	84,000		
Good units completed and transferred out during current period:			
From beginning work in process$^{\|}$	10,000		
10,000 × (100% −100%); 10,000 × (100% − 25%)		0	7,500
Started and completed	51,000$^{\#}$		
51,000 × 100%; 51,000 × 100%		51,000	51,000
Normal spoilage*	6,710		
6,710 × 100%; 6,710 × 100%		6,710	6,710
Abnormal spoilage†	1,290		
1,290 × 100%; 1,290 × 100%		1,290	1,290
Work in process, ending‡	15,000		
15,000 × 100%; 15,000 × 80%		15,000	12,000
Accounted for	84,000		
Work done in current period only		74,000	78,500

$^{\|}$Degree of completion in this department: direct materials, 100%; conversion costs, 25%.

$^{\#}$61,000 physical units completed and transferred out minus 10,000 physical units completed and transferred out from beginning work-in-process inventory.

*Normal spoilage is 11% of good units transferred out: 11% × 61,000 = 6,710 units. Degree of completion of normal spoilage in this department: direct materials, 100%; conversion costs, 100%.

†Abnormal spoilage = Actual spoilage − Normal spoilage = 8,000 − 6,710 = 1,290 units. Degree of completion of abnormal spoilage in this department: direct materials, 100%; conversion costs, 100%.

‡Degree of completion in this department: direct materials, 100%; conversion costs, 80%.

18-19

18-40 (Cont'd.)

PANEL B: Steps 3, 4, and 5—Compute Equivalent Unit Costs, Summarize Total Costs to Account For, and Assign Costs to Units Completed, to Spoilage Units, and to Units in Ending Work in Process

		Total Production Costs	Direct Materials	Conversion Costs
(Step 3)	Work in process, beginning (given: $220,000 + $30,000)	$ 250,000		
	Costs added in current period (given)	2,422,000	$1,480,000	$942,000
	Divided by equivalent units of work done in current period		÷ 74,000	÷ 78,500
	Equivalent unit costs of work done in current period		$ 20	$ 12
(Step 4)	Total costs to account for	$2,672,000		
(Step 5)	Assignment of costs:			
	Good units completed and transferred out (61,000 units)			
	Work in process, beginning (10,000 units)	$ 250,000		
	Direct materials added in current period	0	$0^\S \times \$20$	
	Conversion costs added in current period	90,000		$7,500^\S \times \$12$
	Total from beginning inventory before normal spoilage	340,000		
	Started and completed before normal spoilage (51,000 units)	1,632,000	$51,000^\S \times \$20 + 51,000^\S \times \$12$	
	Normal spoilage (6,710 units)	214,720	$6,710^\S \times \$20 + 6,710^\S \times \$12$	
(A)	Total cost of good units transferred out	2,186,720		
(B)	Abnormal spoilage (1,290 units)	41,280	$1,290^\S \times \$20 + 1,290 \times \$12$	
	Work in process, ending (15,000 units)			
	Direct materials	300,000	$15,000^\S \times \$20$	
	Conversion costs	144,000		$12,000^\S \times \$12$
(C)	Total work in process, ending	444,000		
(A)+(B)+(C)	Total costs accounted for	$2,672,000		

§Equivalent units of direct materials and conversion costs calculated in Step 2 in Panel A.

CHAPTER 19
QUALITY, TIME, AND THE THEORY OF CONSTRAINTS

19-2 Quality of design refers to how closely the characteristics of a product or service meet the needs and wants of customers. Conformance quality refers to the performance of a product or service relative to its design and product specifications.

19-4 An internal failure cost differs from an external failure cost on the basis of when the nonconforming product is detected. An internal failure is detected *before* a product is shipped to a customer, whereas an external failure is detected *after* a product is shipped to a customer.

19-6 No, companies should emphasize financial as well as nonfinancial measures of quality, such as yield and defect rates. Nonfinancial measures are not directly linked to bottom-line performance but they indicate and direct attention to the specific areas that need improvement that would help improve the bottom line. Tracking nonfinancial measures over time directly reveals whether these areas have, in fact, improved over time. Nonfinancial measures are easy to quantify and easy to understand.

19-8 Examples of nonfinancial measures of internal performance are:
1. The number of defects for each product line.
2. Process yield (rates of good output to total output at a particular process).
3. Manufacturing lead time (the amount of time from when an order is received by production to when it becomes a finished good).
4. Employee turnover (ratio of the number of employees who left the company in a year, say, to the total number of employees who worked for the company in that year).

19-10 No. There is a trade-off between customer-response time and on-time performance. Simply scheduling longer customer-response time makes achieving on-time performance easier. Companies should, however, attempt to reduce the uncertainty of the arrival of orders, manage bottlenecks, reduce setup and processing time, and run smaller batches. This would have the effect of reducing both customer-response time and improving on-time performance.

19-12 No. Adding a product when capacity is constrained and the timing of customer orders is uncertain causes delays in delivering all existing products. If the revenue losses from delays in delivering existing products and the increase in carrying costs of the existing products exceed the positive contribution earned by the product that was added, then it is not worthwhile to make and sell the new product, despite its positive contribution margin. The chapter describes the negative effects (negative externalities) that one product can have on others when products share common manufacturing facilities.

19-14 The four key steps in managing bottleneck resources are:
Step 1: Recognize that the bottleneck operation determines throughput contribution of the entire system.
Step 2: Search for, and find the bottleneck operation.
Step 3: Keep the bottleneck operation busy, and subordinate all nonbottleneck operations to the bottleneck operation.
Step 4: Increase bottleneck efficiency and capacity.

19-16 (30 min.) **Costs of quality** (CMA, adapted).

1. The ratio of each COQ category to revenues for each period is as follows:

Semi-annual Costs of Quality Report Bergen, Inc.
(in thousands)

	6/30/2003 (1)	% of Rev. (2) = (1) ÷ 4,120	12/31/2003 (3)	% of Rev. (4) = (3) ÷ 4,540	6/30/2004 (5)	% of Rev. (6) = (5) ÷ 4,650	12/31/2004 (7)	% of Rev. (8) = (7) ÷ 4,510
Prevention costs								
Machine maintenance	$ 215		$ 215		$ 190		$ 160	
Training suppliers	5		45		20		15	
Design reviews	20		102		100		95	
	240	5.8%	362	8.0%	310	6.7%	270	6.0%
Appraisal costs								
Incoming inspection	45		53		36		22	
Final testing	160		160		140		94	
	205	5.0%	213	4.7%	176	3.8%	116	2.6%
Internal failure costs								
Rework	120		106		88		62	
Scrap	68		64		42		40	
	188	4.6%	170	3.7%	130	2.8%	102	2.2%
External failure costs								
Warranty repairs	69		31		25		23	
Customer returns	262		251		116		80	
	331	8.0%	282	6.2%	141	3.0%	103	2.3%
Total quality costs	$ 964	23.4%	$1,027	22.6%	$ 757	16.3%	$ 591	13.1%
Total revenues	$4,120		$4,540		$ 4,650		$ 4,510	

From an analysis of the Cost of Quality Report, it would appear that Bergen Inc.'s program has been successful because

- Total quality costs as a percentage of total revenues have declined from 23.4% to 13.1%.

- External failure costs, those costs signaling customer dissatisfaction, have declined from 8% of total revenues to 2.3%. These declines in warranty repairs and customer returns should translate into increased revenues in the future.

- Internal failure costs have been reduced from 4.6% to 2.2% of revenues

- Appraisal costs have decreased from 5.0% to 2.6%. Preventing defects from occurring in the first place is reducing the demand for final testing.

- Quality costs have shifted to the area of prevention where problems are solved before production starts. Maintenance, training, and design reviews have increased from 5.8% of total revenues to 6% and from 25% of total quality costs (240 ÷ 964) to 45.7% (270 ÷ 591). The $30,000 increase in these costs is more than offset by decreases in other quality costs.

Because of improved designs, quality training, and additional pre-production inspections, scrap and rework costs have declined. Production does not have to spend an inordinate amount of time with customer service since they are now making the product right the first time and warranty repairs and customer returns have decreased.

19-16 (Cont'd.)

2.   To measure the opportunity cost of not implementing the quality program, Bergen Inc. could assume that

- Sales and market share would continue to decline if the quality program had not been implemented and then calculate the loss in revenue and contribution margin.
- The company would have to compete on price rather than quality and calculate the impact of having to lower product prices.

Opportunity costs are not recorded in accounting systems because they represent the results of what might have happened if Bergen had not improved quality. Nevertheless, opportunity costs of poor quality can be significant. It is important for Bergen to take these costs into account when making decisions about quality.

19-18 (30–40 min.) Costs of quality analysis, nonfinancial quality measures.

1. & 2.   **Revenues, Costs of Quality and Costs of Quality as a Percentage of Revenues for Olivia**

Revenues = $2,000 × 10,000 units = $20,000,000

Costs of Quality	Cost (1)	Percentage of Revenues (2) = (1) ÷ $20,000,000
Prevention costs		
Design engineering ($75 × 6,000 hours)	$ 450,000	2.25%
Appraisal costs		
Testing and inspection ($40 × 1 hour × 10,000 units)	400,000	2.00%
Internal failure costs		
Rework ($500 × 5% × 10,000 units)	250,000	1.25%
External failure costs		
Repair ($600 × 4% × 10,000 units)	240,000	1.20%
Total costs of quality	$1,340,000	6.70%

19-18 (Cont'd.)

Revenues, Costs of Quality and Costs of Quality as a Percentage of Revenues for Solta

Revenues: $1,500 × 5,000 units = $7,500,000

Costs of Quality	Costs (1)	Percentage of Revenues (2)=(1)÷$7,500,000
Prevention costs		
Design engineering ($75 × 1,000 hours)	$ 75,000	1.00%
Appraisal costs		
Testing and inspection ($40 × 0.5 × 5,000 units)	100,000	1.33%
Internal failure costs		
Rework ($400 × 10% × 5,000 units)	200,000	2.67%
External failure costs		
Repair ($450 × 8% × 5,000 units)	180,000	2.40%
Estimated forgone contribution margin		
on lost sales [($1,500 – $800) × 300]	210,000	2.80%
Total external failure costs	390,000	5.20%
Total costs of quality	$765,000	10.20%

Costs of quality as a percentage of sales are significantly different for Solta (10.20%) compared with Olivia (6.70%). Ontario spends very little on prevention and appraisal activities for Solta, and incurs high costs of internal and external failures. Ontario follows a different strategy with respect to Olivia, spending a greater percentage of sales on prevention and appraisal activities. The result: fewer internal and external failure costs and lower overall costs of quality as a percentage of sales compared with Solta.

3. Examples of nonfinancial quality measures that Ontario Industries could monitor as part of a total quality-control effort are:
   a. Outgoing quality yield for each product
   b. Returned refrigerator percentage for each product
   c. On-time delivery
   d. Employee turnover

19-20 (25 min.) **Quality improvement, relevant costs, and relevant revenues.**

Relevant costs over the next year of choosing the new lens = $50 × 20,000 copiers = $1,000,000

	Relevant Benefits over the Next Year of Choosing the New Lens
Costs of quality items	
Savings on rework costs	
$40 × 12,000 rework hours	$ 480,000
Savings in customer-support costs	
$20 × 800 customer-support-hours	16,000
Savings in transportation costs for parts	
$180 × 200 fewer loads	36,000
Savings in warranty repair costs	
$45 × 8,000 repair-hours	360,000
Opportunity costs	
Contribution margin from increased sales	600,000
Cost savings and additional contribution margin	$1,492,000

Because the expected relevant benefits of $1,492,000 exceed the expected relevant costs of the new lens of $1,000,000, Photon should introduce the new lens. Note that the opportunity cost benefits in the form of higher contribution margin from increased sales is an important component for justifying the investment in the new lens. The incremental cost of the new lens of $1,000,000 is greater than the incremental savings in rework and repair costs of $892,000. Investing in the new lens is beneficial, provided it generates additional contribution margin of at least $108,000 ($1,000,000 – $892,000), that is, additional sales of at least $108,000 ÷ $6,000 = 18 copiers.

19-22 (20 min.) **Waiting time, banks.**

1.   If the branch expects to receive 40 customers each day and it takes 5 minutes to serve a customer, the average time that a customer will wait in line before being served is:

$$= \frac{\left(\begin{array}{c}\text{Average number} \\ \text{of customers}\end{array}\right) \times \left(\begin{array}{c}\text{Time taken to} \\ \text{serve a customer}\end{array}\right)^2}{2 \times \left[\begin{array}{c}\text{Available time} \\ \text{counter is open}\end{array} - \left[\left(\begin{array}{c}\text{Average number} \\ \text{of customers}\end{array}\right) \times \left(\begin{array}{c}\text{Time taken to} \\ \text{serve a customer}\end{array}\right)\right]\right]}$$

$$= \frac{[40 \times (5)^2]}{2 \times [300 - (40 \times 5)]} = \frac{(40 \times 25)}{2 \times (300 - 200)} = \frac{1,000}{2 \times 100} = \frac{1,000}{200} = 5 \text{ minutes}$$

2.   If the branch expects to receive 50 customers each day and the time taken to serve a customer is 5 minutes, the average time that a customer will wait in line before being served is:

$$= \frac{[50 \times (5)^2]}{2 \times [300 - (50 \times 5)]} = \frac{(50 \times 25)}{2 \times (300 - 250)} = \frac{50 \times 25}{2 \times 50} = \frac{1,250}{100} = 12.5 \text{ minutes}$$

3.   If the branch expects to serve 50 customers each day and the time taken to serve a customer is 4 minutes, the average time that a customer will wait in line before being served is:

$$= \frac{[50 \times (4)^2]}{2 \times [300 - (50 \times 4)]} = \frac{(50 \times 16)}{2 \times (300 - 200)} = \frac{50 \times 16}{2 \times 100} = \frac{800}{200} = 4 \text{ minutes}$$

19-24 (15 min.) **Theory of constraints, throughput contribution, relevant costs.**

1.   Finishing is a bottleneck operation. Hence, producing 1,000 more units will generate additional throughput contribution and operating income.

Increase in throughput contribution ($72 – $32) × 1,000	$40,000
Incremental costs of the jigs and tools	30,000
Net benefit of investing in jigs and tools	$10,000

Mayfield should invest in the modern jigs and tools because the benefit of higher throughput contribution of $40,000 exceeds the cost of $30,000.

2.   The Machining Department has excess capacity and is not a bottleneck operation. Increasing its capacity further will not increase throughput contribution. There is, therefore, no benefit from spending $5,000 to increase the Machining Department's capacity by 10,000 units. Mayfield should not implement the change to do setups faster.

19-26 (15 min.) **Theory of constraints, throughput contribution, quality.**

1.   Cost of defective unit at machining operation which is not a bottleneck operation is the loss in direct materials (variable costs) of $32 per unit. Producing 2,000 units of defectives does not result in loss of throughput contribution. Despite the defective production, machining can produce and transfer 80,000 units to finishing. Therefore, cost of 2,000 defective units at the machining operation is $32 × 2,000 = $64,000.

2.   A defective unit produced at the bottleneck finishing operation costs Mayfield materials costs plus the opportunity cost of lost throughput contribution. Bottleneck capacity not wasted in producing defective units could be used to generate additional sales and throughput contribution. Cost of 2,000 defective units at the finishing operation is:

Loss of direct materials $32 × 2,000	$ 64,000
Forgone throughput contribution ($72 – $32) × 2,000	80,000
Total cost of 2,000 defective units	$144,000

Alternatively, the cost of 2,000 defective units at the finishing operation can be calculated as the lost revenue of $72 × 2,000 = $144,000. This line of reasoning takes the position that direct materials costs of $32 × 2,000 = $64,000 and all fixed operating costs in the machining and finishing operations would be incurred anyway whether a defective or good unit is produced. The cost of producing a defective unit is the revenue lost of $144,000.

19-28 (30 min.) **Quality improvement, relevant costs, and relevant revenues.**

1.   By implementing the new method, Tan would incur additional direct materials costs on all the 200,000 units started at the molding operation.

Additional direct materials costs = $4 per lamp × 200,000 lamps	$800,000

The relevant benefits of adding the new material are:
Increased revenue from selling 30,000 more lamps
$40 per lamp × 30,000 lamps $1,200,000

Note that Tan Corporation continues to incur the same total variable costs of direct materials, direct manufacturing labor, setup labor and materials handling labor, and the same fixed costs of equipment, rent, and allocated overhead that it is currently incurring, even when it improves quality. Since these costs do not differ among the alternatives of adding the new material or not adding the new material, they are excluded from the analysis. The relevant benefit of adding the new material is the extra revenue that Tan would get from producing 30,000 good lamps.

An alternative approach to analyzing the problem is to focus on scrap costs and the benefits of reducing scrap.

The relevant benefits of adding the new material are:

a. Cost savings from eliminating scrap:

Variable costs per lamp, $19[a] × 30,000 lamps	$ 570,000

b. Additional contribution margin from selling another 30,000 lamps because 30,000 lamps will no longer be scrapped:

Unit contribution margin $21[b] × 30,000 lamps	630,000
Total benefits to Tan of adding new material to improve quality	$1,200,000

[a]Note that only the variable scrap costs of $19 per lamp (direct materials, $16 per lamp; direct manufacturing labor, setup labor, and materials handling labor, $3 per lamp) are relevant because improving quality will save these costs. Fixed scrap costs of equipment, rent, and other allocated overhead are irrelevant because these costs will be incurred whether Tan Corporation adds or does not add the new material.

[b]Contribution margin per unit

Selling price		$40.00
Variable costs:		
Direct materials costs per lamp	$16.00	
Molding department variable manufacturing costs per lamp (direct manufacturing labor, setup labor, and materials handling labor)	3.00	
Variable costs		(19.00)
Unit contribution margin		$21.00

On the basis of quantitative considerations alone, Tan should use the new material. Relevant benefits of $1,200,000 exceed the relevant costs of $800,000 by $400,000.

2. Other nonfinancial and qualitative factors that Tan should consider in making a decision include the effects of quality improvement on:
   a. Gaining manufacturing expertise that could lead to further cost reductions in the future.
   b. Enhanced reputation and increased customer goodwill which could lead to higher future revenues through greater unit sales and higher sales prices.
   c. Higher employee morale as a result of higher quality.

19-30 (30–40 min.) **Compensation linked with profitability, on-time delivery, and external quality performance measures.**

1.

	Jan.-March	April-June	July-Sept.	Oct.-Dec.
Detroit				
Add: Profitability				
2% of operating income	$16,000	$17,000	$14,000	$18,000
Add: On-time delivery				
$10,000 if above 98%	10,000	10,000	0	0
Deduct: Quality				
50% of cost of sales returns	(9,000)	(13,000)	(5,000)	(12,500)
Total: Bonus paid	$17,000	$14,000	$ 9,000	$ 5,500
Los Angeles				
Add: Profitability				
2% of operating income	$32,000	$30,000	$36,000	$38,000
Add: On-time delivery				
$10,000 if above 98%	0	0	0	10,000
Deduct: Quality				
50% of cost of sales returns	(17,500)	(17,000)	(14,000)	(11,000)
Total: Bonus paid	$14,500	$13,000	$22,000	$37,000

2.

Operating income as a measure of profitability

Operating income does capture revenue and cost-related factors. However, there is no recognition of investment differences between the two plants. Los Angeles sales are approximately double that of Detroit. This difference gives the Los Angeles plant manager the opportunity to earn a larger bonus due to investment size alone. An alternative approach would be to use return on investment (perhaps relative to the budgeted ROI).

98% on-time benchmark as a measure of on-time delivery performance

This measure does reflect the ability of Pacific-Dunlop to meet a benchmark for on-time delivery. Several concerns arise with this specific measure:

    a.   It is a yes-or-no cut-off. A 10% on-time performance earns no bonus, but neither does a 97.9% on-time performance. Moreover, no extra bonus is paid for performance above 98.0%. An alternative is to have the bonus be a percentage of the on-time delivery percentage.

    b.   It can be manipulated by management. The Pacific-Dunlop plant manager may quote conservative delivery dates to sales people in an effort to "guarantee" that the 98% target is achieved.

    c.   It reflects performance relative only to scheduled delivery date. It does not consider how quickly Pacific-Dunlop can respond to customer orders.

19-30 (Cont'd.)

50% of cost of sales returns as a measure of quality

This measure does incorporate one cost that arises with defective goods. However, there are several concerns with its use:

a. Not all sales returns are due to defective work by the plant manager. Some returns are due to tampering by the customer. Other returns arise from breakage during delivery and installation.

b. It does not systematically incorporate customer opinion about quality. Not all customers return defective goods.

c. It ignores important categories of the cost of defective goods. For example, dissatisfied customers may decline to make any subsequent purchases.

3. Most companies use both financial and nonfinancial measures to evaluate performance, sometimes presented in a single report such as a *balanced scorecard*. Using multiple measures of performance enables top management to evaluate whether lower-level managers have improved one area at the expense of others. For example, did the on-time delivery performance of the Detroit plant manager decrease in the October–December period relative to the April–June period because the manager emphasized shipment of high-margin products to increase operating income?

4. If on-time delivery is dropped as a performance evaluation measure, managers will concentrate on increasing operating income and decreasing sales returns but will give less attention to on-time delivery. Consider the following situation. Suppose a manager must choose between (a) delivering a high margin order that will add to operating income while delaying a number of other orders and adversely affecting on-time performance, or (b) delaying the high margin order and sacrificing some operating income, to achieve better on-time performance. What action will the manager take? If on-time performance is excluded as a performance evaluation measure, the manager will almost certainly choose (a). Only if on-time performance is included in the manager's performance evaluation will the manager consider choosing option (b).

19-32 (60 min.) **Waiting times, relevant revenues, and relevant costs.** (continuation of 19-31).

1.   The direct approach is to look at incremental revenues and incremental costs.

Average selling price per order for Y28, which has average operating throughput time of 350 hours	$ 8,000
Variable costs per order	5,000
Additional contribution per order from Y28	3,000
Multiply by expected number of orders	× 25
Increase in expected contribution from Y28	$75,000

Expected loss in revenues and increase in costs from introducing Y28

Product (1)	Expected Loss in Revenues from Increasing Average Manufacturing Lead Times for All Products (2)	Expected Increase in Carrying Costs from Increasing Average Manufacturing Lead Times for All Products (3)	Expected Loss in Revenues Plus Expected Increases in Costs of Introducing Y28 (4) = (2) + (3)
Z39	$25,000.00[a]	$6,375.00[b]	$31,375.00
Y28	–	2,187.50[c]	2,187.50
Total	$25,000.00	$8,562.50	$33,562.50

[a] 50 orders × ($27,000 – $26,500)
[b] (410 hours – 240 hours) × $0.75 × 50 orders
[c] (350 hours – 0) × $0.25 × 25

Increase in expected contribution from Y28 of $75,000 is greater than increase in expected costs of $33,562.50 by $41,437.50. Therefore, SRG should introduce Y28.

Alternative calculations of incremental revenues and incremental costs of introducing Y28.

	Alternative 1: Introduce Y28 (1)	Alternative 2: Do Not Introduce Y28 (2)	Relevant Revenues and Relevant Costs (3) = (1) – (2)
Expected revenues	$1,525,000.00[a]	$1,350,000.00[b]	$175,000.00
Expected variable costs	875,000.00[c]	750,000.00[d]	125,000.00
Expected carrying costs	17,562.50[e]	9,000.00[f]	8,562.50
Expected total variable and carrying costs	892,562.50	759,000.00	133,562.50
Expected revenues minus expected costs	$ 632,437.50	$ 591,000.00	$ 41,437.50

[a] (50 × $26,500) + (25 × $8,000)   [b] 50 × $27,000
[c] (50 × $15,000) + (25 × $5,000)   [d] 50 × $15,000
[e] (50 × $0.75 × 410) + (25 × $0.25 × 350)   [f] 50 × $0.75 × 240

2. Average selling price per order for Y28, which has average manufacturing
    lead time per order more than 320 hours $ 6,000

    Variable costs per order   5,000

    Additional contribution per order from Y28 $ 1,000

    Multiply by expected number of orders   ×   25

    Increase in expected contribution from Y28 $25,000

Expected loss in revenues and increase in costs from introducing Y28

Product (1)	Expected Loss in Revenues from Increasing Average Manufacturing Lead Times for All Products (2)	Expected Increase in Carrying Costs from Increasing Average Manufacturing Lead Times for All Products (3)	Expected Loss in Revenues Plus Expected Increases in Costs of Introducing Y28 (4) = (2) + (3)
Z39	$25,000.00[a]	$6,375.00[b]	$31,375.00
Y28	–	2,187.50[c]	2,187.50
Total	$25,000.00	$8,562.50	$33,562.50

[a] 50 orders × ($27,000 – $26,500)
[b] (410 hours – 240 hours) × $0.75 × 50 orders
[c] (350 hours – 0) × $0.25 × 25

Increase in expected contribution from Y28 of $25,000 is less than increase in expected costs of $33,562.50 by $8,562.50. Therefore, SRG should not introduce Y28.

19-34 (20 min.) **Theory of constraints, throughput contribution, relevant costs.**

1. It will cost Colorado $50 per unit to reduce manufacturing time. But manufacturing is not a bottleneck operation; installation is. Therefore, manufacturing more equipment will not increase sales and throughput contribution. Colorado Industries should not implement the new manufacturing method.

2.
Additional relevant costs of new direct materials, $2,000 × 320 units,	$640,000
Increase in throughput contribution, $25,000 × 20 units,	$500,000

The additional incremental costs exceed the benefits from higher throughput contribution by $140,000, so Colorado Industries should not implement the new design.

Alternatively, compare throughput contribution under each alternative.

Current throughput contribution is $25,000 × 300	$7,500,000
With the modification, throughput contribution is $23,000 × 320	$7,360,000

The current throughput contribution is greater than the throughput contribution resulting from the proposed change in direct materials. Hence, Colorado Industries should not implement the new design.

3.
Increase in throughput contribution, $25,000 × 10 units	$250,000
Increase in relevant costs	$ 50,000

The additional throughput contribution exceeds incremental costs by $200,000, so Colorado Industries should implement the new installation technique.

4. Motivating installation workers to increase productivity is worthwhile because installation is a bottleneck operation, and any increase in productivity at the bottleneck will increase throughput contribution. On the other hand, motivating workers in the manufacturing department to increase productivity is not worthwhile. Manufacturing is not a bottleneck operation, so any increase in output will result only in extra inventory of equipment. Colorado Industries should encourage manufacturing to produce only as much equipment as the installation department needs, not to produce as much as it can. Under these circumstances, it would not be a good idea to evaluate and compensate manufacturing workers on the basis of their productivity.

19-36 (25 min.) **Quality improvement, Pareto diagram, cause-and-effect diagram.**

1.   Examples of failures in accounts receivable management are:
    a.   Uncollectible amounts or bad debts
    b.   Delays in receiving payments

2.   Prevention activities that could reduce failures in accounts receivable management include:
    a.   Credit checks on customers by salespersons based on company credit policy.
    b.   Shipping the correct copier to the customer
    c.   Supporting installation of the copier and answering customer questions
    c.   Sending the correct invoice, in the correct amount, and to the correct address, promptly
    d.   Following up to see if the machine is functioning smoothly
    e.   Offer cash discounts to encourage early payment of receivables

3.   A Pareto diagram for the problem of delays in receiving customer payments follows:

SOLUTION EXHIBIT 19-36A
Pareto Diagram for Failures in Accounts Receivables at Murray Corporation

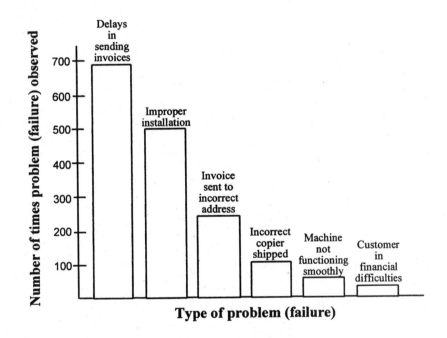

A cause-and-effect or fishbone diagram for the problem of delays in sending invoices may appear as follows:

SOLUTION EXHIBIT 19-36B
Cause-and-Effect Diagram
For Problem of Delays in Sending Invoices at Murray Corporation

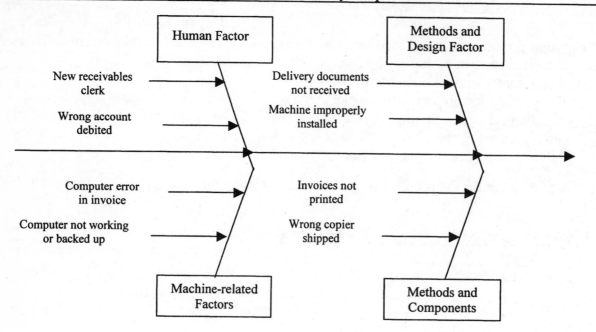

19-38 (45–50 min.) **Quality improvement, theory of constraints.**

1. Consider the incremental revenues and incremental costs to Wellesley Corporation of purchasing additional grey cloth from outside suppliers.

Incremental revenues, $1,250 × (5,000 rolls × 0.90)		$5,625,000
Incremental costs:		
Cost of grey cloth, $900 × 5,000 rolls	$4,500,000	
Direct materials variable costs at printing operation, $100 × 5,000 rolls	500,000	
Incremental costs		5,000,000
Excess of incremental revenues over incremental costs		$ 625,000

Note that, because the printing department has surplus capacity equal to 5,500 (15,000 − 9,500) rolls per month, purchasing grey cloth from outside entails zero opportunity costs. Yes, the Printing Department should buy the grey cloth from the outside supplier.

2. By producing a defective roll in the Weaving Department, Wellesley Corporation is worse off by the entire amount of revenue forgone of $1,250 per roll. Note that, since the weaving operation is a constraint, any rolls received by the Printing Department that are scrapped result in lost revenue to the firm.

An alternative approach to analyzing the problem is to focus on scrap costs and the benefits of reducing scrap.

The relevant costs of Printing Department scrap are:

a.	Direct materials variable costs in the Weaving Department	$ 500
b.	Direct materials variable costs in the Printing Department	100
c.	Contribution margin forgone from not selling one roll $1,250 − $500 − $100	650
	Amount by which Wellesley Corporation is worse off as a result of Printing Department scrap	$1,250

Note that only the variable scrap costs of $600 per roll (direct materials in the Weaving Department, $500 per roll: direct materials in the Printing Department, $100 per roll) are relevant because improving quality will save these costs. Fixed scrap costs attributable to other operating costs are irrelevant because these costs will be incurred whether Wellesley Corporation reduces scrap in the Printing Department or not.

Wellesley Corporation should make the proposed modifications in the Printing Department because the incremental benefits exceed the incremental costs by $125,000 per month:

Incremental benefits of reducing scrap in the Printing Department by 4% (from 10% to 6%)	
4% × 9,500 rolls × $1,250 per roll (computed above)	$475,000
Incremental costs of the modification	350,000
Excess of incremental benefits over incremental costs	$125,000

3.   To determine how much Wellesley Corporation is worse off by producing a defective roll in the Weaving Department, consider the payoff to Wellesley from not having a defective roll produced in the Weaving Department. The good roll produced in the Weaving Department will be sent for further processing in the Printing Department. The relevant costs and benefits of printing and selling this roll follow:

Additional direct materials variable costs incurred in the Printing Department	$ (100)
Expected revenue from selling the finished product, $1,250 × 0.9 (since 10% of the Printing Department output will be scraped and earn zero revenue)	1,125
Net expected benefit of producing a good roll in the Weaving Department	$1,025

By producing a defective roll in the Weaving Department, Wellesley Corporation is worse off by $1,025 per roll. Note that, since the weaving operation is a constraint, any rolls that are scrapped result in lost revenue to the firm.

     An alternative approach to analyzing the problem is to focus on scrap costs and the benefits of reducing scrap.

The relevant costs of Weaving Department scrap are:	
(a) Direct materials variable costs in the Weaving Department	$ 500
(b) Expected unit contribution margin forgone from not selling one roll, ($1,250 × 0.9) − $500 − $100	525
Amount by which Wellesley Corporation is worse off as a result of Weaving Department scrap	$1,025

Note that only the variable scrap costs of $500 per roll (direct materials in the Weaving Department) are relevant because improving quality will save these costs. All fixed scrap costs attributable to other operating costs are irrelevant because these costs will be incurred whether Wellesley Corporation reduces scrap in the Weaving Department or not.

     Wellesley Corporation should make the proposed improvements in the Printing Department because the incremental benefits exceed the incremental costs by $30,000 per month:

Incremental benefits of reducing scrap in the Weaving Department by 2% (from 5% to 3%) 2% × 10,000 rolls × $1,025 per roll (computed above)	$205,000
Incremental costs of improvements	175,000
Excess of incremental benefits over incremental costs	$ 30,000

CHAPTER 20
INVENTORY MANAGEMENT, JUST-IN-TIME,
AND BACKFLUSH COSTING

20-2   Five cost categories important in managing goods for sale in a retail organization are:
1. Purchasing costs
2. Ordering costs
3. Carrying costs
4. Stockout costs
5. Quality costs

20-4   Costs included in the carrying costs of inventory are incremental costs for such items as insurance, rent, obsolescence, spoilage, and breakage plus the opportunity cost of capital (or required return on investment).

20-6   The steps in computing the costs of a prediction error when using the EOQ decision model are:
Step 1: Compute the monetary outcome from the best action that could be taken, given the actual amount of the cost input.
Step 2: Compute the monetary outcome from the best action based on the incorrect amount of the predicted cost input.
Step 3: Compute the difference between the monetary outcomes from Steps 1 and 2.

20-8   Just-in-time (JIT) purchasing is the purchase of goods or materials such that a delivery immediately precedes demand or use. Benefits include lower inventory holdings (reduced warehouse space required and less money tied up in inventory) and less risk of inventory obsolescence and spoilage.

20-10 The sequence of activities involved in placing a purchase order can be facilitated by use of the Internet by having online a complete price list, information about expected shipment dates, and a service order capability that is available 24 hours a day with email or fax confirmation. The cost of placing orders on the Internet is lower than placing orders by telephone or mail.

20-12 Obstacles to companies adopting a supply-chain approach include:
*   Communication obstacles—the unwillingness of some parties to share information.
*   Trust obstacles—includes the concern that all parties will not meet their agreed-upon commitments.
*   Information system obstacles—includes problems due to the information systems of different parties not being technically compatible.
*   Limited resources—includes problems due to the people and financial resources given to support a supply chain initiative not being adequate.

20-14 Traditional normal and standard costing systems use sequential tracking, which is any product-costing method where recording of the journal entries occurs in the same order as actual purchases and progress in production.

Backflush costing omits the recording of some or all of the journal entries relating to the cycle from purchase of direct materials to sale of finished goods. Where journal entries for one or more stages in the cycle are omitted, the journal entries for a subsequent stage use normal or standard costs to work backward to flush out the costs in the cycle for which journal entries were not made.

20-16 (20 min.) **Economic order quantity for retailer.**

1.   D = 10,000, P = $225, C = $10

$$EOQ = \sqrt{\frac{2\,DP}{C}} = \sqrt{\frac{2 \times 10,000 \times \$225}{10}}$$

$$= 670.82$$

$$\cong 671 \text{ jerseys}$$

2. Number of orders per year $= \dfrac{D}{EOQ} = \dfrac{10,000}{671}$

$$= 14.90$$

$$\cong \quad 15 \text{ orders}$$

3. $\dfrac{\text{Demand each}}{\text{working day}} = \dfrac{D}{\text{Number of working days}}$

$$= \frac{10,000}{365}$$

$$= 27.40 \text{ jerseys per day}$$

Purchase lead time = 7 days

Reorder point   = 27.40 × 7

$$= 191.80 \cong 192 \text{ jerseys}$$

20-18 (15 min.) **EOQ for a retailer.**

1. $D = 20{,}000$, $P = \$160$, $C = 20\% \times \$8 = \$1.60$

$$EOQ = \sqrt{\frac{2DP}{C}} = \sqrt{\frac{2 \times 20{,}000 \times \$160}{\$1.60}} = 2{,}000 \text{ yards}$$

2. Number of orders per year: $\dfrac{D}{EOQ} = \dfrac{20{,}000}{2{,}000} = 10 \text{ orders}$

3. Demand each working day

$$= \frac{D}{\text{Number of working days}}$$
$$= \frac{20{,}000}{250}$$
$$= 80 \text{ yards per day}$$
$$= 400 \text{ yards per week}$$

Purchasing lead time = 2 weeks
Reorder point = $400 \times 2 = 800$ yards

20-20 (20 min.)   **Sensitivity of EOQ to changes in relevant ordering and carrying costs.**

1. A straightforward approach to the requirement is to construct the following table for EOQ at relevant carrying and ordering costs. Annual demand is 10,000 units. The formula for the EOQ model is:

$$EOQ = \sqrt{\frac{2DP}{C}}$$

where D = demand in units for a specified period of time

P = relevant ordering costs per purchase order

C = relevant carrying costs of one unit in stock for the time period used for D (one year in this problem.

Relevant Carrying Costs Per Unit Per Year	Relevant Ordering Costs Per Purchase Order	
	$300	$200
$10	$\sqrt{\dfrac{2\times10,000\times\$300}{\$10}} = 775$	$\sqrt{\dfrac{2\times10,000\times\$200}{\$10}} = 632$
15	$\sqrt{\dfrac{2\times10,000\times\$300}{\$15}} = 632$	$\sqrt{\dfrac{2\times10,000\times\$200}{\$15}} = 516$
20	$\sqrt{\dfrac{2\times10,000\times\$300}{\$20}} = 548$	$\sqrt{\dfrac{2\times10,000\times\$200}{\$20}} = 447$

2. For a given demand level, as relevant carrying costs increase, EOQ becomes smaller. For a given demand level, as relevant order costs increase, EOQ increases.

20-22 (20 min.) **JIT production, relevant benefits, relevant costs.**

1.   Solution Exhibit 20-22 presents the annual net benefit of $154,000 to Evans Corporation of implementing a JIT production system.

2.   Other nonfinancial and qualitative factors that Evans should consider in deciding whether it should implement a JIT system include:

   a.   The possibility of developing and implementing a detailed system for integrating the sequential operations of the manufacturing process. Direct materials must arrive when needed for each subassembly so that the production process functions smoothly.

   b.   The ability to design products that use standardized parts and reduce manufacturing time.

   c.   The ease of obtaining reliable vendors who can deliver quality direct materials on time with minimum lead time.

   d.   Willingness of suppliers to deliver smaller and more frequent orders.

   e.   The confidence of being able to deliver quality products on time. Failure to do so would result in customer dissatisfaction.

   f.   The skill levels of workers to perform multiple tasks such as minor repairs, maintenance, quality testing and inspection.

SOLUTION EXHIBIT 20-22
Annual Relevant Costs of Current Production System and JIT Production System for Evans Corporation

Relevant Items	Relevant Costs under Current Production System	Relevant Costs under JIT Production System
Annual tooling costs	–	$150,000
Required return on investment:		
12% per year × $900,000 of average inventory per year	$108,000	
12% per year × $200,000 of average inventory per year		24,000
Insurance, space, materials handling, and setup costs	200,000	140,000[a]
Rework costs	350,000	280,000[b]
Incremental revenues from higher selling prices	–	(90,000)[c]
Total net incremental costs	$658,000	$504,000
Annual difference in favor of JIT production	$154,000	

[a]$200,000 (1 – 0.30) = $140,000
[b]$350,000 (1 – 0.20) = $280,000
[c]$3 × 30,000 units = $90,000

3a.   Personal observation by production line workers and managers is more effective in JIT plants than in traditional plants. A JIT plant's production process layout is streamlined. Operations are not obscured by piles of inventory or rework. As a result, such plants are easier to evaluate by personal observation than cluttered plants where the flow of production is not logically laid out.

Besides personal observation, nonfinancial performance measures are the dominant methods of control. Nonfinancial performance measures provide most timely and easy to understand measures of plant performance. Examples of nonfinancial performance measures of time, inventory, and quality include:

- Manufacturing lead time
- Units produced per hour
- Machine setup time $\div$ manufacturing time
- Number of defective units $\div$ number of units completed

In addition to personal observation and nonfinancial performance measures, financial performance measures are also used. Examples of financial performance measures include:

- Cost of rework
- Ordering costs
- Stockout costs
- Inventory turnover

3b.   The success of a JIT system depends on the speed of information flows from customers to manufacturers to suppliers. The Enterprise Resource Planning (ERP) system has a single database, and gives lower-level managers, workers, customers, and suppliers access to operating information. This benefit, accompanied by tight coordination across business functions, enables the ERP system to rapidly transmit information in response to changes in supply and demand so that manufacturing and distribution plans may be revised accordingly.

20-24 (20 min.) **Backflush costing, two trigger points, materials purchase and sale** (continuation of 20-23).

1.

(a) Purchases of direct materials	Inventory Control	2,754,000	
	Accounts Payable Control		2,754,000
(b) Incur conversion costs	Conversion Costs Control	723,600	
	Various Accounts		723,600
(c) Completion of finished goods	No entry		
(d) Sale of finished goods	Cost of Goods Sold	3,432,000	
	Inventory Control		2,692,800
	Conversion Costs Allocated		739,200
(e) Underallocated or Overallocated conversion Costs	Conversion Costs Allocated	739,200	
	Costs of Goods Sold		15,600
	Conversion Costs Control		723,600

2.

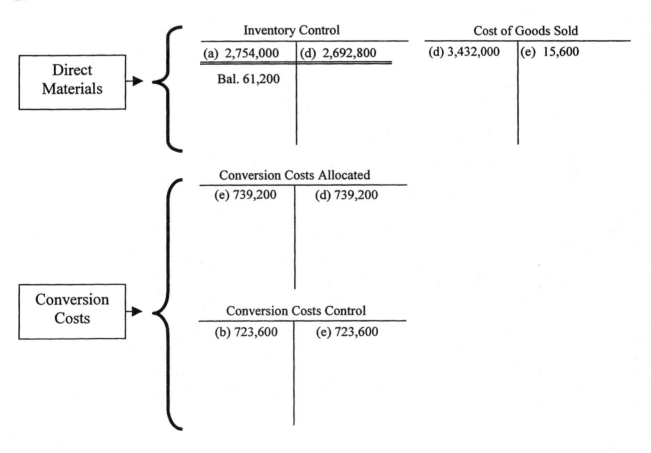

Inventory Control

(a) 2,754,000 | (d) 2,692,800

Bal. 61,200

Cost of Goods Sold

(d) 3,432,000 | (e) 15,600

Direct Materials

Conversion Costs Allocated

(e) 739,200 | (d) 739,200

Conversion Costs Control

(b) 723,600 | (e) 723,600

Conversion Costs

20-26 (30 min.) **Effect of different order quantities on ordering costs and carrying costs, EOQ.**

1. A straightforward approach to this requirement is to construct the following table for different purchase-order quantities.

D: Demand	26,000	26,000	26,000	26,000	26,000
Q: Order quantity	300	500	600	700	900
Q/2: Average inventory in units	150	250	300	350	450
D/Q: Number of purchase orders	86.67	52	43.33	37.14	28.89
(D/Q) × P: Annual ordering costs	$6,240	$3,744	$3,120	$2,674	$2,080
(Q/2) × C: Annual carrying costs	1,560	2,600	3,120	3,640	4,680
Total relevant costs of ordering and carrying inventory	$7,800	$6,344	$6,240	$6,314	$6,760

Minimum
Cost

D = 26,000 units
Q = order quantity
P = $72
C = $10.40

$$EOQ = \sqrt{\frac{2DP}{C}} = \sqrt{\frac{2 \times 26,000 \times \$72}{\$10.40}} = \sqrt{360,000} = 600 \text{ packages}$$

The shape of the total relevant cost function for Koala Blue is relatively flat from order quantities 500 to 700.

2. When the ordering cost per purchase order is reduced to $40:

$$EOQ = \sqrt{\frac{2 \times 26,000 \times \$40}{\$10.40}} = \sqrt{200,000} = 447.2 \text{ packages or } 447 \text{ packages (rounded)}$$

The EOQ drops from 600 packages to 447 packages when Koala Blue's ordering cost per purchase order drops from $72 to $40.

20-28 (20–30 min.) **EOQ, cost of prediction error.**

1. $\quad EOQ = \sqrt{\dfrac{2DP}{C}}$

   $D = 2{,}000; \; P = \$40; \; C = \$4 + (10\% \times \$50) = \$9$

   $EOQ = \sqrt{\dfrac{2 \times 2{,}000 \times \$40}{\$9}} = 133.333 \text{ tires} \approx 133 \text{ tires (approximately)}$

   $TRC = \dfrac{DP}{Q} + \dfrac{QC}{2} \quad$ where Q can be any quantity, including the EOQ

   $= \dfrac{2{,}000 \times \$40}{133.333} + \dfrac{133.333 \times \$9}{2} = \$600 + \$600 = \$1{,}200$

   If students used an EOQ of 133 tires (order quantities rounded to the nearest whole number),

   $TRC = \dfrac{2{,}000 \times \$40}{133} + \dfrac{133 \times \$9}{2} = \$601.5 + \$598.5 = \$1{,}200.$

   Sum of annual relevant ordering and carrying costs equals $1,200.

2. The prediction error affects C, which is now:

   $C = \$4 + (10\% \times \$30) = \$7$

   $D = 2{,}000, \; P = \$40, \; C = \$7$

   $EOQ = \sqrt{\dfrac{2 \times 2{,}000 \times \$40}{\$7}} = 151.186 \text{ tires} = 151 \text{ tires (rounded)}$

20-28 (Cont'd.)

The cost of the prediction error can be calculated using a three-step procedure:

Step 1: Compute the monetary outcome from the best action that could have been taken, given the actual amount of the cost input.

$$\text{TRC} = \frac{DP}{Q} + \frac{QC}{2}$$

$$= \frac{2{,}000 \times \$40}{151.186} + \frac{151.186 \times \$7}{2}$$

$$= \$529.15 + \$529.15 = \$1{,}058.30$$

Step 2: Compute the monetary outcome from the best action based on the incorrect amount of the predicted cost input.

$$\text{TRC} = \frac{DP}{Q} + \frac{QC}{2}$$

$$= \frac{2{,}000 \times \$40}{133.333} + \frac{133.333 \times \$7}{2}$$

$$= \$600 + \$466.67 = \$1{,}066.67$$

Step 3: Compute the difference between the monetary outcomes from Step 1 and Step 2:

	Monetary Outcome
Step 1	$1,058.30
Step 2	1,066.67
Difference	$ (8.37)

The cost of the prediction error is $8.37.

Note: The $20 prediction error for the purchase price of the heavy-duty tires is irrelevant in computing purchase costs under the two alternatives because the same purchase costs will be incurred whatever the order size.

Some students may prefer to round off the EOQs to 133 tires and 151 tires, respectively. The calculations under each step in this case follow:

Step 1: $\text{TRC} = \dfrac{2{,}000 \times \$40}{151} + \dfrac{151 \times \$7}{2} = \$529.80 + \$528.50 = \$1058.30$

Step 2: $\text{TRC} = \dfrac{2{,}000 \times \$40}{133} + \dfrac{133 \times \$7}{2} = \$601.50 + \$465.50 = \$1067.00$

Step 3: Difference $= \$1{,}058.30 - \$1{,}067.00 = (\$8.70)$

20-30 (25 min.) **Relevant benefits and relevant costs of JIT purchasing.**

Solution Exhibit 20-30 presents the $724.50 cash savings that would result if Hardesty Medical Instruments adopted the Just-in-time inventory system in 2003.

SOLUTION EXHIBIT 20-30

Annual Relevant Costs of Current Purchasing Policy and JIT Purchasing Policy for Hardesty Medical Instruments

	Relevant Costs Under	
Relevant Item	**Current Purchasing Policy**	**JIT Purchasing Policy**
Purchasing costs		
$10 per unit × 20,000 units	$200,000.00	
$10.05 per unit × 20,000 units		$201,000.00
Ordering costs		
$5 per order × 20 orders per year	100.00	
$5 per order × 200 orders per year		1,000.00
Opportunity carrying costs, required return on investment		
20% per year × $10 cost per unit × 500[a] units of average inventory per year	1,000.00	
20% per year × $10.05 cost per unit × 50[b] units of average inventory per year		100.50
Other carrying costs		
$4.50 per unit per year × 500[a] units of average inventory per year	2,250.00	
$4.50 per unit per year × 50[b] units of average inventory per year		225.00
Stockout costs		
No stockouts	0	
$3 per unit × 100 units per year		300.00
Total annual relevant costs	$203,350.00	$202,625.50
Annual difference in favor of JIT purchasing		$724.50

[a] Order quantity ÷ 2 = 1,000 ÷ 2 = 500
[b] Order quantity ÷ 2 = 100 ÷ 2 = 50

2. Hardesty may benefit from Morrison managing its inventories if there is high order variability caused by randomness in when consumers purchase surgical scalpels or trade promotions that prompt retailers to stock for the future. By coordinating their activities and sharing information about retail sales and inventory held throughout the supply chain, Morrison can plan its manufacturing activities to ensure adequate supply of product while keeping inventory low. For this to succeed, Hardesty and Morrison must have compatible information systems, build trust, and communicate freely.

20-32 (25 min.) **Supplier evaluation and relevant costs of quality and timely deliveries.**

Solution Exhibit 20-32 presents the $1,450 annual relevant costs difference in favor of purchasing from Quality Sports. Copeland should buy the footballs from Quality Sports.

SOLUTION EXHIBIT 20-32

Annual Relevant Costs of Purchasing from Big Red and Quality Sports

	Relevant Costs of Purchasing from	
Relevant Item	**Big Red**	**Quality Sports**
Purchasing costs		
$ 50 per unit × 12,000 units per year	$600,000	
$ 51 per unit × 12,000 units per year		$612,000
Ordering costs		
$6 per order × 60[a] orders per year	360	
$6 per order × 60[a] orders per year		360
Inspection costs		
$0.02 per unit × 12,000 units	240	
No inspection necessary		0
Opportunity carrying costs, required return on investment,		
15% per year × $50 cost per unit × 100 units of average inventory per year;	750	
15% per year × $51 cost per unit × 100 units of average inventory per year		765
Other carrying costs (insurance, material handling, and so on)		
$4 per unit × 100 units of average inventory per year	400	
$4.50 per unit × 100 units of average inventory per year		450
Stockout costs		
$20 per unit × 350 units per year	7,000	
$10 per unit × 60 units per year		600
Customer returns costs		
$25 per unit × 300 units	7,500	
$25 per unit × 25 units		625
Total annual relevant costs	$616,250	$614,800

Annual difference in favor of Quality Sports ⬆ $1,450 ⬆

[a] Number of orders placed:
    Average inventory per year 100 units
    Average order size = 100 × 2 = 200 units
    Annual demand = 12,000 units
    Number of orders placed = 12,000 units/200 units per order = 60 orders

20-34 (20 min.) **Backflush, two trigger points, materials purchase and sale (continuation of 20-32).**

1.

(a) Purchases of direct materials	Inventory Control Accounts Payable Control	550,000	550,000

(b) Incur conversion costs	Conversion Costs Control
	    Various Accounts
	    (such as Accounts Payable
	    Control and Wages Payable)
		440,000	440,000

(c) Completion of finished goods	No entry		

(d) Sale of finished goods	Cost of Goods Sold
	    Inventory Control
	    Conversion Costs Allocated
		900,000	500,000
			400,000

(e) Underallocated or overallocated conversion costs	Conversion Costs Allocated Cost of Goods Sold Conversion Costs Control	400,000 40,000	440,000

2.

20-36 (30 min.) **Backflush costing, income manipulation, ethics.**

1. Factors SVC should consider in deciding whether to adopt a version of backflush costing include:
    a. Effects on decision making by managers. There is a loss of information with backflushing. Supporters of backflushing maintain, however, that nonfinancial information and observation of production provide sufficient inputs to monitor production and management costs at the shop-floor level.
    b. Costs of maintaining sequential tracking vis-à-vis backflush costing.
    c. Materiality of the differences. If the production lead time is short (say, less than one day) and inventory levels are minimal (as one would anticipate with JIT), the differences between sequential tracking and backflush may be minimal.
    d. Opportunity for managers to manipulate reported numbers.

2. Strong's concerns certainly warrant consideration. Much depends on the corporate culture at SVC. If the culture is that quarterly or monthly reported numbers are pivotal to evaluations, and that managers "push the accounting system to facilitate meeting the numbers," Strong should raise these issues with Brown. Adopting an accounting system with an obvious opportunity for manipulation (backflush with sale as the trigger point) may well send managers the wrong message.

    Strong's concerns, however are not by themselves sufficient to cause SVC to not adopt backflush costing. The factors mentioned in requirement 1 may well be compelling enough to support adoption of backflush costing. Brown has alternative ways to address Strong's quite legitimate concerns—see requirement 3.

3. Ways to motivate managers to not "artificially change" reported income include:
    a. Adopting long-term measures that reduce the importance of short-run financial targets.
    b. Increasing the weight on nonaccounting-based variables—e.g., more use of stock options or customer-satisfaction measures.
    c. Penalize heavily (the "stick approach") managers who are found out to have "artificially changed" reported income. This can include withdrawal of bonuses or even termination of employment.

CHAPTER 21
CAPITAL BUDGETING AND COST ANALYSIS

21-2   The six stages in capital budgeting are:

1.   An *identification stage* to distinguish which types of capital expenditure projects are necessary to accomplish organization objectives and strategies.
2.   A *search stage* that explores alternative capital investments that will achieve organization objectives.
3.   An *information-acquisition stage* to consider the expected costs and expected benefits of alternative capital investments.
4.   A *selection stage* to choose projects for implementation.
5.   A *financing stage* to obtain project financing.
6.   An *implementation and control* stage to get projects underway and monitor their performance.

21-4   No. Only quantitative outcomes are formally analyzed in capital budgeting decisions. Many effects of capital budgeting decisions, however, are difficult to quantify in financial terms. These nonfinancial or qualitative factors (for example, the number of accidents in a manufacturing plant or employee morale) are important to consider in making capital budgeting decisions.

21-6   The payback method measures the time it will take to recoup, in the form of expected future net cash inflows, the net initial investment in a project. The payback method is simple and easy to understand. It is a handy method when screening many proposals and particularly when predicted cash flows in later years are highly uncertain. The main weaknesses of the payback method is its neglect of the time value of money and cash flows after the payback period.

21-8   No. The discounted cash-flow techniques implicitly consider depreciation in rate of return computations; the compound interest tables automatically allow for recovery of investment. The net initial investment of an asset is usually regarded as a lump-sum outflow at time zero. Where taxes are included in the DCF analysis, depreciation costs are included in the computation of the taxable income number that is used to compute the tax payment cash flow.

21-10   All overhead costs are not relevant in NPV analysis. Overhead costs are relevant only if the capital investment results in a change in total overhead cash flows. Overhead costs are not relevant if total overhead cash flows remain the same but the overhead allocated to the particular capital investment changes.

21-12   The categories of cash flow that should be considered are:
  1a. Initial machine investment,
   b. Initial working capital investment,
   c. After-tax cash flow from current disposal of old machine,
  2a. Annual after-tax cash flow from operations (excluding depreciation effects),
   b. Income tax cash savings from annual depreciation deductions,
  3a. After-tax cash flow from terminal disposal of machines, and
   b. After-tax cash flow from recovery of working capital.

21-14 A cellular telephone company manager responsible for retaining customers needs to consider the expected future revenues and the expected future costs of "different investments" to retain customers. One such investment could be a special price discount. An alternative investment is offering loyalty club benefits to long-time customers.

21-16 Exercises in compound interest, no income taxes.

The answers to these exercises are printed after the last problem, at the end of the chapter.

21-18 (30 min.) Capital budgeting methods, no income taxes.

The table for the present value of annuities (Appendix C, Table 4) shows: 10 periods at 14% = 5.216

1a. Net present value

$$= \$28,000(5.216) - \$110,000$$
$$= \$146,048 - \$110,000 = \$36,048$$

b. Payback period

$$= \frac{\$110,000}{\$28,000} = 3.93 \text{ years}$$

c. Internal rate of return:

$110,000 = Present value of annuity of $28,000 at R% for 10 years, or what factor (F) in the table of present values of an annuity (Appendix C, Table 4) will satisfy the following equation.

$$\$110,000 = \$28,000F$$
$$F = \frac{\$110,000}{\$28,000} = 3.929$$

On the 10-year line in the table for the present value of annuities (Appendix C, Table 4), find the column closest to 3.929; 3.929 is between a rate of return of 20% and 22%.
Interpolation can be used to determine the exact rate:

	Present Value Factors	
20%	4.192	4.192
IRR rate	—	3.929
22%	3.923	—
Difference	0.269	0.263

$$\text{Internal rate of return} = 20\% + \left[\frac{0.263}{0.269}\right](2\%)$$

$$= 20\% + (0.978)(2\%) = 21.96\%$$

d. Accrual accounting rate of return based on net initial investment:
Net initial investment = $110,000
Estimated useful life = 10 years
Annual straight-line depreciation = $110,000 ÷ 10 = $11,000

$$\text{Accrual accounting rate of return} = \frac{\$28,000 - \$11,000}{\$110,000}$$

$$= \frac{\$17,000}{\$110,000} = 15.46\%$$

21-2

21-18 (Cont'd.)

2. Factors City Hospital should consider include:
   a. Quantitative financial aspects.
   b. Qualitative factors, such as the benefits to its customers of a better eye-testing machine and the employee-morale advantages of having up-to-date equipment.
   c. Financing factors, such as the availability of cash to purchase the new equipment.

21-20 (25 min.) Capital budgeting with uneven cash flows, no income taxes.

1. Present value of savings in cash operating costs:

$10,000 × 0.862	$ 8,620
8,000 × 0.743	5,944
6,000 × 0.641	3,846
5,000 × 0.552	2,760
Present value of savings in cash operating costs	21,170
Net initial investment	(23,000)
Net present value	$(1,830)

2. Payback period:

Year	Cash Savings	Cumulative Cash Savings	Initial Investment Yet to Be Recovered at End of Year
0	–	–	$23,000
1	$10,000	$10,000	13,000
2	8,000	18,000	5,000
3	6,000	24,000	–

$$\text{Payback period} = 2 \text{ years} + \frac{\$5,000}{\$6,000} = 2.83 \text{ years}$$

3. From requirement 1, the net present value is negative with a 16% required rate of return. Hence, the internal rate of return must be less than 16%.

Year (1)	Cash Savings (2)	P.V. Factor at 14% (3)	P.V. at 14% (4) = (2) × (3)	P.V. Factor at 12% (5)	P.V. at 12% (6) = (2) × (5)	P.V. Factor at 10% (7)	P.V. at 10% (8) = (2) × (7)
1	$10,000	0.877	$ 8,770	0.893	$ 8,930	0.909	$ 9,090
2	8,000	0.769	6,152	0.797	6,376	0.826	6,608
3	6,000	0.675	4,050	0.712	4,272	0.751	4,506
4	5,000	0.592	2,960	0.636	3,180	0.683	3,415
			$21,932		$22,758		$23,619

Net present value at 14% = $21,932 – $23,000 = $(1,068)

Net present value at 12% = $22,758 – $23,000 = $(242)

Net present value at 10% = $23,619 – $23,000 = $619

$$\text{Internal rate of return} = 10\% + \left[\frac{619}{619 + 242} \right] (2\%)$$

$$= 10\% + (0.719)(2\%) = 11.44\%$$

21-20 (Cont'd.)

4. Accrual accounting rate of return based on net initial investment:

Average annual savings in cash operating costs $= \dfrac{\$29,000}{4 \text{ years}} = \$7,250$

Annual straight-line depreciation $= \dfrac{\$23,000}{4 \text{ years}} = \$5,750$

Accrual accounting rate of return $= \dfrac{\$7,250 - \$5,750}{23,000}$

$= \dfrac{\$1,500}{\$23,000} = 6.52\%$

21-22 (30 min.) Payback and NPV methods, no income taxes (CMA, adapted).

1a. Payback measures the time it will take to recoup, in the form of expected future cash flows, the net initial investment in a project. Payback emphasizes the early recovery of cash as a key aspect of project ranking. Some managers argue that this emphasis on early recovery of cash is appropriate if there is a high level of uncertainty about future cash flows. Projects with shorter paybacks give the organization more flexibility because funds for other projects become available sooner.

Strengths
- Easy to understand
- One way to capture uncertainty about expected cash flows in later years of a project (although sensitivity analysis is a more systematic way)

Weaknesses
- Fails to incorporate the time value of money
- Does not consider a project's cash flows after the payback period

1b.
Project A

Outflow, $200,000
Inflow, $50,000 (Year 1) + $50,000 (Year 2) + $50,000 (Year 3) + $50,000 (Year 4)

Payback = 4 years

21-22 (Cont'd.)

Project B

Outflow, $190,000

Inflow, $40,000 (Year 1) + $50,000 (Year 2) + $70,000 (Year 3) + $\dfrac{\$30,000}{\$75,000}$

Payback $= 3 + \dfrac{\$30,000}{\$75,000} = 3.4$ years

Project C

Outflow, $250,000

Inflow, $75,000 (Year 1) + $75,000 (Year 2) + $60,000 (Year 3) + $\dfrac{\$40,000}{\$80,000}$

Payback $= 3 + \dfrac{\$40,000}{\$80,000} = 3.5$ years

Project D

Outflow, $210,000
Inflow, $75,000(Year 1) + $75,000(Year 2) + $60,000(Year 3)

Payback $= 3$ years

2. Solution Exhibit 21-22 shows the following ranking:

	NPV
1. Project C	$27,050
2. Project B	$25,635
3. Project D	$(3,750)
4. Project A	$(19,750)

3. Using NPV, Projects C and B both have positive NPVs and require investment of $250,000 + $190,000 = $440,000 which is less than the $500,000 capital that Cording can raise. Hence, Cording should fund both Projects B and C. Both projects have sizable cash inflows after the payback period. Nonfinancial qualitative factors should also be considered. For example, are there differential worker safety issues across the projects? Are there differences in the extent of learning that can benefit other projects? Are there differences in the customer relationships established with different projects that can benefit Cording Manufacturing in future projects?

21-22 (Cont'd.)

SOLUTION EXHIBIT 21-22

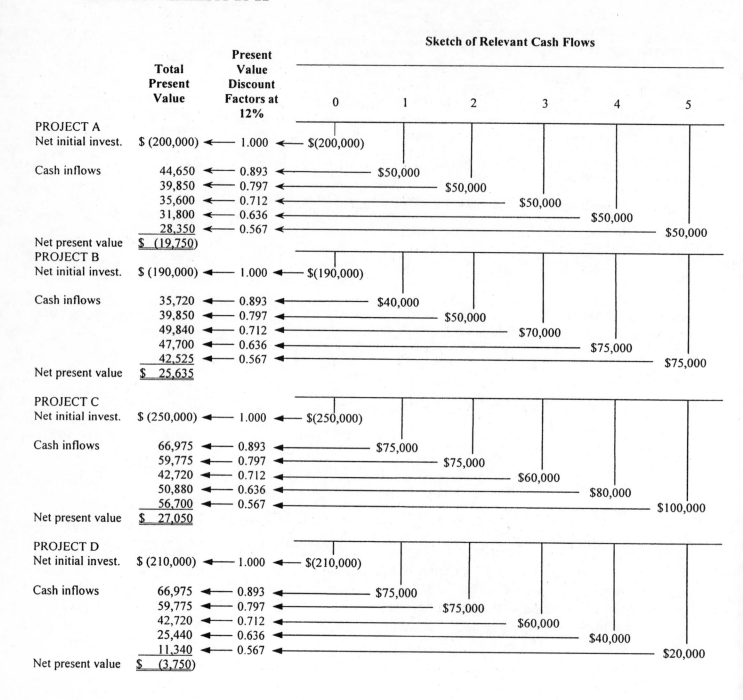

	Total Present Value	Present Value Discount Factors at 12%	Sketch of Relevant Cash Flows					
			0	1	2	3	4	5
PROJECT A								
Net initial invest.	$ (200,000) ◄— 1.000 ◄—		$(200,000)					
Cash inflows	44,650 ◄— 0.893 ◄—			$50,000				
	39,850 ◄— 0.797 ◄—				$50,000			
	35,600 ◄— 0.712 ◄—					$50,000		
	31,800 ◄— 0.636 ◄—						$50,000	
	28,350 ◄— 0.567 ◄—							$50,000
Net present value	$ (19,750)							
PROJECT B								
Net initial invest.	$ (190,000) ◄— 1.000 ◄—		$(190,000)					
Cash inflows	35,720 ◄— 0.893 ◄—			$40,000				
	39,850 ◄— 0.797 ◄—				$50,000			
	49,840 ◄— 0.712 ◄—					$70,000		
	47,700 ◄— 0.636 ◄—						$75,000	
	42,525 ◄— 0.567 ◄—							$75,000
Net present value	$ 25,635							
PROJECT C								
Net initial invest.	$ (250,000) ◄— 1.000 ◄—		$(250,000)					
Cash inflows	66,975 ◄— 0.893 ◄—			$75,000				
	59,775 ◄— 0.797 ◄—				$75,000			
	42,720 ◄— 0.712 ◄—					$60,000		
	50,880 ◄— 0.636 ◄—						$80,000	
	56,700 ◄— 0.567 ◄—							$100,000
Net present value	$ 27,050							
PROJECT D								
Net initial invest.	$ (210,000) ◄— 1.000 ◄—		$(210,000)					
Cash inflows	66,975 ◄— 0.893 ◄—			$75,000				
	59,775 ◄— 0.797 ◄—				$75,000			
	42,720 ◄— 0.712 ◄—					$60,000		
	25,440 ◄— 0.636 ◄—						$40,000	
	11,340 ◄— 0.567 ◄—							$20,000
Net present value	$ (3,750)							

21-24 (40 min.) **New equipment purchase, income taxes.**

1. The after-tax cash inflow per year is $80,000 ($60,000 + $20,000)

Annual cash-operating cost savings	$100,000
Deduct income taxes (0.40 × $100,000)	40,000
Annual after-tax cash-operating cost savings	$ 60,000

Annual depreciation on machine	
[($230,000 – $30,000) ÷ 4]	$ 50,000
Income tax cash savings (0.40 × $50,000)	20,000

a. Solution Exhibit 21-24A reports the NPV computation. NPV = $32,120

b. $\text{Payback} = \dfrac{\$230,000}{\$80,000} = 2.88 \text{ years}$

Solution Exhibits 21-24B and 21-24C report the net present value of the project using 18% and 20%
By interpolation:

$$\text{Internal rate of return} = 18\% + \left[\frac{680}{680 + 8,500}\right] \times 2\%$$
$$= 18.15\%$$

2. Both the net present value and internal rate of return methods use a discounted cash flow approach in which *all* expected future cash inflows and cash outflows of a project are measured as if they occurred at a single point in time. The payback method considers only cash flows up to the time when the expected future cash inflows recoup the net initial investment in a project. The payback method ignores profitability. However, the payback method is becoming increasingly more important in the global economy. When the local environment in an international location is unstable and, therefore, highly risky for a potential investment, a company would likely pay close attention to the payback period for making its investment decision. In general, the more unstable the environment, the shorter the payback period desired.

21-24 (Cont'd.)

SOLUTION EXHIBIT 21-24A

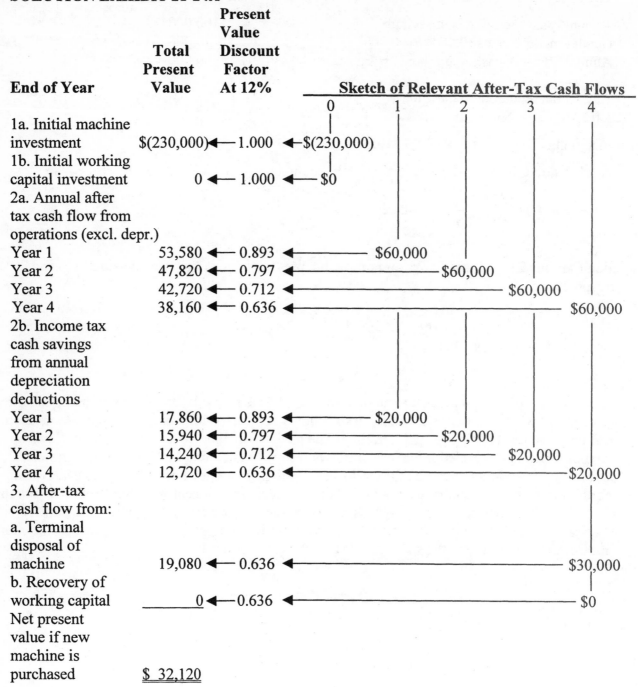

End of Year	Total Present Value	Present Value Discount Factor At 12%	Sketch of Relevant After-Tax Cash Flows
			0 1 2 3 4
1a. Initial machine investment	$(230,000) ◄— 1.000 ◄—$(230,000)		
1b. Initial working capital investment	0 ◄— 1.000 ◄— $0		
2a. Annual after tax cash flow from operations (excl. depr.)			
Year 1	53,580 ◄— 0.893 ◄——— $60,000		
Year 2	47,820 ◄— 0.797 ◄———————— $60,000		
Year 3	42,720 ◄— 0.712 ◄————————————— $60,000		
Year 4	38,160 ◄— 0.636 ◄—————————————————— $60,000		
2b. Income tax cash savings from annual depreciation deductions			
Year 1	17,860 ◄— 0.893 ◄——— $20,000		
Year 2	15,940 ◄— 0.797 ◄———————— $20,000		
Year 3	14,240 ◄— 0.712 ◄————————————— $20,000		
Year 4	12,720 ◄— 0.636 ◄—————————————————— $20,000		
3. After-tax cash flow from:			
a. Terminal disposal of machine	19,080 ◄— 0.636 ◄—————————————————— $30,000		
b. Recovery of working capital	0 ◄—0.636 ◄—————————————————— $0		
Net present value if new machine is purchased	$ 32,120		

21-8

21-24 (Cont'd.)

SOLUTION EXHIBIT 21-24B

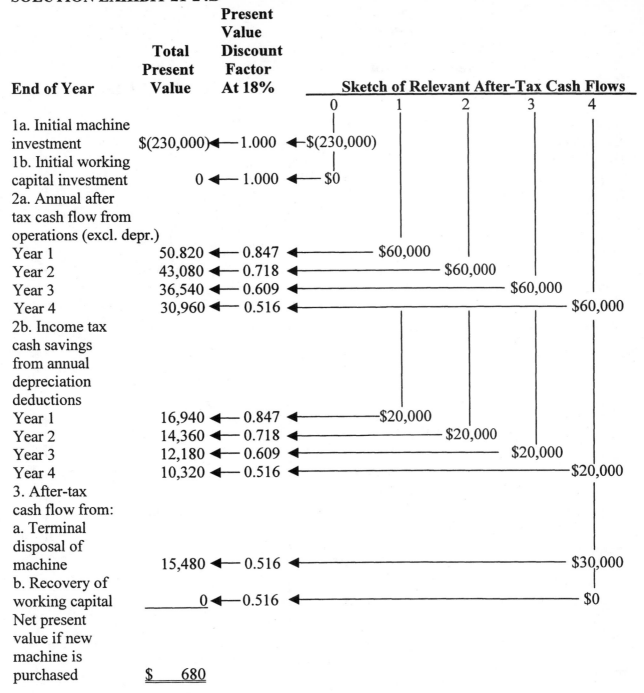

End of Year	Total Present Value	Present Value Discount Factor At 18%	Sketch of Relevant After-Tax Cash Flows
			0 1 2 3 4
1a. Initial machine investment	$(230,000) ← 1.000 ← $(230,000)		
1b. Initial working capital investment	0 ← 1.000 ← $0		
2a. Annual after tax cash flow from operations (excl. depr.)			
Year 1	50.820 ← 0.847 ←		$60,000
Year 2	43,080 ← 0.718 ←		$60,000
Year 3	36,540 ← 0.609 ←		$60,000
Year 4	30,960 ← 0.516 ←		$60,000
2b. Income tax cash savings from annual depreciation deductions			
Year 1	16,940 ← 0.847 ←		$20,000
Year 2	14,360 ← 0.718 ←		$20,000
Year 3	12,180 ← 0.609 ←		$20,000
Year 4	10,320 ← 0.516 ←		$20,000
3. After-tax cash flow from:			
a. Terminal disposal of machine	15,480 ← 0.516 ←		$30,000
b. Recovery of working capital	0 ← 0.516 ←		$0
Net present value if new machine is purchased	$ 680		

21-24 (Cont'd.)

SOLUTION EXHIBIT 21-24C

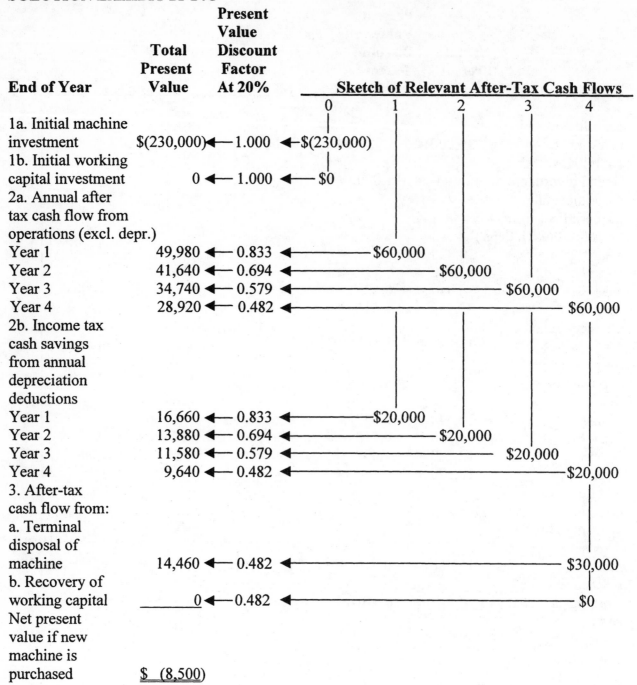

End of Year	Total Present Value	Present Value Discount Factor At 20%	Sketch of Relevant After-Tax Cash Flows
			0 1 2 3 4
1a. Initial machine investment	$(230,000)	← 1.000	← $(230,000)
1b. Initial working capital investment	0	← 1.000	← $0
2a. Annual after tax cash flow from operations (excl. depr.)			
Year 1	49,980	← 0.833	← $60,000 (yr 1)
Year 2	41,640	← 0.694	← $60,000 (yr 2)
Year 3	34,740	← 0.579	← $60,000 (yr 3)
Year 4	28,920	← 0.482	← $60,000 (yr 4)
2b. Income tax cash savings from annual depreciation deductions			
Year 1	16,660	← 0.833	← $20,000 (yr 1)
Year 2	13,880	← 0.694	← $20,000 (yr 2)
Year 3	11,580	← 0.579	← $20,000 (yr 3)
Year 4	9,640	← 0.482	← $20,000 (yr 4)
3. After-tax cash flow from:			
a. Terminal disposal of machine	14,460	← 0.482	← $30,000 (yr 4)
b. Recovery of working capital	0	← 0.482	← $0 (yr 4)
Net present value if new machine is purchased	$ (8,500)		

21-26 (60 min.) **Selling a plant, income taxes** (CMA, adapted).

1. *Option 1*

Current disposal price	$9,000,000
Deduct current book value	0
Gain on disposal	9,000,000
Deduct 40% taxes	3,600,000
Net present value	$5,400,000

Option 2

Waterford receives three sources of cash inflows:

    a. Rent. Four annual payments of $2,400,000. The after-tax cash inflow is:

$$\$2,400,000 \times (1 - 0.40) = \$1,440,000 \text{ per year}$$

    Discount on material purchases, payable at year-end for each of the four years: $474,000

    b. The after-tax cash inflow is:

$$\$474,000 \times (1 - 0.40) = \$284,400$$

    c. Sale of plant at year-end 2006. The after-tax cash inflow is:

$$\$2,000,000 \times (1 - 0.40) = \$1,200,000$$

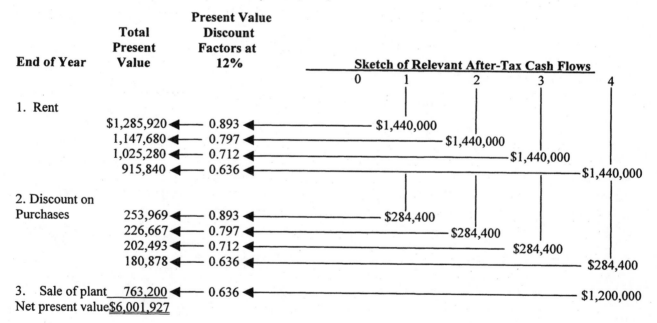

21-26 (Cont'd.)

Option 3

Contribution margin per jacket:

Selling price	$42.00
Variable costs	33.00
Contribution margin	$ 9.00

	2003	2004	2005	2006
Contribution margin $9.00 × 200,000; 300,000; 400,000; 100,000	$1,800,000	$2,700,000	$3,600,000	$900,000
Fixed overhead (cash) costs	200,000	200,000	200,000	200,000
Operating income before depreciation	1,600,000	2,500,000	3,400,000	700,000
Income taxes (40%)	640,000	1,000,000	1,360,000	280,000
Net cash inflow	$ 960,000	$1,500,000	$2,040,000	$420,000

Depreciation:

$$\$1,500,000 \div 4 = \$375,000 \text{ per year}$$

Income tax cash savings from depreciation deduction:

$$\$375,000 \times 0.40 = \$150,000 \text{ per year}$$

Sale of plant at end of 2006:

$$\$3,000,000 \times (1 - 0.40) = \$1,800,000$$

Solution Exhibit 21-26 presents the NPV calculations.

21-26 (Cont'd.)

SOLUTION EXHIBIT 21-26

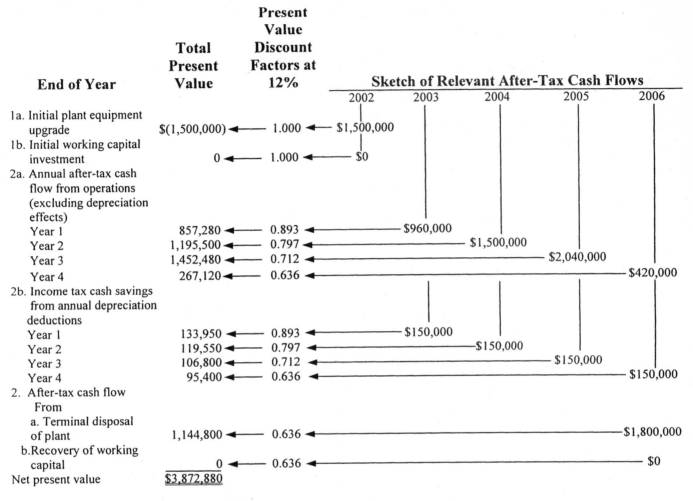

End of Year	Total Present Value	Present Value Discount Factors at 12%	Sketch of Relevant After-Tax Cash Flows				
			2002	2003	2004	2005	2006
1a. Initial plant equipment upgrade	$(1,500,000) ◄— 1.000 ◄—		$1,500,000				
1b. Initial working capital investment	0 ◄— 1.000 ◄—		$0				
2a. Annual after-tax cash flow from operations (excluding depreciation effects)							
Year 1	857,280 ◄— 0.893 ◄—			$960,000			
Year 2	1,195,500 ◄— 0.797 ◄—				$1,500,000		
Year 3	1,452,480 ◄— 0.712 ◄—					$2,040,000	
Year 4	267,120 ◄— 0.636 ◄—						$420,000
2b. Income tax cash savings from annual depreciation deductions							
Year 1	133,950 ◄— 0.893 ◄—			$150,000			
Year 2	119,550 ◄— 0.797 ◄—				$150,000		
Year 3	106,800 ◄— 0.712 ◄—					$150,000	
Year 4	95,400 ◄— 0.636 ◄—						$150,000
2. After-tax cash flow From							
a. Terminal disposal of plant	1,144,800 ◄— 0.636 ◄—						$1,800,000
b. Recovery of working capital	0 ◄— 0.636 ◄—						$0
Net present value	$3,872,880						

2. Option 2 has the highest NPV:

	NPV
Option 1	$5,400,000
Option 2	$6,001,927
Option 3	$3,872,880

Option 1 gives Waterford immediate liquidity which it can use for other projects.

Option 2 has the advantage of Waterford having a closer relationship with the supplier. However, it limits Waterford's flexibility if Auburn Mill's quality is not comparable to competitors.

Option 3 has Waterford entering a new line of business. If this line of business is successful, could be expanded to cover souvenir jackets for other major events. The risks of selling the predict number of jackets should also be considered.

21-28 (40 min.) **Equipment replacement, income taxes**
(continuation of 21-27).

1. & 2. Income tax rate = 30%

Modernize Alternative

Annual depreciation:
$28,000,000 ÷ 7 years = $4,000,000 a year.

Income tax cash savings from annual depreciation deductions:
$4,000,000 × 0.30 = $1,200,000 a year.

Terminal disposal of equipment = $5,000,000.

After-tax cash flow from terminal disposal:
$5,000,000 × 0.70 = $3,500,000.

The NPV components are:

		NPV
1. Initial investment:		
$(28,000,000) × 1.000		$(28,000,000)

2a. Annual after-tax cash flow from operations
(excluding depreciation):

Dec. 31, 2004	8,280,000 × 0.70 × 0.893	5,175,828
2005	9,180,000 × 0.70 × 0.797	5,121,522
2006	10,080,000 × 0.70 × 0.712	5,023,872
2007	10,980,000 × 0.70 × 0.636	4,888,296
2008	11,880,000 × 0.70 × 0.567	4,715,172
2009	12,780,000 × 0.70 × 0.507	4,535,622
2010	13,680,000 × 0.70 × 0.452	4,328,352

2b. Income tax cash savings from annual depreciation
deductions (annuity of $1,200,000 for 7 years):

$1,200,000 × 4.564		5,476,800

3. After-tax cash flow from terminal sale of
equipment:

$3,500,000 × 0.452		1,582,000

Net present value	$ 12,847,464

21-28 (Cont'd.)

Replace alternative

Initial machine replacement = $49,000,000

Sale in Jan. 1, 2004, of equipment = $3,000,000

After-tax cash flow from sale:
$3,000,000 × 0.70 = $2,100,000

Net after-tax initial investment
$49,000,000 − $2,100,000 = $46,900,000

Annual depreciation
$49,000,000 ÷ 7 years = $7,000,000 a year

Income-tax cash savings from annual depreciation deductions
$7,000,000 × 0.30 = $2,100,000

Terminal disposal of equipment = $12,000,000

After-tax cash flow from terminal disposal
$12,000,000 × 0.70 = $8,400,000

21-28 (Cont'd.)

The NPV components are:
1. Net after-tax initial investment
   $$\$(46,900,000) \times 1.000 \qquad\qquad \$(46,900,000)$$

2a. Annual after-tax cash flow from operations (excluding depreciation)

Dec. 31,			
	2004	$11,040,000 × 0.70 × 0.893	6,901,104
	2005	12,240,000 × 0.70 × 0.797	6,828,696
	2006	13,440,000 × 0.70 × 0.712	6,698,496
	2007	14,640,000 × 0.70 × 0.636	6,517,728
	2008	15,840,000 × 0.70 × 0.567	6,286,896
	2009	17,040,000 × 0.70 × 0.507	6,047,496
	2010	18,240,000 × 0.70 × 0.452	5,771,136

2b. Income tax cash savings from annual depreciation deductions
(annuity of $2,100,000 for 7 years)
$$\$2,100,000 \times 4.564 \qquad\qquad 9,584,400$$

3. After-tax cash flow from terminal sale of equipment
$$\$8,400,000 \times 0.452 \qquad\qquad \underline{3,796,800}$$

Net present value $\qquad\qquad \underline{\underline{\$11,532,752}}$

3. Superfast would prefer to:

   a. have lower tax rates,
   b. have revenue exempt from taxation,
   c. recognize taxable revenues in later years rather than earlier years,
   d. recognize taxable cost deductions greater than actual outlay costs, and
   e. recognize cost deductions in earlier years rather than later years (including accelerated amounts in earlier years).

21-30 (40 min.) **NPV and customer profitability, no income taxes.**

1.

Homebuilders	2003	2004	2005	2006	2007	2008
Revenues (5%)*	$45,000	$47,250	$49,612	$52,093	$54,698	$57,433
COGS (4%)*	22,000	22,880	23,795	24,747	25,737	26,766
Op. Costs (4%)*	10,000	10,400	10,816	11,249	11,699	12,167
Total costs	32,000	33,280	34,611	35,996	37,436	38,933
Cash flow from operations	$13,000	$13,970	$15,001	$16,097	$17,262	$18,500
Kitchen Constructors						
Revenues (6%)*	$325,000	$344,500	$365,170	$387,080	$410,305	$434,923
COGS (4%)*	180,000	187,200	194,688	202,476	210,575	218,998
Op. Costs (4%)*	75,000	78,000	81,120	84,365	87,739	91,249
Total costs	255,000	265,200	275,808	286,841	298,314	310,247
Cash flow from operations	$ 70,000	$ 79,300	$ 89,362	$100,239	$111,991	$124,676
Subdivision Erectors						
Revenues (8%)*	$860,000	$928,800	$1,003,104	$1,083,352	$1,170,020	$1,263,622
COGS (4%)*	550,000	572,000	594,880	618,675	643,422	669,159
Op. Costs (4%)*	235,000	244,400	254,176	264,343	274,917	285,914
Total costs	785,000	816,400	849,056	883,018	918,339	955,073
Cash flow from operations	$ 75,000	$112,400	$ 154,048	$ 200,334	$ 251,681	$ 308,549

* Annual increases given in question.

2.

		Homebuilders		Kitchen Constructors		Subdivision Erectors	
Year	P.V. Factor for 10%	Cash Flow from Operations	Present Value	Cash Flow from Operations	Present Value	Cash Flow from Operations	Present Value
2004	0.909	$13,970	$12,699	$79,300	$ 72,084	$112,400	$102,172
2005	0.826	15,001	12,391	89,362	73,813	154,048	127,244
2006	0.751	16,097	12,089	100,239	75,279	200,334	150,451
2007	0.683	17,262	11,790	111,991	76,490	251,681	171,898
2008	0.621	18,500	11,488	124,676	77,424	308,549	191,609
			$60,457		$375,090		$743,374

21-30 (Cont'd.)

Customer NPVs

Homebuilders	$ 60,457
Kitchen Constructors	375,088
Subdivision Erectors	743,374

3. Assuming a 20% discount on revenues for Kitchen Constructors calculated in requirement 1, we have

	2003	2004	2005	2006	2007	2008
Revenues (5%)	$325,000	$275,600	$292,136	$309,664	$328,244	$347,938
Total costs (4%)	255,000	265,200	275,808	286,841	298,314	310,247
Cash flow from operations	$ 70,000	$ 10,400	$ 16,328	$ 22,823	$ 29,930	$ 37,691

Net present value:

Year	P.V. Factor at 10%	Cash Flow from Operations	Present Value
2004	0.909	$10,400	$ 9,454
2005	0.826	16,328	13,487
2006	0.751	22,823	17,140
2007	0.683	29,930	20,442
2008	0.621	37,691	23,406
			$83,929

The 20% discount and reduced subsequent annual revenue reduces the NPV from $375,090 to $83,929. This is a drop of $291,161 in NPV.

Christen should consider whether the price discount demanded by Kitchen need be met in full to keep the account. The implication of meeting the full demand is that the account is minimally profitable. A serious concern is whether Christen's other two customers will demand comparable price discounts if Kitchen's full demands are met. The consequence would be very large reductions in the NPVs of all its customers.

Christen should also consider the reliability of the growth estimates used in computing the NPVs. Are the predicted differences in revenue growth rates based on reliable information? Many revenue growth estimates by salespeople turn out to be overestimates or occur over a longer time period than initially predicted.

21-32 (40 min.) **Replacement of a machine, income taxes, sensitivity** (CMA, adapted).

1. WRL Company should retain the old equipment because the net present value of the incremental cash flows is negative. The computations are presented below. In this format the present value factors appear at the bottom. All cash flows, year by year, are then converted into present values.

	After-Tax Cash Flows				
	2002[a]	2003	2004	2005	2006
Initial machine investment	$(120,000)				
Current disposal price of old machine	40,000				
Tax savings from loss on disposal of old machine[b]	4,000				
Recurring after-tax cash-operating savings:					
Variable ($0.06 × 300,000 × 0.6)[c]		$10,800	$10,800	$10,800	$10,800
Fixed ($1,000 × 0.6)[d]		600	600	600	600
Difference in income tax cash savings from depreciation deductions[e]		6,000	6,000	6,000	6,000
Additional after-tax cash flow from terminal disposal of new machine over old machine ($20,000 − $8,200)[f]					11,800
Net after-tax cash flows	$ (76,000)	$17,400	$17,400	$17,400	$29,200
Present value discount factors	1.000	0.862	0.743	0.641	0.552
Present value	$ (76,000)	$14,999	$12,928	$11,153	$16,118
Net present value	$ (20,802)				

a. Actually January 1, 2003

b.
Original cost of old machine:	$80,000
Depreciation taken during the first 3 years {[(80,000 − 10,000) ÷ 7] × 3}	30,000
Book value	50,000
Current disposal price:	40,000
Loss on disposal	$10,000
Tax rate	× 0.40
Tax savings from loss on disposal of old machine	$ 4,000

21-32 (Cont'd.)

c. Difference in recurring after-tax variable cash-operating savings, with 40% tax rate:
   ($0.20 – $0.14) × (300,000) × (1– 0.40) = $10,800

d. Difference in after-tax fixed cost savings, with 40% tax rate:
   ($15,000 – $14,000) × (1 – 0.40) = $600

e.

	Old Machine	New Machine
Initial machine investment	$80,000	$120,000
Terminal disposal price at end of useful life	10,000	20,000
Depreciable base	$70,000	$100,000
Annual depreciation using straight-line (7-year life)	$10,000	
Annual depreciation using straight-line (4-year life):		$ 25,000

Year (1)	Depreciation on Old Machine (2)	Depreciation on New Machine (3)	Additional Depreciation Deductions on New Machine (4) = (3) – (2)	Income Tax Cash Savings from Difference in Depreciation Deductions at 40% (4) × 40%
2003	$10,000	$25,000	$15,000	$6,000
2004	10,000	25,000	15,000	6,000
2005	10,000	25,000	15,000	6,000
2006	10,000	25,000	15,000	6,000

f.

	Old Machine	New Machine
Original cost	$80,000	$120,000
Total depreciation	70,000	100,000
Book value of machines on Dec. 31, 2006	10,000	20,000
Terminal disposal price of machines on Dec. 31, 2006	7,000	20,000
Loss on disposal of machines	3,000	0
Add tax savings on loss (40% of $3,000; 40% of $0)	1,200	0
After-tax cash flow from terminal disposal of machines ($7,000 + $1,200; $20,000 – $0)	$ 8,200	$ 20,000

Additional after-tax cash flow from terminal disposal of machines: $20,000 – $8,200 = $11,800.

2.	Let the *additional* recurring after-tax variable cash operating savings required to make NPV = $0 be $X each year.

> The present value of an annuity of $1 per year for 4 years discounted at 16% = 2.798 (Appendix C, Table 4)
> To make NPV = 0, we need to generate cash savings with NPV of $20,802.
> That is	$X (2.798)	=	$20,802
> 	X	=	20,802 ÷ 2.798 = $7,435

WRL must generate additional annual after-tax cash operating savings of $7,435.

3.	The nonquantitative factors that are important to WRL Company's decision include the following:

    a.	The lower operating costs (variable and fixed) of the new machine would enable WRL to meet future competitive or inflationary pressures to a greater degree than it could using the old machine.

    b.	If the increased efficiency of the new machine provides a labor or energy cost savings, then additional increases in these costs in the future would make the new machine more attractive.

    c.	Maintenance and servicing of both machines should be reviewed in terms of reliability of the manufacturer and the costs.

    d.	Potential technological advances in machinery over the next four years should be evaluated.

    e.	Space requirements for the new machine should be reviewed and compared with the space requirements of the present equipment to determine if more or less space is required.

21-34 (40 min.) **Ethics, capital budgeting** (CMA, adapted).

1a. Refer to the specific standards of competence, confidentiality, integrity, and objectivity in "Standards of Ethical Conduct for Management Accountants," (Chapter 1, p. 18) George Watson's conduct in giving Helen Dodge specific instructions on preparing the second revision of the proposal is unethical because his conduct violates the following specific standards.

Competence

Watson has the responsibility to perform his professional duties in accordance with relevant technical standards, such as using conservatism and realistic estimates in the net present value analysis. Management accountants should prepare complete and clear reports and recommendations after appropriate analyses of relevant and reliable information.

Confidentiality

Watson should refrain from using or appearing to use confidential information acquired in the course of his work for unethical advantage or personal gain (saving on commuting time and costs).

Integrity

Watson has the responsibility to advise all parties of any potential conflict of interest. Watson should communicate unfavorable as well as favorable information and professional judgments and opinions.

Objectivity

Watson has the responsibility to disclose fully all relevant information that can influence an intended user's understanding of the analysis.

1b. Helen Dodge's revised proposal for the warehouse conversion is unethical because her actions violate the following standards.

Competence

Although the estimates used in the analysis are based on management's judgment, Dodge's action in changing reasonable estimates to assumptions that are less likely to occur is unethical. Management accountants have the responsibility to prepare complete and clear reports and recommendations after appropriate analysis of relevant and reliable information.

Instructors may wish to comment on the low value of historical cost-based depreciation deductions when there is inflation. These depreciation deductions are based on the original cost of the asset and equal $2,000 each year which when discounted at the inflation-adjusted nominal rate of 32% yield a low present value. This leads to a negative NPV for the project.

Integrity

Dodge has the responsibility to avoid conflicts of interest, refrain from subverting the attainment of the organization's legitimate and ethical objectives (profitability), and refrain from engaging in or supporting any activity that would discredit the profession.

Objectivity

Dodge has the responsibility to communicate information fairly and objectively and to disclose fully, all relevant information that can influence an intended user's understanding.

2. Steps that Helen Dodge should follow in attempting to resolve this situation are as follows:

- Dodge should first investigate and see if Evans Company has an established policy for resolving conflict, and she should follow this policy if it does exist.
- Since it appears that George Watson, Dodge's superior, is involved, there is no need to confront Watson or discuss this issue with him any further. Dodge should present the situation to the next higher level, the vice president of finance, for resolution.
- If the issue is not resolved to Dodge's satisfaction, she should continue to successive higher levels, including the Audit Committee and the Board of Directors.
- Dodge should clarify the concepts of the issue at hand in a confidential discussion with an objective advisor, i.e., a peer.
- If the situation is still unresolved after exhausting all levels of internal review, Dodge will have no recourse but to resign and submit an informative memorandum to an appropriate representative of the organization.
- Unless legally bound (which does not appear to be the case in this situation), it is inappropriate to have communication about this situation with authorities and individuals not employed or engaged by the organization.

CHAPTER 22
MANAGEMENT CONTROL SYSTEMS, TRANSFER PRICING,
AND MULTINATIONAL CONSIDERATIONS

22-2   To be effective, management control systems should be (a) closely aligned to an organization's strategies and goals, (b) designed to fit the organization's structure and the decision-making responsibility of individual managers, and (c) able to motivate managers and employees to put in effort to attain selected goals desired by top management.

22-4   The chapter cites five benefits of decentralization:
1.   Creates greater responsiveness to local needs
2.   Leads to gains from faster decision making
3.   Increases motivation of subunit managers
4.   Aids management development and learning
5.   Sharpens the focus of subunit managers

   The chapter cites four costs of decentralization:
1.   Leads to suboptimal decision making
2.   Results in duplication of activities
3.   Focuses managers' attention on the subunit rather than the company as a whole
4.   Increases costs of gathering information

22-6   No. A transfer price is the price one subunit of an organization charges for a product or service supplied to another subunit of the same organization. The two segments can be cost centers, profit centers, or investment centers. For example, the allocation of service department costs to production departments that are set up as either cost centers or investment centers is an example of transfer pricing.

22-8   Transfer prices should have the following properties. They should
1.   promote goal congruence,
2.   be useful for evaluating subunit performance,
3.   motivate management effort, and
4.   preserve a high level of subunit autonomy in decision making.

22-10 Transferring products or services at market prices generally leads to optimal decisions when (a) the market for the intermediate product market is perfectly competitive, (b) interdependencies of subunits are minimal, and (c) there are no additional costs or benefits to the company as a whole from buying or selling in the external market instead of transacting internally.

22-12 Reasons why a dual-pricing approach to transfer pricing is not widely used in practice include:
1. The manager of the supplying division uses a cost-based method to record revenues and does not have sufficient incentives to control costs.
2. This approach does not provide clear signals to division managers about the level of decentralization top management wants.
3. This approach tends to insulate managers from the frictions of the marketplace because costs, not market prices, affect the revenues of the supplying division.
4. It leads to problems in computing the taxable income of subunits located in different tax jurisdictions.

22-14 Yes. The general transfer-pricing guideline specifies that the minimum transfer price equals the additional *outlay costs* per unit incurred up to the point of transfer *plus* the *opportunity costs* per unit to the supplying division. When the supplying division has idle capacity, its opportunity costs are zero; when the supplying division has no idle capacity, its opportunity costs are positive. Hence, the minimum transfer price will vary depending on whether the supplying division has idle capacity or not.

22-16 (25 min.) **Decentralization, responsibility centers**.

1. The manufacturing plants in the Manufacturing Division are cost centers. Senior management determines the manufacturing schedule based on the quantity of each type of lighting product specified by the sales and marketing division and detailed studies of the time and cost to manufacture each type of product. Manufacturing managers are accountable only for costs. They are evaluated based on achieving target output within budgeted costs.

2a. If manufacturing and marketing managers were to directly negotiate the prices for manufacturing various products, Quinn should evaluate manufacturing plant managers as profit centers—revenues received from marketing minus the costs incurred to produce and sell output.

2b. Quinn Corporation would be better off decentralizing its marketing and manufacturing decisions and evaluating each division as a profit center. Decentralization would encourage plant managers to increase total output to achieve the greatest profitability, and motivate plant managers to cut their costs to increase margins. Manufacturing managers would be motivated to design their operations according to the criteria that meet the marketing managers' approval, thereby improving cooperation between manufacturing and marketing.
   Under Quinn's existing system, manufacturing managers had every incentive not to improve. Manufacturing managers' incentives were to get as high a cost target as possible so that they could produce output within budgeted costs. Any significant improvements could result in the target costs being lowered for the next year, increasing the possibility of not achieving budgeted costs. By the same line of reasoning, manufacturing managers would also try to limit their production so that production quotas would not be increased in the future. Decentralizing manufacturing and marketing decisions overcomes these problems.

22-18 (35 min.) Multinational transfer pricing, effect of alternative transfer-pricing methods, global income tax minimization.

1.   This is a three-country, three-division transfer-pricing problem with three alternative transfer-pricing methods. Summary data in U.S. dollars are:

China Plant

Variable costs:	1,000 Yuan ÷ 8 Yuan per $ = $125 per subunit
Fixed costs:	1,800 Yuan ÷ 8 Yuan per $ = $225 per subunit

South Korea Plant

Variable costs:	360,000 Won ÷ 1,200 Won per $ = $300 per unit
Fixed costs:	480,000 Won ÷ 1,200 Won per $ = $400 per unit

U.S. Plant

Variable costs:	= $100 per unit
Fixed costs:	= $200 per unit

Market prices for private-label sale alternatives:

China Plant:	3,600 Yuan ÷ 8 Yuan per $ = $450 per subunit
South Korea Plant:	1,560,000 Won ÷ 1,200 Won per $ = $1,300 per unit

The transfer prices under each method are:

a.   Market price
- China to South Korea = $450 per subunit
- South Korea to U.S. Plant = $1,300 per unit

b.   200% of full costs
- China to South Korea
    2.0 × ($125 + $225) = $700 per subunit
- South Korea to U.S. Plant
    2.0 × ($700 + $300 + $400) = $2,800 per unit

c.   300% of variable costs
- China to South Korea
    3.0 × $125 = $375 per subunit
- South Korea to U.S. Plant
    3.0 × ($375 + $300) = $2,025 per unit

22-18 (Cont'd.)

	Method A Internal Transfers at Market Price	Method B Internal Transfers at 200% of Full Costs	Method C Internal Transfers at 300% of Variable Costs
1. China Division			
Division revenue per unit	$ 450	$ 700	$ 375
Deduct:			
Division variable cost per unit	125	125	125
Division fixed cost per unit	225	225	225
Division operating income per unit	100	350	25
Income tax at 40%	40	140	10
Division net income per unit	$ 60	$ 210	$ 15
2. South Korea Division			
Division revenue per unit	$1,300	$2,800	$2,025
Deduct:			
Transferred-in cost per unit	450	700	375
Division variable cost per unit	300	300	300
Division fixed cost per unit	400	400	400
Division operating income per unit	150	1,400	950
Income tax at 20%	30	280	190
Division net income per unit	$ 120	$1,120	$ 760
3. United States Division			
Division revenue per unit	$3,200	$3,200	$3,200
Deduct:			
Transferred-in cost per unit	1,300	2,800	2,025
Division variable cost per unit	100	100	100
Division fixed cost per unit	200	200	200
Division operating income per unit	1,600	100	875
Income tax at 30%	480	30	262.5
Division net income per unit	$1,120	$ 70	$ 612.5

2. Division net income:

	Market Price	200% of Full Costs	300% of Variable Cost
China Division	$ 60	$ 210	$ 15.00
South Korea Division	120	1,120	760.00
U.S. Division	1,120	70	612.50
User Friendly Computer Inc.	$1,300	$1,400	$1,387.50

22-4

22-18 (Cont'd.)

User Friendly will maximize its net income by using the 200% of full costs, transfer-pricing method. This is because the 200% of full cost method sources most income in the countries with the lower income tax rates.

22-18 Excel Application
User Friendly Computer, Inc.

Original Data

U.S. $ per yuan	0.125	
U.S. $ per won	0.00083	

China Division

Price per memory/keyboard package	3,600	yuan
Variable costs	1,000	yuan
Fixed costs	1,800	yuan
Income tax rate	40%	

South Korea Division

Price per computer	1,560,000	won
Variable costs	360,000	won
Fixed costs	480,000	won
Income tax rate	20%	

U.S. Division

Price per computer	$3,200
Variable costs	$100
Fixed costs	$200
Income tax rate	30%

22-18 (Cont'd.)

Problem 1

	Method A: Internal Transfers at Market Price	Method B: Internal Transfers at 200% of Full Costs	Method C: Internal Transfers at 300% of Variable Costs
China Division			
Division revenues per unit	$450	$700	$375
Deduct:			
Division variable costs per unit	125	125	125
Division fixed costs per unit	225	225	225
Division operating income per unit	100	350	25
Income tax	40	140	10
Division net income per unit	$ 60	$210	$ 15
South Korea Division			
Division revenues per unit	$1,300	$2,800	$2,025
Deduct:			
Transferred in costs per unit	450	700	375
Division variable costs per unit	300	300	300
Division fixed costs per unit	400	400	400
Division operating income per unit	150	1,400	950
Income tax	30	280	190
Division net income per unit	$ 120	$1,120	$ 760
United States Division			
Division revenues per unit	$3,200	$3,200	$3,200
Deduct:			
Transferred in costs per unit	1,300	2,800	2,025
Division variable costs per unit	100	100	100
Division fixed costs per unit	200	200	200
Division operating income per unit	1,600	100	875
Income tax	480	30	262.50
Division net income per unit	$1,120	$ 70	$612.50

Problem 2

Division Net Income	Market Price	200% of Full Costs	300% of Variable Costs
China Divison	$60	$210	$15
South Korea Division	$120	$1,120	$760
U.S. Division	$1,120	$70	$612.50
User Friendly Computer, Inc.	$1,300	$1,400	$1,387.50

22-20 (30 min.) **Effect of alternative transfer-pricing methods on division operating income.**

	Internal Transfers at Market Prices Method A	Internal Transfers at 110% of Full Costs Method B
1. *Mining Division*		
Revenues:		
$90, $66[1] × 400,000 units	$36,000,000	$26,400,000
Deduct:		
Division variable costs:		
$52[2] × 400,000 units	20,800,000	20,800,000
Division fixed costs:		
$8[3] × 400,000 units	3,200,000	3,200,000
Division operating income	$12,000,000	$ 2,400,000
Metals Division		
Revenues:		
$150 × 400,000 units	$60,000,000	$60,000,000
Deduct:		
Transferred-in costs:		
$90, $66 × 400,000 units	36,000,000	26,400,000
Division variable costs:		
$36[4] × 400,000 units	14,400,000	14,400,000
Division fixed costs:		
$15[5] × 400,000 units	6,000,000	6,000,000
Division operating income	$ 3,600,000	$13,200,000

[1] $66 = $60 × 110%

[2] Variable cost per unit in Mining Division = Direct materials + Direct manufacturing labor + 75% of Manufacturing overhead = $12 + $16 + 75% × $32 = $52

[3] Fixed cost per unit = 25% of Manufacturing overhead = 25% × $32 = $8

[4] Variable cost per unit in Metals Division = Direct materials + Direct manufacturing labor + 40% of Manufacturing overhead = $6 + $20 + 40% × $25 = $36

[5] Fixed cost per unit in Metals Division = 60% of Manufacturing overhead = 60% × $25 = $15

22-20 (Cont'd.)

2.   Bonus paid to division managers at 1% of division operating income will be as follows:

	Method A Internal Transfers at Market Prices	Method B Internal Transfers at 110% of Full Costs
Mining Division manager's bonus (1% × $12,000,000; 1% × $2,400,000)	$120,000	$ 24,000
Metals Division manager's bonus (1% × $3,600,000; 1% × $13,200,000)	36,000	132,000

The Mining Division manager will prefer Method A (transfer at market prices) because this method gives $120,000 of bonus rather than $24,000 under Method B (transfers at 110% of full costs). The Metals Division manager will prefer Method B because this method gives $132,000 of bonus rather than $36,000 under Method A.

3.   Brian Jones, the manager of the Mining Division, will appeal to the existence of a competitive market to price transfers at market prices. Using market prices for transfers in these conditions leads to goal congruence. Division managers acting in their own best interests make decisions that are also in the best interests of the company as a whole.

Jones will further argue that setting transfer prices based on cost will cause Jones to pay no attention to controlling costs since all costs incurred will be recovered from the Metals Division at 110% of full costs.

22-22 (25 min.) **General guideline, transfer price range.**

1.   If the Screen Division sells screens in the outside market, it will receive, for each screen, the market price of the screen minus variable marketing and distribution costs per screen = $110 – $4 = $106. The incremental cost of manufacturing each screen is $70. The Screen Division is operating at capacity. Hence, the opportunity cost per screen of selling the screen to the Assembly Division rather than in the outside market is the contribution margin the Screen Division would forgo if it transferred screens internally rather than sold them in the outside market.

> Contribution margin per screen = $106 – $70 = $36.
> Using the general guideline,

$$\text{Minimum transfer price per screen} = \text{Incremental costs per screen up to the point of transfer} + \text{Opportunity costs per screen to the selling division}$$

That is,   Minimum transfer price per screen = $70 + $36 = $106

2.   If the two division managers were to negotiate a transfer price, the range of possible transfer prices is between $106 and $112 per screen. As calculated in requirement 1, the Screen Division will be willing to supply screens to the Assembly Division only if the transfer price equals or exceeds $106 per screen.

If the Assembly Division were to purchase the screens in the outside market, it will incur a cost of $112, the cost of the screen equal to $110 plus variable purchasing costs of $2 per screen. Hence, the Assembly Division will be willing to buy screens from the Screen Division only if the price does not exceed $112 per screen. Within the price range of $106 and $112 per screen, each division will be willing to transact with the other. The exact transfer price between $106 and $112 will depend on the bargaining strengths of the two divisions.

22-24 (30 min.) **Multinational transfer pricing, goal congruence**
(continuation of 22-23).

1. After-tax operating income if Mornay Company sold all 1,000 units of Product 4A36 in the United States is

Revenues, $600 × 1,000 units	$600,000
Full manufacturing costs, $500 × 1,000 units	500,000
Operating income	100,000
Income taxes at 40%	40,000
After-tax operating income	$ 60,000

From Exercise 22-23, requirement 1, Mornay Company's after-tax operating income if it transfers 1,000 units of Product 4A36 to Austria at full manufacturing cost and sells the units in Austria is $112,000. Therefore, Mornay should sell the 1,000 units in Austria.

2. Transferring Product 4A36 at the full manufacturing cost of the U.S. Division minimizes import duties and taxes (Exercise 22-23, requirement 2), but creates zero operating income for the U.S Division. Acting autonomously, the U.S. Division manager would maximize division operating income by selling Product 4A36 in the U.S. market, which results in $60,000 in after-tax division operating income as calculated in requirement 1, rather than by transferring Product 4A36 to the Austrian division at full manufacturing cost. Hence, the transfer price calculated in requirement 2 of Exercise 22-23 will not result in actions that are optimal for Mornay Company as a whole.

3. The minimum transfer price at which the U.S. division manager acting autonomously will agree to transfer Product 4A36 to the Austrian division is $600 per unit. Any transfer price less than $600 will leave the U.S. Division's performance worse than selling directly in the U.S. market. Because the U.S. Division can sell as many units that it makes of Product 4A36 in the U.S. market, there is an opportunity cost of transferring the product internally equal to $250 (selling price $600 – variable manufacturing costs, $350).

$$\begin{matrix} \text{Minimum transfer} \\ \text{price per unit} \end{matrix} = \begin{matrix} \text{Incremental costs per} \\ \text{unit up to the point of} \\ \text{transfer} \end{matrix} + \begin{matrix} \text{Opportunity costs per} \\ \text{unit to the selling} \\ \text{(U.S.) division} \end{matrix}$$

$$= \quad \$350 + \$250 = \$600$$

This transfer price will result in Mornay Company as a whole paying more import duties and taxes than the answer to Exercise 22-23, requirement 2, as calculated below:

U.S. Division	
Revenues, $600 × 1,000 units	$600,000
Full manufacturing costs	500,000
Division operating income	100,000
Division income taxes at 40%	40,000
Division after-tax operating income	$ 60,000

22-24 (Cont'd.)

Austrian Division

Revenues, $750 × 1,000 units`	$750,000
Transferred in costs, $600 × 1,000 units	600,000
Import duties at 10% of transferred-in price, $60 × 1,000 units	60,000
Division operating income	90,000
Division income taxes at 44%	39,600
Division after-tax operating income	$ 50,400

Total import duties and income taxes at transfer prices of $500 and $600 per unit for 1,000 units of Product 4A36 follow:

		Transfer Price of $500 per Unit (Exercise 22-23, Requirement 2)	Transfer Price of $600 per Unit
(a)	U.S. income taxes	$ 0	$ 40,000
(b)	Austrian import duties	50,000	60,000
(c)	Austrian income taxes	88,000	39,600
		$138,000	$139,600

The minimum transfer price that the U.S. division manager acting autonomously would agree to results in Mornay Company paying $1,600 in additional import duties and income taxes.

A student who has done the calculations shown in Exercise 22-23, requirement 2, can calculate the additional taxes from a $600 transfer price more directly, as follows:

Every $1 increase in the transfer price per unit over $500 results in additional import duty and taxes of $0.016 per unit

So, a $100 increase ($600 – $500) per unit will result in additional import duty and taxes of $0.016 × 100 = $1.60

For 1,000 units transferred, this equals $1.60 × 1,000 = $1,600

22-26 (5 min.) **Transfer-pricing problem** (continuation of 22-25).

The company as a whole would benefit in this situation if C purchased from outside suppliers. The $15,000 disadvantage to the company as a whole by purchasing from the outside supplier would be more than offset by the $30,000 contribution margin of A's sale of 1,000 units to other customers.

Purchase costs from outside supplier, 1,000 units × $135		$135,000
Deduct variable cost savings, 1,000 units × $120		120,000
Net cost to company as a whole by buying units from outside		$ 15,000
A's sales to other customers, 1,000 units × $155		$155,000
Deduct:		
Variable manufacturing costs, $120 × 1,000 units	$120,000	
Variable marketing costs, $5 × 1,000 units	5,000	
Total variable costs		125,000
Contribution margin from selling units to other customers		$ 30,000

22-28 (30–40 min.) **Pricing in imperfect markets** (continuation of 22-27).

An alternative presentation, which contains the same numerical answers, can be found at the end of this solution.

1. Potential contribution from external intermediate sale is

$1,000 \times (\$195 - \$120)$	$75,000
Contribution through keeping price at $200 is	
$800 \times \$80$.	64,000
Forgone contribution by transferring 200 units	$11,000

Opportunity cost per unit to the supplying division by transferring internally:

$$\frac{\$11,000}{200} = \$55$$

Transfer price = $120 + $55 = $175

An alternative approach to obtaining the same answer is to recognize that the incremental or outlay cost is the same for all 1,000 units in question. Therefore, the total revenue desired by A would be the same for selling outside or inside.

Let X equal the transfer price at which Division A is indifferent between selling all units outside versus transferring 200 units inside.

$$1,000 \times \$195 = (800 \times \$200) + 200X$$
$$X = \$175$$

The $175 price will lead to the correct decision. Division B will not buy from Division A because its total costs of $175 + $150 will exceed its prospective selling price of $300. Division A will then sell 1,000 units at $195 to the outside; Division A and the company will have a contribution margin of $75,000. Otherwise, if 800 units were sold at $200 and 200 units were transferred to Division B, the company would have a contribution of $64,000 plus $6,000 (200 units of final product × $30), or $70,000.

A comparison might be drawn regarding the computation of the appropriate transfer prices between the preceding problem and this problem:

$$\text{Minimum transfer price} = \begin{pmatrix} \text{Additional } \textit{incremental costs} \\ \text{per unit incurred up} \\ \text{to the point of transfer} \end{pmatrix} + \begin{pmatrix} \textit{Opportunity costs} \\ \text{per unit to} \\ \text{Division A} \end{pmatrix}$$

Perfect markets: $= \$120 + (\text{Selling price} - \text{Outlay costs per unit})$
$= \$120 + (\$200 - \$120) = \$200$

Imperfect markets: $= \$120 + \dfrac{\text{Marginal revenues} - \text{Outlay costs}}{\text{Number of units transferred}}$

$$= \$120 + \frac{\$35,000^a - \$24,000^b}{200} = \$175$$

[a]Marginal revenues of Division A from selling 200 units outside rather than transferring to Division B
$= (\$195 \times 1,000) - (\$200 \times 800) = \$195,000 - \$160,000 = \$35,000.$
[b]Incremental (outlay) costs incurred by Division A to produce 200 units
$= \$120 \times 200 = \$24,000.$

Therefore, selling price ($195) and marginal revenues per unit ($175 = $35,000 ÷ 200) are not the same.

The following discussion is optional. These points should be explored only if there is sufficient class time:

Some students will erroneously say that the "new" market price of $195 is the appropriate transfer price. They will claim that the general guideline says that the transfer price should be $120 + ($195 − $120) = $195, the market price. This conclusion assumes a perfect market. But, here, there are imperfections in the intermediate market. That is, the market price is *not* a good approximation of alternative revenue. If a division's sales are heavy enough to reduce market prices, marginal revenue will be less than market price.

It is true that *either* $195 or $175 will lead to the correct decision by B in this case. But suppose that B's variable costs were $120 instead of $150. Then B would buy at a transfer price of $175 (but not at a price of $195, because then B would earn a negative contribution of $15 per unit [$300 − ($195 + $120)]. Note that if B's variable costs were $120, transfers would be desirable:

Division A contribution is:
$800 \times (\$200 - \$120) + 200\,(\$175 - \$120)$ = $75,000
Division B contribution is:
$200 \times [\$300 - (\$175 + \$120)]$ = 1,000
Total contribution = $76,000

Or the same facts can be analyzed for the company as a whole:

Sales of intermediate product,		
800 × ($200 – $120)	=	$64,000
Sales of final products,		
200 × [300 – ($120 + $120)]	=	12,000
Total contribution		$76,000

If the transfer price were $195, B would not accept the transfer and would not earn any contribution. As shown above, Division A and the company as a whole will earn a total contribution of $75,000 instead of $76,000.

2. a.   Division A can sell 900 units at $195 to the outside market and 100 units to Division B, or 800 at $200 to the outside market and 200 units to Division B. Note that, under both alternatives, 100 units can be transferred to Division B at no opportunity cost to A.

Using the general guideline, the minimum transfer price of *the first 100 units* [901–1000] is:

$$TP_1 = \$120 + 0 = \$120$$

If Division B needs 100 additional units, the opportunity cost to A is not zero, because Division A will then have to sell only 800 units to the outside market for a contribution of 800 × ($200 – $120) = $64,000 instead of 900 units for a contribution of 900 × ($195 – $120) = $67,500. Each unit sold to B in addition to the first 100 units has an opportunity cost to A of ($67,500 – $64,000) ÷ 100 = $35.

Using the general guideline, the minimum transfer price of *the next 100 units* [801–900] is:

$$TP_2 = \$120 + \$35 = \$155$$

Alternatively, the computation could be:

Increase in contribution from 100	
more units, 100 × $75	$7,500
Loss in contribution on 800 units,	
800 × ($80 – $75)	4,000
Net "marginal revenue"	$3,500 ÷100 units = $35

(Minimum) transfer price applicable to first 100 units		
offered by A is $120 + $0	=	$120 per unit
(Minimum) transfer price applicable to next 100 units		
offered by A is $120 + ($3,500 ÷ 100)	=	$155 per unit
(Minimum) transfer price applicable to next 800 units	=	$195 per unit

b. The manager of Division B will not want to purchase more than 100 units because the units at $155 would decrease his contribution ($155 + $150 > $300). Because the manager of B does not buy more than 100 units, the manager of A will have 900 units available for sale to the outside market. The manager of A will strive to maximize the contribution by selling them all at $195.

This solution maximizes the company's contribution:

$$900 \times (\$195 - \$120) \quad = \quad \$67,500$$
$$100 \times (\$300 - \$270) \quad = \quad \underline{\;\;\;3,000}$$
$$\underline{\$70,500}$$

which compares favorably to:

$$800 \times (\$200 - \$120) \quad = \quad \$64,000$$
$$200 \times (\$300 - \$270) \quad = \quad \underline{\;\;\;6,000}$$
$$\underline{\$70,000}$$

ALTERNATIVE PRESENTATION (by James Patell)

1. Company Viewpoint

a: *Sell 1,000 outside at $195*

Price	$195
Variable costs	120
Contribution	$ 75 × 1,000 = $75,000

b: *Sell 800 outside at $200, transfer 200*

Transfer price	$200
Variable costs	120
Contribution	$ 80 × 800 = $64,000

Total contribution given up if transfer occurs[*]
    = $75,000 − $64,000 = $11,000

On a per-unit basis, the relevant costs are:

$$\begin{array}{c}\text{Incremental costs to} \\ \text{point of transfer}\end{array} + \begin{array}{c}\text{Opportunity costs to} \\ \text{Division A of transfer}\end{array} = \text{Transfer price}$$

$$\$120 + \frac{\$11,000}{200} = \$175$$

22-28 (Cont'd.)

By formula, costs are:

$$\left[\begin{array}{c}\text{Incremental costs} \\ \text{to point} \\ \text{of transfer}\end{array}\right] + \left[\begin{array}{c}\text{Lost opportunity to} \\ \text{sell 200 at \$195, for} \\ \text{contribution of \$75}\end{array}\right] - \left[\begin{array}{c}\text{Gain when 1st 800} \\ \text{sell at \$200} \\ \text{instead of \$195}\end{array}\right]$$

$$= \quad \$120 + \frac{200 \times \$75}{200} - \frac{[(\$200 - \$195) \times 800]}{200}$$

$$= \quad \$120 + \$75 - \$20 \;=\; \$175$$

*Contribution of $30 per unit by B is not given up if transfer occurs, so it is not relevant here.

2a. At most, Division A can sell only 900 units and can produce 1,000. Therefore, at least 100 units should be transferred, at a transfer price no less than $120. The question is whether or not a second 100 units should be transferred.

Company Viewpoint

a: *Sell 900 outside at $195*

Transfer price	$195
Variable cost	120
Contribution	$ 75 × 900 = $67,500

b: *Sell 800 outside at $200, transfer 100*

Transfer price	$200
Variable cost	120
Contribution	$ 80 × 800 = $64,000

Total contribution forgone if transfer of 100 units occurs
= $67,500 − $64,000 = $3,500 (or $35 per unit)

$$\begin{array}{c}\text{Incremental costs to} \\ \text{point of transfer}\end{array} + \begin{array}{c}\text{Opportunity costs to} \\ \text{Division A of transfer}\end{array} = \text{Transfer price}$$

$$\$120 \quad + \quad\quad \$35 \quad\quad = \quad\quad \$155$$

2b. By formula:

$$\left[\begin{array}{c}\text{Incremental costs} \\ \text{to point} \\ \text{of transfer}\end{array} + \begin{array}{c}\text{Lost opportunity to} \\ \text{sell 100 at \$195, for} \\ \text{contribution of \$75}\end{array}\right] -$$

$$\left[\begin{array}{c}\text{Gain when 1st 800} \\ \text{sell at \$200} \\ \text{instead of \$195}\end{array}\right]$$

$$= \;\; \$120 + \frac{100 \times \$75}{100} - \frac{[(\$200 - \$195) \times 800]}{100}$$

$$= \;\; \$120 + \$75 - \$40 = \$155$$

Transfer Price Schedule (minimum acceptable transfer price)

Units	Transfer Price

0–100	$120
101–200	$155
201–1,000	$195

22-30 (25 min.) **Goal congruence problems with cost-plus transfer-pricing methods, dual pricing system (continuation of 22-29).**

Two examples of goal congruence problems are:

a. Processing Division manager using an outside supplier when Oceanic Products operating income is maximized by buying from Harvesting Division.

b. Harvesting Division manager selling to an outside purchaser when it is better for Oceanic Products to process internally.

2. *Transfer into buying division at market price*
Harvesting Division to Processing Division = $1.00 per pound of raw tuna
Transfer out to selling division at 150% of full costs
Harvesting Division to Processing Division

$$= 1.5 \times (\$0.20 + \$0.40) = \$0.90 \text{ per pound of raw tuna}$$

Tuna Harvesting Division

Division revenues, $0.90 × 1,000	$ 900
Division variable costs, $0.20 × 1,000	200
Division fixed costs, $0.40 × 1,000	400
Division total costs	600
Division operating income	$ 300

Tuna Processing Division

Division revenues, $5.00 × 500	$2,500
Transferred-in costs, $1.00 × 1,000	$1,000
Division variable costs, $0.80 × 500	400
Division fixed costs, $0.60 × 500	300
Division total costs	1,700
Division operating income	$ 800

3.

	Division Operating Income
Tuna Harvesting Division	$ 300
Tuna Processing Division	800
Oceanic Products	$1,100

The overall company operating income from harvesting 1,000 pounds of raw tuna and its processing is $1,200 (see Problem 22-29, requirement 1).

A dual transfer-pricing method entails using different transfer prices for transfers into the buying division and transfers out of the supplying division. As a result, the sum of division operating incomes do not equal the total company operating income.

4.   Problems which may arise if Oceanic Products uses the dual transfer-pricing system include:

a.   It may reduce the incentives of the supplying division to control costs since every $1 of cost of the supplying division is transferred out to the buying division at $1.50.
b.   A dual transfer-pricing system does not provide clear signals to the individual divisions about the level of decentralization top management seeks.
c.   It insulates the Harvesting Division manager from the frictions of the marketplace because costs, not market prices, affect the revenues of the supplying division

22-32 (30–40 min.) Multinational transfer pricing and taxation.

1.   Anita Corporation and its subsidiaries' operating income if it manufactures the machine and sells it in Brazil or in Switzerland follows:

	If Sold in Brazil	If Sold in Switzerland
Revenue	$1,000,000	$950,000
Costs		
Manufacturing costs	500,000	500,000
Transportation and modification costs	200,000	250,000
Total costs	700,000	750,000
Operating income	$ 300,000	$200,000

Anita Corporation maximizes operating income by manufacturing the machine and selling it in Brazil.

2.   Anita Corporation will not sell if the transfer price is less than $500,000—its outlay costs of manufacturing the machine.

The Brazilian subsidiary will not agree to a transfer price of more than $800,000. At a price of $800,000, the Brazilian subsidiary's incremental operating income from purchasing and selling the milling machine will be $0 ($1,000,000 – $200,000 – $800,000).

The Swiss subsidiary will not agree to a transfer price of more than $700,000. At a price of $700,000, the Swiss subsidiary's incremental operating income from purchasing and selling the milling machine will be $0 ($950,000 – $250,000 – $700,000).

Any transfer price between $700,000 and $800,000 will achieve the optimal actions determined in requirement 1. For prices in this range, Anita Corporation will be willing to sell, the Brazilian Corporation willing to buy, and the Swiss subsidiary not interested in acquiring the machine.

Where within the range of $700,000 to $800,000 that the transfer price will be set depends on the bargaining powers of the Anita Corporation and the Brazilian subsidiary managers. Anita Corporation's main source of bargaining power comes from the threat of selling the machine to the Swiss subsidiary. If the transfer price is set at $700,000, then

Anita's operating income, $700,000 − $500,000	$200,000
Brazilian subsidiary's operating income, $1,000,000 − $700,000 − $200,000	100,000
Overall operating income of Anita and subsidiaries	$300,000

Note that the general guideline could be used to derive the minimum transfer price.

$$\begin{array}{l} \text{Minimum} \\ \text{transfer price} \end{array} = \left(\begin{array}{c} \text{Additional } \textit{incremental } \text{costs} \\ \text{per unit incurred up} \\ \text{to the point of transfer} \end{array} \right) + \left(\begin{array}{c} \textit{Opportunity } \text{costs} \\ \text{per unit to the} \\ \text{supplying division} \end{array} \right)$$

$$= \quad \$500,000 + \$200,000 = \$700,000$$

Anita's opportunity cost of supplying the machine to the Brazilian subsidiary is the $200,000 in operating income it forgoes by not supplying the machine to the Swiss subsidiary. Note that competition between the Brazilian and Swiss subsidiaries means that the transfer price will be at least $700,000.

3. Consider the optimal transfer prices that can be set to minimize taxes (for Anita and its subsidiaries) (a) for transfers from Anita to the Brazilian subsidiary and (b) for transfers from Anita to the Swiss subsidiary.

   a. Transfers from Anita to the Brazilian subsidiary should "allocate" as much of the operating income to Anita as possible, since the tax rate in the United States is lower than in Brazil for this transaction. Therefore, these transfers should be priced at the highest allowable transfer price of $700,000 to minimize overall company taxes.

Taxes paid:	
Anita, 0.40 × ($700,000 − $500,000)	$ 80,000
Brazilian subsidiary, 0.60 × ($1,000,000 − $700,000 − $200,000)	60,000
Total taxes paid by Anita Corporation and its subsidiaries on transfers to Brazil	$140,000

After-tax operating income:	
Anita, ($700,000 − $500,000) − $80,000	$120,000
Brazilian subsidiary ($1,000,000 − $700,000 − $200,000) − $60,000	40,000
Total after-tax operating income for Anita Corporation and its subsidiaries on transfers to Brazil	$160,000

b. Transfers from Anita to the Swiss subsidiary should "allocate" as little of the operating income to Anita as possible, since the tax rate in the United States is higher than in Switzerland for this transaction. Therefore, these transfers should be priced at the lowest allowable transfer price of $500,000 to minimize overall company taxes.

Taxes paid:

Anita, 0.40 × ($500,000 – $500,000)	$ 0
Swiss subsidiary, 0.15 × ($950,000 – $500,000 – $250,000)	30,000
Total taxes paid by Anita Corporation and its subsidiaries on transfers to Switzerland	$30,000

After-tax operating income

Anita, ($500,000 – $500,000) – $0	$ 0
Swiss subsidiary ($950,000 – $500,000 – $250,000) – $30,000	170,000
Total net income for Anita Corporation and its subsidiaries on transfers to Switzerland	$170,000

From the viewpoint of Anita Corporation and its subsidiaries together, overall after-tax operating income is maximized if the machine is transferred to the Swiss subsidiary (after-tax operating income of $170,000 versus after-tax operating income of $160,000 if the machine is transferred to the Brazilian subsidiary). Note that the corporation and its subsidiaries trade off the lower overall before-tax operating income achieved by transferring to the Swiss subsidiary with the lower taxes that result from such a transfer. Hence, (a) the equipment should be manufactured by Anita, and (b) it should be transferred to the Swiss subsidiary at a price of $500,000.

4. As in requirement 2, the Brazilian subsidiary would be willing to bid up the price to $800,000, while the Swiss subsidiary would be willing to pay only up to $700,000. Anita Corporation, acting autonomously, would like to maximize its own after-tax operating income by transferring the machine at as high a transfer price as possible. As in requirement 2, the price would end up being at least $700,000. Since the taxing authorities will not allow prices above $700,000, the transfer price will be $700,000. At this transfer price, the Swiss subsidiary makes zero operating income and will not be interested in the machine. Hence, Anita Corporation will sell the machine to the Brazilian subsidiary at a price of $700,000.

The answer is not the same as in requirement 3, because, acting autonomously, the objective of each manager is to maximize after-tax operating income of his or her own company rather than after-tax operating income of Anita Corporation and its subsidiaries as a whole. Goal congruence is not achieved in this setting.

Can the company induce the managers to take the right actions without infringing on their autonomy? This outcome is probably not going to be easy.

22-32 (Cont'd.)

One possibility might be to implement a dual-pricing scheme in which the machine is transferred at cost ($500,000), but under which Anita Corporation is credited with after-tax operating income earned on the machine by the subsidiary it ships the machine to (in this example, $170,000 of net income earned by the Swiss subsidiary). A negative feature of this arrangement is that the $170,000 of after-tax operating income will be "double counted" and recognized on the books of both Anita Corporation and the Swiss subsidiary.

Another possibility might be to evaluate the managers on the basis of overall after-tax operating income of Anita Corporation and its subsidiaries. This approach will induce a more global perspective, but at the cost of inducing a larger noncontrollable element in each manager's performance measure.

22-34 (40–50 min.) Transfer pricing, utilization of capacity.

1.

	Super-chip	Okay-chip
Selling price	$60	$12
Direct materials	2	1
Direct manufacturing labor	28	7
Contribution margin per unit	$30	$ 4
Contribution margin per hour ($30 ÷ 2; $4 ÷ 0.5)	$15	$ 8

Because the contribution margin per hour is higher for Super-chip than for Okay-chip, CIC should produce and sell as many Super-chips as it can and use the remaining available capacity to produce Okay-chip.

The total demand for Super-chips is 15,000 units, which would take 30,000 hours (15,000 × 2 hours per unit). CIC should use its remaining capacity of 20,000 hours (50,000 – 30,000) to produce 40,000 Okay-chips (20,000 ÷ 0.5).

2. Options for manufacturing process-control unit

	Using Circuit Board	Using Super-chip
Selling price	$132	$132
Direct materials	60	2
Direct manufacturing labor (Super-chip)	0	28
Direct manufacturing labor (Process-control unit)	50	60
Contribution margin per unit	$ 22	$ 42

Overall Company Viewpoint

Alternative 1: No Transfer of Super-chips

Sell 15,000 Super-chips at contribution margin per unit of $30	$450,000
Transfer 0 Super-chips	0
Sell 40,000 Okay-chips at contribution margin per unit of $4	160,000
Sell 5,000 Control units at contribution margin per unit of $22	110,000
Total contribution margin	$720,000

22-34 (Cont'd.)

Alternative 2: Transfer 5,000 Super-chips to Process-Control Division. These Super-chips would require 10,000 hours to manufacture, leaving only 10,000 hours for the manufacture of 20,000 Okay-chips (10,000 ÷ 0.5)

Sell 15,000 Super-chips at contribution margin per unit of $30	$450,000
Transfer 5,000 Super-chips to Process-Control Division	0
Sell 20,000 Okay-chips at contribution margin per unit of $4	80,000
Sell 5,000 Control units at contribution margin per unit of $42	210,000
Total contribution margin	$740,000

CIC is better off transferring 5,000 Super-chips to the Process-Control Division.

3. For each Super-chip that is transferred, two hours of time (labor capacity) are given up in the Semiconductor Division, and, in those two hours, four Okay-chips could be produced, each contributing $4.

$$\begin{array}{l} \text{Minimum transfer price} \\ \text{per Super - chip} \end{array} = \begin{array}{l} \text{Incremental cost} \\ \text{per unit to} \\ \text{the point of transfer} \end{array} + \begin{array}{l} \text{Opportunity cost per unit for} \\ \text{the Semiconductor Division} \end{array}$$

$$= \quad\quad \$30 \quad + \quad\quad \$16$$
$$= \quad\quad \$46 \text{ per unit}$$

If the selling price for the process-control unit were firm at $132, the Process-Control Division would accept any transfer price up to $50 ($60 price of circuit board – $10 incremental labor cost if Super-chip used).

However, consider what happens if the transfer price of Super-chip is set at, say, $49, and the price of the control unit drops to $108. From CIC's viewpoint:

	Using Circuit Board	Using Super-chip
Selling price	$108	$108
Direct materials	60	49
Direct manufacturing labor	50	60
Contribution margin per hour	$ –2	$ –1

Process-Control Division will not produce any control units. From the company's viewpoint, the contribution margin on the control unit if the Super-chip is used is:

Selling price	$108
Direct materials	2
Direct manufacturing labor (Super-chip)	28
Direct manufacturing labor (process-control unit)	60
Contribution margin per unit	$ 18

The contribution margin per unit from producing Super-chips for the process-control unit exceeds the contribution margin of $16 from producing 4 Okay-chips, each yielding a contribution margin of $4 per unit. Hence the Semiconductor Division should transfer 5,000 Super-chips as the following calculations show:

Alternative 1—No transfer (and, therefore, no sales of process-control units)

Sell 15,000 Super-chips at contribution margin per unit of $30	$450,000
Sell 40,000 Okay-chips at contribution margin per unit of $4	160,000
	$610,000

Alternative 2—Transfer 5,000 Super-chips.

Sell 15,000 Super-chips at contribution margin per unit of $30	$450,000
Sell 20,000 Okay-chips at contribution margin per unit of $4	80,000
Sell 5,000 control units at contribution margin per unit of $18	90,000
	$620,000

Therefore, if the price for the control unit is uncertain, the transfer price must be set at the minimum acceptable transfer price of $46.

4.   For a transfer of any amount between 0 and 10,000 Super-chips (which require 2 hours each to produce), the opportunity cost is the production of Okay-chips (which require ½ hour each). In this range, the relevant costs are equal to the transfer price of $46 established in part 3.

If more than 10,000 Super-chips are transferred, the opportunity cost becomes the sale of Super-chips on the outside market. Now the minimum transfer price per Super-chip becomes

$$\begin{matrix} \text{Incremental} \\ \text{cost per Super -} \\ \text{chip up to the} \\ \text{point of} \\ \text{transfer} \end{matrix} \ + \ \begin{matrix} \text{Opportunity} \\ \text{cost per Super -} \\ \text{chip to the} \\ \text{Semiconductor} \\ \text{Division} \end{matrix} \ = \$30 + (\$60 - \$30) = \$60, \text{ the market price.}$$

At this transfer price, it is cheaper for the Process-Control Division to buy the circuit board for $60, since $10 of additional direct manufacturing labor cost is saved.

The Semiconductor Division should at most transfer 10,000 Super-chips.

Internal Demand	Transfer Price
0–10,000	$46
10,000–25,000	60

22-36 (40–50 min.)   **Goal congruence, income taxes, different market conditions.**

1.

	New Engine	Existing Engine Used by Assembly
Selling price	$375	
Savings in purchase costs by making engines inhouse		$400
Manufacturing costs:		
Direct materials	$100	$125
Direct manufacturing labor	40	50
Variable manufacturing overhead	25	25
Total costs of manufacturing	165	200
Contribution margin from New Engine	$210	
Net savings in costs by making existing engine inhouse		$200

If order for the new engine is accepted, San Ramon earns a
contribution margin of $210 × 2,000 units. $420,000

In this case, Engine Division will be in a position to supply only
2,000 units to Assembly, and Assembly will have to purchase 1,200
engines from outside. The incremental cost of buying engines from
outside is $200 × 1,200   240,000

Net benefit from accepting order $180,000

An alternative approach is to compare relevant costs of the accept order and reject order
alternatives.

	Accept Order	Reject Order
1. Contribution margin from selling 2,000 units of new engine, $210 \times 2,000$	$(420,000)	
2. Incremental cost of making and transferring 2,000 units or 3,200 units of old engines, $200 \times 2,000$; $200 \times 3,200$	400,000	$640,000
3. Incremental costs of purchasing 1,200 units from outside, $400 \times 1,200$	480,000	
	$460,000	$640,000

San Ramon Corporation should
- a. make 2,000 units of the new engine in the Engine Division
- b. make 2,000 units of the existing engine for the Assembly Division
- c. have the Assembly Division purchase 1,200 existing engines from the outside market

2. The options facing the Engine Division manager are (a) to sell 2,000 units of the special order engine and make 2,000 units for the Assembly Division, or (b) to make 3,200 units for the Assembly Division. The contribution margin per unit from accepting the special order is $210 per unit. Let the transfer price be $X. Then, we want to find X such that

$$\$210 \times 2{,}000 + (\$X - \$200)\,2{,}000 = (\$X - \$200)\,3{,}200$$
$$(\$X - \$200)(3{,}200 - 2{,}000) = \$420{,}000$$
$$\$X - \$200 = \frac{\$420{,}000}{1{,}200} = \$350$$
$$X = \$550$$

For transfer prices below $550, the Engine Division gets more by selling 2,000 units outside and transferring 2,000 units to Assembly Division. It will not transfer more than 2,000 units to Assembly even though the transfer price is greater than the variable costs of manufacturing the existing engine, $200 plus the contribution margin per unit from accepting the special order of $210 equal to $410 ($500, say). Why? Because by transferring an additional 1,200 units (say), it will have to give up $420,000 ($210 × 2,000) of contribution margin by not accepting the special order. The Engine Division manager would be willing to transfer 2,000 units for which it has capacity (after fulfilling the outside order) to the Assembly Division provided the transfer price covers the Engine Division's variable costs. So, the range of transfer price that will induce the Engine Division manager to implement the optimal solution in requirement 1 is:

TP ≥ $200 for the first 2,000 units

TP ≥ $550 for the next 1,200 units

The Assembly Division manager would be willing to buy from the Engine Division so long as the transfer price is less than or equal to the price at which the Assembly Division can buy the engines on the outside market.

TP ≤ $400

It will not buy the engines from the Engine Division if TP > $400. The range of TP that will result in both managers favoring the optimal actions in requirement 1 are TPs that satisfy the respective constraints described above.

$$\$200 \le TP \le \$400 \text{ for the first 2,000 units}$$

$$TP = \$550 \text{ for the next 1,200 units}$$

This transfer-pricing scheme will induce both managers to transfer 2,000 units between the Engine and Assembly Divisions, but no more. Because the Assembly Division manager is willing to pay no more than $400 and the Engine Division manager is unwilling to transfer unless the transfer price is above $550, no transfers will occur beyond the first 2,000 units.

3a. The full manufacturing costs of the engines transferred to the Assembly Division are:

Direct materials	$125
Direct manufacturing labor	50
Variable manufacturing overheads	25
Fixed manufacturing overheads	

$$\left(\frac{\$520,000}{2} = \$260,000 \div 2,000 \text{ engines} \right)$$

since the engines transferred to the Assembly Division use up half the Engine Division's capacity	130
Total manufacturing cost	$330

b. A transfer price of $330 is in the optimal range identified in requirement 2 and, so, will achieve the optimal actions of selling 2,000 engines to the outside party and transferring 2,000 engines to the Assembly Division as identified in requirement 1. The transfer price for the next 1,200 units should be set at $550 so that the Assembly Division will prefer to purchase engines at $400 from the outside market. The transfer price for the next 1,200 units should not be set at the full manufacturing cost of $330 because the Assembly Division will then want to buy the engines internally. This is not in the best interest of San Ramon Corporation as a whole.

c. One advantage of full cost transfer pricing is that it is useful for the firm's long-run pricing decisions.

One disadvantage of full cost transfer pricing is that costs that are fixed for the corporation as a whole look like variable costs from the viewpoint of the Assembly Division manager. This is because, by choosing not to have a unit transferred from the Engine Division, the Assembly Division manager would appear to save both the variable and fixed costs of the engine. This could lead to suboptimal decisions.

22-36 (Cont'd.)

4a.   To minimize taxes, San Ramon should transfer the engines at the highest price it can, the market price of $400. The Engine Division would pay no taxes on any income that it would report. By setting the transfer price as high as possible, the Assembly Division would minimize the income it would report and, hence, the taxes it would pay.

b.   Yes, as in part 3b, the transfer price of $400 for the first 2000 engines is also within the range identified in requirement 2 and so will achieve the outcome desired in requirement 1 (sell 2,000 engines under the outside offer and transfer 2,000 engines to the Assembly Division).

5.   San Ramon should use a transfer price of $400 for the first 2,000 units and $550 for the next 1,200 units when transferring engines from the Engine Division to the Assembly Division. This transfer price minimizes tax payments for the San Ramon Corporation as a whole and also achieves goal congruence. That is, at the transfer prices indicated, both Divisions will be content with the following arrangement
   a.   The Engine Division will make 2,000 engines for outside customers and 2,000 engines for the Assembly Division
   b.   The Assembly Division will take 2,000 engines from the Engine Division and 1,200 engines from the outside market

   Of course, the Assembly Division manager would like to negotiate a price lower than $400 (but greater than $200) for the first 2,000 engines from the Engine Division, but this would increase San Ramon's tax payments.

   At a transfer price of $400, San Ramon can still evaluate each division's performance on the basis of division operating income because the transfer price of $400 approximates the market prices for the engines transferred from the Engine Division to the Assembly Division. Market-based transfer prices give top management a reasonably good picture of the contributions of the individual divisions to overall companywide profitability.

CHAPTER 23
PERFORMANCE MEASUREMENT, COMPENSATION, AND MULTINATIONAL CONSIDERATIONS

23-2 The six steps in designing an accounting-based performance measure are:
1. Choose performance measures that align with top management's financial goals
2. Choose the time horizon of each performance measure in Step 1
3. Choose a definition of the components in each performance measure in Step 1
4. Choose a measurement alternative for each performance measure in Step 1
5. Choose a target level of performance
6. Choose the timing of feedback

23-4 Yes. Residual income (RI) is not identical to return on investment (ROI). ROI is a percentage with investment as the denominator of the computation. RI is an absolute amount in which investment is used to calculate an imputed interest charge.

23-6 Definitions of investment used in practice when computing ROI are:
1. Total assets available
2. Total assets employed
3. Total assets employed minus current liabilities
4. Stockholders' equity

23-8 Special problems arise when evaluating the performance of divisions in multinational companies because
   a. The economic, legal, political, social, and cultural environments differ significantly across countries.
   b. Governments in some countries may impose controls and limit selling prices of products.
   c. Availability of materials and skilled labor, as well as costs of materials, labor, and infrastructure may differ significantly across countries.
   d. Divisions operating in different countries keep score of their performance in different currencies.

23-10 Moral hazard describes contexts in which an employee prefers to exert less effort (or report distorted information) compared with the effort (or accurate information) desired by the owner because the employee's effort (or validity of the reported information) cannot be accurately monitored and enforced.

23-12 Measures of performance that are sensitive to a manager's performance (measures that change significantly with the manager's performance and not very much with changes in factors that are beyond the manager's control) are the key to designing strong incentive systems in organizations. When selecting performance measures, the management accountant must choose those performance measures that change with changes in the actions taken by managers. For example, if a manager has no authority for making investments, then using an investment-based measure to evaluate the manager imposes risk on the manager and provides little information about the manager's performance. The management accountant might suggest evaluating the manager on the basis of costs, or costs and revenues, rather than ROI.

23-14 When employees have to perform multiple tasks as part of their jobs, incentive problems can arise when one task is easy to monitor and measure while the other task is more difficult to evaluate. Employers want employees to intelligently allocate time and effort among various tasks. If, however, employees are rewarded on the basis of the task that is more easily measured, they will tend to focus their efforts on that task and ignore the others.

23-16 (30 min.) ROI, comparisons of three companies.

1.   The separate components highlight several features of return on investment not revealed by a single calculation:

  a.   The importance of investment turnover as a key to income is stressed.

  b.   The importance of revenues is explicitly recognized.

  c.   The important components are expressed as ratios or percentages instead of dollar figures. This form of expression often enhances comparability of different divisions, businesses, and time periods.

  d.   The breakdown stresses the possibility of trading off investment turnover for income as a percentage of revenues so as to increase the average ROI at a given level of output.

2.   (Filled-in blanks are in bold face.)

	Companies in Same Industry		
	A	**B**	**C**
Revenue	$1,000,000	$ 500,000	$10,000,000
Income	$ 100,000	$ 50,000	$ 50,000
Investment	$ 500,000	**$5,000,000**	$ 5,000,000
Income as a % of revenue	**10%**	**10%**	0.5%
Investment turnover	**2.0**	**0.1**	2.0
Return on investment	**20%**	1%	**1%**

  Income and investment alone shed little light on comparative performances because of disparities in size between Company A and the other two companies. Thus, it is impossible to say whether B's low return on investment in comparison with A's is attributable to its larger investment or to its lower income. Furthermore, the fact that Companies B and C have identical income and investment may suggest that the same conditions underlie the low ROI, but this conclusion is erroneous. B has higher margins but a lower investment turnover. C has very small margins (1/20th of B) but turns over investment 20 times faster.

23-16 (Cont'd.)

I.M.A. Report No. 35 (page 35) states:

"Introducing revenues to measure level of operations helps to disclose specific areas for more intensive investigation. Company B does as well as Company A in terms of income margin, for both companies earn 10% on revenues. But Company B has a much lower turnover of investment than does Company A. Whereas a dollar of investment in Company A supports two dollars in revenues each period, a dollar investment in Company B supports only ten cents in revenues each period. This suggests that the analyst should look carefully at Company B's investment. Is the company keeping an inventory larger than necessary for its revenue level? Are receivables being collected promptly? Or did Company A acquire its fixed assets at a price level that was much lower than that at which Company B purchased its plant?"

"On the other hand, C's investment turnover is as high as A's, but C's income as a percentage of revenue is much lower. Why? Are its operations inefficient, are its material costs too high, or does its location entail high transportation costs?"

"Analysis of ROI raises questions such as the foregoing. When answers are obtained, basic reasons for differences between rates of return may be discovered. For example, in Company B's case, it is apparent that the emphasis will have to be on increasing turnover by reducing investment or increasing revenues. Clearly, B cannot appreciably increase its ROI simply by increasing its income as a percent of revenue. In contrast, Company C's management should concentrate on increasing the percent of income on revenue."

23-16 Excel Application
Performance Measurement, Compensation, and Multinational Considerations

	Companies in Same Industry		
	A	B	C
Revenues	$1,000,000	$500,000	$10,000,000
Income	$100,000	$50,000	$50,000
Investment	$500,000	$5,000,000	$5,000,000
Income as a % of revenues	10%	10%	0.5%
Investment turnover	2	0.1	2
ROI	20%	1%	1%

23-18 (10–15 min.) **ROI and RI** (D. Kleespie).

$$\text{ROI} = \frac{\text{Operating income}}{\text{Investment}}$$

$$\text{Operating income} = \text{ROI} \times \text{Investment}$$

[No. of menhirs sold (Selling price – Var. cost per unit)] – Fixed costs = ROI × Investment

Let X = minimum selling price per unit to achieve a 20% ROI

1. $10,000 (X - \$300) - \$1,000,000$ = 20% ($1,600,000)
    $10,000X$ = $320,000 + $3,000,000 + $1,000,000 = $4,320,000
    X = $432

2. $10,000 (X - \$300) - \$1,000,000$ = 15% ($1,600,000)
    $10,000X$ = $240,000 + $3,000,000 + $1,000,000 = $4,240,000
    X = $424

23-20 (25 min.) **Financial and nonfinancial performance measures, goal congruence**.

1. Operating income is a good summary measure of short-term financial performance. By itself, however, it does not indicate whether operating income in the short run was earned by taking actions that would lead to long-run competitive advantage. For example, Summit's divisions might be able to increase short-run operating income by producing more product while ignoring quality or rework. Harrington, however, would like to see division managers increase operating income without sacrificing quality. The new performance measures take a balanced scorecard approach by evaluating and rewarding managers on the basis of direct measures (such as rework costs, on-time delivery performance, and sales returns). This motivates managers to take actions that Harrington believes will increase operating income now and in the future. The nonoperating income measures serve as surrogate measures of future profitability.

2. The semiannual installments and total bonus for the Charter Division are calculated as follows:

Charter Division Bonus Calculation
For Year Ended December 31, 2003

January 1, 2003 to June 30, 2003

Profitability	$(0.02 \times \$462,000)$	$ 9,240
Rework	$(0.02 \times \$462,000) - \$11,500$	(2,260)
On-time delivery	No bonus—under 96%	0
Sales returns	$[(0.015 \times \$4,200,000) - \$84,000] \times 50\%$	(10,500)
Semiannual installment		$ (3,520)
Semiannual bonus awarded		$ 0

July 1, 2003 to December 31, 2003

Profitability	$(0.02 \times \$440,000)$	$ 8,800
Rework	$(0.02 \times \$440,000) - \$11,000$	(2,200)
On-time delivery	96% to 98%	2,000
Sales returns	$[(0.015 \times \$4,400,000) - \$70,000] \times 50\%$	(2,000)
Semiannual installment		$ 6,600
Semiannual bonus awarded		$ 6,600
Total bonus awarded for the year		$ 6,600

The semiannual installments and total bonus for the Mesa Division are calculated as follows:

Mesa Division Bonus Calculation
For Year Ended December 31, 2003

January 1, 2003 to June 30, 2003

Profitability	$(0.02 \times \$342,000)$	$ 6,840
Rework	$(0.02 \times \$342,000) - \$6,000$	0
On-time delivery	Over 98%	5,000
Sales returns	$[(0.015 \times \$2,850,000) - \$44,750] \times 50\%$	(1,000)
Semiannual bonus installment		$10,840
Semiannual bonus awarded		$10,840

July 1, 2003 to December 31, 2003

Profitability	$(0.02 \times \$406,000)$	$ 8,120
Rework	$(0.02 \times \$406,000) - \$8,000$	0
On-time delivery	No bonus—under 96%	0
Sales returns	$[(0.015 \times \$2,900,000) - \$42,500]$ which is greater than zero, yielding a bonus of	3,000
Semiannual bonus installment		$11,120
Semiannual bonus awarded		$11,120
Total bonus awarded for the year		$21,960

3.   The manager of the Charter Division is likely to be frustrated by the new plan, as the division bonus is more than $20,000 less than the previous year. However, the new performance measures have begun to have the desired effect—both on-time deliveries and sales returns improved in the second half of the year, while rework costs were relatively even. If the division continues to improve at the same rate, the Charter bonus could approximate or exceed what it was under the old plan.

The manager of the Mesa Division should be as satisfied with the new plan as with the old plan, as the bonus is almost equivalent. On-time deliveries declined considerably in the second half of the year and rework costs increased. However, sales returns decreased slightly. Unless the manager institutes better controls, the bonus situation may not be as favorable in the future. This could motivate the manager to improve in the future but currently, at least, the manager has been able to maintain his bonus with showing improvement in only one area targeted by Harrington.

Ben Harrington's revised bonus plan for the Charter Division fostered the following improvements in the second half of the year despite an increase in sales:
   - increase of 1.9% in on-time deliveries.
   - $500 reduction in rework costs.
   - $14,000 reduction in sales returns.

23-20 (Cont'd.)

However, operating income as a percent of sales has decreased (11 to 10%).

The Mesa Division's bonus has remained at the status quo as a result of the following effects
- increase of 2.0 % in operating income as a percent of sales (12% to 14%).
- decrease of 3.6% in on-time deliveries.
- $2,000 increase in rework costs.
- $2,250 decrease in sales returns.

This would suggest that there needs to be some revisions to the bonus plan. Possible changes include:

- increasing the weights put on on-time deliveries, rework costs, and sales returns in the performance measures while decreasing the weight put on operating income.
- a reward structure for rework costs that are below 2% of operating income that would encourage managers to drive costs lower.
- reviewing the whole year in total. The bonus plan should carry forward the negative amounts for one six-month period into the next six-month period incorporating the entire year when calculating a bonus.
- developing benchmarks, and then giving rewards for improvements over prior periods and encouraging continuous improvement.

23-22 (25 min.) **RI, EVA®.**

1.

	Truck Rental Division	Transportation Division
Total assets	$650,000	$950,000
Current liabilities	120,000	200,000
Investment		
(Total assets – current liabilities)	530,000	750,000
Required return		
(12% × Investment)	63,600	90,000
Operating income before tax	75,000	160,000
Residual income		
(Optg. inc. before tax – reqd. return)	11,400	70,000

2.   After-tax cost of debt financing $= (1- 0.4) \times 10\% = 6\%$
After-tax cost of equity financing $= 15\%$

$$\text{Weighted average cost of capital} = \frac{\$900,000 \times 6\% + 600,000 \times 15\%}{\$900,000 + 600,000} = 9.6\%$$

	Truck Rental Division	Transportation Division
Required return for EVA		
9.6% × Investment		
(9.6% × $530,000; 9.6% × $750,000)	$50,880	$72,000
Operating income after tax		
0.6 × operating income before tax	45,000	96,000
EVA (Optg. inc. after tax – reqd. return)	(5,880)	24,000

3.   Both the residual income and the EVA calculations indicate that the Transportation Division is performing better than the Truck Rental Division. The Transportation Division has a higher residual income ($70,000 versus $11,400) and a higher EVA [$24,000 versus $(5,880)]. The negative EVA for the Truck Rental Division indicates that, on an after-tax basis, the division is destroying value—the after-tax economic return from the Truck Rental Division's assets is less than the required return. If EVA continues to be negative, Burlingame may have to consider shutting down the Truck Rental Division.

23-24 (20 min.) **Multinational performance measurement, ROI, RI.**

1a. U.S. Division's ROI in 2003 $= \dfrac{\text{Operating income}}{\text{Total assets}} = \dfrac{\text{Operating income}}{\$8,000,000} = 15\%$

Hence, operating income $= 15\% \times \$8,000,000 = \$1,200,000$.

1b. Swedish Division's ROI in 2003 in kronas $= \dfrac{9,180,000 \text{ kronas}}{60,000,000 \text{ kronas}} = 15.3\%$

2. Convert total assets into dollars at December 31, 2002, exchange rate, the rate prevailing when assets were acquired (8 kronas = $1) equal to

$$\dfrac{60,000,000 \text{ kronas}}{8 \text{ kronas per dollar}} = \$7,500,000$$

Convert operating income into dollars at the average exchange rate prevailing during 2003 when operating income was earned (8.5 kronas = $1) equal to

$$\dfrac{9,180,000 \text{ kronas}}{8.5 \text{ kronas per dollar}} = \$1,080,000$$

Comparable ROI for Swedish Division $= \dfrac{\$1,080,000}{\$7,500,000} = 14.4\%$

The Swedish Division's ROI calculated in kronas is helped by the inflation that occurs in Sweden in 2003. Inflation boosts the division's operating income. Since the assets are acquired at the start of the year on 1-1-2003, the asset values are not increased by the inflation that occurs during the year. The net effect of inflation on ROI calculated in kronas is to use an inflated value for the numerator relative to the denominator. Adjusting for inflationary and currency differences negates the effects of any differences in inflation rates between the two countries on the calculation of ROI. After these adjustments, the U.S. Division shows a higher ROI than the Swedish Division.

3. U.S. Division's RI in 2003   = $\$1,200,000 - 12\% \times \$8,000,000$

                                       = $\$1,200,000 - \$960,000 = \$240,000$

Swedish Division's RI in 2003 (in U.S. dollars) is

$\$1,080,000 - 12\% \times \$7,500,000 = \$1,080,000 - \$900,000 = \$180,000$.

The U.S. Division's RI also exceeds the Swedish Division's RI in 2003 by $60,000 ($240,000 − $180,000).

23-26 (20–30 min.) **Risk sharing, incentives, benchmarking, multiple tasks.**

1. An evaluation of the three proposals to compensate Marks, the general manager of the Dexter Division follows:

(i) Paying Marks a flat salary will not subject Marks to any risk, but will provide no incentives for Marks to undertake extra physical and mental effort.

(ii) Rewarding Marks only on the basis of Dexter Division's ROI would motivate Marks to put in extra effort to increase ROI because Marks's rewards would increase with increases in ROI. But compensating Marks solely on the basis of ROI subjects Marks to excessive risk because the division's ROI depends not only on Marks's effort but also on other random factors over which Marks has no control. For example, Marks may put in a great deal of effort, but, despite this effort, the division's ROI may be low because of adverse factors (such as high interest rates or a recession) which Marks cannot control.

To compensate Marks for taking on uncontrollable risk, AMCO must pay him additional amounts within the structure of the ROI-based arrangement. Thus, compensating Marks only on the basis of performance-based incentives will cost AMCO more money, on average, than paying Marks a flat salary. The key question is whether the benefits of motivating additional effort justify the higher costs of performance-based rewards.

Furthermore, the objective of maximizing ROI may induce Marks to reject projects that, from the viewpoint of the organization as a whole, should be accepted. This would occur for projects that would reduce Marks's overall ROI but which would earn a return greater than the required rate of return for that project.

(iii) The motivation for having some salary and some performance-based bonus in compensation arrangements is to balance the benefits of incentives against the extra costs of imposing uncontrollable risk on the manager.

2. Marks's complaint does not appear to be valid. The senior management of AMCO is proposing to benchmark Marks's performance using a relative performance evaluation (RPE) system. RPE controls for common uncontrollable factors that similarly affect the performance of managers operating in the same environments (for example, the same industry). If business conditions for car battery manufacturers are good, all businesses manufacturing car batteries will probably perform well. A superior indicator of Marks's performance is how well Marks performed relative to his peers. The goal is to filter out the common noise to get a better understanding of Marks's performance. Marks's complaint will be valid only if there are significant differences in investments, assets, and the business environment in which AMCO and Tiara operate. Given the information in the problem, this does not appear to be the case.

Of course, using RPE does not eliminate the problem with the ROI measure itself. To keep ROI high, Marks will still prefer to reject projects whose ROI is greater than the required rate of return but lower than the current ROI.

3.　Superior performance measures change significantly with the manager's performance and not very much with changes in factors that are beyond the manager's control. If Marks has no authority for making capital investment decisions, then ROI is not a good measure of Marks's performance—it varies with the actions taken by others rather than the actions taken by Marks. AMCO may wish to evaluate Marks on the basis of operating income rather than ROI.

ROI, however, may be a good measure to evaluate Dexter's economic viability. Senior management at AMCO could use ROI to evaluate if the Dexter Division's income provides a reasonable return on investment, regardless of who has authority for making capital investment decisions. That is, ROI may be an inappropriate measure of Marks's performance but a reasonable measure of the economic viability of the Dexter Division. If, for whatever reasons— bad capital investments, weak economic conditions, etc.—the Division shows poor economic performance, as computed by ROI, AMCO management may decide to shut down the division even though they may simultaneously conclude that Marks performed well.

4.　There are two main concerns with Marks's plans. First, creating very strong sales incentives imposes excessive risk on the sales force, because a salesperson's performance is affected not only by his or her own effort, but also by random factors (such as a recession in the industry) that are beyond the salesperson's control. If salespersons are risk averse, the firm will have to compensate them for bearing this extra uncontrollable risk. Second, compensating salespersons only on the basis of sales creates strong incentives to sell, but may result in lower levels of customer service and sales support (this was the story at Sears auto repair shops where a change in the contractual terms of mechanics to "produce" more repairs caused unobservable quality to be negatively affected). Where employees perform multiple tasks, it may be important to "blunt" incentives on those aspects of the job that can be measured well (for example, sales) to try and achieve a better balance of the two tasks (for example, sales and customer service and support). In addition, the division should try to better monitor customer service and customer satisfaction through surveys, or through quantifying the amount of repeat business.

23-28 (25 min.) **Historical-cost and current-cost ROI measures.**

1.

	City Plaza	South Station	Central Park
$\dfrac{\text{Operating income}}{\text{Investment at historical cost}}$	$\dfrac{\$90,000}{\$300,000} = 30.0\%$	$\dfrac{\$120,000}{\$500,000} = 24.0\%$	$\dfrac{\$60,000}{\$240,000} = 25.0\%$
$\dfrac{\text{Operating income}}{\text{Investment at current cost}}$	$\dfrac{\$90,000}{\$600,000} = 15.0\%$	$\dfrac{\$120,000}{\$700,000} = 17.1\%$	$\dfrac{\$60,000}{\$450,000} = 13.3\%$

2.   Using investments at historical cost as the denominator, City Plaza has the highest ROI and South Station the lowest. Using investment at current cost as the denominator, South Station has the highest ROI and Central Park the lowest.

The choice of an appropriate measure depends on how Nobillo Corporation judges the performance of its convenience stores.

If Nobillo uses a single benchmark (say, 16%) in judging the performance of each store, the current cost measure will promote comparability among stores that were bought at different times or in areas with different real estate markets. Historical cost will give rise to differences in ROI among convenience stores that are unrelated to differences in operating efficiency. For example, in times of rising prices, the oldest store (City Plaza) will have a lower historical cost investment level than the newest store (South Station) for comparable amounts of square feet of store space in comparable locations. The current cost differences of the investment in the City Plaza and South Station stores, for example, are much smaller than the differences in historical costs, due largely to the different time periods in which the two stores were built. A drawback of current cost is that current cost estimates are difficult to obtain.

If Nobillo tailors the performance benchmark for each convenience store in its budgeting process, then the choice of a specific investment measure is less contentious. For example, if historical cost is used, the budgeted ROI benchmark for the South Station store could be, say, 25% whereas the budgeted ROI benchmark for the City Plaza store could be, say, 30%. Another benefit of tailoring the budget to each manager is that more incentives are provided to managers who are put in charge of poorly performing stations or stations in highly competitive markets.

23-30 (40–50 min.) **Evaluating managers, ROI, value-chain analysis of cost structure.**

1.

	$\dfrac{\text{Revenues}}{\text{Total Assets}}$	×	$\dfrac{\text{Operating Income}}{\text{Revenues}}$	=	$\dfrac{\text{Operating Income}}{\text{Total Assets}}$
Computer Power					
2002	1.111		0.250		0.278
2003	0.941		0.125		0.118
Peach Computer					
2002	1.250		0.100		0.125
2003	1.458		0.171		0.250

Computer Power's ROI has declined sizably from 2002 to 2003, largely because of a decline in operating income to revenues. Peach Computer's ROI has doubled from 2002 to 2003, in large part due to an increase in operating income to revenues.

2.

	Computer Power		Peach Computer	
Business Function	**2002**	**2003**	**2002**	**2003**
Research and development	12.0%	6.0%	10.0%	15.0%
Design	5.0	3.0	2.0	4.0
Production	34.0	40.0	46.0	34.0
Marketing	25.0	33.0	20.0	23.0
Distribution	9.0	8.0	10.0	8.0
Customer Service	15.0	10.0	12.0	16.0
Total costs	100.0%	100.0%	100.0%	100.0%

23-30 (Cont'd.)

Business functions with increases/decreases in the percentage of total costs from 2002 to 2003 are:

	Computer Power	Peach Computer
Increases	Production Marketing	Research and development Design Marketing Customer service
Decreases	Research and development Design Distribution Customer service	Production Distribution

Computer Power has decreased expenditures in several key business functions that are critical to its long-term survival—notably research and development and design. These costs are (using the chapter's terminology) discretionary and can be reduced in the short run without any short-run effect on customers, but such action is likely to create serious problems in the long run.

3.   Based on the information provided, Provan is the better candidate for president of User Friendly Computer. Both Computer Power and Peach Computer are in the same industry. Provan has headed Peach Computer at a time when it has considerably outperformed Computer Power:

a.   The ROI of Peach Computer has increased from 2002 to 2003, while that of Computer Power has decreased.

b.   The computer magazine has increased the ranking of Peach Computer's main product, while it has decreased the ranking of Computer Power's main product.

c.   Peach Computer has received high marks for new products (the lifeblood of a computer company), while Computer Power new-product introductions have been described as "mediocre."

23-32 (20–30 min.) **Division manager's compensation, risk sharing, incentives**
(continuation of 23-31).

1.   Consider each of the three proposals that the management of Mason Industries is considering:

a.   Compensate Grieco on the basis of a fixed salary without any bonus.

Paying Grieco a flat salary will not subject Grieco to any risk, but will provide no incentives for Grieco to undertake extra physical and mental effort.

b.   Compensate Grieco on the basis of division residual income (RI).

The benefit of this arrangement is that Grieco would be motivated to put in extra effort to increase RI because Grieco's rewards would increase with increases in RI. But compensating Grieco largely on the basis of RI subjects Grieco to excessive risk, because the division's RI depends not only on Grieco's effort but also on random factors over which Grieco has no control. Grieco may put in a great deal of effort, but the division's RI may be low because of adverse factors (high interest rates, recession) that the manager cannot control. For example, general market conditions will influence Grieco's revenues and costs.

To compensate Grieco for taking on uncontrollable risk, Mason Industries must pay her additional amounts within the structure of the RI-based arrangement. Thus, only using performance-based incentives costs Mason more money, on average, than paying a flat salary. The key question is whether the benefits of motivating additional effort justify the higher costs of performance-based rewards.

c.   Compensate Grieco using other companies that also manufacture go-carts and recreational vehicles as a benchmark.

The benefit of benchmarking or relative performance evaluation is to cancel out the effects of common noncontrollable factors that affect a performance measure. Taking out the effects of these factors provides better information about management performance. However, benchmarking and relative performance evaluation are effective only when similar noncontrollable factors affect each of the companies in the benchmark group. If this is the case, as it appears to be here, benchmarking is a good idea. If, however, the companies in the benchmark group are not exactly comparable because, for example, they have other areas of business that cannot be separated from their go-cart and recreational vehicle business, or they operate under different market conditions, benchmarking may not be a good idea. If the noncontrollable factors are not the same, then comparing the RI of Grieco's division to the RI of the other companies will not provide useful relative performance evaluation information.

2.   Mason should use a compensation arrangement that includes both a salary component and a bonus component based on residual income. The motivation for having some salary and some performance-based bonus in Grieco's compensation is to balance the benefits of incentives against the extra costs of imposing uncontrollable risk on the manager. If similar noncontrollable factors affect the performance of the benchmark companies that also manufacture and sell go-carts and recreational vehicles, a bonus based on the JSD's residual income relative to the residual income earned by the benchmark companies would be preferred.

23-34 (20–30 min.) **Division manager's compensation (continuation of 23-33).**

Consider each of the three proposals that Rupert Prince is considering:

a. *Compensate managers on the basis of division ROI.*
The benefit of this arrangement is that managers would be motivated to put in extra effort to increase ROI because managers' rewards would increase with increases in ROI. But compensating managers largely on the basis of ROI subjects the managers to excessive risk, because each division's ROI depends not only on the manager's effort but also on random factors over which the manager has no control. A manager may put in a great deal of effort, but the division's ROI may be low because of adverse factors (high interest, recession) that the manager cannot control.

To compensate managers for taking on uncontrollable risk, Prince must pay them additional amounts within the structure of the ROI-based arrangement. Thus, using mainly performance-based incentives will cost Prince more money, on average, than paying a flat salary. The key question is whether the benefits of motivating additional effort justify the higher costs of performance-based rewards. The motivation for having some salary and some performance-based bonus in compensation arrangements is to balance the benefits of incentives against the extra costs of imposing uncontrollable risk on the manager.

Finally, rewarding a manager only on the basis of division ROI will induce managers to maximize the division's ROI even if taking such actions are not in the best interests of the company as a whole.

b. *Compensate managers on the basis of companywide ROI.*
Rewarding managers on the basis of companywide ROI will motivate managers to take actions that are in the best interests of the company rather than actions that maximize a division's ROI.
A negative feature of this arrangement is that each division manager's compensation will now depend not only on the performance of that division manager but also on the performance of the other division managers. For example, the compensation of Ken Kearney, the manager of the Newspaper Division, will depend on how well the managers of Television and Film studios perform, even though Kearney himself may have little influence over the performance of these divisions. Hence, compensating managers on the basis of companywide ROI will impose extra risk on each division manager.

c. *Compensate managers using the other divisions' average ROI as a benchmark.*
The benefit of benchmarking or relative performance evaluation is to cancel out the effects of common noncontrollable factors that affect a performance measure. Taking out the effects of these factors provides better information about a manager's performance. What is critical, however, for benchmarking and relative performance evaluation to be effective is that similar noncontrollable factors affect each division. It is not clear that the same noncontrollable factors that affect the performance of the Newspaper Division (cost of newsprint paper, for example) also affect the performance of the Television and Film studios divisions. If the noncontrollable factors are not the same, then comparing the ROI of one division to the average ROI of the other two divisions will not provide useful information for relative performance evaluation.

23-34 (Cont'd.)

A second factor for Prince to consider is the impact that benchmarking and relative performance evaluation will have on the incentives for the division managers of the Newspaper, Television, and Film studios Divisions to cooperate with one another. Benchmarking one division against another means that a division manager will look good by improving his or her own performance, or by making the performance of the other division managers look bad.

23-36 (30 min.) **ROI, RI, division manager's compensation, nonfinancial measures.**

1. $\text{ROS} = \dfrac{\text{Operating Income}}{\text{Sales}} = \dfrac{1,800,000}{15,000,000} = 12\%$

   $\text{ROI} = \dfrac{\text{Operating Income}}{\text{Total Assets}} = \dfrac{1,800,000}{10,000,000} = 18\%$

2a. $\text{ROI} = 20\% = \dfrac{\text{Operating income}}{\text{Total Assets}} = \dfrac{X}{10,000,000}$

   Hence operating income $= 20\% \times 10,000,000 = \$2,000,000$
   Operating income = Revenue – Costs
   Therefore, Costs $= \$15,000,000 - \$2,000,000 = \$13,000,000$
   Currently,
   Costs = Revenues – Operating income $= \$15,000,000 - \$1,800,000 = \$13,200,000$

   Costs need to be reduced by $200,000 ($13,200,000 – $13,000,000).

2b. $\text{ROI} = 20\% = \dfrac{\text{Operating income}}{\text{Total assets}} = \dfrac{\$1,800,000}{X}$

   Hence X $= 1,800,000 \div 20\% = \$9,000,000$
   PD would need to decrease total assets in 2004 by $1,000,000 ($10,000,000 – $9,000,000).

3. RI = Income – (Required rate of return × Investment)
       = $1,800,000 – (0.15 × 10,000,000)
       = $300,000

4. PD wants RI to increase by 50% × $300,000 = $150,000
   That is PD wants RI in 2004 to be $300,000 + $150,000 = $450,000
   If PD cuts costs by $45,000 its operating income will increase to
       $1,800,000 + $45,000 = $1,845,000

   $\begin{aligned} \text{RI}_{2004} &= \$450,000 = \$1,845,000 - (0.15 \times \text{Assets}) \\ \$1,395,000 &= 0.15 \times \text{Assets} \\ \text{Assets} &= \$1,395,000 \div 0.15 = \$9,300,000 \end{aligned}$

   PD would need to decrease total assets by $700,000 ($10,000,000 – $9,300,000).

5. Barrington could use ROS to some degree. That way there is less focus on cutting costs and reduction in assets and more emphasis on actual revenues and how they translate into operating income.

   Barrington may also want to consider nonfinancial measures such as customer satisfaction and market share, quality, yield and on-time performance as well as monitor employee satisfaction and the development of employee skills.